FX

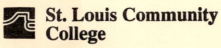
St. Louis Community College

Forest Park
Florissant Valley
Meramec

Instructional Resources
St. Louis, Missouri

The South's Finest

❧

THE FIRST MISSOURI CONFEDERATE BRIGADE
FROM PEA RIDGE TO VICKSBURG

by

Phillip Thomas Tucker

Foreword by
Albert Castel

 WHITE MANE PUBLISHING COMPANY, INC.

This White Mane Publishing Company, Inc. publication
was printed by
Beidel Printing House, Inc.
63 West Burd Street
Shippensburg, PA 17257 USA

In respect for the scholarship contained herein, the acid-free paper used in this book meets
the guidelines for permanence and durability of the Committee on Production Guidelines
for Book Longevity of the Council on Library Resources.

For a complete list of available publications
please write
White Mane Publishing Company, Inc.
P.O. Box 152
Shippensburg, PA 17257 USA

Library of Congress Cataloging-in-Publication Data

Tucker, Phillip Thomas, 1953-
    The South's finest : the First Missouri Confederate Brigade from
Pea Ridge to Vicksburg / by Phillip Thomas Tucker ; foreword by
Albert Castel.
        p.   cm.
    Includes bibliographical references and index.
    ISBN 0-942597-31-1 : $27.95
    1. Confederate States of America. Army. Missouri Brigade, 1st-
-History.   2. Missouri--History--Civil War, 1861-1865--Regimental
histories.   3. United States--History--Civil War, 1861-1865-
-Regimental histories.   I. Title.
E569.4 1st.T83 1993
973.7'478--dc20   93-8732
                                                    CIP

PRINTED IN THE UNITED STATES OF AMERICA

TABLE OF CONTENTS

DEDICATION

FOR A REMARKABLE WOMAN,

SETTA JANE TUCKER

FOREWORD

How do elite military units come into being? To paraphrase Shakespeare, some are born elite, some achieve eliteness, and others have eliteness thrust upon them.

The first way is the best known one, if "born" be understood as synonymous in this context with deliberate designation and creation. Thus a regiment, a brigade, a division, or perhaps an even larger military organization will be established with a special status, assigned men of superior physique or demonstrated fighting proficiency, attired in distinctive uniforms, provided with better weapons and more rigorous training than ordinary outfits, and during battle be used for the most difficult, hazardous, and important missions. Historically, the most famous examples of such units would include the Theban Sacred Band of Ancient Greece, the Roman Praetorian Guards (until they degenerated into barrack politicians), the Polish "Winged Cavalry" of the seventeenth century, Cromwell's Ironsides, Napoleon's Old Guard, and the Waffen SS divisions of World War II such as *Das Reich*. Yet another example, and the only American one of this type, are the Green Berets, who were born of the Vietnam War and died with it, living on only in TV re-runs of the John Wayne movie bearing their name.

Probably most elite troops, though, have become such as a consequence of circumstances, which would be the third way mentioned above of acquiring that status. Thus, thanks to his armor, his horse, and his lance, the medieval knight dominated Europe's battlefields for centuries until firearms rendered him obsolete. Later on, in the eighteenth century, grenadiers became the favored name for crack infantry regiments made up of extra-tall men. Why? Because soldiers of above-average height not only had an advantage in tossing grenades, scaling parapets, and fighting with bayonets, but perhaps even more important they looked impressive on the parade ground (King Frederick William of Prussia had a whole regiment of giants—which, however, he never risked in battle). Likewise, during World War II marines and paratroops became the elite of many armed forces owing to the nature of their missions, which in turn required special training and a high level of physical fitness. In the case of the United States marines, this high status is justified, given their nation's world-wide interests. Paratroops, on the other hand, have not been used on a large scale in combat since World War II (and then with less than auspicious results), nor is it likely they ever will be so used again, as helicopters provide a much more effective way of striking at an enemy's rear.

The First Missouri Confederate Brigade illustrates the second of the categories we have presented: it achieved eliteness. In most armies, in most wars, this occurs with a number of units, perhaps a goodly number. Yet—and here is the crucial distinction—these units are not formally designated as "elite," "crack," or "special." They are just known to be so and used that way by the commanders under whom they serve. This certainly was the case with the First Missouri, whose troops were described by a Mississippi officer as being "the brag of this or any other army, they fight better, drill better and look better than any other men in the army." The First Missouri originated from a hodge-podge of ill-trained, often untrained, militia outfits. Far from having distinctive uniforms, most of its men began the war without any uniforms at all and the first uniforms they eventually did receive were more bizarre than impressive! As for weapons, they fought for nearly a year and a half before being issued rifled muskets; prior to then, those who were equipped with a semi-obsolete smoothbore considered themselves fortunate.

Three things, basically, made them "the South's Finest." First, they were highly motivated. Having taken up arms to, as they saw it, save Missouri from Yankee-abolitionist domination, by 1862, when they formally joined the Confederate service, their state had been overrun by Northern troops and hence their sole hope of liberating it was to fight, and fight hard, for Southern victory on the battlefields of Arkansas, Mississippi, Louisiana, Georgia, Tennessee, and Alabama, and this they did. Second, and even more important, after being formed into a Confederate brigade they enjoyed the advantage of being commanded, trained, and led into battle in their crucial initial engagements by Brigadier General Henry Little, a first-class regular army officer and a veteran of the Mexican War during which he was brevetted for gallantry in combat. Then, following Little's death at the Battle of Iuka, Mississippi, in September 1862, they came under the command of an exceptionally able West Pointer, Brigadier General John S. Bowen, who led them during the Vicksburg Campaign. These two generals, plus such outstanding colonels as Elijah P. Gates and Francis Marion Cockrell, both of whom served as acting commanders of the brigade, gave the Missourians a quality of leadership without which no military unit, regardless of the quality of its rank and file, can be truly elite.

But the main reason for the Missouri Brigade's elite status was its combat performance. Starting with the Battle of Pea Ridge, Arkansas (March 7-8, 1862), and going on to the battles of Iuka and Corinth in Mississippi in the fall of 1862, it spearheaded the Confederate attacks and gained its assigned objectives, only to have to relinquish them because of the failure of the other Confederate forces to attain similar success necessitated retreat—a retreat from victory in so far as the Missourians were concerned. These exploits gave them a reputation for bravery, determination, and fighting skill which henceforth they felt that they had to sustain. And this too they did, in battle after battle, right to the end of the war, by which time they were reduced to a mere remnant of three hundred men. Major General Dabney H. Maury, a Virginian who saw them in action at Pea Ridge and Corinth, did not exaggerate when he declared after the war that the soldiers of the First Missouri "were not surpassed by any troops in the world." He simply spoke the truth.

In *The South's Finest* Dr. Phillip Thomas Tucker, himself a Missourian, tells the story of the First Missouri Confederate Brigade from its beginnings as a motley collection of raw volunteers on through to the siege of Vicksburg, by which time it had become one of the most fearsome and feared brigades in the entire Confederate army. He does so vividly, accurately, and in great detail, in the process utilizing an awesome amount of sources, many of them unpublished and hitherto unused diaries, letters, and memoirs. In his pages we not only learn of the First Missouri's battles and campaigns, we also become acquainted with its men, from the top generals down to the lowliest privates. When we read the final page, we will share Dr. Tucker's obvious and infectious admiration for these men and what they did and endured. We also will look forward to the second volume of Dr. Tucker's work in which he relates the rest of their story. This, readers can be assured, is just as thrilling and even more poignant than the first part.

Albert Castel

Author of *General Sterling Price and the Civil War in the West* and of *Decision in the West: The Atlanta Campaign of 1864*

PREFACE

The tragic experience of the Missouri Confederates best epitomizes the meaning of the brothers' war and the horror of America's fratricidal conflict. These Missourians—the forgotten Rebels of the Confederacy—suffered more severely and paid a higher price during the Civil War than any other Americans, both on the battlefield and on the home front. While struggling far from their Union-occupied home, the exiled Missouri Confederates repeatedly performed better and more effectively in combat than any other troops in the Civil War, North or South. Of the more than 8,000 Missouri soldiers, in total, who fought in the Missouri Brigade, only about 300 were left after the last battle in April 1865.

In the decades after the war, a proud North and South boasted of the respective fighting prowess of their most famous brigades in the great sectional conflict. But, ironically, one Confederate brigade that rightly deserved the most recognition and fame for its superior fighting qualities and accomplishments on the battlefield has received the least notice by historians during the last 130 years. The Missouri Brigade maintained its unrivaled level of excellence in combat in more key engagements, for a longer period, in more theaters, and more consistently than the legendary Stonewall, Orphan, Iron, Texas, and Irish brigades, which historians have long considered the best fighting units of the war.

Indeed, if any command in the Civil War truly deserved the coveted title of the "Iron" or "Stonewall" brigade, it was the Missouri Brigade. By any measure, the Missouri Brigade was the elite of the elite: a distinction long ignored by the leading Civil War historians. No soldiers on either side saw as much combat, or more often faced greater battlefield challenges than the ill-fated Missouri Rebels. Though always outnumbered, the Missouri Brigade was never out-fought while repeatedly demonstrating a superior level of performance as *the* key player in some of the bloodiest and most decisive engagements of the war.

Even though the Missouri Brigade won widespread acclaim *during* the war years across the South, and also in the North, that legendary and unmatched reputation quickly faded *after* the conflict, as mythology began to replace fact. Meanwhile, the reputations of other hard-fighting units, such as the Orphan, Texas, Iron, Stonewall, and Irish brigades, grew steadily during the postwar years. These brigades gained much publicity and widespread recognition, becoming increasingly more famous and far outshining the fast-fading record of the Missouri Brigade both in the popular mind and in the annals of Civil War history.

How and why was the distinguished role of the hardest fighting command of the Civil War ignored by historians of the most written-about period in the nation's history? Many good explanations can be found. First, the victors of wars always interpret history, naturally glorifying the accomplishments of the winners, such as the Union Iron and Irish brigades. Second, when Southerners wrote their lost cause histories, a romanticism began to replace reality, and further muddied the historical record.

Indeed, the South was as guilty as the North in dooming "the South's Finest" to obscurity. Powerful Southern veteran organizations, including highly-active brigade associations, along with cavalier nostalgia, lost cause sentimentality, publicity bestowed upon the more popular brigades which had fought east of the Mississippi, and the dominance and glorification of the Army of Northern Virginia and Robert E. Lee school, resulted in a one-sided public relations battle that was easily won by the promoters of those other units long after the last shot had been fired. Hence, the Missouri Brigade's reputation as the best combat unit of the Civil War was relegated to oblivion.

Also, during the postwar period the misconception was born that Missouri was a "western" state devoid of a distinctive Southern heritage. This led to the myth that Missouri made no substantial contributions to the Confederate war effort. Even worse, the Missouri Brigade's legacy also has been ignored by the people of Missouri and Missouri historians as Southern consciousness diminished after the war. Some of today's descendants of Missouri Brigade members still feel a sense of shame in regard to their forefathers' service in the Confederacy, believing that these Rebels were nothing but lawless renegades and bushwhackers and not the elite troops of the Civil War.

Another reason why the Missouri Brigade's reputation faded was that so few survivors were left in 1865 to perpetuate the unit's history. The mystery of the fates of the Missouri Confederates who never came home after four years of war haunted Missourians for generations. Near the beginning of the Twentieth Century, a leading St. Louis newspaper attempted to solve the 30-year riddle surrounding the disappearance of hundreds of Missouri Brigade soldiers, for "much interest is felt and many inquiries are made of the people of Missouri and elsewhere as to the fate of those who left this State at the beginning of the war, joined the Confederate Army, and never returned."

Even today, many of the descendants of Missouri Brigade soldiers have no knowledge of the exact fate of their ancestors who vanished somewhere in the vastness of the South during 1861-65. "The family has always wondered what had happened to great-grandfather," wrote a Missouri Brigade descendant to the author in 1990, before being informed of the date and location of his ancestor's death on a Mississippi battlefield. The answer to the mystery was simple: an unusually high percentage of the Missouri Confederates were left lying hundreds of miles from home in solitary graves and burial trenches across the South and in the prison cemeteries of the North.

Another key factor contributing to the Missouri Brigade's obscurity lies in the fact that most of the battlefields across the seven states where the Missourians fought are either today underdeveloped or not developed as historic sites at all. The hallowed grounds of Iuka, Corinth, Port Gibson, Champion Hill, and Big Black River have no monuments or markers to the Missouri Brigade or its leaders. And because the Trans-Mississippi Theater remains today's most neglected and least appreciated arena in Civil War historiography, the crack Rebel troops from the Trans-Mississippi were likewise fated for obscurity in part because of geography.

In telling the long-overlooked story of the Missouri Confederates, another group of forgotten Southerners has likewise been illuminated for the first time: the Irish immigrants of the Confederacy, whose role in the conflict has also been ignored by historians for 130 years. These Missouri Irish Confederates played a prominent role throughout the Missouri Brigade's history.

A study of the Missouri Brigade fills a void in Civil War, Southern and Missouri historiography, further enriching our understanding of the nation's greatest national tragedy. For Americans today, the saga of the Missouri Confederates from the western frontier is relevant and meaningful because their tragic odyssey still exemplifies some of the noblest aspects of the American character under severe adversity, and in a hopeless struggle against a cruel fate and impossible odds.

During their 40-month journey across the South, those exiled western Rebels experienced a magnitude of defeat, both on the battlefield and the home front, unparalleled in the American experience, often losing their homes, land, and family members. And they also lost the dream of an independent nation, the Confederacy. The few who returned to Missouri in 1865 could hardly recognize a once bountiful land which had been ravished by four years of the worst guerrilla war in the nation's history. While their unprotected homeland was devastated by the savagery of a no-quarter conflict on a scale unseen in any other section of the country, those Missouri Confederates continued to fight faithfully in the South far from home.

My efforts have focused upon analyzing the personal experiences and struggles of the common soldier of the First Missouri Confederate Brigade. Because of the Missouri Brigade's distinguished military record, a strong temptation exists for any military historian to become enmeshed in the minute details of the maze of battles, strategies, and campaigns, losing touch with the intimate history of a unique command. Indeed, the real history of the Missouri Brigade revolves around the personal lives and stories of these frontier yeomen of common origins who fought and died in the ranks.

More than enough has already been said about the standard cast of great leaders and climactic battles, which continue to appear in a steady and much-acclaimed flow of "new" works with monotonous regularity. An in-depth personal interpretation of the heart and soul of this western unit—the common soldiery—was essential for a thorough understanding of the Missouri Brigade's history, because the most important story of this exiled command lies far beyond the perspective that this brigade was simply a cold, killing machine without a soul or spirit, performing mechanically on a series of chessboard battlefields.

I show both positive and negative aspects of the Missouri Brigade's history and personnel to present a balanced view. It was also important for me to incorporate the good, the bad, and the ugly to escape the trap of romanticizing and glorifying these Missouri soldiers, who were ordinary men caught in extraordinary times.

Consequently, I have made a 20-year effort to collect and rely as much as possible on unpublished letters, diaries, and journals instead of the standard secondary and postwar sources. The goal was to secure the least biased and most accurate primary documentation to help answer the key question as to why and how these young Missouri farm boys were transformed into "the South's Finest," by the challenges and experiences of war.

Hence, this history has been based primarily upon the fertile repository of unpublished, primary Civil War source material yet untapped in the United States today: the wealth of private collections, mostly in possession of soldiers' descendants, which constitute the last and best remaining unexploited resource of primary Civil War material in the country. A thorough understanding of the personal history of the Civil War cannot be glimpsed from the seemingly endless volumes of the *Official Records*. Fully understanding the history of this little-known Missouri

Brigade could only be accomplished by reaching beyond the over-used standard sources and into this least accessible, but richest, lode of unpublished and primary Civil War material which historians most often overlook because of the difficulty in finding the sources.

This cache of previously unpublished letters, journals, diaries, photographs, and paintings from private collections has been utilized to present a comprehensive, balanced, scholarly, and personal history of the First Missouri Confederate Brigade. In addition, thousands of daily editions of Southern newspapers and more than 8,000 individual service records of Missouri Brigade soldiers have been closely analyzed to correct the often inaccurate and erroneous post-war accounts and the *Official Records* version of history.

Those primary source materials have been relied upon also to strip away the unrealistic and idealized versions of history that many of today's arm-chair historians find in the majesty and glory of the Civil War. Indeed, there was nothing romantic or glorious in a frightened teenage farm boy from Polk County dying of dysentery in a soiled bed of wet straw in a dirty Mississippi field hospital or a drummer boy from the Bootheel region of Southeast Missouri being blown to pieces by an exploding shell, or a gut-shot St. Louis Confederate begging to be relieved of his pain by a bullet through the head and taking weeks to die without anesthesia.

I located and used family papers and private collections of more than 20 descendants of Missouri Brigade members to tell the story of the common soldier of this command. In addition, to better analyze and more fully understand the Missouri Brigade's impressive role in combat I thoroughly explored and studied the Southern battlefields upon which the Missouri Brigade fought over the years.

I would like to thank the following people of the academic and professional community throughout the country, who have assisted and contributed advice and encouragement over the years: Dr. Leslie Anders, Dr. Perry D. Jamieson, Dr. Richard J. Sommers, Dr. John McGlone, Dr. Michael H. Gorn, Dr. Richard P. Hallion, Dr. Martin G. Towey, Dr. T. Michael Ruddy, Dr. Roy Stubbs, Dr. Martin K. Gordon, Dr. James Neal Primm, and Father William Barnaby Faherty. A number of National Park Service personnel likewise gave invaluable assistance: Terrence J. Winschel, Doug Harding, Douglas Keller, and Edwin C. Bearss. Also, I would like to thank Margie Riddle Bearss and Louise Richardson, of Paragould, Arkansas, for their generous and unsolicited support. Others deserve mention for important contributions as well: Robert L. Hawkins III, and Dr. Thomas P. Sweeney, and the always helpful and gracious staffs of the Missouri Historical Society and the State Historical Society of Missouri. Dr. Diane R. Gordon helped with the editing of this manuscript. I would like to especially thank Dr. Albert Castel, preeminent Civil War historian of the War in the West, for his gracious assistance.

Washington, D.C.   Phillip Thomas Tucker
March 6, 1991

INTRODUCTION

The Winter of Decision

The cold, blustery winds that howled across the brown woodlands and prairies of the western border state of Missouri brought the full wrath of winter by December 1861. But winter's fury could not compare to the fierce sectional storm caused by human folly, cursing this picturesque land torn by the deepest sectional divisions in the nation. The insanity of American killing American with a ferocity never seen before announced what seemed to be the end of the great republican experiment. This fratricidal conflict had already unveiled some startling new realities. By the end of 1861, some unexpected military lessons in the first modern war had become apparent. For instance, the failure of the scrappy Missouri State Guard, under Major General Sterling Price, to wrest control of Missouri from the Unionists in 1861 pointed to one important lesson: a revolutionary state army founded upon the outdated militia model and with an improvised support system could not compete in a lengthy conventional war of attrition against a better organized opponent with superior resources galvanized by a strong centralized government.

In the old days, Americans could leave their farms, fight for a short time, and then return to the fields after a battlefield success, but this was no longer the case. During the summer of 1861, unexpected Rebel victories in Missouri at Wilson's Creek and Lexington demonstrated that a loosely organized, militia-based Missouri army could launch an invasion into Union-held territory, but could win nothing but pyrrhic victories. "Upon every field the brave Missourians have gloriously triumphed over the Hessians," crowed one Southern newspaperman, but the Missouri Rebels could never deliver a decisive knock-out punch. Victories could not be fully exploited, especially without substantial contributions of manpower and materiel from the newly formed Confederacy. Despite General Price's successes across Missouri, strong Union forces continued to occupy the key city of St. Louis, the state capital of Jefferson City, and most of the state by the end of 1861.

A remarkable victory at Lexington in September of 1861 was the high-water mark of the Missouri State Guard. In typical frontier fashion, a large percentage of Price's command melted away during the winter of 1861 almost as quickly as it had formed the previous spring and summer, when states rights and Southern sentiment were high. Poor discipline, no pay, the cold weather, and loose organization caused the unraveling of a volunteer Rebel army, which had initially fought more on behalf of the home state than the South. As the idealism of the Missouri Rebels faded with increased hardships and a new awareness of the war's harsh realities, and the need to return home to tend farms emerged, it became apparent that the antiquated militia system that had brought success in America's earlier conflicts was inadequate to meet the demands of a lengthy modern war that knew few limits.

To win the contest for Missouri, a new solution was urgently needed on the western border. The "Missouri sons of liberty" could gather by the thousands to defend their homes, families, and lands from invading Iowa, Kansas, Missouri, and Illinois troops, but they lacked both the capabilities and the desire to take the war to the Northern homeland to win decisive victory. As often demonstrated by the colonial militia during the American Revolution, Price's State Guard simply could not sustain a long, exhaustive struggle or a successful invasion without adequate organization, manpower and materiel and without a reliable logistical support system. A force more stable than volunteer state militia was needed in Missouri to win this geopolitically and strategically important border state, if the Confederacy were to achieve success in the western war and gain independence. To secure the vital western border for the South, Missourians had to serve as Confederate soldiers for years with support from the Confederate government. Newly-elected President Jefferson Davis eventually came to this realization, writing how, "we are anxious that the troops of Missouri should be tendered to the Confederate Government [since] their efficiency will be increased, and that they will be relieved from the anomalous position they now occupy, as militia [and] without being a part of their organized army."[1]

A practical solution to bolster the effort to win Missouri called for the Missouri Guardsmen to enlist in the Confederate army, after the expiration of their six-month term of state service. With Missouri having "boldly taken her position in line with her sister Slave States, in their struggle for life and freedom," wrote one Southern journalist, the strategic and symbolic importance of Missouri Rebels fighting for the Confederacy was paramount to the future of the new Southern nation in 1861. To help win the war in the West and enhance prospects of independence, the South desperately needed to secure as early as possible the strongest and richest of both the Trans-Mississippi and the all-important border states, Missouri. Many advantages would go to the side which gained possession of this frontier slave state where the South and West met and mingled as one.

A concentrated Confederate military effort in Missouri was vital for the South's future. But instead Confederate leadership pursued a fatal strategy of protecting practically all areas of the South rather than concentrating against Union threats at crucial points. Even geography favored a Confederate effort in Missouri. Indeed, Missouri's bountiful river system and rail network offered the Confederacy an opportunity to concentrate for an early offensive. Control of Missouri meant a firm hold on the key resources necessary for victory in this war: the most miles of railroad track in the Trans-Mississippi, a higher population than any Southern state except Virginia, the largest concentration of valuable natural resources west of the Mississippi, and important lines of commerce and transportation along the state's natural arteries, the Mississippi and the Missouri Rivers. But only belatedly did Southern leaders, politicians, and strategists fully understand the importance of the mobilization of Missouri Rebels and the importance of the struggle for this vital northwestern corner of the Confederacy. By December 1861, not much time remained to make up for this negligence since the war's beginning, but the Confederacy had one last chance to save Missouri before the state was out-flanked on the east by the Union push to victory in Kentucky and Tennessee during early 1862.

The westernmost border state of Missouri held almost unlimited strategic possibilities for the Confederacy: a fact long overlooked by modern historians. A Confederate Missouri promised much, offering a secure Rebel grip on not only the Missouri River, but also on the Mississippi and its important valley, which the South had to retain for independence. The "Father of Waters" was a natural avenue for Union invasions that pointed south like a dagger toward the heart of the South and the way to decisive victory, as subsequent events showed. Out-flanking Illinois on the west, Missouri could serve as a vital staging area for Confederate invasions into Federal territory like neighboring Illinois, and could protect Kentucky and Tennessee and thereby, perhaps could help save the all-important Southern heartland. A Confederate Missouri also meant isolating Kansas and providing key support for Rebel uprisings in Southern Illinois and Kentucky. In addition, a Confederate invasion north from Missouri and up the Mississippi to the Great Lakes region might split the Union in half. As one Deep South Rebel accurately stated in 1861, "Our interest as well as our duty to our co-laborers in Missouri, demands that they be assisted." "If Missouri," wrote a journalist, "is not sustained, Arkansas, Texas and Louisiana, and other States south of us, will suffer." A Confederate Missouri could best "preserve the other States of the Confederacy South": a reality eventually proven by the relentless course of Union victory in the West.

By the winter of 1861, therefore, the wisest Confederate strategy west of the Mississippi would have called for "keeping this war as high up the Mississippi valley as possible," pleaded one Southerner. In addition, if Missouri were won for the Confederacy, it could change the inequality of resources between North and South. The winning of Missouri could have provided the Southern nation with an early taste of important strategic military-political success before Bull Run, strengthening Confederate morale and nationalism, lengthening the war, and sapping the will of the Northern war effort. The largest United States Arsenal in the South was located just south of St. Louis, and presented an easy target in the war's beginning. The weakly-defended arsenal held not only sufficient arms, cannon, and munitions for a successful revolution on the frontier and a Confederate offensive, but also its capture might have determined the outcome of the war in Missouri and the Trans-Mississippi, the forgotten theater of the Civil War. A concentrated Confederate effort in Missouri offered the earliest and best political possibilities for the important western victories that would enhance the prospects of foreign recognition and slow the political attrition that eventually destroyed the fragile fabric of Southern nationalism. But a successful Confederate political and military strategy to win Missouri was never developed. Ironically, Missouri has long been considered by Civil War historians to be the least important border state.[2]

The transformation of Missouri Guardsmen into Missouri Confederates became politically possible when the exiled rump Missouri assembly passed an ordinance of secession on October 21, 1861. Both houses of the legislature reached a quorum at the small agricultural community of Neosho, in southwest Missouri. At a plain Masonic Hall Missouri became the twelfth state of the Confederacy. Wild celebrating erupted in the Missouri soldiers' encampments with the addition of a new star to the Confederate banner. The bold prediction of one Southern journalist that "Missouri will be with [her] Southern sisters at an early day" had finally come true. Now, the Confederacy had gained more credibility and prestige. But official declarations had little meaning in the war on the western border. Indeed, the Confederacy would have to take Missouri by force if the leadership gained the far-sighted vision necessary for victory in the West. At that time the naive farm boys under General Price believed that substantial Confederate aid and reinforcements would soon be forthcoming. But the amount of Confederate assistance necessary for Rebel victory in Missouri never arrived.

A short-sighted Davis government in Richmond, Virginia, embraced a militarily and politically unsound strategy of defensive warfare, attempting to protect too much Confederate territory instead of concentrating for a coordinated effort in Missouri. In failing to embrace the long-term view, this fatal flaw in strategic planning would guarantee the loss of what the South could not afford to lose: the initiative, the western border and the Mississippi. But some Southerners possessed enough insight to comprehend Missouri's strategic and geopolitical significance. "The results flowing from [the winning of Missouri] cannot be over estimated. They extend far beyond the boundaries of Missouri. They reach the frontiers of New Mexico, and involve the destinies of Kansas, the Indian Nation, Arizona and New Mexico," accurately analyzed one Rebel.

For most of 1861 the sole responsibility for guarding vulnerable Missouri had lain primarily with the outnumbered state guardsmen of Price's Missouri army. Missouri, the gateway to the vital Mississippi Valley and the Trans-Mississippi, and much of the western theater, was gradually slipping away from the South by the end of 1861, while the Confederacy contributed little to the struggle that had raged across the state for more than six months. "But for the Missouri army, [Union forces] would have moved over [the Mississippi] valley and met [Major General Benjamin] Butler at New Orleans. For one whole year these devoted men had, without support, held 50,000 Federal troops in Missouri, and prevented their marching on the Southwest...," proclaimed one Mobile newspaperman. By the end of 1861, almost double that number of Federal troops were tied down in Missouri by Price's Rebels, who bought precious time for the Confederacy but none for themselves. Primarily because the Missouri Rebels never received sufficient aid or support from the Davis Government, the Union cause eventually triumphed by first turning the Confederacy's left flank in Missouri, then slicing down the Mississippi Valley, and steamrolling to decisive victory by winning control of the Mississippi.[3]

With the winter respite, Price's Missouri army reorganized throughout December of 1861. Amid the rolling and forested hills of southwest Missouri, Confederate recruitment among guardsmen leaving state service began near the forks of the Sac and Osage Rivers and near Osceola, Missouri, which had been recently burned by Kansas Jayhawkers. The exciting news spread across the South that in Missouri, "the State troops under Gen. Price's command are rapidly volunteering for the Confederate service organized into a brigade [the First Missouri Confederate Brigade, to] drive back the armies of Lincoln, and let the people rise and assent their choice," recorded a journalist.

But the Southern people could hardly have realized that Confederate recruitment in far-away Missouri would result in the formation of a brigade that would become the elite of the elite. Indeed, the First Missouri Confederate Brigade would become famous across the Confederacy as the best drilled and finest combat unit of the South. The Missouri Brigade gained its reputation during, and not after, the conflict, and was compared to "the Macedonian Phalanx, the Tenth Legion of Caesar, and the Old Guard of Napoleon." It played more key roles in more strategically important battles and more often than the most famous brigades of both sides. But for more than 130 years, this historical record has been obscured and largely forgotten, in part because of the Missouri Brigade's tragic fate during the first half of the war: every major battle in which the Missouri Confederates fought so magnificently were Southern reversals except one, Grand Gulf. The First Missouri Brigade was a distinguished combat unit of the Civil War and "the South's Finest." In fact, the Missouri Brigade was one of the supreme fighting machines in American military history.

As fate would have it, the Missouri Brigade never fought a major battle in Missouri. The Missourians struggled for 37 of their 40 months in service as exiles east of the Mississippi. Few units in the Civil War fought in as many different theaters or in so many states—Missouri, Arkansas, Mississippi, Alabama, Louisiana, Georgia, and Tennessee—as did the Missouri Brigade. Ironically, the Missouri Brigade's superior record guaranteed that the Missourians would fight and die for years east of the Mississippi and would never return to the struggle for their home state.

Successive Confederate leaders repeatedly gave the most dangerous assignments to the Missouri Brigade because of its reputation. Hundreds of miles from home, isolated from domestic and political support, and manipulated by an apathetic government in Richmond, the exiled Missourians were expendable and exploited as few other troops. They were repeatedly placed in suicidal, no-win situations during some of the most important battles of the war. One Missouri Brigade member explained in a letter: "The boys have taken up the idea that Missourians are outsiders that will do very well to do the rough fighting..." These Missourians were killed off at a higher rate more consistently and for a longer period than any other Rebel troops, often serving as little more than cannon fodder.[4]

Many factors explain why the Missouri Brigade acquired the hard-earned reputation as not only the elite combat brigade of the Confederacy, but also of the Civil War. First, these Missouri Confederates had been tempered and toughened by the frontier experience, an agricultural and outdoor life. Hardships had been a way of life long before military service. These frontiersmen were fiercely individualistic, believing that they had to fight anyone who got in their way, including Uncle Sam. These hardy westerners were hunters, woodsmen, horsemen, and marksmen, who knew how to survive on their own, endure the elements, and live off the land. Such well-honed skills partly explain why Missouri Brigade members fought so well in the forests and rough terrain of the South. Some of these soldiers became Whitworth Sharpshooters, the Confederacy's best marksmen. Largely because to the frontier experience, few units were so egalitarian, and contained so few class distinctions as the Missouri Brigade, which was a factor forging solidarity.

But more important, long before Southern cannon fired on Fort Sumter in Charleston Harbor, many of these self-reliant yeomen had already acquired much military experience. In 1861, these men were seasoned veterans unlike the vast majority of soldiers of both sides. Many of these Missouri guardsmen had been engaged in a wide variety of ante-bellum military and paramilitary activities, including the Mexican and Indian Wars, epic treks to the Far West in search of gold and new lands, the Mormon difficulties, excursions in Latin America and Mexico, suppression of slave revolts, the hot and cold war in "Bleeding Kansas" from 1855-1860, and the Southwest Expedition to the Kansas border during the winter of 1860-61.

Missouri Volunteer Militia of St. Louis during the Southwest Expedition of 1860. Two of these men became soldiers in the Missouri Brigade, C.S.A.

Courtesy Edmund J. Boyce, St. Louis, Mo.
(Unpublished Painting)

Of these varied experiences the militia tradition and militia service, including duty in the infantry, cavalry, and artillery, had the greatest impact. This invaluable prewar training helped to lay a solid foundation explaining why an iron discipline among the Missouri Confederates remained so strong, while enduring a degree of adversity that few others would share. This long-overlooked ante-bellum experience had smoothly integrated large numbers of these Missourians into the world of the military, conditioning them to regulations, discipline, tactics, drill and organization. But, unlike other troops on both sides, it was the unique fusing of the dual influences of prewar militia service and Missouri State Guard service of 1861 which most deeply sowed the seeds that blossomed to maturity by early 1862, transforming these roughhewn Missouri Confederates into the elite troops of the Civil War.

In terms of political philosophies, the Missouri Confederates held to the Jeffersonian faith and the Democratic tradition, believing in the principles of a decentralized democracy and states rights. Beliefs rooted in traditional values, conservatism, and heritage explain why these Missourians took up arms against a newly elected Republican administration. In the minds of these Missouri Rebels, the United States government no longer represented their interests, instead representing the antithesis of a Jeffersonian Democracy: an urbanized Northern society that was industrialized, modernized, and culturally alien. According to the Missourians' interpretation of Jeffersonian philosophy, the centralized power of the Federal government was the greatest threat to the most natural form of democratic society, which was represented by the small farmer, who owned the land he worked. Because it was thought that the Lincoln government represented the radicalized economic, political, and social values of an industrial, urban and business-first society, secession offered the security of the past, a solution to counter Northern extremists, and a conservative haven in a rapidly changing and more progressive world, while preserving the traditional values of the Founding Fathers, the Constitution, and the "true" political philosophies of the republic. Private Isaac Vincent Smith, and his Missouri Brigade comrades fought simply because "they thought that their civil rights were being taken away from them."

Hence, identification with the South's struggle came easily. For instance, one Missourian analyzed in 1861, "our people [were] as intensely Southern as those of South Carolina." Commitment to the Southern faith often ran deeper than familial bonds on the traumatized border. Along with many other Missouri Brigade members, Private James Hearny Wells, age twenty-two, fought not knowing if the opponents whom he faced in battle were his three brothers in Yankee blue. Another Missouri Brigade soldier, Private John T. Wickersham, wrote to his grandson how, "even our own family was divided, and we fought to kill each other." As State Guardsmen, some Missouri Brigade members had captured brothers, cousins, and uncles during fighting across Missouri in 1861.

To fully understand the personal motivations of the Missouri Brigade members and to help place their distinctive role in a proper historical perspective, it must be noted that most of them owned no slaves. For the vast majority of these men, this was a righteous struggle comparable to the American Revolution, and they did not fight in support of the institution of slavery, as evidenced by scores of these soldiers' letters and diaries. The influence of slavery, however, can not be dismissed for Missouri was a "Southern frontier state." Even though most of these young men owned no slaves, it cannot be ascertained how many of them had aspirations toward owning slaves in the future.

Despite the fact that these Missouri Confederates were not fighting primarily to defend slavery, many of these soldiers either owned a small number of slaves, or hailed from families which owned a few slaves. But slave-owning Confederates of the Missouri Brigade were a minority. Clearly, it would be a mistake to dismiss slavery as a non-factor in the personal motivation of Confederates from a western slave state that contained more than 100,000 African Americans in bondage in 1860. The profitable staples of tobacco [northeast Missouri] and hemp [northwest Missouri] were primary cash crops in areas which contributed heavily to the Missouri Brigade. These mostly non-slave-owning yeomen raised typical western products, primarily corn, oats, and hogs, like generations of their Upper South forefathers and like their Union counterparts of the west. Cornmeal and pork were the principal dietary staples on the western border, both North and South.

Whenever the theme of black slavery served as the principal motivation for the enlistment of Missouri Brigade members, it sprang primarily from a fear of slave revolt and racial war reminiscent of St. Domingue [Haiti], when the French were victims of the most successful slave rebellion in history. John Brown's 1859 raid on Harper's Ferry, Virginia had fanned the fears of slave revolt throughout Missouri and the South. An ancient paranoia, this obsession was not entirely an unfounded fear for while the Missouri Brigade's soldiers were fighting across the South, Kansas Jayhawkers attempted to incite slave insurrections in western Missouri.

The often overlooked factor of "white slavery," and not black slavery, played a larger role in the motivations of Missouri Brigade members. The fear was widespread that a strong centralized government, the Lincoln administration, would first strip the yeomen of their property, then individual rights and liberties. Private Absalom Roby Dyson wrote in a letter that he was determined never to return to a Union-occupied Missouri, for "I cannot think of going back until I can go as a Free-man. You are well aware that I told you that I never expected to return to Mo. until I could go as a white-man and not as a slave." This interpretation was analogous to the revolutionary ideology of colonists who fought against the British. Offering no resistance equated to enslavement. In another letter, Private Dyson described the struggle as one for "freedom and prosperity." A deeply religious schoolteacher, Dyson found comfort in the belief that he would have at least "died in the service of our country nobly battling for Liberty and free institutions," as he wrote in one of his final letters before his death. Private George William Warren, a young merchant of Franklin County, wrote to his family in a letter how, "if the sacrifice of my life is necessary to our independence, and the freedom of those I hold most dear, I will not shrink from the sacrifice..."

The Missouri Brigade's quality was also immeasurably strengthened by a well-trained and seasoned cadre of leaders, who had learned much of their trade before the war. Besides being hardened graduates of the natural school of the frontier, distinguished alumni of private Southern military schools and West Point enhanced the quality of the Missouri Brigade's leaders. Another invaluable prewar factor that helped the leadership quality of the Missouri Brigade was service in the volunteer fire companies of St. Louis. This long ignored urban influence that benefited the officer corps applied most especially to the St. Louis Irish, such as Captains Patrick Canniff and Martin Burke, who were also militia members. These two sons of Erin early became two of the unit's best officers in part because of the discipline, teamwork, leadership, and organizational skills learned with the volunteer fire companies.[5]

The Missouri Brigade was primarily a young unit, and the command consisted of the best of a western frontier society. As one soldier wrote, "The Brigade was made up of the youths of the first families of Central and Northern Missouri." These zealous young men, mostly from the Mississippi and Missouri River valleys, "were the flower of the [rural] communit[ies] in which they lived," explained another Missouri Brigade member. Soldiers of fourteen and fifteen fought beside fathers and even grandfathers. Among the more than 8,000 Missouri Confederate volunteers, who served in the Missouri Brigade, more than 95 percent were of English and Scotch-Irish ancestry. In addition, these men were the descendants of Southern ancestors, who were among the most enterprising people of an agrarian middle-class from Kentucky, Tennessee, Virginia and North Carolina. The majority of these restless and adventurous spirits had migrated west across the Upper South in the early 1800's to start a new life on the frontier and fulfill the Jeffersonian dream. Leaving behind worn-out farms, these early settlers had trekked up the Missouri and Mississippi River Valleys, taming an incredibly rich and productive land, including a culturally distinct region of north-central Missouri known today as "Little Dixie," because of its strong Southern roots.

The Missouri soldiers had a distinctive physical appearance which impressed many observers. Even among the hardened Rebels of the Missouri State Guard, Missouri Brigade members were viewed as being rough-looking and "a damned hard set." Southerners wrote that the Missouri soldiers appeared "more intelligent and finer-looking, as a whole, than the men from the states farther south." Missouri Brigade members were healthier and more hardy than the average Southern soldiers. Therefore, the Missourians were more likely to survive wounds and disease, which assisted them in becoming the Confederacy's most dependable troops in the West. This quality was especially important, for the Missouri Brigade was cut off from the home state's manpower pool for almost its entire service.

It would be fiction to maintain that these western frontiersmen were all stainless heroes. The Missouri Brigade had its fair share of drunkards, thieves, deserters, cowards, stragglers, criminals, adulterers, and misfits as in every military unit, North or South. Disgruntled substitutes and mutineers could be found in the ranks. Some members of the Missouri Brigade were cursed with alcoholism, passions for prostitutes, ugly cases of venereal disease, and "fits of insanity." Other soldiers ran away in every battle and never fired a shot in anger, while some became notorious "hospital rats," who faked illness to escape duty. Some Missourians murdered comrades in camp disputes, exchanged Confederate gray for Federal blue, later rode with William C. Quantrill's raiders, schemed to kill at least one high-ranking officer, whipped male body servants, hanged one African American for committing an alleged crime, sexually exploited slave women, and committed other acts generally associated with the darker side of human nature. Unlike the rural soldiers, some of the more worldly Rebels from the harsh streets of St. Louis, one of the nation's major urban centers, were probably con artists, pimps, pickpockets and hustlers, who were as dangerous to civilians as to enemy soldiers. One Missouri Brigade officer lamented, "when far away from all the wholesome restraints of social life, soldiers are sad dogs." But once the fighting began, most of these unsavory characters were transformed into "the South's Finest" on the battlefield. However, these incidents were few, and did not tarnish the overall high caliber and deeply religious character of the majority of Missouri Brigade Confederates.

The cultural, emotional and historical identification with the South was natural for these volunteers. For instance, Private William Henry Kavanaugh explained the strong Southern bonds that had taken root and thrived in Missouri for generations after ancestors had migrated west: "My Parents being of Southern blood it was only natural for me to espouse the cause of the South." For most Missouri Brigade members, this decision was almost automatic for those of Southern heritage.

The importance of Missouri State Guard service can hardly be overestimated in laying the solid groundwork for "the South's Finest." These newly enlisted Confederates had gained invaluable experience during the six months' service in Price's State Guard. As members of Missouri's "Army of Liberation," the guardsmen had eventually won respect from their adversaries by their sheer determination. In 1861 Price's army had awakened Union leaders in Washington, D.C. to an unexpected threat in the West. Price's surprising victories at Carthage and with Ben McCulloch's Confederate volunteers and Arkansas State Guard at Wilson's Creek, Dry Wood Creek and Lexington and in dozens of skirmishes across Missouri caused a New York newspaperman to say: "What the [C.S.S.] Sumter is on the seas, Gen. Price is on the land—everywhere present, yet never to be caught. Now he is up on the Missouri river, now on the Osage, and now away down among the Ozark hills; now he skirts along the Kansas border, skulks down into Arkansas or rushes towards the red man's reserve [Indian Territory]; now he turns his front towards St. Louis."

The embryonic Missouri Brigade was the beneficiary of "the best and most buoyant material of the State Guard," wrote one soldier. In late 1861, these volunteers brought an esprit de corps from Guard days with them into Confederate service. The fusing of frontier self-reliance, prior military experience, and regular army discipline eventually forged this fledgling unit into "the best drilled & disciplined Brigade in [Confederate] service," wrote one Rebel. The western border state unit was known throughout the South during the war as "The Fighting Missouri Brigade." Without the many benefits of State Guard experience, the Missouri Brigade would not have acquired such a level of combat effectiveness, dependability and discipline during the war years.[6]

At the unit's formation, the Missourians' potential and tough western fiber could have been best gauged from the 1846-47 exploits of Colonel Alexander Doniphan's expedition during the Mexican War. In traveling almost 4,500 miles by foot, by horse and by steamboat and winning the battles of El Brazito and Sacramento and capturing El Paso and Chihuahua, Doniphan's Missourians compiled a one year record that reads much like a Homeric epic during the longest military expedition in American history. But the Missouri Brigade's soldiers would march on foot more than 4,000 miles and travel more than 1,500 miles by railroad and steamboat during their 40 month trek across seven states on both sides of the Mississippi, exceeding the legacy of Colonel Doniphan. Appropriately, many of Doniphan's veterans were sprinkled throughout the Missouri Brigade, serving as an invaluable cadre of experienced leaders, both among the officer and enlisted ranks.[7]

Another important factor that contributed to the Missouri Brigade's quality was a sturdy moral foundation, buttressed by sacrifice, a strong sense of duty, and firm commitment, which steadily increased as time passed. High morale stemmed from the all-consuming desire to reclaim the homeland from Federal occupation forces. The early invasion of Missouri by Kansas, Illinois, and Iowa troops had been perhaps the most decisive factor in transforming farm boys into fanatical defenders of the state and then revolutionaries of a new nation. To these young men who had never strayed far from behind the plow, Union soldiers, who thought and spoke differently, were as much invaders as the Redcoats of their grandfathers' day, and "foreigners" of different political and cultural beliefs. As one Missouri Brigade member explained, "When the Yankees came in our part of the country, we got after them." And another Missouri Brigade soldier recorded how his comrades "were mostly young men who had spent their lives in the open: physically strong and crack shots. Had it not been for the [abusive] conduct of [Union occupation troops], probably not more than one in ten of these would have cast his lot with the South." For perhaps a majority of Missouri Brigade members, the reason to fight was to resist the invasion of home soil. When Union troops gained control of St. Louis after the capture of Camp Jackson on May 10, 1861, Private Ephraim McDowell Anderson reasoned that "this at once was invasion, outrage, war." Motivation was also fueled because these former guardsmen had once been ridiculed as "Turnip Skinners," "Hazel-nut chargers" and "Blackberry Cavalry." Now Confederate service presented them an opportunity to yet prove their worth to themselves, their people, and their new nation.

Another key factor that strengthened the unit's esprit de corps was the Missouri Brigade's unique role as the largest body of Missouri Confederates serving east of the Mississippi River for most of the war. These soldiers felt that the eyes of the entire South were upon them, and they took much pride in their distinctive role of representing Missouri. Despite years of defeats and setbacks, a powerful unit loyalty continued to bolster the Missouri Brigade.

Revenge also served as a primary source of motivation, for families suffered under Union occupation. A good example of how Federal abuses fueled the common soldiers' determination came from Missouri Brigade member Lieutenant Avington Wayne Simpson, who wrote in his diary in 1863 how he "recd. the Sadest [sic] news of [my] life, Murder of [my] Aged Father" by the Federals in Missouri. Most of all, the exiled Missouri soldiers only "wish[ed] to protect [their families in Missouri] from the insults of their overbearing conquerors," wrote Lieutenant Warren in a letter to his father, who was persecuted by the Unionists. Such intense emotional and psychological factors helped to make the Missouri Confederates a highly motivated soldiery and the South's best troops, kindling a superior elan and fighting spirit.[8]

Colonel John Quincy Burbridge
Courtesy Missouri Historical Society, St. Louis
(Unpublished Painting)

CHAPTER ONE

The First Missouri Brigade

Throughout December 1861 Missouri enlistment in Confederate ranks continued. Not even an epidemic of measles and a groundless fear that the soldiers would not be allowed to elect their own commanders impeded the flow of volunteers. With Confederate commissions in their pockets, officers continued vigorous recruitment. By early December the first body of Missouri infantry destined for regimental status in the Missouri Brigade was organized by a devout Catholic, John Quincy Burbridge. This contingent became the First Missouri Confederate Infantry Regiment, a temporary designation. The sons of Johnson, Lincoln, Morgan, Pike, St. Charles, Callaway, Monroe, Ralls, Pettis, Atkinson, Boone, Linn, and Chariton Counties contributed most heavily to the new unit. Other Missouri counties made less substantial, but no less important, contributions. More than three-fourths of the 1,314 soldiers who served in the regiment were middle-class farmers, or yeomen of the frontier. Most were in their 20's, in good health and in the prime of life.

Colonel Burbridge, a banker from Louisiana, Missouri, had been born along the fertile bottom lands of the Mississippi River. The businessman and civic leader in the small port community, upriver and slightly northwest of St. Louis, had an Ireland-born indentured servant who attended his family. Burbridge, age thirty-one, had been educated at St. Louis University, the premier Jesuit institution of higher learning in the West. He had prewar militia experience, which provided invaluable leadership training. As an officer and drill master of the Louisiana militia company of Pike County, Burbridge and his followers had captured a cache of militia arms at Louisiana to resist the Illinois invaders, including prizes won during Doniphan's Expedition. Employing guerrilla tactics, Burbridge often had "outgeneraled the federals" in northeast Missouri during 1861. The roughhewn and heavily-bearded Catholic colonel was popular with his Protestant soldiers, who knew him informally as "Jack."

The colonel's younger brother, Clinton D. Burbridge, was a lieutenant in Company A, First Missouri Regiment, and later became a daring Rebel mail carrier. "Clint" had been a steamboat clerk in Louisiana, Missouri, and felt that if Confederate armies were defeated, then he and his comrades "would take it gurrilla [sic] fashion and fight us till the day of judgment," wrote one Yankee. And when confined in a St. Louis prison, he wrote defiantly to his brother how "if they shoot me you shall never have any reason to be ashamed of me [for] I will show them how a rebel can die." At the war's end, Colonel Burbridge would find a dying Clinton in St. Louis's streets after his release from prison, "sick with tuberculosis and hardly recognized his brother. He was siting [sic] on the sidewalk with his feet in the gutter—just sitting there," penned Clinton Burbridge, Sr., to Clinton

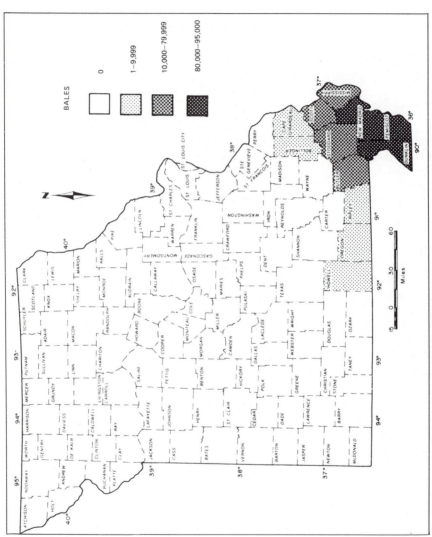

County Map of Missouri also showing Cotton Production

Courtesy Historical Atlas of Missouri

Burbridge III, in a personal, hand-written 1965 centennial tribute from grandfather to grandson. The colonel brought the emaciated Clinton home to die in his beloved Pike County.

In a solemn ceremony at the Confederate encampment near Osceola, General Price formally received Burbridge's new Missouri Confederate regiment. Colonel Burbridge's regiment contained a nucleus of officers and enlisted men who were Mexican War veterans. One of the best Mexican War veterans was Captain Peter Creed Flournoy, a physician of Linn County, who owned no slaves although his father had owned slaves. Born in Virginia and destined to have three horses shot from under him, Flournoy now commanded Company K at age thirty-three. When not leading a charge, he treated his sick and injured soldiers as if back at home in the small community of Linneus. Another such dependable leader was Captain William Fuqua Carter, a former mason. He led Company F after having gained valuable experience with Colonel Burbridge in the Louisiana, Missouri, militia company. Carter showed much promise for higher rank at only age twenty-three.[1]

Reconfirming the societal values of the frontier, the common soldiers voted overwhelmingly to serve under their community leaders. Following Colonel Burbridge's example, two other leaders recruited for Missouri Confederate regiments during the cold weather of December 1861, Dr. Benjamin Allen Rives and Elijah P. Gates. Hundreds of eager volunteers poured forth. All classes were represented in the ranks, from lowly bondsmen, who had worked like slaves on farms, to the respected pillars of the community, including physicians, merchants, and teachers. The vast majority of Missouri Brigade members were young farmers "ranging from 18 to 30 years old and picked from the flower of her best [agrarian] citizenship," analyzed one Rebel. This group served as the backbone of the Jeffersonian Democracy on the western frontier. Practically entire communities and large family clans enlisted en masse to fight and die together in an enthusiastic community response across Missouri to resist invasion. In large part, the Missouri Brigade was a frontier unit of relatives.[2]

The family of the Reverend James Duvall exemplified the fusion of revolutionary, militant religion and Southern nationalism in the Missouri River Valley. The Duvall family had prospered for generations on a fine seven-hundred-acre farm along the Crooked River in Ray County. The minister's four Virginia-born sons enlisted in Colonel Rives's new regiment, Privates David Henderson, William Russell, Thomas Isaac, and Joseph F. Duvall. Only a battle-scarred Joseph would survive to return to Ray County in 1865, after losing his three brothers to Yankee bullets.

Also in Colonel Rives's regiment were brothers Sergeant Nathaniel G. Mothershead, Jr. and Lieutenant Joseph R. Mothershead. Serving with the Mothershead boys in Company I was their sprightly grandfather, who fought beside them like a youngster. Private Nathaniel Mothershead, Sr., was the Missouri Brigade's eldest soldier at age eighty-five! He had voted for Thomas Jefferson in the presidential election of 1800. Mothershead fought against the United States to defend the Jeffersonian society that he admired.

Important symbolically in bestowing more legitimacy to that Second American Revolution, as many have called the Civil War, Jefferson's descendants served in the Missouri Brigade. One of the relatives of the third president of the United States was Captain Archer Christian Bankhead, who had been raised near Monticello.

Now leading the northeast Missouri men of Company B, Burbridge's regiment, young Captain Bankhead was Jefferson's great-grandson. He was also related to the Confederate Secretary of War, George Wythe Randolph, and to General John Bankhead Magruder. Captain Bankhead commanded soldiers primarily from Pike and Lincoln Counties, which consisted of fertile lands bordering the Mississippi River between St. Louis and Hannibal.[3]

Colonel Rives supplied another example of large family groups forming into community-like companies. One nephew acted as the colonel's aide-de-camp. And the colonel's brother, Lieutenant Robert Rives, served in Company F. In addition, four more of Colonel Rives's nephews enlisted in the regiment, temporarily designated as the Second Missouri Confederate Infantry. Such heavy concentrations of relatives within companies resulted in much grief on the home front when multiple deaths occurred on the same Southern battlefield.

Colonel Rives's Second Missouri consisted of western and northwestern Missouri soldiers, with most hailing from Ray County, which bordered the Missouri River. 1,107 men served in this infantry regiment. After Ray County, east of Kansas City, the counties of Clay, Gentry, Randolph, Daviess, DeKalb, Clinton, Jackson, Buchanan, Carroll, and Livingston, respectively, gave most freely of their sons to Colonel Rives's regiment. The majority of the Rebels of the Second Missouri were Missouri-born. However, at least 180 regimental members were born in Kentucky, 46 in Tennessee, 35 in Virginia, and another 12 in North Carolina. The Second Missouri regiment also contained more soldiers born in the old Northwest Territory—Indiana, Ohio and Illinois—than those men born in the Deep South. The Missouri Brigade's other regiments contained a comparable breakdown which exemplified historical migration patterns.

The close, family-like bonds among elected leaders, the home community, and the enlisted men was obvious when scurvy swept the encampment of Rives's regiment. Colonel Rives wrote a long letter home describing the brutal ravages of disease, which had almost immediately sent young men to early graves before meeting their first Yankees. In response to the colonel's letter, Rives's mother and other relatives brewed a giant batch of onion pickle broth, then sent a large barrel of the broth by wagon on the long journey south from Ray County. Soon nutrition-deprived and medicine-short Rebels dipped out onions from the barrel and drank the broth, declaring, "God bless old Mother Rives." And the familial character of Burbridge's regiment was evident when the colonel's wife from Louisiana, Missouri, presented the best drilled company of the command with a battle-flag.[4]

Colonel Rives's natural military abilities complemented his former occupation as a Richmond, Missouri, physician. He also had been a successful farmer, who used the latest scientific methods to make the rich lands near the Missouri River even more productive. Unlike most of his soldiers, the Virginia-born Doctor Rives was from the frontier upper-class. He owned many slaves obtained through marriage to a young woman, "who had more pewter [money] than a couple of mules could pull down a slippery hill," wrote an obviously thankful Rives in the year of his marriage [1846] not long before migrating to Missouri. Demonstrating enlightenment that was considered unwise in ante-bellum Missouri, Colonel Rives was a benevolent slave-owner, teaching his wife's slaves how to read and write. He showed a comparable sincere paternalistic concern for his Rebel soldiers. Such egalitarian qualities made Colonel Rives especially popular among his free-thinking frontiersmen.

The colonel's distinguished background included an impressive list of accomplishments including a medical education from the University of Virginia. He was an active member of the Missouri State legislature from 1858 to 1860; a respected, leading citizen of Richmond, Missouri; a widespread reputation for performing brilliant medical operations which amazed older physicians; and the distinction of being one of Missouri's best public speakers. But unlike a detached aristocrat, Rives had found much personal satisfaction in tilling the fertile land of western Missouri like the most humble farmer. Rives's scientific agricultural experiments won him trophies for superior products. Of French Huguenot and Scotch-Irish extraction, Rives was a good-natured, gentleman-planter mingling well with people of all classes. Tall and slender, he cut a dashing figure in his new Confederate uniform. A tawny beard accented a handsome face, blue eyes and long reddish-blond hair.

Despite sympathy with his native Virginia and the South, Rives had not been a radical fire-eater in early 1861. Like most Missourians, he initially opposed secession. With Lincoln's success in the November 1860 presidential election, for instance, Rives had declared: "The South has never had a fair construction of her principles, but let us give Lincoln a trial." But Rives's deep kinship, emotional and cultural ties with Virginia were key factors which eventually changed his mind, when the Old Dominion seceded from the splintered Union in mid-April 1861. Like most Americans in 1861, the physician from a small rural community had been thrust into the conflict by events beyond his control. The invasion of Missouri and the capture of Camp Jackson by the Unionists were the catalysts which caused pro-Southern Missourians to fight for the South. Rives was one of the first to organize a cavalry company of his friends and neighbors. Most of these soldiers were now in the Second Missouri, ready to follow their physician-leader to hell and back if necessary. Throughout his State Guard career, Colonel Rives compiled an impressive record, especially at the Battles of Wilson's Creek and Lexington. After exhibiting leadership qualities that placed him far above the majority of State Guard commanders, Colonel Rives was "the idol, not only of the [regiment], but [also] of the whole [Missouri] brigade," wrote one soldier. By 1862 Colonel Rives was ready for command of the Missouri Brigade.[5]

A natural leader without a military background at age thirty-two, Colonel Elijah P. Gates had more influence and achieved more popularity among the Missouri Brigade members than only one other leader, Francis Marion Cockrell. Gates was a self-reliant, middle-class tiller of the soil. General Price swore that among his whole army, the hot-tempered farmer from northwest Missouri "had no superior for bravery." Broad-shouldered and stoutly built, Gates's commanding presence and high-spirited nature accomplished what a West Pointer would consider almost impossible, inspiring respect and discipline among some of the most individualist Rebels of the Confederacy. But another key characteristic made Colonel Gates one of the finest cavalry commanders in the West—a tough and stubborn "bull-dog tenacity."

Of Virginia and Kentucky antecedents, like most of his horse soldiers, Colonel Gates rose up in life on his own ability and hard work, mastering a harsh frontier environment. He had trekked to the Sierra Nevada Mountains of northern California in search of gold during 1852. After failing to find instant wealth in the mountains of California, Gates had migrated to Missouri with his wife and eventually settled on nearly two hundred acres in Buchanan County. The native Kentuckian had raised hemp along the rolling hills and the bottom lands along the Platte River, finally discovering the riches that had escaped him in California in the fertile soil of Missouri. Despite producing a plantation culture crop, Gates was an agriculturalist without slaves, who supported a wife and four children. With the call to arms, he had enlisted as a cavalry private in the Easton Guards of northwest Missouri, and then joined General Price. Gates later helped raise one of the State Guard's best cavalry regiments, and served with distinction as lieutenant colonel. Colonel Gates had compiled a reputation second to none among cavalry commanders during the Missouri campaigns of 1861.[6]

Forged from the frontier experience and early teachings of guerrilla-style fighting in Missouri, an unorthodox nature and unrestricted freedom of thought helped Colonels Gates and Rives to become open-minded, flexible and innovative tacticians on the battlefield. Neither of these commanders had prior military experience, but they employed their own initiative with considerable success on the battlefield. They were not artificially restricted or limited tactically by the out-dated axioms of formal military training. During the prewar period, both Gates and Rives were so unconventional as to refuse to join any organized religion and both defied other orthodox social constraints. Natural leadership ability and an aggressive nature would help transform Colonel Gates into perhaps the best horse commander in the Trans-Mississippi by early 1862. Likewise, Colonel Rives had been "a bold, independent thinker" as a cavalry leader and tactician during the campaigns of 1861. Both of these capable regimental commanders had used frontier ways of fighting among the forest and hills of the West. Colonels Gates, Rives, and Burbridge all had brothers who were destined to forfeit their lives while serving in the Missouri Brigade.[7]

Two Missouri Confederate artillery units began organizing in December of 1861 at the Confederate encampment near Osceola. Battle-tested gunners with a plentiful amount of State Guard experience and raw recruits volunteered for Confederate artillery service. In contrast to the Missouri Brigade's infantry and cavalry leaders who hailed from rural areas, the two artillery commanders of the Missouri Brigade were products of an urban environment. Both Captains William Wade and Samuel Churchill Clark were raised in Missouri's largest city, St. Louis. Many of these volunteers of Clark's new Confederate Battery had seen duty in the State Guard battery that he had commanded since the autumn of 1861.

With the addition of artillery units, almost all of Missouri was represented in the Missouri Brigade, including the state's major urban centers, St. Louis, St. Joseph, Kansas City, and Springfield. But the majority of Missouri Brigade members hailed from the rural areas of the great river valleys of the Missouri, which cut across the state's midsection, and the Mississippi, the state's eastern border. Both socioeconomically diverse groups managed to get along reasonably well in the Missouri Brigade despite some differences that were wider than those between them and the Yankees. As in most revolutionary movements, the earliest resistance had developed in Missouri as a response to the perceived threat of repressive measures of a strong, centralized government, which forged bonds between rural and urban Rebels, who forgot differences and fought side by side. So many St. Louis Rebels rose up in revolt that an early attempt had been made to form a Missouri brigade composed entirely of St. Louis soldiers, under the command of Captain Clark's father, Meriwether Lewis Clark.

The fewest Missouri Brigade members hailed from the wilds of southern Missouri, a mountainous, densely forested region with a small population and few slaves. The most forgotten Missouri Brigade members came from the Bootheel region, named for its geographic shape, of southeast Missouri. Recently reprinted post-war memoirs of Missouri Brigade members from northern and mid-Missouri and local historians have fostered the myth that the contribution of Southeast Missouri soldiers to the unit's historical record was insignificant.

The urban influence was especially prevalent in the six-gun battery of Captain Wade. A large number of these hardy cannoneers hailed from the bustling city environment of St. Louis. Private Jennings P. Orr exemplified the quality of Wade's artillerymen. He had won fame as a daring color bearer, who demonstrated heroics at the Battle of Wilson's Creek. Orr continued his flag bearing tradition with Wade's battery.

Captain Wade was energetic and resourceful, an ideal choice for command of the First Missouri Confederate Artillery. The native Marylander had served with distinction as an artillery major in the Missouri State Guard. A combative and spirited nature highlighted his lively personality. According to one Rebel, the forty-two-year-old Wade "was in the prime of life, of medium height and rather slender, but sinewy, active, and muscular in his movements and development [and] his manners were plain and unassuming." These characteristics were a source of the captain's popularity among his artillerymen. During prewar days, Wade demonstrated a gritty side when he held a group of workers at gun-point in a downtown St. Louis office, while General Daniel Marsh Frost, commander of the Missouri Volunteer Militia of St. Louis, settled a personal score. But Captain Wade also had a compassionate disposition. During the Southwest Expedition to the Kansas border in 1860, he had raised and donated money for a destitute Missouri family so that they might survive the winter, after the family head had been killed in a Jayhawker raid.

Captain Wade's most valuable military experience was gained as a captain of a company of high-spirited, troublesome and hard-drinking Irishmen of the Missouri militia of ante-bellum St. Louis. He and his men had been captured at Camp Jackson. After signing a parole and returning home, Wade was a marked man because of his political beliefs. In June of 1861, the Wade family house in St. Louis was surrounded by Federals eager to arrest Wade, but he fled south to Memphis. Here at the Mississippi River port in western Tennessee, he gathered and enlisted his first recruits for his Missouri artillery unit.

By 1861 Wade had suffered the deaths of three young children from disease in 1855-1857; capture at Camp Jackson; exile from home and family and the loss of his St. Louis business interests and investments to the Unionists. Nevertheless, Captain Wade "was always cheerful and alert, and never grumbled." Wade and his battery left Memphis and headed northwest to link with General Price's army during the autumn of 1861. The St. Louisan also brought twenty-five cannon which had been cast at the Quinby & Robinson Foundry in Memphis. The timely resupply brought new confidence to "the Patriot Army of Missouri." Captain Wade would become the best artillery commander in the Missouri Brigade and the chief of artillery for one of the finest Confederate divisions in the West by the 1863 Vicksburg Campaign.[8]

Also possessing an abundance of both natural and taught ability was Captain Samuel Churchill Clark, or "Churchy." He was the only West Point graduate unit commander in the Missouri Brigade. After two years of learning his trade at West Point and with civil war on the horizon, the teenager left the military academy on the Hudson River. To join his idol, General Price, and his army, Clark left the beautiful family mansion called "Minoma," just west of St. Louis, in the summer of 1861. The handsome, athletic "Churchy" planned to marry a relative of General Price, a wish that would be unfulfilled. The West Pointer was so eager for action that he offered to serve in the ranks as a private. But General Price wisely knew that he had to utilize Clark's martial talents to the fullest. Enthusiastic and popular, Clark immediately became a favorite of "Old Pap" Price.

Like Colonel Burbridge, Clark was a Catholic who had attended St. Louis University. He carried a Bible that his father had given him before he left Missouri for West Point in 1859. "Churchy" was the grand-nephew of the famous Virginian and American Revolutionary hero, George Rogers Clark. The sectional conflict had split the Clark family, with the captain's favorite older brother wearing Federal blue and his father serving as a Missouri State Guard general. "Churchy" was also the gifted grandson of explorer William Clark of the Lewis and Clark Expedition. In addition, Clark's father was a veteran of Doniphan's Expedition. Most people expected the young man to rival the deeds of his famous ancestors.

Captain Clark soon won a widespread reputation as "the [John] Pelham of the [Western] army..." A boyish demeanor hid the fierce determination of the young commander of the Second Missouri Confederate Light Artillery. "Conquer or die, and die I will before they shall take me," wrote the captain in a letter to St. Louis. During his first engagement with Price's army, he won much acclaim and a gold medal for blasting a United States flag off the earthworks of Lexington with a miraculous shot. But Clark later wrote to this family and admitted that he "felt a little queer when I saw the stars and stripes fall by my own hand, but still went on," less than six months after he had paraded as a zealous cadet on the drill ground of West Point. Personable and still innocent in many ways but always a fighter, Clark liked the ladies and carried locks of hair of different colors. But now the captain's top priority was focused on fine-tuning his newly formed Confederate battery so that they would always be "ready to give the 'Feds' 200 rounds at a moment's notice."

By early 1862 Captain Clark was considered the finest artillery commander in Price's army. Clark was an invaluable addition to the Missouri Brigade, enhancing the unit's overall quality and fighting prowess. The captain was popular among his artillerymen, who were mostly from western Missouri and consisted of "the best blood of Missouri['s]" frontier yeomanry. A fine example of the soldiers who served in Clark's battery was Private George Thomas Martin, a seventeen-year-old. As a cannoneer of this reliable artillery unit that included Union guns captured at Lexington, Martin was characterized by a "bravery [which] abounds to recklessness," wrote one comrade. Although eager for action, young Captain "Churchy" Clark most of all feared a slow, painful death from "a Minie ball in the bowels."[9]

The lack of West Point training among the Missouri Brigade's unit commanders did not prove as serious a liability as might be expected. Instead, in a brutal western war in which both sides would be slaughtered in part because of an over-emphasis on obsolete military tactics of the Mexican War, the absence of the rigid West Point indoctrination often worked to the advantage of Missouri Brigade leaders.

Along with experience gained from the frontier environment and partisan warfare, the dearth of West Point training allowed Colonels Gates, Rives, Burbridge, and Captain Wade to develop and mature naturally as leaders, relying more heavily upon their own instincts and resourcefulness in developing their own tactics and ways of fighting. Tight bonds of mutual trust and respect between the enlisted men and their officers were forged early, strengthening the Missouri Brigade's cohesion.

But, conversely, it was crucial that a West Point-like leader with regular army experience be given overall command of the Missouri Brigade. Recently from Richmond, a competent and talented officer with a colonel's commission in his pocket and with more than twenty years of experience in the United States Army, Lewis Henry Little had been appointed by General Price to organize and command the Missouri Confederate troops. Henry Little, as he preferred to be known, was the right man to undertake the difficult job of transforming quarrelsome and rowdy ex-Guardsmen into "the South's Finest." Only an experienced and mature officer like Colonel Little could gradually and carefully, but firmly, instill the necessary discipline without causing widespread discontent or unit disloyalty. A Missouri Brigade member described his new commander as "a fine tactician, an accomplished soldier, and won for himself the love and esteem of the men he commanded..." As General Price's adjutant-general, Colonel Little played a key role in transforming the Missouri State Guard into a respectable fighting force; Colonel Little soon became General Price's top lieutenant.

Like Colonel Rives and other regimental commanders, Colonel Little was forced to make an anguished decision before taking up arms against the United States government. Little's dilemma was especially complex and anxiety-provoking. The emotional pull of his love for his native Maryland, another deeply divided border state, and his sympathy for the South clashed with his devotion to "Old Glory," which he had served faithfully for twenty-two years. A Mexico War hero cited for bravery at the Battle of Monterrey, son of a Maryland Congressman, and from a leading Baltimore family, Little had been tormented by the plight of both his Maryland and his self-destructing nation.

The news of the war's outbreak had caused Little to write in his diary, "My poor Country! I fear you are gone—God help us!" Besides the trauma of the sectional struggle, Little wrestled with conflicting feelings, including a longing for a return to his Maryland to join in that struggle, debating resignation from the United States Army, contemplating the loss of much personal property in the North if he went South, the lingering pain of the recent death of his four-year-old daughter, the recent miscarriage of his wife, and concern about finding a home for his family if he decided to forsake the Union. Ironically, the gentleman from the easternmost border state found himself in command of a Confederate Brigade of frontiersmen from the westernmost border state. With much tactical ability and potential, the long-haired and dark-featured Colonel Little was the perfect commander to lead the first Confederate Brigade from Missouri. This struggle for national identity was a "fight for liberty," as he wrote in his diary.[10]

Not even official entry into Confederate service was enough to tame the boundless individualism of these frontiersmen, however. For instance, when Captain Peter C. Flournoy of Burbridge's regiment "quarrelled [sic] with [a] Sergt about beef," wrote one soldier, the heated argument escalated "from high words [then] they got to blows." After being knocked down by the enlisted man, Flournoy

Chaplain John B. Bannon
Painting in author's collection. Artwork by Dennis Scanio, St. Louis
(Unpublished Painting)

proceeded to brutally "beat [the] Sergt of his Company." Then, in another clash, a feisty private of Wade's Battery fought for his "rights," viciously "striking a Superior officer with a [horse] whip." Other examples of such defiance and outbursts of frontier rowdiness among the enlisted ranks were legion. Not long after enlistment, for instance, most of Colonel Burbridge's men ignored the colonel's order not to burn a farmer's fence rails. Immediately after Colonel Burbridge walked away after threatening to arrest any man who burnt a rail, "the campfires were lighted almost at his heels," wrote one private who never forgot this early disregard for the rules and regulations.

To help control such free-spirits, something more than West Point-like discipline was necessary. Playing the most important role in providing a strong spiritual foundation to toughen the soldiers' moral fiber by fusing religion and nationalism were the regimental chaplains. The man of God who provided the most spiritual inspiration was Father John B. Bannon, the chaplain of the Missouri Brigade. Father Bannon, as much of a soldier as a chaplain, and his fellow chaplains deserve much credit for providing the inspiration that enabled the Missouri Brigade to rebound after frightful casualties and successive defeats year after year to face the next challenge. Despite the fact that the Missouri Brigade members were overwhelmingly Protestant, the dark-bearded, six-foot-four Irish priest from St. Louis served as the spiritual guiding light for the Methodists, Baptists, Episcopalians, Presbyterians and Catholics of the frontier unit. In this war, no chaplain accomplished as much important work for the South, both on the battlefield or in camp, as Father Bannon.

Along with Captain Wade, the soldier-priest had served on the Southwest Expedition as chaplain of the Missouri Volunteer Militia during the ante-bellum period. Then he had been captured at Camp Jackson, while acting as brigade chaplain of the militia of St. Louis. Father Bannon sacrificed much in joining Price's army, leaving one of the finest churches of St. Louis shortly after it was dedicated, and forsaking a bright future and high leadership position within the Catholic Church. Bannon reached Price's command while the organization of the Missouri Brigade continued. Over the next year and a half, Bannon's heroics on the battlefield and unceasing efforts to strengthen the soldiers' Christian virtues became legendary, earning him a widespread reputation as the Confederacy's "Fighting Chaplain" and "the Catholic Priest who always went into battle." Father Bannon was especially close to the St. Louis boys, including many of his former parishioners of St. John the Apostle and Evangelist Church [which stands today in St. Louis], in the Missouri batteries. He always "joked and laughed with them in bivouac and went with them into action [and he] helped serve the guns in desperate emergencies, and who prayed with the dying on the battlefield," wrote one Rebel. Father Bannon was personable, witty and good-humored, and popular among the common soldiers. On many battlegrounds, Father Bannon would prove more of a soldier than a man of God, especially if angered.

A native of Ireland, Chaplain Bannon was a pillar of strength, inspiration, and spiritual refuge for these young men and boys. For Bannon and the Irish Catholic Rebels, the South's struggle for self-determination was almost identical to the yearnings of Irish nationalism against another strong, centralized power, the British Empire. Along with the regimental chaplains, Bannon's influence in the Missouri Brigade strengthened unit cohesion, instilling the belief of the righteousness of waging a holy war, which enhanced the unit's fighting quality by creating a moral soldiery.[11]

All in all, Colonels Little, Rives, Gates, Burbridge, and Captains Wade and Clark would soon have much excellent raw material with which to work: more than 2,000 young farm boys of the western frontier. These Rebels were quite unlike the Confederate troops found among the more polished soldiery and cavalier types of the Army of Northern Virginia in the east.

In appearance, these new Confederates looked little different from their State Guard comrades. Only a few new arms and no new Confederate uniforms were issued with the initial enlistment. Some infantrymen who brought shotguns and flintlocks from home exchanged these weapons for muskets. Colonel Gates's horsesoldiers retained their shotguns, which would soon prove more of an asset than a liability. One Missouri Brigade member reflected with much pride how "though our clothes were rough and not very good, our guns and bayonets were bright and polished." By the time of their first battle as Confederates, many of the Missourians were armed with .69 caliber smoothbore muskets, which were formidable weapons with "buck and ball," a ball and three buckshot ammunition. In addition, Colonel Little's men soon received cartridge-boxes and belts with "C.S." brass plates. Colonel Little immediately began drilling his men with an intensity unknown in State Guard days. The Missouri Brigade suffered its first loss, when one Rebel's musket fired accidentally during the manual of arms, killing an unfortunate soldier nearby. Colonel Little and a young staff officer from a leading St. Louis family, Captain Wright C. Schaumburg, conducted the military funeral in regular army fashion.

Although in Confederate service, the Rebels of the Missouri Brigade continued to maintain not only their individualist frontier attitudes, but also their homespun appearances. One Southerner soon wrote in a newspaper that among the Missouri Confederates, "I have been forcibly struck by the remarkable personnel of a majority of the men. They are heavy, large headed, rough, brown faced fellows, who look as if [they could] 'whip their weight in wild cats!' Fully over three-fifths of them are over six feet in hight [sic] [and] nearly every man...is a splendid shot." For instance, colorful dress was worn by such soldiers as William and Thomas Duvall. Both brothers in Colonel Rives's regiment wore sturdy pull-over hunting shirts, or "battle-shirts," which were also adopted by Missouri guerrillas. These durable garments had been lovingly sewn by mothers, wives, and grandmothers for "their boys." Just like another country private, General Price donned a homespun "war-coat" in battle.

The Missouri Brigade's organization continued, even after General Price's army was forced to withdraw southward to occupy Springfield. This timely decision to retire from the Osceola area was wise, solving logistical problems by reducing the length of the supply line to Arkansas. In addition, Price's position was too far north, an exposed salient with Union forces on each side. To consolidate gains and to protect the resource-abundant region of southwestern Missouri, including the all-important Granby lead mines necessary for making bullets for Rebel armies on both sides of the Mississippi, and the largest city in this corner of the state, Price made a stand in the last week of December 1861 at Springfield. Here, the Missouri boys settled into winter quarters while the Federals remained quiet. At the Missouri Brigade's picturesque encampment at Fullbright Spring, Colonel Little drilled his regiments for long hours in snowy fields and under wintry skies. When not drilling, the Missouri Confederates wrestled, drank rot-gut whiskey, played cards like riverboat gamblers, and danced to fiddles far into the night, after building log cabins for what they thought would be a long winter respite. Young soldiers continued to die from a variety of diseases at a steady rate. Much-feared pneumonia and dysentery kept the chaplains busy trying to save souls before they laid more soldiers in the cold ground of Greene County.

Through the end of December and throughout much of January of 1862, meanwhile, the filling of the Missouri Brigade's ranks continued. By the end of January, the organization of the Missouri Brigade was finally complete, and these Rebels were now in better shape to engage the Federals than ever before. Only two of the five unit commanders of the Missouri Brigade, Colonel Burbridge and Captain Clark, had been born in Missouri, while an ex-United States officer from the aristocratic east, Colonel Little, led the new brigade of western frontiersmen. And the Missouri Brigade, which had been organized to help win Missouri for the Confederacy, remained in the state for less than two weeks, before departing and heading south, never to return. But worst of all, a high percentage of these young soldiers from the Trans-Mississippi fought and died for years on the east side of the Mississippi far from home.[12]

CHAPTER TWO

Mr. Cox's Tavern

The tranquillity of Price's winter quarters at Springfield was interrupted in the second week of February by the advance of the Union Army of the Southwest under Brigadier General Samuel R. Curtis. In the attempt to permanently secure the Union grip on Missouri, Curtis's relentless drive southwest from Rolla, Missouri was focused upon hurling Price's Rebels out of the state once and for all. The Union offensive threatened not only to gain control of Missouri, but also to win Arkansas and the resource-rich Indian Territory for the North. Without support from the Confederacy, unable to tap the rich manpower pool of pro-Southern Missourians north of the Missouri River because of Union control of the vital waterway, and with too few troops, Price's only alternative was withdrawal southwest into northwestern Arkansas to link with McCulloch's division. Missouri had to be abandoned without a fight.

Expecting a quiet winter in southwest Missouri, General Price was caught by surprise on February 12, when skirmishing erupted east of Springfield and on the main road leading from the Union-held railroad terminus of Rolla, Missouri. The advance elements of Curtis's 12,000 troops were rapidly closing in on the outskirts of the unfortified winter encampment, and Price had no time to marshal an adequate defense. Panic spread in Springfield, and Price ordered an immediate evacuation. With the beating of drums, the Missouri Brigade's log cabin community, named Camp Price, swirled with activity. Even if the Rebels left immediately, the Missouri Army of barely 7,000 soldiers might yet be cut to pieces on the open road to Arkansas by Curtis's pursuit.

"Old Pap" Price ordered the newest Confederate cavalry unit in the West, the First Missouri Confederate Cavalry, to perform a key mission: buy time for the Rebel army's evacuation and safe withdrawal from Springfield with a bold diversion, taking the offensive to slow the advance of Curtis's army. With a blast of bugles, Colonel Gates and his butternut troopers were soon thundering east to strike a blow to allow the escape of Price's army and enhance the possibility that the forces of Price and McCulloch might link for a chance to reverse sagging Confederate fortunes in the Trans-Mississippi. This was a critical first assignment for the newly-organized Confederate regiment, and a harbinger of the Missourians' arduous duty in the years ahead.

Upon nearing the peaceful Yankee encampments along McPherson's Creek and on the main road about eight miles east of Springfield, Colonel Gates ordered an immediate attack. He led a daring charge that smashed through the advance outposts of the First Missouri Volunteer Cavalry, U.S.A. To exploit the success and create the impression that "Price's whole army was bearing down upon them,"

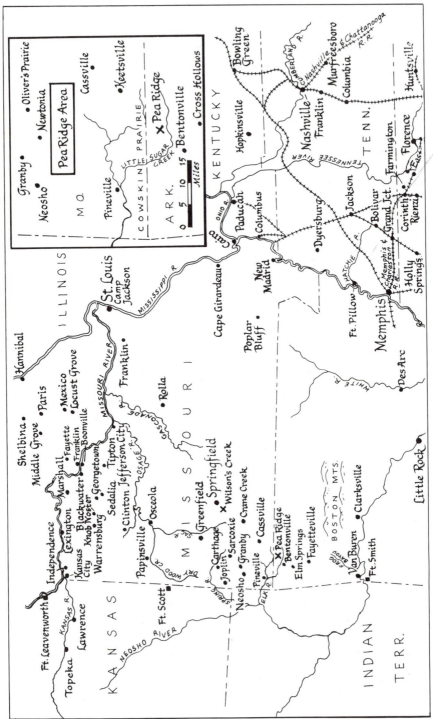

The Region around the Battle of Pea Ridge

Courtesy *First Missouri Confederate Brigade* by Anderson and Bearss

Colonel Gates ordered the attack continued. Gates wanted to hit the quiet Union camps in the late afternoon of February 12, when the Federals were relaxing and cooking. But the alerted Yankees quickly responded to the threat and advanced. With bluecoats swarming toward the lone Confederate regiment, Colonel Gates assessed the situation, then wisely ordered his frontiersmen to dismount and take ambush positions on timbered, advantageous terrain. Union artillery hammered the dismounted Rebels, but the cavalrymen refused to budge. Gates's boys unleashed a volley with shotguns from concealed positions in the underbrush when the Federals closed in for the kill. The brisk skirmishing continued into the night, with Colonel Gates audaciously holding his position and buying all the time he possibly could after stirring up "a hornet's nest."

Eventually, the Unionists threatened to flank the Rebels' position. Gates finally ordered his cavalrymen to mount up and retire to Springfield, after having caused havoc in the Yankee encampments with "Stonewall Jackson tactics" and accomplishing his difficult mission. Colonel Gates's surprise attack made the Federals more cautious, delaying the capture of Springfield, and, most important, distracting the Unionists from their main objective, General Price's army. Meanwhile, Price's columns had left Springfield and were moving down the Telegraph Road that led southwest to the safety of Arkansas. Colonel Gates's strike helped guarantee that one of the principal Rebel forces in the Trans-Mississippi would live to fight another day for the possession of Missouri.[1]

During the risky ten-day withdrawal into the vastness of the Boston Mountains of northwestern Arkansas, Colonel Little and the Missouri Brigade, as a whole, were given the first opportunity to prove themselves by playing the vital role as the rear-guard for Price's army. Aggressive pursuit of Yankee cavalry and artillery, combined with Price's slow-moving, badly disorganized army and cumbersome train of 200 wagons that had to be saved, forced the Missouri Brigade to halt, turn around, and make numerous stands to parry each Federal thrust. Skirmishes were especially hot at numerous creek crossings in obscure and narrow valleys amid the wilderness. Repeatedly, Colonel Little demonstrated extraordinary ability in choosing excellent defensive terrain and skillfully deploying his forces to check-mate each threat which endangered Price's army. Captains Clark's and Wade's cannon were also effective in dispersing Union cavalry thrusts and keeping Federal artillery at a distance. While serving as the army's guardians, the soldiers suffered severely in the bitterly cold weather, with ragged clothes freezing stiff and beards turning half-white with frost.[2]

Colonel Gates's First Missouri Cavalry performed brilliantly during the long and hazardous withdrawal through southwestern Missouri and into the dense forests of Arkansas. Like the protective role that the Missouri Brigade played in guarding the rear of Price's army, so Gates's horse regiment acted as the rear-guard protector of Colonel Little's Missouri Brigade. Day after day across the frozen fields and brown woodlands of Missouri and Arkansas, Colonel Gates judiciously employed frontier tactics—ambush, hit-and-run, and dismounted cavalry fighting as infantry—, with much success and at a time when these tactics were uncommon in conventional armies.

This frontier way of waging war came naturally for Gates's regiment, which had been forged from hard-riding partisan units, which were initially organized to combat Union occupation forces in Missouri. More of Gates's soldiers had been involved in bitter years of prewar fighting against the Kansas Jayhawkers than the members of any other Missouri Brigade unit or of any other Confederate cavalry regiment. Years before the Civil War, these troopers had learned about frontier-style cavalry tactics of reconnaissance, lightning-quick raids, flank maneuvers, striking at night, scouting, fighting on the run and hiding in the bush from experience gained in Indian conflicts, the Mexican War, the struggle for Kansas, and in Missouri State Guard cavalry service.

Colonel Gates's regiment was primarily a northwest Missouri unit. Of the 1,288 horse soldiers who served in the First Missouri Cavalry, Platte County contributed the majority of regimental members, followed by Buchanan County. Poised on the Missouri River with Kansas on the west side, Platte County had long served as the headquarters and staging area for the pro-Southern Missouri effort in "Bloody Kansas" during the 1850's. Most of the other hard-riding First Missouri Cavalrymen hailed from Andrew, Holt, Nodaway, and Atchison Counties in northwest Missouri. In early 1861 some of these Rebels from Atchison and Nodaway Counties could look north and view their future adversaries in Iowa from cabins nestled amid the sprawling sea of prairie grass.

The invaluable experience of irregular warfare gained by Gates's seasoned veterans now paid dividends, being instrumental in enhancing the Missouri Brigade's effectiveness in saving Price's army from defeat on the difficult road to Arkansas. No other unit in the Rebel army matched Gates's regiment for "the sturdy pluck and game of the men," wrote one soldier. These frontier cavaliers rode their own horses and carried the weapons brought from home in the militia tradition.

Another key to the efficiency of Colonel Gates's command can be found in the experienced and high quality of leadership. Company commanders, such as Captain Silas M. Gordon, had first organized resistance and partisan bands when their communities were overrun by Federal troops in 1861. Captain Gordon of Company I and other company commanders were experts at the frontier tactics of mobile and guerrilla warfare. In establishing a reputation across both Missouri and Kansas, Captain "Si" Gordon had been wounded during the border clashes with Kansas bands under such Jayhawker leaders as John Brown.

Another of Colonel Gates's top lieutenants and company commanders was Captain John Thrailkill, who led Company F. He had the distinction of being the only Missouri Brigade member of Russian descent. Thrailkill's experience in the vicious border war with Kansas rivaled that of Captain Gordon. The wild-riding, twenty-two-year-old Missouri "Cossack" from Holt County was a frontier dandy, wearing his hair long and perfumed. Commanding Company K and a veteran of Doniphan's Expedition during the Mexican War, Captain Charles Austin Rogers was another example of the type of veteran leader who helped to make the First Missouri Cavalry the best horse unit in terms of effectiveness, quality of leadership and overall level of experience.

Also some of Gates's troopers had played key roles in capturing the United States arsenal at Liberty, Missouri in April 1861. This early coup in western Missouri by many veterans of the Kansas conflict resulted in the arming of troops of Price's army with United States weapons, including artillery. Some of the regiment's best leaders, such as Lieutenant Colonel Richard B. Chiles, Captains Gordon and Thrailkill and others, later left Confederate service to ride with Quantrill's raiders across the plains of Missouri and Kansas.[3]

The most severe threat to Price's army during the arduous withdrawal south through the rough countryside of Arkansas and the harsh winter weather came on February 16 at Potts' Hill. The Union advance struck Colonel Little's guardians immediately south of the Missouri state line in a determined effort to tear into the rear of Price's army. Suddenly in the cold evening and fading light, Union cavalry charged through the open fields, smashing into a retiring company of Gates's regiment, which was protecting the Missouri Brigade's and the army's rear. The blue cavalry onslaught caught the First Missouri cavalrymen at the most vulnerable moment. Attacked from behind, the butternut horsemen turned and fired double-barrel shotguns at point-blank range, while Unionists cut down Rebels with sabers and pistols.

A mob of struggling troopers of both sides surged down the road en masse, shooting, cursing, and plowing into the Missouri Brigade's rear. Captain Clark's artillerymen had no time to unlimber their guns before the hand-to-hand fighting engulfed them and swirled around the battery. Farther down the Telegraph Road to the south, the Missouri Brigade's infantrymen were screened by heavily-timbered Potts' Hill, and had not seen the Yankee cavalry swooping down upon their comrades like an avalanche. Without support and badly outnumbered, Clark and his cannoneers made a seemingly suicidal stand around their field pieces. Rebel artillerymen swung sponge-staffs and fired revolvers at the blue plague swarming around them. Some Confederates were quickly sabered and ridden down, but Clark's men refused to run in the unequal contest for possession of the battery. Before Captain Clark and his gunners were wiped out, Colonel Rives's infantrymen about-faced and charged forward to drive away the Yankee cavalry and save the battery. Afterward, the Rebel withdrawal south continued along with the ever-present danger to Price's army. Lieutenant Warren described the Missouri Brigade's arduous duty, writing in his diary how, "we are completely worn out marching [and] counter-marching & skirmishing. We are covering the retreat of our Army—and the [Missourians] must be ever on the alert. The cold is piercing and hunger often pinches us."[4]

But the Missouri Brigade's resistance bought time, allowing Price's army to reach the safety of the rugged Boston Mountains at Cove Creek, after linking with General McCulloch's forces. Lieutenant Warren wrote in his diary, bragging that the Missouri Brigade handed out a few hard lessons "of what they may expect from us when brought to bay." The timely uniting of the two principal Rebel commands in the Trans-Mississippi, Price and McCulloch, was in no small part due to the steadfast performance of the protective guardians of Price's army, the Missouri Brigade. This contribution was critical, helping to provide the Confederacy with one last opportunity to reclaim Missouri.

One of Colonel Little's staff officers from St. Louis, Captain William Clark Kennerly, a veteran of the Doniphan and Southwest Expeditions, a St. Louis University graduate and a cousin of Captain "Churchy" Clark, bestowed an appropriate compliment upon the vital performance of the Missouri Brigade during this risky withdrawal down the Telegraph Road through Missouri and Arkansas, writing "never have I seen anything so masterful as Sterling Price's retreat from Springfield..." Amid the wooded hills and rough countryside around Cove Creek about thirty miles south of Missouri, Colonel Little's Confederates rested, savoring their hard-won reputation. They gained a much needed respite after the vigorous Yankee pursuit finally ended when the forces of Price and McCulloch united.

By this time, Colonel Little's soldiers hardly looked like the most reliable fighters of Price's army with the issuance of perhaps the most unusual uniforms ever handed to Confederate soldiers. From a Memphis warehouse the troops of Colonels Rives and Burbridge at Cove Creek were given an odd-looking uniform of a jean material. These new Confederates were not at all flattered with their first uniforms, for these garments were the typical clothing of slaves on the cotton plantations of the Deep South. The jean material consisted of an undyed wool, white in color and with wooden buttons. But worst of all, these unorthodox Confederate uniforms still reeked of the odor of sheep. Looking like anything except "the South's Finest," the Missouri boys, nevertheless, could not have been issued a more durable uniform. Other Rebels later laughed and bleated like sheep in poking fun at Colonel Little's veterans clothed in white. Fortunately for the ridiculed members of the Missouri Brigade, these uniforms later turned a dirty brown from wear and the elements. This unusual "Confederate" uniform actually enhanced morale and camaraderie, giving Colonel Little's troops a distinctive look, which strengthened unit identity and pride and seemingly early signified the Missourians' role as crack troops in this war.[5]

To soothe the escalating states rights friction and to establish a working relationship between a pro-Arkansas McCulloch and the pro-Missouri Price and restore harmony for a combined effort to confront Curtis, President Davis sent Major General Earl Van Dorn west in early 1862 to take overall command of both forces. At long last, the vast possibilities in the Missouri-Arkansas theater had not been completely forgotten by Richmond. The Confederacy was about to make a belated attempt to win the Trans-Mississippi. This was the last serious attempt of the Davis Administration to make up for many months of a fatal negligence. With the prospects now bright to reclaim the home state, the Missouri soldiers were elated. As one Missouri Rebel penned in his diary, "Van Dorn has arrived and now we will have some fun with the Yanks." And another recorded that "the boys were eager to get into a battle with Curtis, thinking they would drive him back and then we could return to Missouri again"; the dream of the Missouri Confederates. Indicating his disdain for defensive warfare, General Van Dorn boasted that he "would not allow a spade in his camp."

The newly styled Army of the West prepared to take the offensive to win Missouri. In the late winter of 1862 fortunes of war in the West could be tipped to the South's favor, if Van Dorn could whip Curtis, conquer Missouri, and capture St. Louis, and then take the war into the Northern states in an audacious campaign. Also, a successful campaign could upset the powerful Union offensive that was beginning to rip through northwestern Tennessee deeper into the strategic Confederate heartland in an attempt to gain the all-important Mississippi Valley. Three separate Union offensives were about to push south in a coordinated effort to win the Mississippi Valley and secure the "Father of Waters": Curtis in northwestern Arkansas, General John Pope in southeast Missouri, and General Ulysses S. Grant in northwestern Tennessee, respectively from west to east. Lincoln was employing the concept of simultaneous Union advances, exploiting the Confederacy's limited manpower and negating the potential for Rebel concentrations via an internal network of rail lines. An effective strategy for a nation with superior manpower, materiel and resources, Lincoln's well-conceived means of waging war was a key factor in achieving Union success in this fratricidal conflict.

One insightful Southern journalist pinpointed the strategic significance of Van Dorn's forthcoming offensive in northwest Arkansas, writing "if we succeed in destroying [Curtis's] powerful army, the fame of the triumph will equal its consequences, which will be a powerful diversion in our favor as bearing on the enemy's operations in Tennessee and the Mississippi Valley." Indeed the most important and bloodiest engagement west of the Mississippi was about to be fought, with the fate of Missouri, the Trans-Mississippi, and much of the West at stake.

The people of the South, consequently, now turned their eyes upon military developments in the wilderness of northwestern Arkansas, where the strategists of both sides had not expected a big battle. As one Southern newspaperman said "when the conflict comes it will be a dreadful one, and unless overborne [sic] by numbers, the sons' of liberty [now in the] Boston Mountain[s] will make [those] eminence [s] as famous in history as Bunker's Hill." Across the Confederacy, General Van Dorn was looked upon as the nation's savior, being described as "a man of energy and Napoleonic celerity of movement," wrote one Rebel journalist. In the first of all modern wars, early Nineteenth Century tactics that had been successful on the Napoleonic battlefields of Europe would shortly prove to be especially out-dated and obsolete in the rugged hills, forests, and hollows of northwest Arkansas.[6]

Curtis was now vulnerable as never before. The aggressive Federals had advanced too deeply and too quickly into the mountainous labyrinth of Arkansas. Expecting a quiet winter and burdened with an ineffective logistical line that stretched more than 200 miles south from Rolla, Curtis's units were now dispersed over the rough countryside of northwest Arkansas to forage. Winter weather made movement more difficult. These Unionists were too far from both support and their railroad base and too close to Van Dorn's 16,000 Rebels, who were eager to strike. To exploit Curtis's dilemma, the jaunty Army of the West swung north under dark wintry skies of March 4 to accomplish great things. The weather of the Ozark highlands was especially cold and windy in early March, but it soon turned even harsher. However, not even the biting cold could dim the spirits of Colonel Little's soldiers, who dreamed of redeeming Union-held Missouri. Around 2,000 Confederates of the Missouri Brigade advanced north toward their home state. At the head of Van Dorn's Army, Colonel Gates's hard-riding troopers led the way through the blinding snow flurries and the northeasterly winds that howled across the hilly terrain draped in the brown tint of winter.

In their new uniforms of white that served as a sort of camouflage on the snow-covered landscape, the swiftly-marching Missourians headed straight into the strong gusts of wind and toward the Federal Army with only a few handfuls of parched corn in their jean pockets. In a wild attack across a wide prairie, Colonel Gates's cavalry smashed into the Union rear guard at Bentonville, Arkansas, on March 6. After failing to trap a Union corps at Bentonville, both Price's and McCulloch's horsemen chased the retiring bluecoats north through the cold woodlands and deep valleys which resembled gorges. During the running fight, Gates's Missourians repeatedly struck the Yankees at close range. Demonstrating tactical ability throughout the hot skirmishing, Colonel Gates led "the pursuers with great activity and skill" during the chase and running fight.[7]

Despite the rapid Southern pursuit, Curtis's Army was not as scattered across the mountainous terrain as anticipated. The fight at Bentonville bought Curtis precious time to organize a defense. Curtis hurriedly recalled and concentrated his forces along high ground on the north bank of Little Sugar Creek a couple of miles south of Elkhorn Tavern. Now more than 10,000 Federals were aligned in fine defensive positions astride the Telegraph Road—the main route leading from northwest Arkansas to southwest Missouri—and atop the bluffs above the clear, fast-flowing creek. Frontal assaults hurled against such a strong position would be suicidal. Readily understanding this tactical reality, Van Dorn set into motion a bold plan worthy of Napoleon, which resembled Winfield Scott's Mexican War successful strategy at Cerro Gordo. The audacious plan called for a long flank march around the right flank of Curtis's army via an obscure road, the Bentonville Detour, which circled west off the Telegraph Road south of Curtis's forces and then east and around Pea Ridge to enter the Telegraph Road north of Curtis and in the Yankees' rear.

Again assigned to lead Van Dorn's army, Colonel Little's warriors broke camp and shouldered muskets that felt like ice at 8:00 p.m. on March 6, after only a two-hour rest in the biting cold. The already exhausted Missouri soldiers were ill-prepared to follow the complicated Rebel strategy that meant a grueling all-night march along the detour on empty stomachs and in bitterly cold weather without sufficient clothing. During the previous three days, these Confederate soldiers had trudged more than fifty miles north across the rough terrain of the Arkansas wilderness on little more than high hopes. As young Lieutenant Warren wrote in his diary, "since the 13th of February, we have eat little [but] idle bread." With no adequate issue of rations in haversacks, no winter gear and wet from crossing Little Sugar Creek, Missouri Brigade members plunged into the freezing night and pushed north along the thin dirt trail, the Bentonville Detour, hewn through the silent forests. With Colonel Gates's horse soldiers in front, Burbridge's troops led the Missouri Brigade's infantry, followed by Price's State Guard divisions and then General McCulloch's forces.[8]

Success hinged upon almost perfect timing and a stealthy flank march with no lengthy delays during the eight mile, all-night march along the detour to get around Pea Ridge and behind Curtis's army, which faced south. According to Van Dorn's grandiose plan, the nighttime trek along the detour that first led north before turning east through the dense woodlands would allow enough time for the Army of the West to reach the Telegraph Road and then launch the attack south into the Union Army's rear by dawn of March 7. But this was an extremely delicate and complex maneuver across unfamiliar and rugged terrain in pitch-blackness. Any unforeseen delay could easily jeopardize the entire plan, but General Van Dorn, a careless planner who often overlooked significant details, had failed to reconnoiter the Bentonville Detour. Consequently, the Rebels continued to march blindly onward for hours into the night and into the frigid wilderness. The young Confederates kept quiet, and hoped for the best in the seemingly not too difficult push to reach the Telegraph Road before dawn, during one of the greatest flank marches of the war. After passing near the western end of Pea Ridge and turning east behind the several mile-long ridge, the Missouri Confederates continued to trudge forward, with some soldiers hobbling barefoot across the rocks and gullies of the frozen detour.[9]

But around midnight trouble developed, when the column piled up in the blackness behind Pea Ridge. Union soldiers had felled timber and erected barricades to effectively block the narrow detour. Thick forests on each side prevented the

Confederates from making a detour of the detour. Racing the sunrise, the stoutest Rebels of Burbridge's regiment began cursing Yankee ingenuity and furiously heaving logs and brush from the roadbed that resembled a trail. Clearing the detour took much longer than anyone expected. But finally after much time had been wasted, Colonel Little's Confederates resumed their march to gain the rear of the Union Army and glory, continuing east through the dark forests. Then the Rebels swung into the even rougher terrain along the environs of Big Sugar Creek, hurrying in an attempt to make up for lost time. Captains Wade's and Clark's artillerymen kept up with the infantry, laboriously pushing their guns through the paths cut through the felled obstacles. Then the cannon were pulled and man-handled across the ravines and gullies that drained toward the creek. The frantic race to reach the rear of the Union Army by daylight continued, and some lost time was regained.

But just when it seemed as if the Telegraph Road in Curtis's rear might be reached in time, a second, larger blockade across the Bentonville Detour was encountered around 2:00 a.m., according to Father Bannon's pocket watch. A frustrated Chaplain Bannon wrote in his diary that the Confederates "found the ravine entering [Big Sugar] Creek blocked by fallen timber." Once more the Rebel column came to a halt. Chances for success and hours slipped away, while the worn Missourians again waited for the narrow road to be cleared by Burbridge's hardworking soldiers. A faint light on the eastern horizon proclaimed a failed Confederate strategy on March 7. A cold dawn found thousands of General Price's Rebels bunched-up behind Pea Ridge, dozing in column and strung-out for miles in the woods.[10]

Finally, the march resumed at 7:00 a.m. One hour later, Colonel Little's soldiers at last reached the Telegraph Road and the rear of the Yankee army, but several hours late. In fact, twelve hours had elapsed since the Missouri boys had optimistically departed from camp and embarked upon their flank march. Even worse, the road-blocks and difficult terrain had left McCulloch's division even further behind schedule and a long distance behind Price's troops. Now, Van Dorn realized that he would have to launch the attack in two widely-separated wings. McCulloch would strike southeast on the west side of Pea Ridge, while Price attacked south on the east side of the imposing forested ridge. With Van Dorn forced to fight two separate battles instead of one, this division of strength and the two-pronged assault invited disaster.[11]

Scattered firing between pickets shortly alerted Colonel Little and his sleepless followers that the battle was about to begin. Little quickly began deploying the Missouri Brigade astride the Telegraph Road, barring the route of the anticipated Federal retreat. But the racket of musketry had alerted the Yankees of the danger to the rear and they quickly responded to the threat. In front, the terrain to the south rose more sharply up the wooded hollow, Colonel Little realized the importance of meeting the first challenge of the day at once, when the First Iowa Battery unlimbered above and in front of them about 400 yards north of the country inn owned by Jesse Cox, Elkhorn Tavern. The rustic, former stage coach stop and post office was perched on strategic high ground. South of the Missouri Brigade's advancing ranks on the high ground, the Iowa cannon were aligned in an ideal position to sweep the hollow and command the road, as it plunged north and down into the deep hollow now filled with Rebels. For Confederate success on March 7, these foremost Union guns had to be pushed aside as soon as possible. Also Colonel

Little's units had to escape the depths of the hollow and take the high plateau covered in farmers' fields and upon which stood the Cox tavern decorated with a massive elk rack.

Burbridge's soldiers quickly aligned on the wooded hillsides to the right, or west, of the road. Demonstrating his unit's versatility, Colonel Gates dismounted his troopers, while every fourth soldier held horses, and then boldly advanced. With a good eye for terrain, Colonel Gates led his boys forward and hurriedly occupied the most dominant elevation to the left of the road, the wooded rim of Williams Hollow. If the Yankees gained this high ground, Little's Missouri Brigade would be at the Unionists' mercy, especially if Federal artillery was planted on the rim. "Old Pap" Price understood the importance of Gates securing as soon as possible this "very commanding position [from which Rebel artillery could] not only check the enemy's advance upon our left, but also to support our right in its advance upon the enemy," wrote the general.

The narrow, forested gorge of Cross Timber Hollow prevented full deployment of the Missouri Brigade, however. During the rapid advance up the slopes, Gates's cavalrymen skirmished and charged on foot, capturing a handful of forage wagons and some bluecoats in a rematch of the clash east of Springfield on February 12. The homespun Rebels of the First Missouri Cavalry, C.S.A., again captured their fellow staters in blue of the First Missouri Cavalry, U.S.A., who thought they were safe in the army's rear. This was another example of the Missourians' own intimate brand of the brothers' war, and during the next two days there would be more such clashes between Missouri soldiers of opposite sides.

Encountering less opposition as the timbered and brushy gorge widened higher up the slope toward the plateau, Colonel Little hurriedly attempted to complete deployment of the Missouri Brigade. On the double, Colonel Rives led his regiment to a hill on the left of the road to support the advance of Gates's dismounted troopers. Among Rives's soldiers taking position on the wooded hill was Private Thomas Jefferson Yager, age twenty-five. One of Yager's comrades of Company G had picked up two pieces of Yankee hardtack from the dirt roadbed. Although half-starved, Yager refused to take a hardtack when offered and said to his comrade, "I don't need it, you eat them." The surprised friend responded by saying that "he needed it as much as he did." But a despondent Yager, a Pike County farmer, ended the conversation by announcing that, "I'm going to be killed in this battle," a premonition that proved true on March 7.

Meanwhile, the full deployment of the Missouri Brigade was completed on both sides of the road. With much effort, Captains Wade and Clark ran their cannon up the steep and underbrush-covered slopes by hand, positioning the guns on the timbered southern rim of Williams' Hollow. Aligning on the all-important rim, the Missouri Brigade's artillerymen had taken commanding positions along the wooded ridge and held the highest ground east of the road, along with the rest of Price's batteries. This strategic elevation, crowned with artillery lined up almost hub to hub and overlooking the tavern and the plateau, had been secured by Colonel Gates and his dismounted cavalrymen. As soon as his field piece was placed onto its elevated position, Captain "Churchy" Clark initiated the artillery contest for Elkhorn Tavern by pulling a lanyard and letting a shell fly toward the Federal cannon.[12]

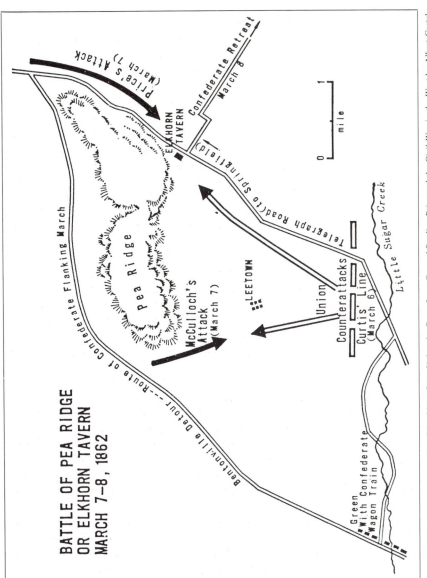

BATTLE OF PEA RIDGE OR ELKHORN TAVERN MARCH 7–8, 1862

Price's Attack (March 7)

Confederate Retreat
March 8

ELKHORN TAVERN

Telegraph Road (to Springfield)

Pea Ridge

--- Route of Confederate Flanking March

Bentonville Detour

McCulloch's Attack (March 7)

LEETOWN

Counterattacks

Union

Curtis' Line (March 6)

Little Sugar Creek

Green With Confederate Wagon Train

0   1
mile

The Missouri cannon roared at the targets below them. Having been granted precious time by the Bentonville detour delays that sabotaged the Rebel strategy, Curtis quickly about-faced his forces. Van Dorn's Napoleonic strategy of hitting the Union army's rear had self-destructed. Divided by Pea Ridge, the two wings of the Southern army fought at a severe disadvantage on March 7. After Curtis countered the emergency in his rear by turning his forces around, a concentrated mass of Union infantry and artillery held the crucial high ground at the head of Cross Timber Hollow. On the high level plateau covered with the cornfields of last year and bounded by woods, these Yankee troops were aligned in good defensive positions before the tavern.[13]

As opposing rows of blue and gray artillery dueled in the crisp morning air of early March, Colonel Little's Confederate formations rolled forward, while the State Guard units deployed on the Missouri Brigade's left. The Rebel advance proceeded steadily south along both sides of Telegraph Road. With a clatter of accouterments, the Missouri Brigade's lengthy line surged past a tanyard, a half-mile north of the tavern, and up the timbered gorge as the terrain rose higher. Knowing the importance of pushing the Yankees off the plateau, Little called upon Colonel Gates to launch a lightning-quick attack to surprise and overrun the defenders. Young buglers, such as Charles Shipley, Jacob Bechtel, a twenty-one-year-old baker born in Germany, and John L. Debard, a printer from Platte County, blew the shrill notes of the cavalry charge, which eerily cut through the cool air. Gates's troopers charged forward on foot with wild cheers to carry the high ground, after Captains Wade's and Clark's artillery blew up several caissons and disabled three guns of the First Iowa Battery. Smashed by the barrage, the Hawkeye unit from Dubuque, Iowa, was effectively eliminated with half of its cannon knocked out of action. With the Union artillery mostly silenced, Colonel Little knew that he had to exploit the advantage immediately, and Gates was the perfect commander for the job.

Anxious to join the fight but unable to leave his rear post, the commissary officer of Colonel Gates's regiment felt that his new rifled-musket was being wasted. He, therefore, went up to Gates and asked, "Colonel, show me the man who has the bravest horse in the regiment." This strange request was a tribute because according to Gates: "It was a delicate compliment to my men, for it implied that there was no difference in their bravery, ..." Colonel Gates gave the gun to Captain Thrailkill. But not all Missouri Brigade members were so heroic at Pea Ridge. Lieutenant Fontaine H. Ketchum deserted the ranks of Company F, or Burbridge's regiment, running for the rear.[14]

Remounting after gaining more ground, the First Missouri cavalrymen shortly again charged up the slope, with the blowing of brass horns, and colorful guidons waving through the trees. Screaming butternut riders from northwest Missouri spurred horses through the scrub oaks and underbrush on both sides of Telegraph Road. Among Company D's attackers were nine relatives named Blain from Camden, Ray County. Half-way to the top, Colonel Gates again ordered his command to dismount to fight on foot, taking advantage of favorable terrain. With machine-like precision, the Rebel horsemen leaped off mounts, then surged forward once more as infantry. Gates's attack crashed headlong into a solid wall of Federals, consisting of the Ninth Iowa Volunteer Infantry, which was supported by the Twenty-Fourth Missouri, Fourth Iowa, and Thirty-Fifth Illinois Volunteer Infantry Regiments.

A point-blank volley of musketry and shell-fire from the guns of the Third Iowa Battery, which had replaced the smashed First Iowa Battery, poured down the gorge. This withering fire riddled Price's cavalry. Young troopers, such as Private William Henry Hartman, age seventeen, were killed. With his usual aggressiveness, Colonel Gates had stirred up a hornet's nest. After unleashing a volley in return, Colonel Gates's horse soldiers retired further down Cross Timber Hollow, then took cover among the trees to resume the contest with renewed fury.[15]

The withdrawal of Gates's cavalry caused Lieutenant Colonel Francis J. Herron and his Ninth Iowa Volunteer Infantry to take the initiative. Gates's cavalrymen had just taken defensive positions to Rives's left, when the blue formations flooded into the hollow to wipe out the pesky Rebel horsemen. In preparation for meeting the attack, Colonel Little made wise dispositions, hustling Colonel Rives's regiment into position to the road's left, while Burbridge's regiment aligned on Rives's right. The brown, winter-hued woodlands grew quiet as the artillery duel subsided before the inevitable clash of infantry. With cocked muskets, the Missouri Confederates awaited the Federal advance, while listening to Union officers' orders and the pounding drums, which echoed down the canyon-like valley from the head of Cross Timber Hollow. Perhaps Colonel Burbridge once more reminded his men to aim carefully at the Federals' "breeches' buttons," because a wound in that area "nearly always gives the victim time to prepare to meet his Maker."[16]

Advancing splendidly as if on parade, the Iowans pushed to within close range. Letting the Yankees ease nearer and deeper into the depths of the gorge, Colonel Rives finally roared, "Fire!" Many Federals fell, but others shortly returned fire and "shot well, for our wounded fell on every side," recorded one Missourian in his diary. After the bloodied Federals retired and the Rebels again pushed forward, the entire Union brigade surged into the hollow. But the Yankee assaults were beaten back. The last attack was a bayonet charge, which was only scattered with the volleys of Colonel Rives's soldiers and a vicious hand-to-hand contest with musket-butts, swords, and bayonets amid the chilly, tangled woodlands. Anticipating such bitter fighting, Colonel Little had bolstered Rives's unit with Gates's tough horse soldiers. Colonel Little described how "Colonel Rives sternly [held] his position, from which his men did not yield an inch of ground." After taking severe punishment from Little's infantry and the raking fire of the Missouri cannon on the high ground, the battered Unionists retired uphill through the trees and smoke, leaving their dead scattered like fallen autumn leaves. The Yankees then established their line on the open, commanding terrain before the tavern. Because of the struggle's tenacity, Price hurried a Guard division to reinforce Little in case the Federals launched more attacks from the commanding terrain. Taking advantage of the respite, Colonel Little carefully placed the guardsmen to Burbridge's right, extending the line before resuming the offensive.[17]

To exploit the repulse of the Unionists, the Missouri Rebels swarmed forward with yells and bayonets flashing in the pale winter sunlight. The regiments of Colonels Gates, Rives and Burbridge, from left to right, charged forward, pouring uphill as if to avenge the death of comrades. Ignited by the sparks from paper cartridges, small brush fires burned along the slopes, raising clouds of low-hanging smoke and the fear of an agonizingly slow death for those injured soldiers lying helpless on the ground. Rings of fire swept over some of the helpless wounded. Colonel Gates, meanwhile, had ordered his rough riders to remount and charge. Hundreds of wild-looking troopers galloped up the hollow in hot pursuit of the withdrawing Unionists. The charging Rebel cavalrymen shortly found the Yankees deployed along the lip of the hollow. Butternut troopers again swung out of saddles to fight on foot. But shotgun volleys were no match for Springfield rifled-muskets. Colonel Gates, therefore, ordered his horse soldiers to retire downhill toward Little's advancing infantrymen, upon receiving a heavy fire. Gates's "eyes and ears" of the Missouri Brigade had once more pinpointed the Unionists' dispositions and strength, providing intelligence for Colonel Little. Colonel Gates positioned his regiment along the Missouri Brigade's line to Rives's left, after fulfilling his mission and helping to ensure that the Federals would not regain the initiative.[18]

After clashing once more, both sides stood up face-to-face in a ritualistic contest of combat. Union pressure mounted on the Missouri Brigade's right, held by Burbridge and the Second Missouri Confederate Brigade to his right. After bolstering Colonel Burbridge with a State Guard unit, Colonel Little ordered a general advance. Cheering Rebels surged through the stunted scrub oak and blackjack and slammed into the blue formations on the high ground. Point-blank exchanges of gunfire continued for almost an hour and a half. Despite paying a fearful price in casualties, the Missouri Brigade finally gained the head of the hollow and the northern tier of the plateau, where the Union artillery had been placed. By the mid-afternoon, Colonel Little's Rebels had escaped the heavily-timbered hollow and now could fight on more equal terms. One Federal was shocked when from the hollow's depths, "the enemy pored [sic] out of the Brush on to us by the Thousands."[19]

The relentless Southern advance up and out of Cross Timber Hollow cost much in lives, time, and momentum, a payment for the detour delays and a failed strategy. But worst of all, a solid Union defense had been skillfully organized in the vicinity of Elkhorn Tavern, with the arrival of additional Federal troops and artillery. On the smoke-covered plateau, Colonel Eugene Asa Carr, a hard-fighting West Pointer commanding the Fourth Division, effectively slowed the Rebel advance by hurling infantry down into the hollow and planting batteries at intervals. Carr's success in delaying the Southern assault saved the day, winning him a Medal of Honor.[20]

Only 300 yards south of the Missouri Brigade was Elkhorn Tavern, which stood just beyond the brown cornfields now filled with dead stalks, lying limp in the March sunshine. Long formations of bluecoated soldiers, of two brigades, stretched across the wintry landscape in full view. Hardly were the Confederates deployed for more action, when shells from the Third Iowa Battery, positioned around the tavern, and infantry volleys pounded the Missouri Brigade at the timbered edge of the hollow. One of Rives's privates recorded how the exploding shells and bullets "going zip, zip all around and the dust flying out of the trees and the limbs and twigs [caused] a commotion from the concussion of the guns..." A torrent of shells and canister forced the Confederates a short distance back into the shelter of the hollow's depression and into the forest's edge.

The brief reprieve from the carnage gave the Confederates time to prepare for launching an assault all along the front. On the Southern battle-line now coiled and again ready to spring forward, Colonel Little commanded the center. Price's State Guard divisions held the left and right. Colonel Burbridge's regiment had lost so heavily that it had to be supported by another Guard division. Hundreds of resolute Unionists, meanwhile, prepared "to hang on to the last extremity" around Elkhorn Tavern.[21]

Meanwhile, the Missouri Brigade waited for Price's guardsmen, to the east, to open the attack. The air grew cooler as the sun sank behind Pea Ridge to the west. Taking advantage of the lull, a Yankee force attempted to cut off and turn Burbridge's, and the Missouri Brigade's, right flank. Indeed, Colonel Burbridge's regiment was vulnerable, positioned slightly ahead of the Missouri Brigade's main line in the thick woodlands. But the advance of Rives's regiment and a Second Brigade battalion drove the foremost Unionists off with a volley. As one soldier remembered, "Col Rives crying forward we advanced and drove them on before us, and occupied their position. Our attack enabled Burbridge to drive them before him [and] compelled their whole line to fall back" closer to Elkhorn Tavern at the southeastern edge of Pea Ridge. Not long afterward, the booming of artillery and the crashing of musketry rattled over the hills to the left, signaling the beginning of the Rebels' general assault. In the front lines as usual, Chaplain Bannon checked his watch and scribbled in his diary that it was then 4:30.[22]

The Missourians' charge that repulsed the Yankees' flanking movement coincided with the launching of Price's attack. According to one Missouri soldier, "Like magic the word 'charge!' ran along the line, and with a wild shout it sprang forward, ..." With Colonel Gates's regiment on the left, Colonel Rives's regiment in the center and Colonel Burbridge's regiment now on the right, the howling Missourians rushed forward astride both sides of the road. Beardless drummer boys beat their drums with all their might. Without slowing the assault's momentum, the attacking Rebel soldiers jumped over a split-rail fence at the wood-line, spilling onto the plateau with bayonets flashing. Hundreds of Little's frontiersmen poured through the cornfields with red Confederate battle-flags and blue Missouri state banners flying above the rows of bent and lifeless stalks, while Rebel yells rang over Elkhorn Tavern. The long Confederate formations swept onward like an avalanche in a desperate bid to reverse the Southern nation's destiny in the brown fields and woodlands of northwest Arkansas.[23]

Exploding shells rippled down the charging ranks, knocking attackers to the ground. In Burbridge's regiment, twenty-year-old drummer boy J. Martin West of Morgan County dropped dead when a minie ball whistled through his lungs. After hurling back an initial Union force before the main line, the howling Rebels slowed briefly before the final rush to victory or death, as if catching their breath or contemplating the formidable concentration of two brigades of Yankee artillery and infantry around the country inn, now the eye of the storm. But the momentary pause ended when Confederate officers screamed, "On to the battery!" Double loads of canister plowed through the onrushing Rebel waves, but "above all, 'forward Missourians' could be distinctly heard," wrote one soldier. Gaining momentum, the charge rolled south through the fields and toward Cox's house-tavern. Shouting and shooting on the run in an angry swarm, the Confederates rushed onward through the choking smoke. Now recalled one attacker, "Nothing could withstand the charge of the First Missouri Brigade."[24]

Colonel Gates's versatile troopers on the Missouri Brigade's left flank also charged forward as infantry. Upon nearing the Federals, the fast-moving cavalrymen blasted away with shotguns, while shouting as if their lungs would burst. Likewise, salvos of ball and buckshot from the muskets of Burbridge's and Rives's attackers tore into the blue ranks. During the charge, Colonel Gates's brother, Private John Gates, age twenty-six, fell mortally wounded. A mounted Colonel Gates was "in the thickest of the fight," while leading his dismounted horsemen in the rush upon the tavern.[25]

In a jumbled mass, the howling Missouri tide poured over Elkhorn Tavern like locusts and at the point of "the bayonet," wrote Chaplain Bannon in his diary. The Missouri attackers struck hard, killing and driving back the bluecoat defenders. These veteran Confederates targeted artillery horses for slaughter, firing and loading on the run, and cutting down animals with well-placed shots. Unable to escape, Federal gunners fell while trying to hitch pieces to limbers. During the hand-to-hand contest around the two cannon of the Third Iowa Battery, Colonel Gates's homespun warriors used double-barrel shotguns with deadly effect. Shotgun blasts toppled many defenders, demonstrating the destructive firepower of these frontier hunting pieces at close range. Now unstoppable, Little's soldiers plowed savagely into the Federals of the Twenty-Fourth Missouri, a tough unit of Colonel William Vandever's mauled brigade. Neighbors only months before, Missourians on opposing sides now had no qualms about killing each other during a vicious struggle with fists, bayonets, musket-butts, knives, and sabers.

The bloody fighting became especially nightmarish around the Cox residence. During the fierce struggle, Captain Thrailkill fell with a saber wound delivered by a Union officer. Like so many of his men, Colonel Herron went down, when his horse was killed. One of Gates's troopers, "a tall fellow in a butternut coat and trousers," thrust a shotgun into Herron's face and captured the commander of the Ninth Iowa. Rebel bayonets, musket-butts and swords finally dropped the last Unionists. At last, Elkhorn Tavern and its surrounding area, the key to the Union position on the high ground, fell to the Missouri Brigade.[26]

Despite heavy losses, Colonel Little's troops kept charging forward like men possessed, surging past the log tavern, down the road, and through the fields littered with Yankee dead and wounded. Tasting victory, the Missourians rolled onward to complete an amazing success. Wrote Lieutenant Mothershead in his diary, "Our gallant men had by this time become wildly enthusiastic and scarcely halting at the first battery they moved on towards another, planted some hundreds of yards in rear of the first." With many officers shot down, hundreds of cheering enlisted men pressed onward in the fading daylight.

Commanding the right of Rives's regiment, Colonel James A. Pritchard and his troops swarmed over a final remaining pocket of resistance. Here, Colonel William P. Chandler had rallied many Thirty-Fifth Illinois Infantrymen, near the Missouri Brigade's left flank, and boldly counter-attacked straight into more Rebels than they had ever seen before. Pritchard, a Mexican War veteran, led his soldiers forward through the choking smoke and surrounded the hard-fighting Unionists. After a sanguinary contest in Cox's darkening woodlot to the tavern's southwest and to the road's right, nearly 100 Federals threw down weapons and surrendered to the victorious Missourians.[27]

Colonel Rives was enraged by the fragmenting of his regiment. Only "after much effort, he succeeded in halting the regiment; and reformed it," in the smoky woodlot, recalled Lieutenant Mothershead in his diary. Then Rives's soldiers raised a cheer and continued to push farther south. Like the Missouri Brigade's other units, Colonel Rives's regiment paid dearly for its success, being cut up badly. Wrote Lieutenant Mothershead, whose eighteen-year-old brother, Nathaniel, had already fallen with a fatal wound: "but in these charges all were not permitted to go through unscathed, many of those noble spirits who dashed bravely forth to meet the foe went not far before they fell." Ignoring the losses, Rives instinctively knew when to press the attack, day or night. Wanting to further exploit this success before it was too late, he led a portion of his regiment through the fields and belts of forest in an audacious attempt to capture a Yankee battery on the flank. But the Rebel attack dissolved in the blackness after the Confederates charged so close to the Union artillery that, said Mothershead, "the fire from the guns would pass in jetting streams, through our lines." Also slowing Rives's charge were the volleys from the Second Missouri Confederate Brigade, which blasted away wildly in the twilight, raking the Second Regiment and causing confusion and damage. Nevertheless, some of Rives's attackers continued to charge onward through Samuel Ruddick's corn-field east of the road and "pursued [the Federals] quite into his wagon trains." Of all the Missouri Brigade's units, Colonel Rives's regiment penetrated the farthest southwest, hurling the Yankees about a half-mile south of the tavern.

The Missouri Brigade's artillery likewise advanced, with gunners somehow pushing guns uphill through the timber and out of the hollow, before unlimbering on the high ground around Elkhorn Tavern. Ever-enthusiastic Captain Clark "joyously move[d] his battery into battle [and] not grudgingly, but as if he loved the sound of his guns as they thundered [and] it was a grand sight to see him move the boy battery in the very paths of the bluecoats and open great lanes through their brave ranks and to behold him in the very gates of death and hear his orders given as cool as on a field day." For his performance that day, which included per-sonally dismounting one of the Iowa guns, Captain Clark was conferred a major's rank by General Price on the battleground that would soon become his grave.[28]

Darkness failed to end the bloody struggle, which had taken a heavy toll on the Missouri Brigade during its advance of more than a mile. At the front, Chaplain Bannon recorded in his diary that the Missouri Brigade's struggle on March 7 finally ended at half-past six, and "after 7½ hours [of hard] fighting." Curtis's forces had been roughly handled, but were not yet beaten, and much fighting spirit re-mained. Federal units rallied and took defensive positions farther south down the Telegraph Road, after being bolstered with reinforcements. Heavy losses and nightfall prevented additional gains by General Price's troops on March 7. Little's decimated regiments regrouped and consolidated their positions about a half-mile to the tavern's south and astride the road, where a cold sunset found them amid the acres of dead and wounded. After fighting for almost eight hours and driving the Yankees back more than a mile, surviving Missouri Brigade members rested on the field, while a near-freezing darkness dropped over the horror of Pea Ridge. The multitudes of Rebel wounded were collected, and then taken to Elkhorn Tavern, now an infirmary, or field hospitals.

Colonel Little's Confederates had captured a vast amount of Union supplies, a couple of hard-earned Yankee cannons, and the bluecoats' encampments. After gobbling down captured Federal provisions, many worn soldiers slept in prepara-tion for another hard day's work to begin with the sunrise. One Rebel wrote, "we all expected to capture the entire Federal army" on the following day, while posi-tioned defiantly across the main road that led to Missouri. Another half-hour of daylight on March 7 might have brought a complete Confederate victory in Price's sector.[29]

But fate dictated otherwise. Van Dorn's other wing had been defeated after the killing of General McCulloch and the death or capture of other leading Southern officers. Around 1:00 a.m. on the cold morning of March 8, recorded Chaplain

Bannon in his diary, the ominous sounds of noisy activity drifting over the field in the darkness told of Curtis shifting thousands of troops from his left to bolster his right flank and to concentrate before Price, after McCulloch's defeat. Price's troops would have to struggle alone and against the full might of Curtis's army on March 8. The failure to complete the march around Pea Ridge had created an ugly scenario for Confederate fortunes. With the Rebels' separation of force, Van Dorn had created the ideal tactical situation and handed it to the Federal commander: divide and conquer. The dismal news of the disaster on Van Dorn's right wing came to Price's left wing late in the night, while the wounded of both armies cried out for assistance.[30]

During Curtis's hasty redeployment, a Yankee caisson blundered toward Rives's position in the early morning hours. The noise alerted those vigilant Missourians too cold or too fearful of the ghosts of Pea Ridge to sleep on this eerie night around the body-strewn Telegraph Road. Colonels Rives and Pritchard and a few others rode out to investigate the disturbance. Shortly, the Missourians surrounded the Federal interlopers and ordered them to surrender. Instead of giving up, however, one Federal raised his rifled-musket. Colonel Pritchard immediately slashed the Unionist across the head with his sword, forcing him to surrender. After a thirty-six hour famine, meanwhile, many of the Missouri Rebels continued to help themselves to the commissary supplies housed around the tavern, now also serving as Little's headquarters, and in the nearby captured Union encampments.[31]

Missouri Brigade troops fighting around Elkhorn Tavern
Courtesy Museum of The Confederacy, Richmond, Va.

CHAPTER THREE

Counterattack

Daylight found Curtis's army concentrated for a massive counterattack. On the cold morning of March 8, the sun's rays poked through the heavy blanket of smoke that had not blown off the field during the windless night. For the inevitable confrontation, Colonel Little consolidated his position and redeployed the Missouri Brigade along better defensive terrain in the center of Van Dorn's line. East of the road, the native Maryland colonel aligned his soldiers in the timber skirting the north side of Ruddick's extensive cornfield, and astride the Telegraph Road. About 1,200 yards south of the tavern, Colonel Burbridge's regiment held the line's right in Cox's woodlot and east to the road, in an area now covered with bodies and debris. Taking a fine defensive position, Captain Wade unlimbered his battery near the road to Burbridge's left-rear, concealing his guns in the oak thickets. On the artillery's left stood Colonel Rives's command, then farther to the east came Gates's dismounted troopers, who were poised on good defensive terrain. After marching and fighting for most of the last month, enduring the arduous rear-guard duty during the long withdrawal to Arkansas, and trudging along the all-night trek around Pea Ridge, the Missouri soldiers were more worn-out, both mentally and physically, than any other troops in either army on the morning of March 8. But the spirits of Colonel Little's Confederates remained high, for they still dreamed of the victory that could lead to an attempt to reclaim Missouri.

For the coming attack, State Guard troops had aligned themselves on the Missouri Brigade's left, providing a solid anchor on the flank. Between Little's Brigade and Price's regiments stood the Sixteenth Arkansas Confederate Infantry. The early sunlight of another cold morning glistened off an abandoned Yankee caisson between the lines, illuminating the human wreckage. A group of Wade's gunners dashed forward to claim the trophy. Other Missouri Confederates, meanwhile, hurriedly collected and stacked fence rails to form a light breastwork, which offered some shelter from the fast-approaching storm. A slight, cold breeze ruffled the dead leaves of the snarled oaks and made the tall grass gently sway above the bodies of the dead. All hell was about to break loose.[1]

The fate of Missouri, and perhaps much of the West, would soon be determined in the sprawling cornfield, about one mile long and half a mile wide, and in the fallow fields and brownish woodlands along both sides of the Telegraph Road. Opposing armies were drawn up on either side of Ruddick's cornfields. Here, on the relatively level plateau, surrounded by high, forested hills on the east and west, was a European-style arena and a perfect killing ground, which was open and adaptable for extensive maneuvering. But the battleground was to the Southerners' disadvantage despite their being on the defensive. A lengthy stand-up fight against better-armed and supplied Union troops meant slim chances of success for these western Rebels, especially since they were handicapped by an ammunition shortage. Consequently, this upcoming contest would largely be determined by superior Union organization, resources, logistics and firepower.[2]

Artillery of both sides growled in anger as the morning mists rose from the frozen ground. Amid one of the most fierce artillery duels of the war, Captains Wade's and Clark's hard-working gunners fired from higher ground behind Ruddick's field, and were "cheering gaily at every discharge." With nearly 60 Rebel cannon blazing away, Van Dorn employed the largest concentration of Southern artillery in any Trans-Mississippi battle, outnumbering the Union guns that day. But again the Bentonville Detour haunted the Rebels and negated the Confederate superiority in artillery, for ammunition could not be transported along the path-like detour. These munition trains were mistakenly hauled even farther south with McCulloch's defeat, and more out-of-reach at the most critical moment.[3]

Colonel Little's troops, along with Price's guardsmen, other Confederate units, and some of McCulloch's units, withstood the wrath of the Union artillery that morning, without knowing how badly fate had already turned against them. One of Rives's soldiers wrote in his journal that, "the roar of artillery shook the hills [and] wild tumult was created in air, by bursting shells and hissing shot." Quickly gaining the advantage, some Federal artillery advanced to unlimber on a slight ridge southwest of the tavern amid the frosty cornfield and almost directly across from the Rebel right flank. In a woodlot to the right, or west, of the road, Colonel Burbridge's regiment and Captain Wade's battery, now aligned astride the road, took the most punishment from the vicious enfilade fire pouring in from the west. Among the many of Burbridge's soldiers falling to rise no more was twenty-one-year-old Private Franklin A. Taylor, who was dropped by the concussion of an exploding shell.[4]

The Southern logistical breakdown was shortly keenly felt. Rebel artillery fire slowed after only two hours of dueling with an opponent who knew no shortages on March 8. Already, Confederate artillery ammunition reserves were largely expended. To exploit their advantage, lengthy Union infantry waves now surged forward, as if knowing that they had the Rebels in a bad fix. Blueclad Missourians were among those who charged toward Colonel Little's Missourians for another bloody home state reunion in northwest Arkansas. More Federal batteries pressed ever-closer, closing in for the kill. Unlike their opponents, Union cannon maintained a devastating fire from a plentiful ammunition supply. This relentless cannonade blew holes in the Confederate lines and knocked out artillery pieces. The punishment that the Missouri Brigade now suffered caused one astonished Yankee cannoneer to write in a letter how, "I had never believed that artillery was capable of such havoc."[5]

From its position astride the road, Captain Wade's battery drove one Federal artillery unit to the rear with accurate shell-fire, but more fresh Union batteries replaced it. But soon Wade's cannoneers expended their ammunition, while taking a pounding under the enfilade cannonade. Unable to return fire, the First Missouri Confederate Battery retired north. Captain Clark's guns thundered down the narrow dirt road and unlimbered into position in Wade's stead north of, and on the right flank, of Rives's regiment, after Little's units east of the road had fallen back a short distance north beyond Ruddick's cornfield. Here, the Missourians realigned to more effectively confront the Union onslaught. Behind Little's formations, Captain Wade and his powder-stained boys witnessed the terrible plight of the Missouri Brigade's infantry, which suffered under a murderous frontal and crossfire. But when one of Van Dorn's batteries, with ammunition, galloped to the rear because of the Unionists' blistering fire, Captain Wade jumped at the opportunity. The St. Louis captain, "a great favorite with Van Dorn," now went up to the commanding general with a bold request. Wade proposed: "General Van Dorn, the limbers of this battery are full of ammunition; may I not transfer some of it to my own boxes and go back into the fight?" General Van Dorn consented. Shortly thereafter, Wade's eager gunners returned to the contest, "cheering and in high glee..." But Captain Wade's last rounds were soon used. Then the desperate Missouri cannoneers loaded guns with anything handy, including gravel, wagonnuts, links of chain from wagons and horse harnesses, and stones. These emergency "projectiles" raked the advancing Yankees, but nothing could slow the blue avalanche.[6]

Without a chance the Rebel artillery was quickly and easily overpowered as the last Confederate rounds were expended. Torn and battered, Wade's Battery was forced to retire. In his diary, Lieutenant Mothershead recorded the fatal turning point: "Some of our batteries were withdrawn, and after awhile others were taken away [and] this continued untill [sic] but one battery [Captain Clark's unit] of ours was heard to respond to the angry roar from the enemy's side." Resplendent in frock coat, high boots and plumed hat with one side turned up, Captain Clark eagerly accepted one of the day's most difficult challenges: while under a heavy artillery barrage, attempting to hold masses of converging Union infantry at bay to help keep Little's formations from buckling, as Van Dorn withdraw his beaten army. As more of his comrades fell around him, one of Rives's bewildered soldiers, nineteen-year-old Private Asa N. Payne, was "wondering why the rest of our artillery [besides Clark's cannon] did not open." This young Confederate did not realize that most of the Rebel artillery was out of ammunition. On a slight, lonely ridge in the open southeast of the tavern, Clark's position, both on and just to the left of the road just behind the Missouri Brigade's riddled lines, was a death-trap.[7]

About to be engulfed by mile-long lines of blue and the combined might of most of Curtis's four powerful divisions, Colonel Little frantically galloped over to General Van Dorn for specific withdrawal orders. Trying desperately to take his army off the field before being overwhelmed, Van Dorn ordered the Missouri Brigade to hold its advanced position "as long as possible" and against impossible odds. Dirt-grimed Missouri Brigade members, the foremost Rebel command, braced for the inevitable clash with the attacking waves of Yankees. Colonel Little recalled the crisis, "the enemy advanced. On, on they came, in overwhelming numbers, line after line." No Missouri Brigade soldiers were more at a disadvantage than Colonel Gates's cavalrymen, who were exposed in the open and armed only with shotguns! These Confederates, consequently, suffered terribly from the volleys of the Yankees' rifled-muskets, for they had to wait for the Unionists to get practically on top of them before they could return fire. The open terrain, which gradually sloped upward toward a high point of the plateau around the tavern, gave the Unionists fine targets with Little's soldiers exposed on the elevated ground. Colonel Gates's dismounted troopers, nevertheless, weathered the leaden storm, taking the punishment but holding firm. In one cavalryman's frontier analogy which described the Missouri Brigade's tenacity: "Several heavy charges was made to

Watch of Private Albert W. Simpson, killed at Pea Ridge
Courtesy Pea Ridge National Military Park
Pea Ridge, Ark. Photo by Clifton Eoff
Photographers, Rogers, Ark.

break our lines (but we was like the trees in the forest [they] stand till they are cut down.)'' But not all the Missourians were so steady. A private of Burbridge's unit named Jackson McVey, age twenty-four, was shot and killed as he ran for his life. After the Second Missouri brigade left the field and safely withdrew, Little's Brigade, the largest unit to remain behind, struggled alone. Federal artillery concentrated their salvos on Little's vulnerable regiments. Raked by the scorching frontal and crossfires, more Missouri soldiers dropped to the ground, dead and wounded. One young man of Rives's unit who fell in the artillery hell was twenty-eight-year-old Sergeant Albert W. Simpson, who had a cannonball tear completely through his body. Only his pocket watch later made the journey back to his Ray County home and relatives, a painful reminder of their young son. Knowing that he had to slow the overwhelming Federal onslaught somehow, General Van Dorn quickly dispatched a courier to Colonel Rives with a suicidal, but necessary, directive, "Tell him to hold [his position] at all odds!"[8]

In a swirl of dust, a desperate Colonel Rives shortly galloped up to Van Dorn and other officers and pulled up hard, informing him that his badly-exposed regiment was being cut to pieces and was about to be overwhelmed. But General Van Dorn only shouted back an urgent order that exemplified the full extent of the crisis, "Do anything you can, Col.—the day is going against us." Now Colonel Rives understood that there was only one way to slow the Federal advance and to ensure the Army of the West's escape: an immediate frontal attack against overwhelming odds! As Colonel Rives disappeared in the battle-smoke, riding back to his hard-hit regiment, south of the tavern and north of Ruddick's cornfield, one leading Rebel officer commented: "What a noble looking fellow he is." These commanders would never see Colonel Rives again.

Colonel Rives's attack also had to be launched to cover the Missouri Brigade's precarious withdrawal under heavy pressure. Amid the hail of lead, Rives's sacrificial regiment, east of the road, prepared to attack south down the Telegraph Road sector, which was now full of advancing Yankees confident of victory. Colonel Rives's regiment was the foremost Rebel infantry command offering resistance before the onslaught of the bulk of Curtis's army. In the Missouri Brigade's ranks was Father Bannon, who recorded in his diary how the deafening exchanges of musketry "continues in one voley [sic] for [every] 20 [of] the enemy." Not long thereafter, the Irish chaplain for once forgot about saving souls and attending to the wounded. He soon joined the St. Louis Irish cannoneers of Captain Henry Guibor's battery near the tavern, taking the place of a fallen cannoneer and serving on a gun crew.

Most Missouri Confederate cartridge-boxes were now empty. So far Little's troops had held firm, successfully covering the rear of Van Dorn's retiring army against the advance of Curtis's forces. But these rear-guard regiments of the Missouri Brigade faced destruction before the massive Yankee attack all along the line, which threatened to turn Little's flanks and bury the ever-dwindling unit under the blue waves. Responding to the crisis, Colonel Rives galloped to the front of his regiment, drew his saber and screamed, "Forward Missourians!" Color bearer James Spencer, age twenty-two, led the suicidal advance that had to be made to ensure the army's escape, carrying the regimental banner to lead the way. Against impossible odds, the cheering soldiers of Colonel Rives's regiment charged straight ahead, slamming into the foremost Federals. The short counterattack threw the surging blue legions off balance and bought brief, but precious, time for Colonel Little to disengage his troops on the west side of the road and hurry them east and rearward toward the tavern. Then, with the time won, Little rallied and formed his ammunition-less regiments around the tavern and near the intersection of the Telegraph and Huntsville Roads. Colonel Rives's rear-guard defenders were "slaughtered like hogs" in buying time with audacity and surprise. Switching to canister, Union artillery unleashed blasts of iron hail that swept viciously through the regiment, tearing gaps in Colonel Rives's formations. Out-flanking Rives's command, Unionists on the west side of the road now even more severely punished Little's Rebels with a merciless flank fire.[9]

After the unexpected Rebel attack that momentarily halted the Federals' momentum, Colonel Rives ordered his hard-hit troops to retire slowly through the belt of woods toward the tavern. All the while, Rives's survivors maintained a scattered fire and protected the Telegraph Road sector, and the vulnerable rear of Colonel Little's decimated brigade, while retiring through the stream of projectiles. As the remainder of the Missouri Brigade left the gory field via the Huntsville Road, Rives's steadfast guardians slowly fell back toward the tavern and through the drifting smoke, firing what few rounds that remained. Perhaps now a young fifer in the regiment's rank uplifted spirits by playing the only tune he knew, "The Girl I Left Behind Me," which would have carried through the sulfurous air. Facing almost certain destruction, veteran Missouri soldiers in their once-white uniforms, now stained with dirt, powder and blood, steadily dropped to the Yankees' volleys and the exploding shells. But these Rebels administered some final punishment of their own, "doing fearful execution" at close range.

To encourage his troops under the pounding when the regiment was nearly abreast of Captain Clark's guns, making a last stand around the tavern, Colonel Rives rode down his hard-pressed lines. Bullets whistled all around and soldiers continued dropping under a murderous fire, which seemed to pour from all sides. A minie ball staggered Colonel Rives in the saddle, when it tore through his abdomen. That mortal wound was the exact fate which the colonel had most dreaded.[10]

Just southeast of the Elkhorn tavern and immediately to the left of the Telegraph Road, Colonel Rives realized that he had been fatally wounded. The colonel requested one final wish from his nephew, a young aide: "Help me to keep my seat until I ride down the line to encourage my men. They will break if they see me fall." Despite severe pain, the dying colonel made one last gallop across the regiment's front, with his tearful nephew supporting him in the saddle. Colonel Rives's death ride raised a chorus of cheering. Heartened by their commander's inspiration,

**Captain Samuel Churchill
Clark, killed at Pea Ridge**
Courtesy of Missouri Historical
Society, St. Louis
(Unpublished Photo)

**Colonel Benjamin Allen Rives,
mortally wounded at Pea Ridge**
Courtesy Missouri Historical Society,
St. Louis (Unpublished Photo)

the Missourians continued to act as guardians and withdrew in good order. Enough rounds remained for Rives's soldiers to unleash a final "voley [sic] of small arms [into] the side of the federals," wrote Father Bannon in his diary. This was the Missourians' last volley fired into the Yankees, who were close to outflanking Rives's regiment on the right. One high-ranking Confederate officer never forgot how the last band of Missouri Confederates defiantly "faced about with cheers, believing they were only changing front to fight in some other position." Despite devastating losses, no ammunition, and fighting mostly alone during the closing phases of the Battle of Pea Ridge, Colonel Little's troops refused to break on March 8.

In practically sacrificing itself, the Missouri Brigade ensured that the Army of the West would live to fight another day. As rationalized an embittered Lieutenant Mothershead in his diary: "It seems that Gen. Van Dorn, who all the day before had witnessed the terrible courage of [Rives's] regiment, determined to leave them on the field, while the rest of the army withdrew. They were to hold the enemy in check untill [sic] the whole army had well retired [and] our noble regiment although it lost its gallant commander, and many brave men, accomplished its purpose, for the troops were enabled to easily withdraw." Perhaps all that had saved Colonel Rives's command from being destroyed where the palls of "smoke from the gunfire [which] was so dense that the springtime sunshine was turned into a dull copper haze."[11]

To cover the withdrawal of Colonel Rives's regiment and the retirement of the army's batteries, Captain Clark's guns roared like thunder. General Van Dorn was brought to tears by witnessing the slaughter of his best troops and the discouraging news from an aide who reported, "Colonel Rives is down, sir!" But Captain Clark's example inspired the Mississippi general at this dark hour. Earlier Van Dorn had asked what artillery officer could most be counted upon to stem the blue tide. Price had unhesitatingly answered "Churchy." Captain Clark, consequently, had positioned his battery "very near the advancing column [and] without sufficient infantry support," to protect the retiring Missouri Brigade and the withdrawing Rebel army.[12]

Clark's veteran cannoneers "kept up a galling fire" into the very faces of the charging Unionists. These Confederate gunners were steadily cut down beside their pieces, while the might of Curtis's batteries concentrated on the Rebel battery exposed on the open terrain. General Price, slightly wounded, had earlier dashed up one last time to encourage "Churchy" and his busy cannoneers. Price had implored his "boy" to hold his position to allow the Southern army so slip away from Curtis's grasp. In response, the ex-West Point cadet had taken off his brown felt hat, with side turned up and decorated with a squirrel's tail, and waved it at "Old Pap" in a final salute. He had then shouted above the din, "General, we will hold our own," while his cannon fired against the encroaching blue tide.[13]

Making a bold last stand before the Federal onslaught, the few cannon of Clark's isolated battery blazed away as never before. Colonel Clay Taylor, of Price's staff, rode up and Captain Clark turned and yelled, "Clay, if either of us fall, I hope it will not be you, for you have both wife and children, but I have none." Shell explosions ripped up sod and cut down more Confederate artillerymen and horses. But by then the Second Missouri Confederate Artillery had bought precious time, fulfilling its critical mission in slowing the Union army's advance to allow the Army of the West's survival. One projectile whizzed so close to the teen-age captain that it brushed his mustache. Enveloped in smoke, Clark responded to the near-miss with a smile, remarking to his hard-working artillerymen "God! That was a close shave!"[14]

Finally the artillerymen had to try to save themselves before it was too late. Captain Clark yelled for his gunners to limber up and retire. Smoke-grimed cannoneers worked frantically, hitching field pieces to caissons and limbers amid the torrent of shells and bullets. Most of the battery's guns shortly bounced north, racing through the body-strewn cornfield to escape. Now only one Rebel cannon stood along, bellowing defiance and homemade canister. Captain Clark stayed behind, lingering to make sure that the final gun was safely withdrawn, while the Federals charged ever-closer.[15]

The last field piece of Clark's Battery then pulled out amid the barrage. As Captain Clark prepared to turn his horse and follow, a shell struck "Churchy" in the forehead. The projectile decapitated the St. Louisan, horrifying his cannoneers nearby. In the late morning Captain Clark fell from his coal-black horse, toppling off and falling toward the strategic plot of ground for which he had died. Lieutenant Houston King caught Clark's headless body, which splashed him with a gory mess. With the Federals so close, "Churchy" had to be abandoned on the field. Captain Clark's death deeply affected General Price, who grieved and choked out upon learning the sad news, "My God! Is my Boy Dead?" Both Colonel Rives and Captain Clark had been fatally cut down within minutes and near the same spot, along a slight ridge immediately southeast of the tavern. In a tribute to the Missouri Brigade's last stand, hundreds of Yankees "took off their hats and gave three cheers, which were heartily responded to" by Colonel Little's survivors.[16]

With Union cavalry pursuit harassing the rear, heavy losses and rough terrain, Van Dorn's withdrawal quickly turned into chaos. Much of the Army of the West simply fell apart, with fragments drifting off in three directions, north, east, and west. But most of Colonel Little's Missouri Brigade remained intact, fighting and retiring east through the timber down the Huntsville Road and toward the White River. Other Missouri Brigade members drifted north up the Telegraph Road. Despite losing their Colonel Rives, the soldiers of the Second Missouri stopped on their own and made repeated stands against a vigorous Yankee pursuit. The Federals relentlessly badgered the rear of the withdrawing Rebel column, resulting in hand-to-hand combat amid the hilly, forested terrain. During one bitter clash, Colonel Gates turned his survivors about-face to beat back a serious threat. A young private named Absalom C. Grimes, of Gates's regiment, was knocked unconscious by a Yankee musket-butt in the close, rear-guard fighting. These Missouri defenders provided invaluable service, despite being outnumbered and "badly armed [, for they continued to] fight like devils." A safe retrograde movement of Van Dorn's scattered army was ensured by other successful rear-guard actions of Missouri Brigade veterans. None of these last stands were more important than that of Captain Thrailkill, despite being wounded, and about 60 other First Missouri Cavalrymen. These roughhewn Confederate horsemen rescued from capture and then guarded "33 pieces of cannon [whose caissons and teams had] stampeed [sic] along the [Telegraph] road" and north toward Cassville, Missouri, wrote one of Colonel Little's Rebels immediately after the battle.[17]

Also performing timely service during the confused withdrawal were six of Burbridge's companies, which had been cut off from the Missouri Brigade. Lingering behind the main column and guarding the rear, these companies "saved the Artillery of the Army of the West," in one soldier's words not long after the feat. Despite having suffered at least one-third casualties and isolated from most of the Missouri Brigade, the six decimated companies under Captains Francis Marion Cockrell, Pembroke S. Senteny, Thomas M. Carter, and George Butler, and along with other commanders had quickly formed a line to repel a cavalry attack. The pointblank fire with the few remaining cartridges among Burbridge's veterans repulsed the charge, allowing the escape of the bulk of Van Dorn's artillery. This spontaneous defensive stand by Colonel Burbridge's six First Missouri Regiment companies across the Telegraph Road, north of Pea Ridge, also bought more time for the safe withdrawal of Van Dorn's mauled army. Captain Carter was one soldier who fell wounded during this delaying action. Private Isaac V. Smith, of Colonel Rives's regiment, summarized the role of the Missouri Brigade in thwarting the Yankee pursuit throughout March 8: "We had given the enemy such a drubbing that they did not follow" in large enough numbers to threaten the destruction of Van Dorn's army.

Such rear-guard defensive stands by the scattered elements of the Missouri Brigade further enhanced the unit's reputation. Despite heavy losses and practically no ammunition, these isolated bands of Missouri boys fought on their own without orders. One factor that explains the Missouri Brigade's performance during such a disadvantageous situation lies in the quality of leadership on the company level. Indeed, the captains of Burbridge's six companies, who helped save the day immediately after the Battle of Pea Ridge, were among the Missouri Brigade's best leaders.

For instance, Captain Butler, forty-two, hailed from a distinguished South Carolina family and had organized the Morgan County Rangers at the war's beginning. He led Company D of Burbridge's regiment, consisting mostly of Morgan County soldiers. One of his men killed at Pea Ridge was Private Joseph S. Thruston, age sixteen. He and four brothers had served in Butler's Morgan County Rangers. They had been raised on the farm of their father, a slave owner and Mexican War veteran. One brother, Fayette Thruston, had been killed at the Battle of Wilson's Creek. Another brother, Henry C. Thruston, was "the tallest Confederate" to fight for the South. Presenting an ideal target at Pea Ridge, Thruston stood more than seven feet, gaining a widespread reputation as "the Rebel Giant" because of his size and his bravery.

Captain Senteny had been born and raised in Kentucky. Senteny demonstrated a restless spirit, migrating from the Kentucky Bluegrass in the 1850's to Missouri to seek new opportunities working as a merchant. At age twenty-six, he became colonel of Burbridge's regiment. To the Company A soldiers from Ralls, Pike, and Marion Counties, Senteny was "a friend and an efficient and galant officer [and] he was beloved by all his men" of northeast Missouri, penned one Rebel in his diary.

Another one of Colonel Burbridge's best leaders on the company level, one who helped conduct the rear-guard stands at Pea Ridge, was Captain Carter. He had been a tobacconist from the rich lands bordering Big Creek near the Eagle Fork community. This fertile area of Lincoln County, Missouri, had been mostly settled by Virginians. In 1849, Carter had trekked to the gold fields of California, then later married a pretty girl named Alabama. Leading Company F, the thirty-five-year-old Carter rose swiftly up the Missouri Brigade's leadership hierarchy. The infantrymen of Company F hailed primarily from Pike, Laclede, Jefferson, Lincoln, Vernon, St. Charles, and Callaway Counties, Missouri. Another capable company leader who played a key role in the rear-guard fighting was Captain Cockrell, commanding the Johnson County boys of Company H. Cockrell eventually became the Missouri Brigade's best commander.[18]

After a miserable one-week withdrawal south through the Boston Mountains of western Arkansas, the battered Army of the West finally gathered on the Arkansas River at Van Buren, Arkansas. The Rebels had marched about 80 miles through cold rains, rough country, and fields barren of food, living without rations and wading rain-swollen creeks. At Van Buren, south of Pea Ridge, the beaten Confederates recuperated from the nightmare of Elkhorn Tavern. Fortunately for Van Dorn's army, Curtis mounted no energetic pursuit, failing to exploit his success in Benton County. Pea Ridge had been a disaster for the Confederacy, costing the South 1,300 casualties, while Union losses were comparable. But worst of all for Southern fortunes, Pea Ridge was the high-water mark of the Confederate effort in the Trans-Mississippi. Never again would the Confederacy make a more determined or concentrated attempt to win Missouri or to save the resource-rich Trans-Mississippi. Not only was Missouri lost forever, but also Arkansas and the Indian Territory were now open to invasion. All in all, the Richmond government had been negligent, and awoke only belatedly to the importance of the Trans-Mississippi, consequently, the Confederate bid to reclaim Missouri in March of 1862, had simply been a case of too little, too late. Union victory at Pea Ridge secured the western-most flank for the Federal push to decisive victory in the Mississippi Valley to the east. Also, the Yankee success in the wilderness of northwest Arkansas resulted in political gains for the Union, strengthening the will of the North and solidifying the domestic consensus to prosecute the war to the end.

The exact losses suffered by the Missouri Brigade during its baptismal fire have never been fully tabulated because of incomplete records. Colonel Burbridge's regiment lost at least a third of its strength, or about 175 soldiers. Colonel Rives's unit suffered a comparable loss during the two-day action. While fighting both mounted and on foot, the cavalrymen of Colonel Gates's regiment probably suffered more than those two infantry regiments. In addition, many Missouri Brigade members never reached Van Buren, falling out of column when too exhausted to go farther. Other soldiers were cut off and captured during the chaotic withdrawal. An unknown number of Missouri Brigade Rebels were captured at Pea Ridge and during the long withdrawal south. A tough sergeant and Mexican War veteran of Burbridge's regiment, Oliver G. Pitts, was one soldier taken prisoner.

Most Confederate wounded had to be abandoned on the field, which was the cost of gaining the Union army's rear, losing the fight, and suddenly having the Federals in the Confederate rear. As best as can be determined, the Missouri Brigade's loss was close to 600 soldiers, including the casualties among the artillery units. Captain Wade's Battery lost 1 killed and 8 wounded. The battery of Captain Clark probably suffered heavier casualties. In its first big battle, Colonel Little's Missouri Brigade suffered heavily in officers, with every regimental or battery leader killed or wounded except two. Colonel Rives and Captain Clark were killed, while a third unit commander, Colonel Burbridge, was wounded. Only Colonel Gates and Captain Wade survived the engagement without a scratch.[19]

The Battle of Pea Ridge was a reversal that the Confederacy could ill-afford, especially in early 1862. Rebel defeat around rustic Elkhorn Tavern was the trumpet that sounded the end of Confederate aspirations to regain Missouri and left the Trans-Mississippi open to Union domination as never before. Van Dorn's defeat at Pea Ridge eliminated any realistic possibility of a strong Rebel army ever capturing St. Louis or reclaiming Missouri. In addition, the Southern reversal in northwest Arkansas led to the eventual transfer of the Army of the West to the east side of the Mississippi River. Only a year later, Grant took a giant step in winning the war in the West by slicing down the west side of the Mississippi through eastern Louisiana, bypassing Vicksburg in order to land his army on the east side of the river to gain the citadel's rear.

In the gloom of the Pea Ridge defeat, the Missouri soldiers rested and prayed with their chaplains for the many comrades, dead and wounded, who had been left behind in the blood-soaked cornfields and woodlands around Elkhorn Tavern. Three days after the battle, the news reached the Missouri camp of Colonel Rives's death. Perhaps the best tribute to Rives came in the battle report of General Van Dorn, who wrote that the colonel's fall "was a great loss to us. On a field where there were many gallant gentlemen, I remember him as one of the most energetic and devoted of them all." In his honor, the encampment outside Van Buren was christened Camp Rives.

The survivors learned of the ordeal of Colonel Rives. Rives had been gently carried and left in a log cabin on the battlefield by his brother, Lieutenant Robert Rives, and some of his nephews. Colonel Rives remained defiant until the end, declaring that, "I only wish I had a hundred lives, that I might die again and again for Missouri." Although dying and in severe pain, Rives argued politics during a heated sectional debate with a Union division commander with the unlikely name of Colonel Jefferson C. Davis. Colonel Rives explained his personal motivation, and that of the majority of his followers, proclaiming, "Sir, I have not fought for slavery, but for Constitutional rights!"[20]

Colonel Rives soon died an agonizing death on the Pea Ridge battlefield, leaving a widow and six children in Ray County. No one better than Colonel Little understood the impact of Rives's death on the entire Missouri Brigade, writing that,

> in the fall of Colonel Rives the brigade sustained a severe loss, such a one as the Army of Missouri could not many times encounter and yet preserve its prestige as a band of gallant and devoted patriots; for true as may be the courage of the individual soldiers who fill our ranks, yet of a truth we have but few such officers as was our late brother in arms. A brave and gallant soldier; a prudent and accomplished officer, and, as every man of his command knows from experience, a dear, kind friend, ever solicitous for their comfort, ever interested in their well-being. Peace to his ashes, and may his name be held in veneration.

Colonal Rives had not died alone. The faithful chaplain of Rives's regiment, George Washington Rogers, had been beside the colonel during his final moments. Chaplain Rogers, age twenty-six, performed the sad burial service for Colonel Rives near Elkhorn Tavern with many Union officers in attendance. Most, but not all, Federals were respectful, but one Yankee stole the beautiful saber which had been presented to the colonel by the people of Lexington, Missouri. After Rives's burial in Benton County, two young nephews of Colonel Rives, Private Adrian Collier Ellis, a twenty-two-year-old attorney from Richmond, Ray County, and his brother later brought the colonel's body back to Richmond during a pathetic journey north to Missouri. Colonel Rives found a permanent home amid the beautiful rolling countryside of his beloved Ray County.[21]

Around the war-torn fields and forests of Pea Ridge, the Confederate wounded continued to die and suffer for weeks after the battle. The victorious Unionists generally gave good medical support and comfort to the vanquished. Colonel Rives, for example, had been given decent medical treatment by the blueclads in a farmhouse-turned-infirmary before he died. But not all of the Yankees were so compassionate, which was discovered by Private Parker H. Watkins of Rives's regiment in a make-shift hospital. A twenty-one-year-old farmer from Clay County, Watkins would shortly be "killed by the enemy before he was able to get about," wrote one enraged comrade. Many injured Missouri Brigade members received medical and spiritual comfort from Surgeon E. McDowell Coffey, the regimental physician of Gates's regiment, and Chaplain Rogers. Other Rebels also stayed behind to nurse their wounded relatives. For example, Sergeant David Hardin Chism, age forty-five, had carried his seventeen-year-old son, crippled by a leg mangled by a bullet, off the battlefield and took him to a lob cabin. There, young Private Jacob Chism, also in Company D, of Burbridge's regiment, recovered, and returned to Versailles with the help of his father, who was imprisoned by the Unionists upon reaching home.

In a sacred pilgrimage to reclaim for the Missouri Brigade what had once been its own, Colonel Little ordered Captain Schaumburg to lead a detail back to the battlefield to bury the Rebel dead and to retrieve the body of a popular St. Louis officer. Despite almost being fired upon by nervous Unionists, the Confederate burial party flying a white flag accomplished their psychologically important mission, and brought the body of the young captain back to Van Buren. Now "Churchy" rejoined his comrades for one last time. During an emotional service by his artillerymen and the Missouri Brigade's chaplains, Captain Samuel Churchill Clark was laid to rest on March 29 along the green hills near the majestic Arkansas River hundreds of miles from his St. Louis home and family.[22]

Fortunately for the decimated Missouri Brigade, a highly qualified cadre of leaders survived the disaster of Pea Ridge to replace the many officers who had been cut down during the two-day battle. For example, Lieutenant Colonel James Avery Pritchard was a worthy replacement for Colonel Rives. Like the vast majority of Missouri Brigade personnel, Pritchard's roots were in the Upper South, the Kentucky Bluegrass, and the mountains of Virginia. The handsome, scholarly Pritchard was a distant cousin of Lieutenant General Thomas Jonathan "Stonewall" Jackson. Frontier life, the Mexican War, and the California gold fields provided Pritchard with the conditioning, leadership skills, and experience that helped to prepare him for regimental command. Like the lamented Colonel Rives, Pritchard had been a member of the Missouri legislature from 1858-60.[23]

Colonel Pritchard had been a solid Union man as late as 1860. As a noted legislator, he had sensed the worst for his increasingly polarized nation, feeling that "there has been a dark, gloomy cloud of foreboding hanging over my mind for several years in regard to my country. I have resisted disunion in every shape that it has presented itself." Pritchard was commanding one of the best regiments in an elite Confederate Brigade, which had been proven its caliber at the Battle of Pea Ridge. Like his soldiers, Pritchard felt much pride in the complimentary words of General Van Dorn, who wrote an appropriate tribute to the Missouri Brigade: "During the whole of this engagement [Pea Ridge], I was with the Missourians under Price, and I have never seen better fighters than these Missouri troops, or more gallant leaders than General Price and his officers. From the first to the last shot, they continually rushed on, and never yielded an inch they had won; and when at last they received orders to fall back, they retired steadily and with cheers." Clearly, these were the words of a West Pointer who had gained a new respect for the citizen-soldiers from the western frontier. In addition, General Van Dorn believed that "many of [the Missourians'] charges would have done credit to Napoleon's old guard." Indeed, the Missouri Brigade's reputation was now firmly established as the "Old Guard" of Price's army. News of the Missouri Brigade's exploits were spread by a journalist at the Confederate capital of Richmond, who wrote that "the Missourians surpassed all ancient and modern history of valor," by their performance at the battle of Pea Ridge.

From the beginning, Pritchard, a prosperous farmer, had compiled a distinguished record. During Missouri State Guard service, Pritchard had served under Colonel Rives, and had acquired a fine reputation for ability and inspired leadership. He had three horses shot from under him at the Battle of Wilson's Creek, and two more of his mounts were cut down during the attacks on Lexington. An innovative and natural tactician, his reckless bravery placed him in the same category as Colonel Gates and Colonel Rives. The tall, dark and long-haired Pritchard cut a dashing figure on the battlefield, and he always escaped injury despite bullets often cutting through his uniform. More close calls had come for Pritchard at Pea Ridge. Among the Missouri Brigade, therefore, a belief had spread that the minie ball to cut him down had not yet been molded. Colonel Pritchard "seemed for a time to bear a charmed life," which was another quality that inspired his soldiers to supreme heights.[24]

Mathilda Pritchard took no comfort in her husband's battlefield heroics and his repeated brushes with death. Therefore, she sought out an old black woman and slave of Carroll County, who was deeply religious, spiritual, and a respected psychic in their frontier community. For some time, the African American woman concentrated upon the fate of Mathilda's husband in the far-away South and gained insights that proved prophetic. She informed Mrs. Pritchard that her colonel would be safe from harm only as long as he never rode a reddish-brown horse into a charge. Mathilda, thereafter, wrote desperate letters to Colonel Pritchard, warning him of the slave's prophecy and begging him to heed the warning. But Pritchard failed to heed the warning, ignoring the portent that would prove true in Mississippi.[25]

Replacing Captain "Churchy" Clark was Lieutenant James L. Farris. The Kentucky-born Farris commanded the battery, but this unit would forever be known throughout the army as "Captain Clark's Artillery," another tribute for the Missouri Brigade's first battery commander killed in action. Despite taking a wound at Pea Ridge, Colonel Burbridge continued to lead his regiment.[26]

Not long after Pea Ridge, the Missouri Brigade's infantry regiments were redesignated. These numerical redesignations were made because Colonel John Stevens Bowen had recruited a Missouri Confederate regiment in the summer of 1861. Since this was the first Confederate regiment organized from Missouri, Bowen's unit was designated as the First Missouri Confederate Infantry. Con-

sequently, Colonel Burbridge's unit, formerly the First Missouri Confederate Infantry, now became the Second Missouri Confederate Infantry. This was no simple
bureaucratic matter to the proud soldiers in the ranks, because the highest honor
went to the regiment with the lowest numerical designation. Also, Colonel Rives's
Second Missouri Confederate Infantry was now redesignated the Third Missouri
Confederate Infantry.[27]

To resume the struggle for Missouri, Van Dorn planned to take the offensive.
But unknown to him, Confederate strategists in Richmond had already decided
otherwise. Indeed, Missouri had been forsaken for the interests of the war east of
the Mississippi. Nevertheless, for the next year and a half, the exiled soldiers of
the Missouri Brigade continued to engage in the decisive "struggle for the master-
ship of the Mississippi river and valley," wrote one Southern journalist.[28]

A difficult 200-mile trek east across the wet landscape of central Arkansas began
toward the end of March. Van Dorn still wanted to continue the contest for Missouri
with an offensive in southeast Missouri. To cut the logistical and communications
network in Curtis's rear to keep him from reinforcing the Union forces around New
Madrid, Missouri, Van Dorn ordered Colonel Gates's regiment into action. The
First Missouri Cavalry galloped north as part of a six-regiment cavalry raid to smash
Curtis's communications line leading to Springfield and Rolla, while the Army of
the West pushed east through Arkansas and toward southeast Missouri. But the
cavalry raid was aborted when the butternut troopers were stopped by the rain-
swollen White River near Forsyth, Missouri, south of Springfield. For all their efforts, Gates's cavalrymen accomplished little.[29]

But more important developments had occurred while Colonel Gates's horsemen
engaged in their last mounted assignment of the war. Orders came in the final days
of March for the Army of the West to cross immediately to the east side of the
Mississippi to join the largest concentration of Confederate forces in the West at
Corinth, Mississippi. At last, the Davis Government decided to mount a maximum
offensive effort to reverse the recent series of disasters in the West. In addition to
the Pea Ridge defeat, the transfer of this Rebel army equated to the abandonment
of Missouri to the Federals for the remainder of the war. Likewise, with Missouri
being the key linchpin of the entire Trans-Mississippi, that theater was also doomed,
even though the struggle for its possession continued. On April 6, the hard-marching
Missouri soldiers reached Des Arc, Arkansas, the departure point on the White River
for the trip by steamboat to gain the Mississippi. Flooded streams, seas of mud,
and cold rains had slowed the long march through the rolling hills and farm lands
of mid-Arkansas. For the first time in their lives, the yeomen from the frontier state
to the north viewed the unfamiliar plantation world of northeastern Arkansas:
sprawling fields of cotton, an economy built upon a Southern staple, gangs of slaves,
and a wealthy planter class and fine mansions.

Much precious time had been lost in the long march east, which slipped away
along with Confederate fortunes. Indeed, on the same day that the Missourians
reached the muddy White River and the fleet of steamboats awaiting them, General
Albert Sidney Johnston and the principal Rebel army in the West had already advanced northeast from Corinth and smashed into General Ulysses S. Grant's Army
at Shiloh, amid the dense forests along the Tennessee River. The Army of the West,
mired in flooded east-central Arkansas and on the west, or wrong, side of the
Mississippi, missed this all-important battle around Pittsburg Landing on the

east side of the Mississippi. Ironically, the express purpose of the Army of the West's transfer east of the Mississippi had been to reinforce Johnston for the South's western offensive to revive sagging Confederate fortunes. But, without the 20,000 veterans of the Army of the West, Johnston's chance to defeat Grant at Shiloh on April 6-7 and to regain the initiative to save the Mississippi Valley was lessened considerably.

As at Pea Ridge, poor Confederate timing and coordination, and bad luck at Shiloh resulted in another bloody Rebel defeat. With the Army of the West, Johnston might have driven Grant's forces into the Tennessee on the first day at Shiloh. The lack of an east-west railroad line in north or central Arkansas to transport Van Dorn's army had cost the Confederacy dearly. Mistakenly, the Missouri soldiers thought that the news of the first day at Shiloh pronounced a decisive victory. Captain Wade's artillerymen fired victory salutes and the Missouri boys, wrote Private Sam Dunlap in his diary, celebrated with wild cheering, and a great many hats "were thrown in the air."

As fate would have it on a rainy April 7, the jubilant Missourians boarded steamboats with little reason to celebrate the beginning of the long journey southeast down the flooded White River and then northeast up the Mississippi to Memphis, before an overland trip by rail to northeastern Mississippi. The steamboats pulled away from the wharf despite the fact that the primary purpose of the Army of the West's mission to the other side of the "Father of Waters" had already been negated.[30]

Some organizational changes were made with the transfer to the east side of the Mississippi. A fine Arkansas unit, the Sixteenth Arkansas Confederate Infantry, was attached to the Missouri Brigade. These hardy Rebels, formerly of McCulloch's Division, had stood firmly beside the Missourians on that awful last day at Pea Ridge. This reliable frontier command had been organized in the same county, Benton, where the Battle of Pea Ridge had raged so fiercely. An exiled unit with its homeland occupied by the Yankees like the Missouri Brigade, the Arkansas regiment was commanded by Colonel John F. Hill, a capable leader from the wilds of northwest Arkansas, a Mexican War veteran, and, best of all in the Missourians' opinion, "a fighter."[31]

Also with the transfer of the Army of the West came orders to transfer Van Dorn's cavalry to infantry service. For Colonel Gates's wild riders, this unexpected directive was taken almost as hard as losing Missouri. The horses that Gates's troopers had brought from home had to be left behind at Des Arc with Richmond's orders. Perhaps the best Confederate horse unit in the Trans-Mississippi had now died an early death. Consequently, Gates's regiment, hereafter, was designated the First Missouri Confederate Cavalry (Dismounted). But this change did not diminish the combat effectiveness of Gates's command, because this unit became "one of the most effective infantry regiments in the army." Double-barrel shotguns were soon traded for .58 caliber Mississippi rifles, Model 1841. The soldiers' discontent knew no bounds, fated to walk instead of ride and endure endless infantry drill to transform horsemen into foot-sloggers. Consequently, Colonel Gates's ex-cavalrymen would remain some of the most disgruntled and most difficult soldiers to manage in the Missouri Brigade, refusing ever to relinquish their dream of returning to cavalry service.[32]

For days, the Missouri soldiers rode the transports like curious spectators in homespun uniforms, consisting of butternut, militia uniforms, civilian clothes, and undyed wool of dirty white. But these slow-moving steamboats crowded with jovial Rebels were only carrying them to a cruel destiny east of the Mississippi.[33]

CHAPTER FOUR

Exiled East of the Mississippi River

After disembarking at the Mississippi port of Memphis from their "leaky old Tub[s]," the Missouri troops were welcomed as liberators by a cheering populace. Sergeant Edward C. Robbins, a Missouri artilleryman, wrote a letter to Union-occupied St. Louis and described "how enthusiastically Price's army was received in Memphis and we of St. Louis thank the people for so receiving our *brave Missourians*. We have every confidence that the right will triumph when such brave, noble hearted men as we have on the Southern side are spilling their blood for the maintenance of their cause. May God watch over and save all near and dear to me from death by a Federal hand." Indeed, the welfare of those at home under the rule of Union occupation troops was a never-ending source of anxiety for Colonel Little's exiles. From Memphis, the Missouri regiments moved southeast by rail, heading swiftly through the pine forests for Corinth, Mississippi. After reaching the vital railroad center of Corinth, the Missouri Brigade proceeded south down the Mobile & Ohio Railroad to Rienzi, in northeastern Mississippi. Less than a dozen miles below Corinth, the Missourians erected a tented city near the railroad, within a quick train trip to bolster strategic Corinth if necessary. Wrote Colonel Pritchard in his diary, "the encampment is designated as camp 'Rives,' in memory, and honor of our late gallant Colonel, who fell at the battle of 'Elkhorn' Whilst nobly discharging his duty to his country and State."

At Corinth General Pierre Gustave Toutant Beauregard commanded the principal Rebel army in the West, after General Johnston's death and Confederate defeat at Shiloh. Bad luck, Southern reversals, and an apathetic Richmond bureaucracy had seemingly conspired to cast the Missourians' fate with Beauregard's Army of the Mississippi. Most of Colonel Little's soldiers were farther from Missouri than they had ever been before in their young lives. As fate would have it, the majority of the Missouri Brigade's soldiers, including Colonel Little, would never see their home state again. During this tranquil period in northeast Mississippi, "the Missouri troops were the centre of attraction, and a great many thronged our camp to look at us. Some said that they imagined that the Missourians had horns, but they saw we were 'just like any body else' and seemed to be surprised." But the most unusual attraction in Price's encampment was the Missouri Brigade's former mascot from the mountains of northwestern Arkansas. This pet was a fat and sassy black bear, which had been presented by Little's followers to "Old Pap."[1]

As the spring of 1862 slipped toward summer, both North and South expected the war's most decisive engagement to erupt at Corinth. The small railroad town in northeastern Mississippi was the Confederacy's most important strategic point in the West. There, the great communications arteries of the east-west Memphis

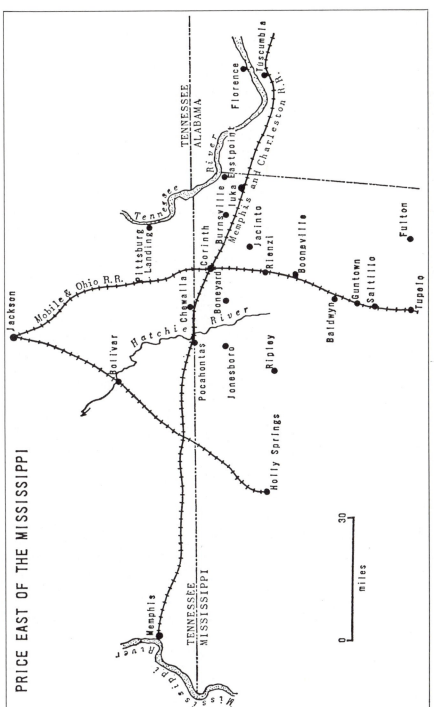

PRICE EAST OF THE MISSISSIPPI

& Charleston Railroad and the north-south Mobile & Ohio Railroad connected all corners of the South. To protect such a strategic communications and logistical hub, reported one journalist, "the Confederate Government is bending its energies with desperate earnestness to maintain the position at Corinth; with the loss of the latter, that of Mobile, New Orleans and the Gulf States could immediately follow." Likewise the Confederacy foresaw no less dramatic results from a Rebel success at Corinth, which could unleash a Confederate offensive thrust north to the Ohio River.[2]

But the climactic showdown between the two rival armies in northeast Mississippi never developed. Some of the foremost military minds of the South continued to understand a fundamental reality of the Civil War. "It grows more and more apparent every day that the great contest for freedom in which the Confederate States are now engaged is to be decided in the valley of the Mississippi." Despite an army eventually swelling to more than 120,000 troops, Major General Henry W. Halleck failed to strike a killing blow against a defending Southern army less than half the size of his command. Recently sent from his St. Louis headquarters, Halleck had done much to ensure that Missouri remained in Union hands, earning the hatred of the Missouri Confederates. The marshaling of Northern forces was in part made possible because of the Army of the West's transfer across the Mississippi in its futile bid to reach Shiloh. Now, the "great chess board [game]" for control of Corinth continued throughout the increasingly hot Mississippi weather.[3]

But no great clash of armies was almost as good as victory to a young, agrarian nation on the resource-short end of a war of attrition against an industrial giant. Avoiding a decisive defeat not only lengthened the life of the Dixie republic, but also enhanced the possibility for foreign recognition, which was the South's primary diplomatic and political goal to ensure independence. Further, an avoidance of a decisive Confederate reversal in the West might sap the will of a Northern populace to fight for years to the death. Most Americans had naively believed that this would be a short war, and the expected climactic battle in northeastern Mississippi proved to be yet another illusion.[4]

During the spring of 1862, the conflict in the West was still very much a West Point-like business of maneuver and bluff, without the nightmarish fighting seen later. And no general on either side was more adept at an Eighteenth Century-style of waging war than "Old Brains" Halleck. General Halleck's primary weakness was that he thought harder than he fought. Commanding more than 120,000 troops only made Halleck more cautious instead of more aggressive. Burdened by logistical problems, muddy roads, and the daily process of entrenching to avoid being caught by surprise like Grant at Shiloh, the Unionists' approach south upon Corinth was reduced to a crawl.

During a scorching May at Camp Churchill Clark, the Missourians re-enlisted in Confederate service for three years. This voluntary decision committed them more firmly to the destiny of the South. With each passing day, a subtle transformation had been taking place in the Missouri soldiers' definitions and understanding of the meaning of states rights and its relationship to a larger Southern nationalism. Amid the hot Mississippi forests, the fusing of these two conflicting ideological concepts was now gradually occurring in the hearts and minds of the common soldiers. Private Dyson, a Franklin County teacher, who would see several of his former students-comrades killed in action, described to his wife in a letter, "all of us boys are stronger for the South [than when] we left home." Feeling much like Private Dyson, three Jefferson County brothers of Company F, Second Missouri, re-enlisted in Confederate service. Of French ancestry, Privates Elias and Jerome Gamache, ages twenty and twenty-five respectively, would be killed in battle. The youngest brother, John Gamache, would die of disease ot age eighteen. Also, the Missouri soldiers now received State Guard back-pay for the first time. Wrote the frugal merchant Lieutenant Warren, "The boys have more [money] than they know *what to do with* [and consequently] the gaming runs *high*."

Colonel Pritchard was baptized by Father Bannon on May 8 in preparation for meeting the Yankees and perhaps his Maker. Fighting erupted at Farmington, just northeast of Corinth, on May 9. Price's division, including the Missouri Brigade, advanced northeast from Corinth's forti-

Private William Jackson Haydon, Company G, 2nd Missouri Infantry, taken at time of the battle for Lexington, Missouri
Courtesy Dorothy G. Haydon, Springfield, Missouri

fications to ascertain the Federals' strength and dispositions, and soon collided with the Yankees. The skirmish at Farmington made Halleck more cautious. But complained one Missourian, "had it not have been for the almost unimpenetrable swamp through which we had to pass [that] retarded our progress [General Price] should have succeeded in completely cutting off the enemy's retreat." Instead of striking the Unionists with a punishing blow, Missouri Brigade members marched for hours, floundered in thickets, and splashed through swamps. Although the fight at Farmington was only a skirmish, some Rebels gloated that the Yankees "ran like sheep." After the Federals retired "in true Bull Run fashion" the Corinth front returned to its nerve-wracking quiet.[5]

Since the arrival in Mississippi, scorching weather and disease continued to cause more damage to the Missouri Brigade than Yankee bullets and shells. Poor rations, horrid sanitation, rainy weather, campsites in swampy lowlands, legions of lice, ticks, and fleas, and brackish drinking water sent hundreds of Missourians to the hospitals. Always the greatest killer, diarrheal diseases spread like wildfire. Young Lieutenant Warren complained in his diary that, "we have had no cessation in the rains [and] everything is saturated with water." The rages of disease greatly reduced the Missouri Brigade's strength, almost as if a great battle had been fought. Within the first month of service in northeast Mississippi, for instance, only 13 soldiers of the 84 who crossed the Mississippi were able to perform duty in one Third Missouri company.

Regimental chaplains, such as Benjamin Franklin Kavanaugh of the First Missouri Cavalry (Dismounted) and William N. Dodson of the Second Missouri, laid more and more soldiers to rest in the red soil of Tishomingo County. Living amid an unfamiliar environment of low-lying swamps and almost daily soaked with rains, the Confederates from Missouri died steadily from a wide range of diseases, including pneumonia, typhoid fever, the "mumps," and dysentery. Wide fluctuations of daily temperatures were unhealthy, causing a mystified Lieutenant Warren to write "the nights in these swamps are colder than the nights in Mo are in November." So deadly was this killing summer in Mississippi that one of Colonel Burbridge's unacclimated soldiers recalled how, "Corinth was long remembered, and often called the graveyard of our army." A detailed survey of incomplete individual service records indicates that at least 10 soldiers of the First Missouri Cavalry (Dismounted), 16 of the Second Missouri, and 13 of the Third Missouri died of disease during the summer of 1862. Including those soldiers who died of illness in Captain Wade's Battery, the Sixteenth Arkansas, and those men whose deaths went unrecorded, probably more than 50 Missouri Brigade members perished of disease in Mississippi that summer. Typical deaths from illness included two brothers, Privates Jacob and Michael Vineyard, seventeen, of the Third Missouri, who died within days of each other. In addition, Pea Ridge-wounded in Arkansas and Mississippi hospitals and private homes continued to die of wounds during this period.

Even Little, now promoted to brigadier general, fell ill in the humid, gloomy woodlands around Corinth. General Dabney H. Maury led the sickly Missouri Brigade while General Little recuperated. Fortunately, General Little received good physical and spiritual care from Father Bannon, who effectively administered the comforts of heaven and earth as few others could. The chaplain of the Missouri Brigade probably saved the general's life more than once that summer with his tireless care. Bannon centered his activities around Captain Wade's Battery and a Rienzi storehouse that he had turned into a church. As always, the fiery Irish priest instilled faith in as many soldiers as possible, regardless of denomination. More than any other Missouri Brigade chaplain, Father Bannon strengthened the soldiers' bonds between religion and the Confederate experiment in nationhood, fortifying the concepts of Southern nationalism and the moral foundation to struggle to the end.[6]

Beauregard's Rebels were understandably nervous with Halleck's immense force hovering nearby. Several times during this period, the Missouri Brigade and other Confederate troops rushed north to repel attacks that never came. Confined to a sick bed, General Little often anguished while "the army [went] to march out & meet the enemy—God grant us victory & oh! that I were able to lead my command in the coming conflict." Toward the end of May, the contest for Corinth came to an unexpectedly quiet end. For weeks Halleck's forces had crept closer, erecting fortifications for a siege, and extending the blue lines until they threatened the Rebels' flanks. With Corinth becoming a vulnerable salient because the Federals gained territory in Alabama, and along the Mississippi River after the fall of Island Number Ten, and with Memphis threatened, General Beauregard decided to escape the trap and evacuate the West's great prize before being surrounded.

After the thousands of Rebel sick were sent deeper into the safety of Mississippi, Confederate units quickly entrained on the boxcars of the Mobile & Ohio Railroad during the escape south from Corinth, without alerting the Yankees of their departure. As noiselessly as possible, the Missourians eased out of Camp Churchill Clark on the evening of May 29, heading for Corinth's depot, while protecting the rear. During the hasty evacuation, the "1st [Missouri] Brigade [acted as the] rear guard of the army," wrote a proud Father Bannon in his diary of yet another honor bestowed upon the ever-reliable frontier unit. As in serving as the rear-guard for a Trans-Mississippi army during its risky withdrawal from Missouri to Arkansas, the Missouri Brigade veterans were now the principal guardians for the major western Rebel army, which was engaging in its most dangerous withdrawal to date. To deceive the Federals, meanwhile, Confederates about to embark on the journey south cheered the arrival of the trains of empty box cars, as if welcoming reinforcements from the Deep South.

Taking the bait, "the [Yankee] Doodles," lampooned one Southern newspaperman, failed to detect the stealthy withdrawal from Corinth between the sunset of May 29 and sunrise of May 30. Lieutenant Mothershead was jubilant at the army's escape, writing in his diary: "Beauregard has successfully fallen back from Corrinth [sic], bringing away all his Ordnance, Commissary, and Quartermaster stores, and without loss of men. By this retrograde movement from Corrinth [sic], the deep laid schemes of the enemy are again baffled." After slipping out of Halleck's noose, the Army of the West retired south to the Tupelo, Mississippi area. There, more than 50 miles south of Corinth, Beauregard's command found a safer and healthier region to recuperate from the disease-plagued stay at Corinth, since Halleck failed to pursue.[7]

Some Federal cavalry, however, thundered deeper into the Magnolia State and in the Confederates' direction to reconnoiter. To help parry this threat, Colonel Gates returned briefly to cavalry service. Colonel Gates, consequently, led a 600-1,000-man mounted expedition to repel the Federal horse soldiers. A follow-up strike by Halleck was not forthcoming, and the Confederates soon relaxed.[8]

In one Southerner's assessment, "We think that Halleck's summer campaign is fairly spoiled. The process of subjugation by his army is as completely checked as if he had lost a battle." But, in reality, the strategic consequences of the loss of Corinth were far-reaching. Historians have long underestimated the importance of Halleck's bloodless capture of Corinth. The successful strategic turning movement that won Corinth resulted in greater Yankee control of West Tennessee, made the fall of Memphis inevitable, and secured a tighter Union grip on the Mississippi Valley. But more important, the Federal hold on the vital railroad terminus at Corinth deprived the Confederacy of its most direct and efficient means by which to utilize interior rail lines to most easily reinforce the vital Mississippi Valley with the Army of Northern Virginia or other Rebel armies to the east. With the loss of Corinth and the most direct east-west line, the Memphis & Charleston Railroad, Vicksburg was more vulnerable than ever before. If Vicksburg was now threatened, Rebel reinforcements could not be drawn from all corners of the South to reinforce Vicksburg as speedily as before. A lenghty and time-consuming detour via Mobile was now the alternative route to reinforce the Mississippi Valley from the east.

The Mississippi summer quickly passed, while active campaigning in Price's sector subsided. As if worn down by the heat, both sides ceased active operations in northeastern Mississippi. Saddled with logistical difficulties, Halleck's mighty army was mostly dismantled and shuffled to other theaters during the respite. The Missouri Brigade paid more heavily in economic terms than in battlefield losses.

Colonel Gates's First Missouri cavalrymen collected and donated $2,350 of their meager pay for the welfare of wounded Confederates in Virginia. Perhaps such donations were easier because the Missouri homeland was under Union control and money could not be sent to families. As Private Dyson explained to his wife, "I would send you some money if I could get any that would be of any account to you but confederate money is not worth anything in Mo." Colonel Gates described this generous donation, "The officers and men of the Missouri cavalry having a lively appreciation of the gallantry and fortitude of our brothers in arms before Richmond [during Major General George B. McClellan's Peninsula Campaign] and not being able to share with them the dangers and glory of driving the invader from before our capital, desire [now] to give material evidence of [our] gratitude to, and consideration for, those who were so unfortunate as to receive wounds in the late glorious conflict." Only a week later, these same dismounted horsemen petitioned General Price for the immediate return of their horses and transfer back to cavalry service. But this wish, like the dream of reclaiming Missouri and the winning of the Confederacy's independence, would never be realized.[9]

Reorganizations within the army came with some of the summer's hottest weather. By mid-June, General Little had been promoted to divisional command, taking charge of the First Missouri Brigade and the Second Brigade, which consisted of Texas, Missouri, Louisiana, and Arkansas troops under Brigadier General Louis Hebert, who had recently been exchanged after his capture at Pea Ridge. Little's steadfast performance at Pea Ridge earned him divisional command, while General Price went to Richmond in a futile effort to have his Missouri troops transferred west of the Mississippi. In addition, the Clark battery had been reassigned to one of Price's other brigades, leaving only Captain Wade's battery with the Missouri Brigade.

Some key personnel changes had been made as well. Colonel Burbridge had left the Second Missouri because of his Pea Ridge wound and sickness. He refused to quit the struggle, however. Returning to the guerrilla-style of fighting that had launched his military career in Missouri, Burbridge led Rebels into action in the Trans-Mississippi theater once again. Winning promotion to colonel in Burbridge's stead was Captain Francis Marion Cockrell, an attorney at age twenty-seven. The serious-minded Cockrell was the prototype of the citizen-soldier leader from the frontier, who found religion and Southern nationalism inseparable. Without formal military training and as "green as a gourd in military affairs" at the war's beginning, the taciturn, homespun leader, who never drank or cursed, combined natural instinct, common sense, and aggressiveness on the battlefield. One of his soldiers tried to explain the secret of Cockrell's success: "While the other fellows were fussing and fuming about the ranks and grades, Cockrell was fighting, and between battles was lying flat on his belly in his tent studying Hardee's tactics." Such dedication had long made Cockrell the best captain of the Second Missouri. A crusader in butternut, the "praying captain" fought as hard as he sought God's blessing. In battle he carried Hardee's *Tactics* in one coat pocket and the Bible in the other. For four years, Cockrell would fight and pray "that the land of his forefathers [both Missouri and the South] would be freed from invasion and its independence won." Fueling personal resolve and a yearning for revenge, Cockrell's Johnson County birthplace of Columbus lay in ashes, after being burned down by Kansas Jayhawkers in January of 1862.

Cockrell's Cromwellian demeanor and stoic nature had been strengthened by a 1859 tragedy: his wife's death in child birth, leaving him a single parent with two young sons. But he was not embittered, remaining positive about all aspects of life and keeping faith in God. One secret of his popularity was the ability to remain the same person despite his high rank and success, giving privates and generals the same consideration. He acted as a father to the boys in the ranks. Strengthened by a frontier Presbyterianism, Cockrell waged a holy war as the commander of the Second Missouri. Energetic and intelligent, he was an ideal revolutionary for the South's independence movement and a perfect leader of the Missouri exiles far from home. Colonel Cockrell possessed an inspiring command presence, for he "was one of the finest looking officers in the army," wrote one soldier, "being large and having an air of command [and the] men would have followed him anywhere." Like General Little, Cockrell was a tough disciplinarian. One Rebel would still be complaining decades after the war, writing with some lingering bitterness how "when he wasn't fightin', [Cockrell] used to turn loose and drill us till the tongues hung outen [sic] our mouths." Colonel Cockrell played a key role in making these troops "the South's Finest."

In the Second Missouri, some of the best soldiers were coming to the fore, such as Captain Senteny. He advanced to a major's rank because of his leadership qualities and his Pea Ridge performance. Athletic and clean-shaven, Pembroke Senteny had been born in Ohio. The farm of his birth bordered that of the father of Ulysses S. Grant. He had early excelled in scholastics, teaching school after migrating to Missouri from Kentucky. While serving as a Missouri militiaman, Senteny had been captured at Camp Jackson in early May of 1861. The Missouri Rebels never forget "the polished Senteney [sic], so grateful and gracious and good," recalled one soldier.[10]

In the steamy encampments amid the tall oaks and pines near Tupelo, the Missourians stayed busy with drilling, improving discipline, and conditioning. As Lieutenant Warren scribbled in his diary, "The weather is excessively warm, but we still continue to drill & it is pretty tough [in] this hot weather." In lieu of a cool breeze, religious revivals swept the Missouri Brigade, after being sparked by the hard-working chaplains and the sobering sight of disease continuously stealing Missouri boys from the ranks. Much of the soldiers' free time was spent this summer in picking blackberries, gambling, hunting for Mississippi belles and liquor, sinking wells to find decent drinking water, writing letters to loved ones, and reading the Bible. But the most fun came with the latest rage in camp, consisting of "chicken fights," revealed Lieutenant Warren in his diary, and "there is quite a demand among the Soldiers, for pugalistic [sic] fowls [and] the excitement is generally great & the Stakes High." The religious revival failed to dissuade the First Missouri Cavalrymen from mischief, however. That summer, for example, the dismounted cavalry "soldiers made a charge on a [railroad] car load of Watermelons last night [and] took two hundred dollars worth (the way they sold them)." And on another occasion, the disgruntled horsemen without mounts raided the Missouri Brigade's commissary. The thieves in dirty butternut hauled off the Missouri Brigade's supply of bacon and flour and a barrel of whiskey, which initiated a festive celebration in honor of "John Barleycorn," and for obtaining some revenge against the Confederate government for having taken away their horses. Clearly, with no battle imminent, these western frontiersmen were capable of causing considerable mischief.

Despite the epidemics of disease, the scorching heat of summer, and the boredom of camp life, morale improved by the efforts of one of Colonel Gates's ex-soldiers, Absalom C. Grimes. The importance of letters from Missouri was indicated by Private Dyson, who emotionally described in a letter to his wife how, "it would be a source of greater enjoyment to me to get a small scrape of a pen from you than anything else that I could think of aside from knowing that we had gained our independence." But letters from home brought relief only if they contained no news of harm inflicted on families by the Union occupation troops and Home Guards. As the war lengthened, the number of letters that failed to report outrages steadily decreased.

After his capture at Pea Ridge, recovery from a head wound, and exchange, Grimes became the Missouri Brigade's principal mail runner. This hazardous duty performed by the twenty-five-year-old Grimes consisted of carrying soldiers' letters back to Missouri and returning to Mississippi with relatives' letters. A steamboat pilot from Hannibal, Missouri, and old friend of Samuel Clemens, or Mark Twain, Grimes had a thorough navigational knowledge of the Mississippi River by which he usually traveled by skiff. But the Kentucky-born Grimes was only the middle man in a vast clandestine postal network of dedicated female Rebels, who gathered mail across much of Federal-occupied Missouri. To boost the morale of their boys at the front, these courageous Missouri women risked much in defying Federal authorities, and occasionally they sacrificed their homes, property, and possessions. These resourceful women, who often had sons, brothers, or husbands in the Missouri Brigade, remain some of the forgotten players in the drama of the little-known Trans-Mississippi war. The official military records and reports fail to tell the story of these unsung heroines of the Confederacy.

Letters from families often fueled the fighting spirit of the exiles in the far-away South. Tales of abuses committed by Unionists, often neighbors, in Missouri heightened the desire for revenge among the common soldiers. For instance, Lieutenant Warren reflected in his diary how a year had passed since he had "left my distant Mo home, and bid adieu to those 'kind ones,' to join the standard of Liberty & Freedom. Little did I then think, that to day, I would be so far distant in the Old Miss State, an Exile from home and friends, & that good old State, the Home of those I hold most dear, trampled and crushed under the foot of the oppressor. How often do I wish to be with them to share their oppression, to protect them with my feeble arm, from the insults of their overbearing Conquerors. I feel proud that I am a Confederate Soldier, and know that I am serving them, as well as my Native South."[11]

More organizational changes came within the army during that disease-riddled summer. Enigmatic and competent, General Braxton Bragg replaced Beauregard as the commander of the Army of Mississippi. The Seminole War veteran and Mexican War hero took command with the intent to improve the army's health and morale, and regain the offensive. With Vicksburg, Mississippi, under serious threat from the Union Navy, General Van Dorn left the Army of the West to take charge of that all-important citadel in western Mississippi. Then General Price replaced Van Dorn, earning command of the Army of the West, consisting of two divisions, whose assignment was to protect the Mobile & Ohio Railroad. General Little retained leadership of Price's old division. Already, Little's First Division was fast acquiring the reputation as one of the finest such units in the West. The First Missouri Brigade continued to improve in the capable hands of Colonel Gates, who knew how to fine-tune the command, and was idolized by the common soldiers.

Commanding General Little's Third Brigade was Brigadier General Martin E. Green. In one Southern journalist's words, the fiery and silver-haired Green was "an old veteran [and] the Yankee hordes have reason to remember him. For many months he was to them a terror in North Missouri. Many were the schemes to entrap and overwhelm him; and as many were the failures and discomfitures of the foe. Many were the bloody conflicts, and many a hundred invaders bit the dust before the invincible riflemen of Green." Of course, quality officers of this fine division were not exclusively Missourians. General Hebert's brigade was attached to the First Division, and the regiments of Colonel John D. Martin's brigade by mid-July.

The Missourians' old interim commander, Brigadier General Maury, led the Second Division of Price's Corps. Maury, a West Pointer and Mexican War veteran, demonstrated leadership qualities and dedication which "justly entitled him to be classed, in the possession of these high attributes of character, along with the officers and soldiers of Missouri. That is the highest praise we know how to bestow," complimented a Mississippi newspaperman. Reflecting the Missouri Brigade's widespread reputation which continued to grow with each passing month, this non-Missouri journalist was already using the quality of General Little's Missouri troops as the standard measure by which to gauge others.[12]

A new aggressive Confederate strategy was developing. General Bragg prepared to launch an offensive north into Tennessee and Kentucky, and take the war to Northern soil to reap the military-political gains that were so desperately needed to win foreign recognition. Toward the end of summer the Army of the West's assignment was crucial, keeping Grant's forces around Corinth pinned down, so that they could not reinforce those Unionists facing Bragg's northern invasion. With Grant not countering Bragg's thrust, the arena of northeastern Mississippi around Tupelo remained quiet, as if the heat and humidity had made it too hot to fight.[13]

Long hours of drilling in the choking dust and under the blistering Mississippi sun paid dividends. General Bragg, a West Pointer and an old army martinet, had improved the army discipline. The Missouri Brigade's overall quality was likewise enhanced by the efforts of Generals Bragg and Little during this lull before the storm. Now, the Missouri boys "are still hopefull [sic] & feel that all will yet be well at least they are determined & the Feds will feel their power in the next engagement," wrote one Rebel in his diary.

General Bragg complimented General Little and his troops during a review. While the Missourians swung across the fields in perfect step, Bragg had turned to Little and marveled: "You had the reputation of having one of the finest companies in the old army. General, this is certainly as fine a division as I have ever seen."[14]

On September 1 the Missouri Brigade gained a new regiment, when the regimental organization of the Fifth Missouri Confederate Infantry was finally completed. Nine companies of two Missouri Confederate infantry battalions had united after Pea Ridge and this command, although one company shy of being a full regiment, was listed as the Fifth Missouri in official records. But it was not until September 1 when an independent company composed of southeast Missourians joined these two united Confederate infantry battalions, under Lieutenant Colonels Robert S. Bevier and James C. McCown, that the formation of the Fifth Missouri Confederate Infantry was at last completed. Those two Confederate infantry battalions had served with the Missouri Brigade since the spring of 1862, after having fought at Pea Ridge as

Colonel James C. McCown
Courtesy Dr. Thomas P. Sweeney, Springfield, Missouri
(Unpublished Photo)

part of the Second Missouri Confederate Brigade. In the words of a proud Lieutenant Warren, "We have now Ten Companies [since] we received a company from [General] Jeff Tompson [sic]. We are *now* the 5th Mo Regiment." Most of these soldiers of the southeast Missouri company from the Bootheel region had been either born in Tennessee or had Volunteer State ancestors, who had crossed the Mississippi from Tennessee to southeast Missouri. These Rebel soldiers were not recruits, but tested and disciplined veterans of State Guard and Confederate service.

Leading the Fifth Missouri was a commander of much promise, Colonel McCown. A native of Virginia and a second generation Irishman, the forty-five-year-old McCown commanded the regiment from beginning to end, the only regimental commander of the Missouri Brigade fortunate enough to survive long enough to accomplish this rather remarkable feat. McCown had been a large landowner, a long-time Johnson County official, and civic leader in the same community that Colonel Cockrell called home, Warrensburg. During a March 1861 political confrontation which had hurled western Missouri closer toward civil war, McCown's son killed a leading Union spokesman at the Johnson County courthouse. An angry mob sought to hang both McCown and son. Only the last-minute intervention of a young attorney, Cockrell, had saved father and son from the hangman's noose.

In March 1862, the McCown family home in Warrensburg had been burned to the ground by the Federal militia in retaliation for the family head being a Confederate soldier: not an uncommon fate to befall the homes of Missouri Brigade members while they fought hundreds of miles away in the Deep South. One Northern officer felt outraged by the act, "leaving the [McCown] family, consisting of his wife and some four or five children, without anything to support or protect them," in the cold of late winter.[15]

The most distinguished body of soldiers within the Fifth Missouri were the boys of Company F. Those Confederates consisted of an unpolished group of wild "Irishmen from St. Louis [and rural areas]—all Irish from the captain down. They were recruited from the wharves of St. Louis. Brave men and good soldiers they proved themselves to be," wrote young Albert Carey Danner, who would eventually become the Missouri Brigade's quartermaster. The Missouri Brigade could draw upon much such material, for Missouri contained an Irish population which was second only to Louisiana in the South. No one could control the turbulent spirits of these sons of Erin. They were, wrote one officer, "the best soldiers on duty and the worst off, the best fighters and the most troublesome men in the army." Not even Father Bannon, a native Dubliner with a hot temper and an imposing physique whom they loved like a saint, could keep these high-spirited Irishmen from raising hell across the South. But they were not just successful in creating chaos, drinking whiskey, fist-fighting, and talking back to officers. Those troublesome and rebellious Celtic warriors were the elite soldiers of a crack brigade, earning fame as the "Fighting Irish Company" of the Southern Army in the West. Many of these Rebels from St. Louis had gained skills in the ante-bellum militia service. As one Confederate officer said, "This company [F] was like regulars in every movement it made. They were veterans, for they had been in all the [State Guard] engagements [and] it [would become] the pride of the Missouri division."

Almost rivaling their zeal for fighting, the Irish lads of Company F had a legendary fondness for "John Barleycorn." Disbelieving officers sometimes found every Company F soldier "as drunk as Bacchus." Paradoxically, these hardy men were among the pious of the Missouri Brigade. Remaining faithful to the Celtic heritage of their native Ireland, the Roman Catholic Rebels closely embraced religion, especially if Father Bannon was nearby and if no alcohol was available.

In command of the hard-fighting Celts of Company F, Fifth Missouri, was Captain Patrick Canniff. He had marched with Captain Wade's Emmet Guards of the prewar Missouri militia, including service on the Southwest Expedition. The auburn-haired saddler from St. Louis, twenty-four, had compiled a distinguished State Guard and Confederate record on previous battlefields across Missouri, Arkansas, and Mississippi. Almost reckless in combat and equating Southern independence with his native Ireland's longing for freedom from British rule, Canniff embodied the essence of the Confederacy's foreign-born revolutionaries: a young, hardworking, dedicated immigrant who struggled in a new land of opportunity.

A devout Catholic and often a helpful disciple for Father Bannon, Captain Canniff had a warm, compassionate side to his dashing personality. On long marches, the captain often dismounted to allow a sick or weary soldier to ride, while he walked for miles through dust and heat. Such a mixture of compassion, determination, and bravery created many faithful followers of the popular Irish officer from St. Louis. Canniff's most significant contribution came as the best skirmish leader of the Missouri Brigade. For most of the Missouri Brigade's history, Company F was employed consistently by both regimental and brigade commanders for hazardous skirmish duty, to spearhead an advance, or to protect a withdrawal during the most dangerous situations.[16]

The new regiment was a good one, containing not only seasoned troops but also an excellent cadre of experienced leaders. For example, those veteran Fifth Missouri officers, Lieutenants William Algernon Crow, a St. Louis merchant age twenty-seven, and Ireland-born Walter Marnell, a twenty-six-year-old clerk from St. Louis, were invaluable in making this unit the finest regiment of the Missouri Brigade. These two young officers and many of their soldiers were products of the middle or lower upper-classes of St. Louis and were either first or second generation Irishmen. In addition, they had been members of Captain Joseph Kelly's Washington Blues, an elite Missouri Volunteer Militia unit.

Besides the uncontrollable St. Louis Irish of the Fifth Missouri, soldiers of this new regiment from the rural counties of Missouri likewise had gained their own experience in a fine militia unit of prewar days, the Polk County Rangers. These tough and radically independent cavaliers from the southwest Missouri frontier had been the defenders of their beautiful Ozark highlands against the Kansas Jayhawkers. Reputedly able to grab a rifled-musket and a horse and be ready for active duty within minutes, the Rangers had been the latter-day "Minute Men" of the western frontier. The military experience gained during the ante-bellum period by these young rural Missourians produced some of the best and most experienced fighters and leaders in the Missouri Brigade.

Three Missouri counties were most represented in the Fifth Missouri's ranks: Polk County, Macon County, and Johnson County. Natives from every region of the state could be found in this infantry regiment, with soldiers from 55 of the state's 115 counties. The vast majority of the 1,092 Rebels who served in the Fifth Missouri had been middle-class farmers. Contrary to the myth of an uneducated Confederate soldiery from the western frontier, the second highest occupational group represented in the regiment were students. Fifth Missourians generally were literate and educated, more so than a typical Deep South regiment. Many regimental members, both officers and enlisted men, had attended Chapel Hill College [Colonel Cockrell was an alumnus], McGee College, and Christian University, and other Presbyterian academic institutions in rural Missouri.

The third most represented occupation in the Fifth Missouri was that of laborer. Then merchants and carpenters [both having an equal number] were fourth. Clerks, ministers, and printers [the same amount] ranked in fifth place, and blacksmiths, physicians, lawyers, and teachers [an equal number] were sixth. Some of the more interesting occupations of Fifth Missourians consisted of stage driver, steamboat-man, wagon maker, United States soldier, baker, circuit rider [the regimental chaplain], hotel keeper, peddler, news agent, hatter, gunsmith, "clown," watch maker, engineer, minister, bondsman, miner, trader, etc. This diverse variety of occupations occurred in every other unit of the Missouri Brigade.

A number of key influences can be ascertained from the names of Fifth Missourians. For instance, the strong Protestant roots of the western frontier translated into a heavy Biblical influence on the names of the Missouri soldiery. For example, many of these Rebels had the first names of Joshua, Elijah, Jeremiah, Ephraim, Ezekiel, Zachariah, Ezra, etc. Also in the first and middle names of these Confederates can be seen the influence of the American Revolution, which was appropriate for these Rebels believed that they were engaged in the Second American Revolution. In the Fifth Missouri, for example, there were 20 men with the name of George Washington, 7 soldiers with the name Benjamin Franklin, 7 Rebels with the name of Thomas Jefferson, and 4 Confederates with the name of Francis Marion, and one Confederate named John Paul Jones. The influence of the American Revolution was especially apparent to a young Ray County farmer and private of the Third Missouri, who had been severely wounded at Pea Ridge, Independence Mann.[17]

CHAPTER FIVE

The Battle of Iuka

In preparation for the next battle, the Missouri Brigade's soldiers continued to drill for hours each day amid the heat and humidity of summer. Spirits soared with the slightly milder weather of September, and then the swarms of "ticks and tobacco are like the dream of things that were, and malarias [sic] and mosquitoes are likely to leave together," wrote one thankful Rebel. Morale was high at the prospects for a new fall campaign, one that might reverse the South's fortunes. Union strategists were understandably apprehensive about Price's ever-unpredictable army since its transfer across the Mississippi after Pea Ridge. Now that the Army of the West was again on its own, the anxious Federals expected the unexpected from these veteran western Rebels.

Concerned about the next strike by Price's hardened soldiers, one Northerner warned that "there is one thing in the way of the execution of this programme [of conquest] more 'dangerous' than all the delays in the world; that is Price's army." As a Memphis journalist boasted: "Price is the only one of all our generals who originally brought into the field an army without the aid of the War Bureau. At his call a body of men assembled who, in order to battle for their homes, had to conquer arms, ammunition, and supplies, from their enemy. What they did in the West, Lexington, Oak Hill, Carthage, and other glorious fields, testify; their feats east of the river are familiar to all."

For the impending fall campaign, the Missouri Confederates had adopted an appropriate motto which exemplified their desperation, "Conquer or Die." By this time, General Price held the reputation as "the Fox of the West," while leading his homespun Rebels on a war-horse, whose name reflected a primary motivation of the Missouri Confederates, "Revenge."[1]

With the gradual breakup of General Halleck's huge army before Corinth, "Old Pap" began to realize that he could no longer afford to watch Grant's forces, but must strike a blow to support Bragg's invasion effectively. Price found a good opportunity to the northeast at Iuka Springs, a quiet mineral spring long visited by wealthy Southerners. General Price saw a potential victim in Major General William Starke Rosecrans's forces at Iuka, twenty miles southeast of Corinth. Rosecrans commanded the left of Grant's over-extended line, stretching west all the way to Memphis to protect the Memphis & Charleston Railroad. The Federals had eased down the Memphis & Charleston Railroad from Corinth to Iuka, which was a vulnerable salient dangling at the end of the Unionists' line.

The possibilities looked inviting to the ex-Mexican War militia commander. It was true, as predicted a Southern newspaperman in September of 1862, that "if General Price is not...tied down by orders from some superior officer [then] he will soon have his name in the mouths of our entire people, with Jackson, Lee, Morgan and Smith." Also to win the victory that might release him and his troops for a march of "liberation" upon Missouri, General Price was about to take the initiative.

Since Rosecrans might be on his way to oppose Bragg in Kentucky and Tennessee, Price planned to strike immediately. When Price's two divisions swung forward through northeast Mississippi to meet the Yankees, that motley force was "as strangely and colorful an army as ever human eye rested upon." The Missouri Brigade added its own distinctive style to the western army. Many Missouri boys wore uniforms which were as multicolored and varied as the autumn-hued woodlands now covering northeast Mississippi. After pushing swiftly northeast, Generals Little's and Maury's Divisions, comprising the Army of the West, easily overran Iuka on September 14. Only light skirmishing between opposing cavalry erupted in the valley of Iuka, for "they did not know we were coming," wrote Lieutenant Warren in his diary. But Rosecrans had retired toward Corinth with two divisions and three other Union divisions already had been sent to help stop Bragg's sweep north into Kentucky.[2]

Iuka's fall, nevertheless, paid dividends. Taking a page from Missouri State Guard history, the Army of the West took a large supply and commissary depot and secured a hold on the Memphis & Charleston Railroad close enough to threaten Corinth. A jubilant Lieutenant Simpson penned in his diary, "The Yankees got up and dusted [and we] got all their commissary stores and many other things." This relatively bloodless victory was another example of Price's style of waging war, taking what his army needed from the Yankees. But much had changed since the Missouri State Guard days of 1861. Unlike in Missouri, "Old Pap" Price now faced the North's best commander in the West, General Grant, and his Army of the Tennessee.

At that time optimism for the success of Price's troops was high across the South. According to the prediction of one Rebel journalist, General Price and his soldiers would shortly "strike a characteristic blow in an unexpected quarter...it may be in the direction of Memphis, Corinth or Nashville. Let the Yankees 'guess'." The Rebel victory at Iuka had only set the stage for another clash.[3]

Price was torn by conflicting orders from superiors. General Van Dorn, protector of Vicksburg and the Mississippi River sector, wanted to combine forces for a joint attack on Corinth, and General Bragg continued to request support. General Price, therefore, decided to remain at Iuka. But General Price made a serious error in staying too long at Iuka, while his troops rested and subsisted splendidly off Mr. Lincoln's bountiful commissary. In Price's common sense view, lingering at Iuka to watch Rosecrans was safer than advancing recklessly north into Tennessee and deeper into Grant's domain as Bragg advocated. Almost any sector in Grant's jurisdiction was dangerous for Price's Rebels, who had already lost the initiative. General Grant, fearing that Price's Army of the West would join Bragg's offensive, took immediate advantage of Price's decision to remain at Iuka. The Army of the West's vulnerability, without support and exposed in the Union-held country, was greater than the Rebels at Iuka realized. With the instincts of a great captain, Grant formulated plans to trap and destroy the Army of the West.

The leaves of the oaks and hickories turned yellow and red on the rolling hills of Tishomingo County, announcing the advent of an early autumn, the slow approach of winter, and more important, the approach of Grant's forces. Correctly assuming that Price's Army of the West would take time to replenish itself at his captured supply depot, Grant intended to hit the Confederates from three sides: front, rear and flank. General Rosecrans, with his two divisions, would slam into Price's flank and rear. After advancing from the northwest and holding Price in place, General Edward Otho Cresap Ord's troops would attack in the Rebels' front. Striking from below, or south of, Price at Iuka, Rosecrans would cut off the Southerners' line of retreat. Then, the two Union forces would crush the Army of the West, as a nut-cracker smashed a walnut.[4]

But the complicated Federal strategy amid Mississippi's dense pine forests, rough terrain, hot weather, and path-like roads was practically impossible to execute on schedule. The simultaneous Union attacks failed to materialize as planned. General Rosecrans finally smashed into an unsuspecting Price on the humid afternoon of September 19, while Ord demonstrated to the northwest in the Southerners' front. But Rosecrans's gunfire, which should have launched the Union assault from the northwest, could not be heard by Ord. A stiff northwest breeze blew toward Confederate fortunes and away from Ord. Grant's pincer movement remained unclosed.

Expecting the Federals to advance from the direction of Corinth, General Price was caught by surprise by the sudden attack from the south. Yankee shells exploding around his headquarters finally alerted "Old Pap" of the Unionists' position south of Iuka. But luckily Price had some vigilant Rebels picketed along the Jacinto Road, who skirmished and made the Yankees more cautious about the dark, tangled woodlands before them. In the midst of trying to withdraw to link with Van Dorn for a joint attack on Corinth, the Army of the West hurriedly attempted to shift to meet the threat to the rear, where Rosecrans's forces were pushing north up the Jacinto Road. Grant had struck before Price and Van Dorn could unite.

Despite facing only one attacking Union force instead of two, the Southern force was in serious trouble. Price's route of escape south could be blocked if the Federals gained the eastern road leading south out of Iuka, the Fulton Road. But General Little's timely efforts saved the day. As at Pea Ridge, the Missouri Brigade's first commander again demonstrated tactical skill and boldness during an emergency. In spite of a premonition of death and weak from disease, General Little galloped south down the Jacinto Road to marshal a defense. He hurried all available Rebel troops, including the Missouri Brigade, south and hurled the foremost units headlong into Rosecrans's onslaught. Little's attack blunted the Union drive and ensured that the Fulton Road was not secured by Yankees. General Little heard booming guns of "Churchy" Clark's old battery, which was the only Confederate artillery engaged during the battle.

But the capable General Little soon accomplished much more than simply slowing the Federal onslaught. General Little's aggressiveness in a fierce counterattack not only halted the Unionists' momentum, but also nearly carried the field. Characteristically, General Little struck hard and with the conviction that "if the line would move forward [one final time before dark], the battle could soon be won." Only bad luck, too few troops and artillery at hand, and approaching nightfall robbed General Little of a more impressive success at Iuka. According to one attacker, "one hour of daylight and the entire Yankee [command] would have been captured."

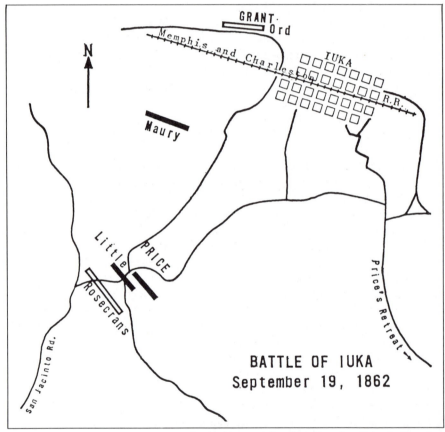

BATTLE OF IUKA
September 19, 1862

While discussing strategy with "Old Pap" as the battle raged around them, General Little was hit in the forehead by a bullet and fell dead off his horse near the place where the cannon of Clark's old battery roared. To avenge Little's death, the Missourians double-quicked into the battle. While charging onward in the fading light, Colonel Gates's soldiers waved their slouch hats in a salute to General Price and cheered. Missouri Brigade soldiers fought that day in memory of the inspirational officer who had been the most responsible for molding them into "the South's Finest."[5]

Unlike almost every other battle that it fought, the Missouri Brigade was spared from the worst fighting at Iuka by entering the struggle at twilight. Though worn-out after a hard six-mile run without a rest, Gates's onrushing

General Henry Little, killed at Iuka, Mississippi
Courtesy Missouri Historical Society
(Unpublished Painting)

Rebels stumbled over the blue and gray bodies littering a pasture. A horrified Lieutenant Warren wrote in his diary that "the dead & wounded are lying around so thick that you can scarcely help steping [sic] on them." Upon nearing the blue line during the charge south, the cheering Missourians stopped and unleashed a volley in the smoky near-darkness. A return fire swept the Missouri Brigade's ranks, but the bullets mostly whistled high. Only a handful of men were hit, falling into the grassy pasture. One Federal unit that Gates's soldiers exchanged volleys with was the Eleventh Missouri Volunteer Infantry. Already the Missouri Brigade's fame had spread to these Missouri Unionists. Indeed, the Missouri Brigade's reputation as the "famous flower" of the Confederate Army was not only known across the South, but also among the Federals who respected and feared the fighting qualities of the Missouri Rebels.

Ten of Gates's Missourians fell wounded in the near-darkness of September 19. More Missouri Brigade members were lost during the subsequent withdrawal when fifteen Missouri boys were left sick in Iuka and another eleven diseased Rebels were abandoned along the Fulton Road. The Battle of Iuka had been a sharp, nasty affair, resulting in almost 800 Federal casualties and more than 500 Confederate losses. One of the wounded was Lieutenant Simpson, who described Iuka as "one of the hardest little fights imaginable."

That night the Missouri Brigade remained in place near the body-littered Jacinto Road. Far ahead of the Missouri Brigade's position and too close to the Yankees, Captain Canniff's skirmishers were in a bad fix, with the Unionists only a few yards away. A close, deadly fire between skirmishers flared up throughout the night.

The exposed skirmishers were easy targets, for "the enemy would give us a volley, when ever we made the least noise," recalled Warren in his diary. Hour after hour the cries of hundreds of wounded soldiers of both sides filled the night air. Some of Gates's butternuts risked their lives, leaving the Missouri Brigade's advanced position on their own and slipping into no-man's-land on errands of mercy. Despite a scattered fire coming from the Yankees who expected more trouble, those foremost Missouri Rebels let the injured Federals drink from their canteens.[6]

General Price became aware of the full extent of the danger during the night, realizing that the Army of the West was still sandwiched between two Union forces. Therefore, Price altered his plans to renew the battle on the morning of September 20. Instead he ordered a withdrawal south down the open Fulton Road, General Little's last and most important gift to the Army of the West. In the darkness, Price's army began slipping out of Grant's trap. At Little's busy headquarters, meanwhile, the body of the brilliant general, who had come close to bringing victory on September 19, was tenderly laid to rest behind a Iuka private house, "Twin Magnolias," during a hasty nighttime funeral. The Confederacy in the West had suffered another severe blow, for "no more efficient soldier than Henry Little ever fought for a good cause. The magnificent Missouri brigade, the finest troops I had ever seen, or have ever seen since, was the creation of his untiring devotion to duty and his remarkable qualities as a commander...his eyes closed forever upon the happiest spectacle they could behold, and the last throbs of his heart were amidst the victorious shouts of his charging brigade," wrote one Confederate general.[7]

Father Bannon performed Little's funeral service in a stirring manner that deeply affected those present. In the blackness, Bannon spoke a solemn tribute by torch light to his dead friend from Maryland. The chaplain's Irish brogue and eloquence rang clear in the cool September air, while some of the army's top leaders held candles and wept during the emotional eulogy. Hardened soldiers witnessing the scene never forgot Chaplain Bannon's service on this haunting night in northeastern Mississippi.[8]

Shielded by the darkness, the Missouri regiments slipped away from the front around 3:00 a.m., "by the left flank with as little noise as possible," wrote Lieutenant Warren, who was one of the last Rebels to leave the field. Just before sunrise Captain Canniff's elite skirmishers likewise retired from their advanced positions and brought up the rear. While Union artillery shelled Gates's withdrawing column, the Army of the West passed quickly through Iuka. As if in tribute to General Little's key influence in the Missouri Brigade's development, the Missouri troops effectively covered the army's rear like guardian angels. The Army of the West escaped during the night and day, pushing down the Fulton Road. According to the diary entry of one First Missouri Cavalryman, "This is the grandest retreat that southern troops ever made [and] we came almost out of the mouth of the yankees cannon & surrounded too." The Confederate withdrawal continued south toward Baldwyn, about 30 miles southwest of Iuka and on the Mobile & Ohio Railroad, while Captain Canniff and his crack skirmishers protected the rear of both the Missouri Brigade and the Army of the West. Several days after the struggle at Iuka, the worn Southerners reached Baldwyn and safety. Thanks to General Little's influence, the Missouri Brigade would continue to compile the best combat record on either side during the Civil War.[9]

CHAPTER SIX

"Corinth Must & Shall Be Ours."

General Price's Army of the West was bloodied at Iuka, but not beaten. General Van Dorn, long proclaimed throughout the South as "the terror of the Lincolnites," breathed new life into Confederate aspirations in the West with an ambitious plan: the capture of Corinth and the destruction of Rosecrans's army. The Army of the West swung northwest through the heat of late September for Ripley, Mississippi. There Van Dorn's forces waited to link with Price's troops before launching another strike, hoping to reverse the Confederacy's fortunes in the West. Price's army, and the Missouri Brigade, reached Ripley on September 29, after four days of dusty and hot marching. Both Rebel forces were now united in an infrequent example of Confederate cooperation in the West.[1]

Southern morale sky-rocketed with orders to embark upon a hard 50-mile march to take the all-important terminus of those key "railroads that, like great arteries, have given to the heart of the [West's most strategic] position—Corinth—life and strength," analyzed one perceptive Confederate. Since the war's beginning, tons of Trans-Mississippi supplies and thousands of troops had poured east from Louisiana, Arkansas, and Texas via the Memphis & Charleston Railroad. Likewise, large quantities of materiel and many Southern regiments from the Deep South Gulf region had been hauled north along the tracks of the Mobile & Ohio Railroad. A successful northern offensive by Van Dorn's and Price's troops could result in an attempt to reclaim Missouri, after taking Corinth, linking with Bragg's army, and planting Confederate battle-flags on the banks of the Ohio River. The uniting of Van Dorn's and Price's forces at Ripley created the Army of West Tennessee, composed of 22,000 veterans who wanted badly to whip Yankees. This combined Rebel effort to take Corinth was only one phase of a three-part offensive, the Confederacy's high water mark during the decisive autumn of 1862. Rivaling Bragg's Kentucky invasion, the Army of Northern Virginia had swept into Maryland to win the easternmost border state, before pushing farther north. The triple Rebel threat of Lee—Bragg—Van Dorn sought to gain the decisive battlefield victories, which would deflate the will of the Northern populace and influence Northern elections, and might bring foreign recognition and independence to the young Southern nation.

When Van Dorn's Confederates swung north for the Tennessee state line in a feint to Corinth's northwest, dreams of taking the war into Northern territory burned vividly. One soldier predicted that whenever the Missouri Confederates came "again in contact with the Federal forces, it is not unreasonable to predict an overthrow, a rout, a victory complete, or one of the bloodiest pictures of history [since we] prefer death to disgrace or defeat [and] with [our] faces and hearts set upon home, no power on earth can arrest [our] march."[2]

The Missouri Brigade had never been led by better commanders than in the autumn of 1862 with an important engagement imminent. Colonel McCown continued to command the Fifth Missouri, while Colonel Pritchard led the Third Missouri. About to take a regiment into a big battle for the first time, Colonel Cockrell had well-prepared his Second Missouri for the upcoming challenge. The hardy backwoods "Razorbacks" of the Sixteenth Arkansas Infantry were now under the steady influence of Colonel David Provence. Captain Wade's ever-reliable battery completed the Missouri Brigade.

With Colonel Gates leading the Missouri Brigade, Colonel William D. Maupin, age twenty-three, now commanded the First Missouri Cavalry (Dismounted). The farmer from the fertile lands of Buchanan County had grown up in the same small northeastern Missouri neighborhood, Easton, as Colonel Gates. He had capably led this trouble-making regiment since June, filling the giant void left by Gates. With a realist's cynicism, Colonel Maupin referred to the most bitter clash of arms as only "a little piece of work." The common soldiers of the Missouri Brigade were in fine shape, both physically and psychologically. Morale remained exceptionally high, with these Rebels wanting desperately to make up for what they perceived as a missed opportunity at Iuka and to avenge the death of General Little. At that time the Missourians looked more like authentic Rebels than ever before in their wool uniforms which were now a dingy brown instead of the embarrassing white. Also, the stain from the nut of the white walnut and the dirt and grease of everyday wear during the last seven months had given these uniforms a brownish-butternut color.[3]

Meanwhile, the arduous push north continued in the blistering weather which felt like July in Missouri to soldiers burdened with heavy equipment during a long march across a rough and dusty countryside. As part of Van Dorn's plan to keep the Unionists guessing as to his true objective, Bolivar, Tennessee, or Corinth, Mississippi, the swiftly-moving Rebels crossed into Tennessee, just south of Pocahontas, on the first day of October. For the first time, a large percentage of the Missouri Confederates returned to the state of their birth and the land of their ancestors.

Marching on sore feet instead of riding, one of Gates's former cavalrymen wrote that invasion fever spread through the ranks as never before, for when "we got into Tenn [it] seemed to put joy & mirth in all the Missourians hearts to get out of the State of Miss, not that we disliked the state but we wanted to go north [and] every fellow said when we crossed the line that he didn't want to cross it again." Upon entering Tennessee after a rough three-day march, Lieutenant Warren wrote in his diary, "I hope we have bid farewell to Miss for a long time." During the last six months, Mississippi had been a land of disease, misery, and death for the Missouri exiles. In reality, however, the bloody trials in the Magnolia State were only beginning for the Missouri Brigade.[4]

Once in southwestern Tennessee, Van Dorn's forces quickly turned southeast for Corinth in the hope of catching Rosecrans before he could recall reinforcements to Corinth from surrounding garrisons. The abrupt swing southeast to attack Corinth from the northwest was calculated to deceive Rosecrans as to the Army of West Tennessee's intentions. In attempting to outwit his old West Point classmate [Class of 1842], General Van Dorn had also based this strategy on the belief that Corinth's defenses on the northwest were the weakest. As at Pea Ridge, the native Mississippi general had undertaken another lengthy and difficult march to bypass the Yankees on the west in order to launch a swift surprise attack from the north but without a careful reconnaissance. As with the strategy based upon the Benton-ville Detour at Pea Ridge, the best laid plans of General Van Dorn began to go awry long before the battle started.[5]

A rapid and problem-free advance was essential for success. First, wrecked bridges across both the Hatchie and Tuscumbia Rivers had to be repaired. Then, when close to Corinth on October 3, the Confederate push southeast toward the railroad center was again slowed upon finding the "road blockaded [and the march was once more] delayed," wrote a frustrated Chaplain Bannon in his diary. This was another time-consuming delay because of Van Dorn's failure to conduct a reconnaissance. After the obstacles were removed and after some light skirmishing, thousands of Rebels converged on the outer defensive line of Corinth. These powerful fortifications pro-tected Corinth on the northwest. Ironically, the Missouri Rebels had stood behind these works in facing Halleck's army less than six months before.

To hit the Yankees before they escaped to Corinth, Price's corps, of two divi-sions, swung east and took up positions on the left and center of Van Dorn's battle-line. General Louis Hebert, leading Little's Division, positioned the Missouri Brigade and three other brigades in front of the strong fortifications to the south. With Green holding the left flank of the Confederate battle-line, Colonel Gates's troops were aligned on a timbered hill to the right of Green's brigade. However, the vigilant Rosecrans had not been fooled by Van Dorn's Tennessee detour, and had adroitly rushed reinforcements from nearby garrisons to bolster Corinth. In the struggle for Corinth, Van Dorn would face almost as many defenders as he had attackers. With characteristic abandon, Van Dorn planned to order his eager Confederates forward immediately.[6]

In a cloud of dust, Captain Wade unlimbered his guns on high ground to rake the Union defenses. A spirited artillery duel ensued, booming like a summer storm across the wide prairies of western Missouri. Lieutenant Samuel Farrington, a St. Louisan, former Missouri militiaman, and veteran of the Southwest Expedition, performed commendable service in directing the battery's fire. A projectile shortly tore through the upper body of Captain Wade's top lieutenant, toppling him from his horse in a bloody heap. Not long after baptizing Captain Clay Taylor in a nearby muddy creek, Father Bannon ignored the exploding shells to conduct a hasty funeral service, and buried the Massachusetts-born Farrington beside a cotton gin amid the brown cotton fields. A St. Louis cannoneer wrote home weeks after the battle, lament-ing that Farrington's "death is universally regreted [sic] as he was much beloved in the army." Later, General Rosecrans would allow Lieutenant Farrington's body to be exhumed by his family for transport to St. Louis.[7]

All was ready shortly after noon, and Colonel Gates finally screamed, "Charge!" The Missouri Brigade's brownish-hued lines sprang forward with red battle-flags flap-ping in the oppressive heat. A thick abatis of felled timber protected the fortifica-tions, but failed to stop this attack which rolled over every obstacle in its path. According to one of Gates's soldiers, "Every fellow began to hollow [sic] charge and over the down timber we went like a drove of Sheep and was soon over their brest [sic] works (with a small loss) they ran like hens running from a hawk, hiding behind every log & every place they could find." In only minutes, the Missourians stormed across the defenses, shouting victory and driving the Unionists rearward. Van Dorn's attacks made gains all along the line, and it appeared that the battle-plan was working as intended.[8]

Losses in the Missouri Brigade's sector, on the left, were relatively light, for Rosecrans had made the stand at Corinth's outer defenses primarily to slow Van Dorn, ascertain the Rebel strategy, and buy time. One Missouri Brigade member bragged how the beaten Federals "left several pieces of cannon [,], 1 siege piece & some rifled ones [and] we got sev Horses [,] 100 Barrels of Flour [,] 25 Bbs of pickled pork [,] some clothing &c together with several prisoners." To reap further gains from the success, the Missourians continued onward in pursuit with high-pitched, fox-hunt yelps, charging through the captured Union camps and past the bodies of fallen bluecoats. Vicious, close-range skirmishing flared in the hot forests and the parched fields during the fierce attack that covered hundreds of yards.

When Green's brigade smashed into stiff resistance and suffered high losses, the Missouri Brigade shifted to the left to protect the flank of these heavily-engaged Missouri and Mississippi troops. At the most seriously threatened point on the extreme left, Colonel Cockrell led his cheering Second Missouri Confederates forward in a desperate charge that drove away the Union forces, which were punishing Green's brigade with a vicious enfilade fire. Colonel Cockrell and his regiment succeeded in their timely mission, taking the pressure off General Green's battered and shaky left flank, and perhaps preventing Van Dorn's battle-line from being rolled-up. Soon another serious threat developed when several regiments of Union reinforcements attempted to tear into Van Dorn's left flank, but instead rushed through a gap between the advancing Southern units and then eased behind the attacking Missouri Brigade. Aware of their advantage, these Unionists in the Confederate rear surged forward to capture Price's busy artillery, which had no infantry protection. At the last moment, however, the vulnerable Rebel guns, including those of Wade's Battery, quickly turned in time to face their opponents.

Sergeant Robbins, a Missouri artilleryman from St. Louis, recorded in a letter, "The whole [Confederate] line [had] advanced into the woods which the enemy had but lately held. About half an hour after our men had disappeared in the woods, what did we see in the edge of the cornfield [but] a "Star Spangled Banner," & a long line of glistening bayonets. Their position was directly in rear of our infantry [the advancing Missouri Brigade]. At first we hardly [believed] that it was the enemy but in a moment we opened on them with shell & grape, & they "skedaddled" in double-quick time."

The wild chase after the Yankees continued for the attacking Missourians. According to one of Gates's soldiers: "We followed them for a qr [quarter] mile but they out ran us..." Before the Missouri Brigade's charging ranks, the bluecoats fell back to better defensive positions at the inner line closer to Corinth and along the ridges encircling the small community on the north and west.[9]

As a reddish sun began to set over the battlefield and its horrors, the Confederates were poised before Corinth's final defensive line. The dusty, sweat-soaked Rebels of Colonel Gates's Missouri Brigade found shelter behind the high dirt embankment of the Mobile & Ohio Railroad before Rosecrans's right-center. Captain Canniff, leading Company F, Fifth Missouri, and Captain Thomas B. Wilson, commanding Company G, Second Missouri, led their skirmishers forward through the dark shadows of the trees, driving back the Federal skirmishers.

While Van Dorn telegraphed victory dispatches to Richmond, many Rebels, including General Bowen, felt that the best chance to capture Corinth had vanished with the falling sun. As subsequent events proved, the probability of a successful

Confederate assault upon Corinth might have been greatest during the late afternoon and early evening of October 3. Many of Van Dorn's units, including the
Missouri Brigade, had aligned for the final charge in the fading light and awaited
the expected order to advance. But during the crucial half-hour while the sun
dropped, the directive that might have resulted in Corinth's capture never came.
To General Van Dorn such a last-ditch assault was unnecessary, because the victorious Confederates would march nearly unopposed into Corinth on the following morning. Throughout the night of October 3, however, the energetic Rosecrans
repositioned his troops with great skill, readied his reserves at key locations, and
shifted his artillery to strong defensive positions.[10]

An early autumn coolness settled over the pastures and woodlands filled with
thousands of Rebels poised before Corinth. Those soldiers either caught a few hours
of sleep or were too anxious to rest. As if realizing their tragic fates, many young
and grizzled Catholic warriors in faded butternut gave the final confessions of their
lives to Father Bannon in the pale moonlight of a night in northeast Mississippi.
For the entire night, the Irish chaplain performed God's work as rapidly as possible,
hoping to complete his ministrations before the sunrise of October 4.

The final showdown for the possession of Corinth was opened by the Confederates "with artillery at 4½ [o'clock] in the morning," wrote Father Bannon
in his diary with pocket watch in hand. The Missouri Brigade chaplain recorded
that the terrific outburst of responding Union artillery hurled a torrent of "24
[pounder shells which] passed us for 2 hours [and the] firing [continued] with intervals" throughout the humid morning. As if to avenge the recent death of popular
Lieutenant Farrington, Captain Wade's bronze guns growled in the early morning
light. More and more Federal artillery growled back in angry defiance. While a bright
red sun inched higher and the cannonade intensified, the Missouri Confederates
hugged the dirt embankment beside the iron railroad tracks swept by shell-fire,
sweated in the heat, and no doubt prayed to survive the barrage. Meanwhile, the
Rebel skirmishers, under Captains Canniff and Wilson, had gone to work with
business-like efficiency, clearing the Missouri Brigade's front of an exceptionally
stubborn unit of Yankee sharpshooters, who fought as skirmishers. Captain Canniff urged his men onward in the close-range contest between skirmishers. In the
struggle for Corinth, Company F lost more than 70 percent of its personnel.

Among the Missouri Rebel skirmishers, Private William Ray, age thirty-two,
was one who fell dying during the escalating action. The Kentucky-born Ray had
anticipated his death with remarkable clarity. He had written a final good-bye to
his wife in a diary only a few hours before. The Second Missouri soldier had requested that his diary and a lock of his hair be kept for his family in the Boone's
Lick country of central Missouri.

As the skirmishing heated up to almost a full-scale engagement, Colonel Gates
hurriedly dispatched troops from his old regiment to reinforce the two heavily-engaged
skirmish companies. Company C of the First Missouri Cavalry (Dismounted),
under Captain Lucius P. Johnson, hastened forward to assist their busy comrades.
Captain Johnson, age thirty-six, was killed in the day's fighting. Lieutenant Davis
Lanter, a veteran of Doniphan's Expedition and a farmer who had formed a militia
company in Platte County to oppose the invasion of Federal troops, then took
command of the skirmish company.

Additionally, Colonel Gates dispatched Company E, Fifth Missouri, to bolster the hard-fighting Irish comrades of Company F. Neither captain of these two reinforcing companies survived October 4. Captain James W. Fair, a twenty-seven-year-old Englishman, led Company E into battle for the last time. Punishing the Missouri Brigade's skirmishers were the keen-eyed Missouri bluecoats of the "Western Sharpshooters." These Missouri Unionists were led by a former St. Louis militia officer, who had once commanded some of the St. Louisans of the Missouri Brigade. Like Captain Canniff, who had served with him in the Missouri militia, the skilled Union officer, Colonel Patrick E. Burke, was an Irishman from St. Louis. Now in front of a small railroad town in the Deep South, Captain Canniff and Colonel Burke faced each other in command of opposing parties of skirmishers from the same state. Throughout the morning, the deadly skirmishing was hot and furious. Ireland-born Sergeant Thomas Hogan, age twenty-two, later wrote in a letter to St. Louis, "I escaped unhurt, although the men next to me, on both my right and left, were shot."[11]

After pushing through some open woods and following behind their hard-fighting skirmishers, the onrushing troops of the Missouri Brigade finally reached the vast expanse of cleared terrain lying before the network of fortifications. Hundreds of Missouri men were now awed by the imposing sight of "the strongest Federal position on the continent," wrote one Southerner. Across the 300-400 yards of open slopes leading to the ridge-top, "there was not a single bush to screen a person," wrote Sergeant Hogan. Shouting orders and encouragement, Colonel Gates galloped down his long lines, raising dust and making sure that the alignment of his five regiments was complete. Battle-inscribed banners waved above the Missouri Brigade's ranks, which stretched for hundreds of yards.

While tight formations, an iron discipline, and the glitter of well-maintained weapons all betrayed a superior quality among the Missouri Brigade's veterans, the appearance of these soldiers failed to impress anyone. As a Missourian explained in a letter, "Before the battle we had marched hard day & night & it was so dusty [that] we was dusty as dogs before going in to this fight." In addition, most stomachs were empty, feet were sore, and many soldiers had slept little the night before. Those few of Gates's soldiers with rations had only a handful of dirty kernels of parched corn in haversacks. Before one of the most important battles in the West, the shortage of rations, shoes, and uniforms symbolized the weak logistical capabilities of a western Rebel army during an invasion. Nevertheless, the Missouri Confederates were especially eager for action and morale was exceptionally high, because General "Price had told them he was leading them home by way of [Corinth]."[12]

In the battle-line of Hebert's Division on Van Dorn's left, Colonel Gates's Missourians were aligned as the second brigade on the right, east of the Mobile & Ohio Railroad. To Gates's right, or west, Green's brigade held Hebert's right flank. Occupying the Missouri Brigade's left flank was Colonel Cockrell's Second Missouri. The Third Missouri stood on the Missouri Brigade's right flank. Between these two solid commands spanned the neat formations of the Sixteenth Arkansas, the First Missouri Cavalry (Dismounted), and Colonel McCown's Fifth Missouri. As the racket of skirmishing intensified, the Missouri soldiers remained standing patiently in line northwest of Corinth, awaiting the signal to charge. Not long after crossing to the east side of the Mississippi, Gates's Rebels had warmly welcomed these veteran Sixteenth Arkansas soldiers as sturdy additions to the Missouri Brigade, for "the Missourians esteem those brave Arkansans as among 'the best of their band'," wrote one Southerner.

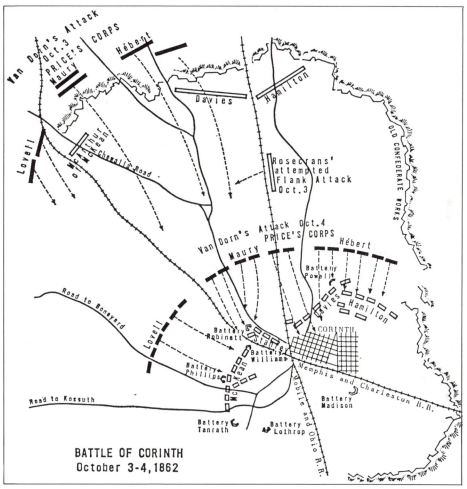

BATTLE OF CORINTH
October 3-4, 1862

From the Missouri Brigade's position, it looked as if all of Rosecrans's forces were deployed along the ridge before them. These grim "fortifications in front were gay with streaming banners, defiant with glittering bayonets and bristling cannon," recalled a survivor. One Missourian sensed that he would not be lucky today, telling his comrades that "he would rather lose his legs than his arms, so he could [continue to] play the violin." Instead, however, the young man in dirty brown lost his life, when a bullet ripped through his head.[13]

The stage was now set for one of the most bloody engagements of the war. From right to left stood the divisions of Major General Mansfield Lovell, a Mexican War veteran, and Brigadier Generals Maury and Hebert. As at Pea Ridge, Rebel confusion, disorganization, and lack of communication had caused Van Dorn's assault plan to self-destruct. According to the battle-plan, Hebert's division was to begin the advance, striking Rosecrans's right. Then the remainder of Van Dorn's army would attack. But hours passed and Hebert remained motionless, after failing to receive his orders to advance at the scheduled time, while much of the morning wasted away. Then a sickly General Hebert reported to Van Dorn, explaining that he was unfit for duty. General Green replaced Hebert, but the damage had been done.

Father Bannon took advantage of the lengthy delay, offering last-minute spiritual guidance and moral support. Ignoring the whistle of bullets and shells, he rapidly went "along the line, [to] hear the men as they stood in the ranks." Sinful and roughhewn soldiers found comfort and salvation in Bannon's words of inspiration, for most of these Rebels understood that they now were standing "face to face with eternity," and wanted one last chance to make peace with their God. Within only a few hours, the best and brightest of the Missouri Brigade would be slaughtered like cattle on that beautiful October day.[14]

About 9:30 a.m. orders finally came to advance on one of the season's warmest days. With a wild yell, the Missouri Brigade's soldiers leaped forward. In front of the sprawling ranks, drummer boys pounded away on instruments and fifers blew their tunes. About two thousand Missourians swarmed forward with flags fluttering and their distinctive war-cries, common among Southern units.

According to Father Bannon, "When the time came for advancing, I made a sign for them all to kneel, and gave them absolution [and] I then went to the second line, or the reserve, till it was their turn also to advance." With a frontal assault on such powerful fortifications a virtual death-sentence, God certainly needed to be with the Missourians during their first big battle east of the Mississippi.[15]

After charging some distance across the barren slopes and taking quite a few losses, the Missouri Brigade halted briefly to redress ranks. Colonel Cockrell galloped before his formations on his favorite war-horse, "Old Yellow," waving his saber. Above the deafening roar from the rows of Yankee cannon, Cockrell screamed, "Forward, my boys; we must capture that battery!" Unleashing a chorus of shouts, hundreds of Missourians poured uphill, as if a dam had burst. Caught in a shooting gallery, the charging Confederates were terribly exposed and cut to pieces on the open slopes. Union batteries blasted away at targets they could not miss. More attackers dropped, piling together in ugly clumps on the bloody plain of Corinth. The attack was becoming a slaughter unlike anything ever seen by those veterans. Sergeant Hogan later scribbled in a letter that it "looked like if hell had been let loose. Shells bursting all around you; round shot plowing the ground everywhere;

grape and cannister [sic] sweeping down the hill almost by the bushel; it is a miracle how anyone escaped." Indeed, thousands of soldiers on both sides did not escape the holocaust of October 4.[16]

Explosions ripping into the Missouri Brigade's charging ranks caused one Second Missouri Rebel to swear that "the very earth shook." Because the Missouri skirmishers in blue were chased in by the Missourians in butternut until the Federals were crowded before the earthworks attempting to rejoin their comrades, the musketry from the main line erupted belatedly. But when the first volley exploded, heaps of Gates's soldiers fell to rise no more. Worst of all, Union artillerymen switched from shell to canister to increase the destruction. Leading the charge, Colonel Cockrell went down when "Old Yellow" dropped like lead, as a cannon ball tore through the animal's body. The wiry, athletic Cockrell "jumped over its head, lighted on his feet, and waving his sword above his head marched straight toward" the defenses. Then the blasts from the Federal cannon sent hundreds of iron shot tearing into the Missouri Brigade's charging waves, inflicting horrendous damage.[17]

Battery Powell, which was the strongest artillery bastion and most formidable earthwork anchoring Rosecrans's right-center and dominating one of the highest points of the ridge stood in front of Colonel Gates's attackers. That fortified redoubt jutted north, forming a powerful salient. Immediately to Powell's left-rear, or to the southwest, along the same bare ridge rose Fort Richardson, its red clay earthworks and artillery glistening in the sunlight. Fort Richardson had been constructed during the previous night by the herculean efforts of Yankees and impressed slaves, indicating the error of the Confederates not pressing the attack the evening before. Filled with artillery and fresh Unionists, Battery Powell and Fort Richardson loomed atop the ridge like great earthen citadels. This strong defensive network was the key to Rosecrans's position north of Corinth. From these bastions, from the Yankee batteries, and from the seemingly endless infantry formations along the ridge came a continuous sheet of fire. Fluttering in a slight breeze, United States and regimental colors dotted the high ground, indicating that the key position was held by hundreds of defenders.

Leading his First Missouri Cavalrymen on foot, Lieutenant Colonel Maupin grabbed his regiment's banner, after two color bearers were killed. Soon thereafter Maupin was knocked to the ground mortally wounded. Through the raging inferno, however, the Missouri Brigade's lines steadily converged on the fiery salient of Battery Powell, which stood imposingly before the blue lines like the Rock of Gibraltar. With each passing minute, more Rebel soldiers were cut down along the bullet-swept hillside that had become a killing field.

An exposed target in the open, Colonel Cockrell had another brush with death, when "my whiskers were cut off by a bullet and my throat grazed, but no blood was drawn." "I felt sure that my throat had been cut; but when I reached up my hand I found only a bunch of loose whiskers which the ball had torn out by the roots...." In spite of the close call, Cockrell continued encouraging his troops onward toward the northernmost apex of Rosecrans's line at Battery Powell, the primary objective of Gates's Brigade. Ringing above the rattle of hundreds of muskets and the crash of cannon, the cries of "On to the battery! Capture the battery!" echoed down the onrushing ranks.

Color Sergeant William Walsh, an Irishman from St. Louis, fell with a bullet through the brain, going down with the Fifth Missouri's flag. After picking up the banner stained with Walsh's blood, Captain Fair fell mortally wounded. The Fifth Missouri's color guard had already been wiped out. Well-served Yankee cannon of Battery Powell and Fort Richardson continued to hurl thousands of iron balls of canister point-blank into the advancing Confederates converging on the forts enveloped in fire and smoke.[18]

To the Missourians' right, meanwhile, Green's brigade hit the defenders with a vicious enfilade fire. Raked with this gunfire and unnerved by the sight of about two thousand screaming Rebels of Gates's Missouri Brigade charging forward as if nothing could stop them, groups of Federals along the ridge began to waver. After the howling Missourians tore through the tangle of abatis gradually more Unionists buckled under the pressure from flank and front, fleeing over the ridge for the safety of Corinth. Yankee support on each side of Battery Powell grew more shaky, but the whole ridge-line of blue formations continued to punish the Missouri Brigade mercilessly. Finally, the Missouri Rebels reached the high ground and swarmed across the ridge-top with wild cheers. A savage hand-to-hand clash erupted on the crest as Gates's attackers slammed into the blue defenders, and fought with musket-butts, swords, fists, rocks and bayonets.[19]

With the red Confederate battle-flags finally near the summit, the first hand-fuls of soldiers in filthy butternut scaled the parapet and swarmed into Battery Powell. There six pieces of the Sixth Wisconsin Light Artillery and six 20-pounder Parrott rifled guns of the First United States Artillery were either crammed into the fort or positioned nearby for a massive concentration of firepower. But with dozens of howling Missourians charging over the parapet, the Federal guns that had killed so many could not be withdrawn in time. Defiant to the end, many Union gunners refused to leave doomed Battery Powell and desert their field pieces. Against an elated Missouri tide that could not be stopped, those Federal artillerymen continued to load and fire, trying to destroy as many Rebels as possible before they themselves were killed.[20]

Eager for revenge after losing so many comrades, the Missouri soldiers hurriedly shot down and bayoneted the fiercely resisting cannoneers. Lieutenant Henry Gillispie, a twenty-seven-year-old farmer of the Second Missouri, was one of the first Rebels inside Battery Powell. With drawn saber, Gillispie rushed one Yankee gunner about to pull a lanyard and forced him to surrender before discharging the cannon. The lieutenant's quick-thinking spared his comrades from a point-blank blast of canister. In the chaotic, noisy bastion, Confederates swung musket-butts like clubs and slashed with bayonets in the choking dust and smoke.[21]

Among the foremost attackers were Lieutenant William Russell Duvall and his three brothers of the Third Missouri, who all charged over the top together. Nearby, two soldiers of Colonel Pritchard's unit attempted to plant the colors of the Third Missouri upon the parapet, but both men were almost instantly cut down. One of these Rebels was Sergeant James H. Barger, age eighteen, who had placed the regimental banner atop the fortifications, while "a myriad of bullets were flying around his head." Then Sergeant Barger blasted away with a musket from his perch until shot in the hip. After the sergeant fell, Lieutenant Duvall grabbed the flag and replanted the colors on the earthworks, while the brutal fighting swirled around him. Lieutenant Duvall was shot and killed, while waving his saber and crying, "Victory!"[22]

Not far from Lieutenant Duvall was Colonel Pritchard, who encouraged his troops forward through the smoky haze. Pritchard jumped off his mount at the edge of the deep ditch before the parapet because of the steep, high earthen wall and perhaps heeding the slave prophecy of his death while on horseback. Then, with sword in hand, the colonel scaled the defenses on foot, mingling with the attackers pouring over the fortifications. While standing on top of the parapet, shouting directives and inspiring his Confederates onward, Pritchard was hit by a bullet which slammed into his shoulder with a sickening thud. Knocked off his feet by a shot fired only a few feet away, Colonel Pritchard tumbled down the works and then yelled to his soldiers, "My God, I am shot! Boys, take me off the field— don't let me fall into the hands of the Yankees." As the mortally wounded colonel was carried to the rear, he shouted his last order, "Boys, do your duty!" Major Finley Lewis Hubbell, commanding the Third Missouri, had to convince the dying Pritchard to leave the battle.[23]

One of the Missouri Brigade's best horsemen, Colonel Gates had stayed mounted upon reaching the deep ditch, unlike most other officers. From yet another color bearer shot down, Gates snatched the fallen regimental flag of his First Missouri Cavalry (Dismounted) off the ground and then "rode along the embankment cheering his comrades in arms," recorded a Southern journalist in a widely-read newspaper column. Such inspiring leadership spurred the efforts of the enlisted men to fanatical heights amid the inferno engulfing Battery Powell. Finally, the tattered banner of the First Missouri Cavalry (Dismounted) was planted on top of the earthworks, after three color bearers had been killed and another one wounded during the charge.

More attackers gained the ridge-top, and soon additional powder-stained Rebels flooded into Battery Powell. The wild struggle within the earthen bastion was nightmarish, with the screaming Missourians leaping inside the works and "fighting like demons incarnate, with bayonets, clubbed guns, bowie knives." Twenty-seven-year-old Private Ezekiel H. Ragan, of the First Missouri Cavalry, captured the colors of the hard-fighting Fiftieth Illinois regiment, after some furious hand-to-hand combat in the melee. The Indiana-born "Zeke" Ragan shortly fell mortally wounded, dying beside the United States flag. After a free-swinging contest, Confederate victory cheers resounded over the bloody ridge as both Battery Powell and Fort Richardson fell to the Missouri Brigade. The colorful Missouri regimental flags, shredded from numerous projectiles, waved on top of Battery Powell and Fort Richardson above the grim piles of bodies. In an infrequent example of a successful frontal assault against strong fortifications, the Missouri Brigade had punched a hole in the right-center of Rosecrans's battle-line, after a "charge [which] in the history of the war [there was none] more daring or bloody," wrote one Southerner who witnessed the attack.[24]

Colonel Gates's troops had captured more guns than they had ever seen together. Including the cannon in and around Battery Powell and Fort Richardson, and some of Rosecrans's reserve artillery, at least 40 Union artillery pieces had been captured by the Missouri Brigade. Colonel Hubbell was astounded by the magnitude of the success won by the Missouri Brigade, writing in his diary that "never will I forget the sight that now presented itself to my eyes as I stood upon the breast-works. That our small force had obtained the position they now occupied, could hardly be believed; around us stood about forty pieces of artillery, deserted

The Rebel Charge at Corinth
Courtesy Library of Congress, Washington, D.C.

**Colonel James Avery Pritchard,
mortally wounded at Corinth**
Author's collection

Storming the defenses of Corinth
Courtesy Library of Congress, Washington, D.C.

**Colonel Elijah P. Gates,
1st Missouri Cavalry**
Courtesy State Historical Society
of Missouri, Columbia

by the enemy." And Sergeant William Aaron Ruyle, a twenty-two-year-old farmer of the Fifth Missouri, was equally amazed by the amount of the artillery pieces won by the Missouri Brigade, writing in his diary, "We had possession of a large number of cannons which they had deserted. This was one of the bloodiest places I ever saw." Indeed the Missouri Brigade had captured almost twice as many artillery pieces as General Price's Army of the West during the advance on Iuka.[25]

The successful Rebel charge toward the town of Corinth continued. On the Missouri Brigade's right, Green's brigade likewise smashed through the Federal line, helping to rip an ever-widening gap into Rosecrans's disintegrating right-center and center. Exploiting the break, hundreds of howling Rebels from Colonel Gates's and General Green's brigades steadily pushed south toward the great prize of Corinth and ever-deeper into Rosecrans's rear. However, those Confederates were the only attackers to pierce the Union lines on October 4. The victorious Missourians continued to rush forward without support, believing that a decisive victory was finally within reach. Thousands of Rebels "swarmed like tigers" off the high ground and down into the valley of Corinth, which became a valley of no return.

Hit by murderous crossfire from both left and right where other Southern attacks were repulsed, some Missouri Brigade soldiers remained on the ridge in defensive positions. There they caught their breath, reloaded muskets, and waited for the expected Confederate reinforcements before resuming the offensive. Those Rebels also stayed on the high ground to keep a firm grip on the captured artillery. Meanwhile many of Colonel Gates's soldiers continued to charge forward, racing for Corinth with screams and red battle-flags flying in the haze.[26]

But Rosecrans was ready for the Rebels who had torn savagely through his center and right-center, having adroitly massed heavy reserves in Corinth for just such an emergency. Consequently, dense blue formations and batteries stood ready and waiting less than 500 yards behind Battery Powell between the bloody ridge and the railroad town. One of the reasons those Yankee reserves were in the right place at the right time was the fact that Lowell's division failed to press the assault on the far right. On October 4 Price's corps, the Army of the West's two divisions under Generals Maury and Green, fought the battle mostly on their own. Amazingly, the assault almost succeeded. Southwest of Battery Powell, large numbers of Rebels, chiefly Green's troops but also elements of the Missouri Brigade, charged into the streets and main plaza of Corinth, fighting from house to house, almost capturing Rosecrans's headquarters. But those Confederate attacks were heading straight toward more well-positioned blue reserves and artillery.

The assault's momentum was shattered by massed volleys, double-loads of canister from artillery, and vicious hand-to-hand fighting. After gun-fire from the blue line exploded in their faces, Confederate survivors were pushed out of Corinth's bloody valley and back up the ridge, leaving behind piles of dead and wounded, torn battle-flags, and the dreams of victory lying amid the gory fields around Corinth.[27]

Badly mauled but not yet beaten, Colonel Gates's survivors returned to their ridge-top and took cover to make one last stand. They rejoined comrades who were already awaiting the Yankee counterattack. The isolated band of Missouri defenders continued to suffer under the brutal crossfire from other sectors to the left and right, which had both been recaptured by the Unionists or which had never been penetrated by the Rebels. They held the key high ground in the hope that successful Confederate assaults elsewhere or reinforcements in the Battery Powell and Fort Richardson sector might still save the day. One member of Wade's Battery, Benjamin Von Phul, rode frantically to the rear to urge reinforcements forward with the cry, "Colonel Gates has captured forty guns, but cannot hold them unless you reinforce him at once!" But help did not reach the pinned-down Missouri Confederates in time. After Van Dorn's attacks had been stopped at every point, thousands of Union reserves and rallied units prepared to drive Colonel Gates's seemingly suicidal Rebels off the ridge overlooking Corinth, before any of Van Dorn's reinforcements arrived to assist the badly out-numbered Confederates.[28]

Rapidly loading and firing their muskets, Gates's Missouri boys held their positions on the high ground for forty minutes, taking more punishment and still believing that "Corinth was ours." However, no support arrived for the ever-dwindling number of Missouri Brigade survivors. As in their first major battle, many of the Missouri Rebels had expended their last rounds, and awaited the inevitable counterattack with only fixed bayonets.[29]

Major Hubbell best described the Missouri Brigade's dilemma in his diary: "With deep mortification and regret than I ever before experienced, I noticed that no reinforcements came to our assistance, and that the lines on our right [General Green's brigade] were beginning to falter, after we had, by the most exalted valor and desperate charge on record, won the whole day— but on threads hang the decision of battles [and] the fate of armies." As the counter-attacking blue waves neared Battery Powell, the Missouri Brigade's survivors unleashed one final volley into the Yankee ranks. Facing a bayonet charge, the fire of the Missouri Confederates sputtered, after the last bullets struck down the foremost Unionists, who included attackers of the Tenth Missouri Volunteer Infantry, U.S.A. Private James H. Fauntleroy, an eighteen-year-old farmer of the First Missouri Cavalry (Dismounted), bitterly wrote in his diary, "We took 40 pieces of cannon but had to leave them."

Consequently, the battered remnants of the Missouri regiments melted away. Without order, soldiers fled downhill for their lives. Since no one had brought the necessary tools, the captured Federal guns could not be spiked. Then the rows of Union cannon which had killed so many attackers stood as silent sentinels watching over the heaps of dead and wounded. Near the rows of captured cannon, Major Hubbell commanded the last Confederates left unwounded at Battery Powell. In his diary he recorded the final moments on the ridge-top when, "a panic seemed to seize all the men on the right and left, until I stood alone, with only about fifty of my own brave [Third Missouri] boys, who all offered to die with me. But I thought it would be sacrificing their lives to no purpose, and finally gave the painful order to fall back..." On this fateful day in northeast Mississippi, Major Hubbell's "determined valor elicited the admiration" from the entire Missouri Brigade and army, wrote a Southern newspaperman. The Confederates abandoned Battery Powell, Fort Richardson and the Yankee artillery after the charging bluecoats of the Tenth Missouri, and other attacking Yankee regiments, pushed the last remaining defenders out of Battery Powell with musket-butts and bayonets. At last the Union center and right-center were secure, after some of the most savage fighting of the war.[30]

More men died during the pell-mell withdrawal from the bloody ridge, when hundreds of the counterattacking blueclads aligned on the commanding terrain and blasted away, as if enjoying target practice. But upon reaching relative safety on the low ground, the surviving Missourians rallied in the open woods near the creek.

At last the Corinth nightmare had ended, except for the hundreds of Missouri wounded left behind, after another reversal for Southern fortunes. The Missouri Brigade suffered losses of 53 killed, 332 wounded and 92 missing, a total of 477 men. However, a detailed survey of individual soldiers' records indicates a higher loss suffered by the Missouri Brigade, more than 500 Confederates, and even these records are incomplete. Many Missouri Rebels were last "seen in the works during the charge of 4 Oct and when we were repulsed was seen no more," wrote one survivor, who never forgot the horror of Corinth. The fearful price that the Missouri Brigade paid at Corinth caused Colonel Hubbell to write in his diary that Americans of future generations should "pause and cast a kind regret over the graves of [Missouri's] fallen heroes who fell far away from home and friends, battling for a principle dearer to them than life, and valuable to their survivors. When our liberty is gained it will have cost a precious boon." The Missouri Brigade's dead rest in some obscure burial trench under the streets and sidewalks of modern Corinth, known only to God.

During the Battle of Corinth, the Second Missouri suffered the highest losses in the Missouri Brigade, losing 19 killed, 122 wounded and 21 missing, a total of 162. But losses in the Fifth Missouri were a higher percentage than the Second Missouri, because 100 soldiers killed and wounded out of the 225 engaged constituted a 44 percent casualty rate. Many factors led to the disaster in which the Confederates suffered twice as many losses as the defenders, 5,000 Rebel losses versus 2,500 Union casualties. Van Dorn's recklessness and overly-ambitious strategy were key culprits in defeat. The Confederates' lack of careful planning and reconnaissance and poor coordination resulted in confusion, ill-timing and dismal logistical support. All of these factors led to the decimation of Price's corps. In the words of one Southern journalist, Van Dorn "sacrificed the flower of Price's army in his crazy attack upon Corinth." Once more superior firepower, generalship, manpower, logistics, and materiel had saved the day for the Union in a formula for victory that would often be repeated in the western war.

Despite the high losses and another defeat, the fighting spirit remained strong among the Johnny Rebs from Missouri. As one St. Louis Confederate explained the defeat in a letter: "We were defeated badly in our attempt to take Corinth, but we failed not from cowardice but from want of men & incompetency & disobedience of orders in some of our Brigadiers. We went to Corinth with too few men. The next [time that] we go, we will take it mind that. Corinth must & shall be ours." Corinth was lost to the South for all time. The most important junction on the vital Memphis & Charleston continued under Union control for the rest of the war, depriving the manpower-short Confederacy of the ability to shuffle reinforcements rapidly from east to west by the most direct route in a conflict in which the railroad had revolutionized warfare. The lack of the most direct east-west rail line makes Vicksburg more vulnerable than ever before.

The role of the Missouri Brigade at Corinth further nourished the growing reputation of the unit's fighting prowess. For example, the *Memphis Daily Appeal* recognized the deeds of the Missouri Brigade at Corinth in October of 1862, writing that "surely such a charge was never made before as the Missourians made here." He also complimented the Missouri Brigade: "The devotion of these troops, their daring their heroic, unfaltering courage rises to the moral sublime. No record of history can show an instance where patriotic men have better won their title to immortality. Human nature is not capable of higher perfection in the attributes of moral courage and patriotic devotion." Such acclaim for those Confederates from the distant frontier fueled a pride among Southerners throughout the Confederacy in the accomplishments of these warriors from the west side of the Mississippi.

People across the South also learned of the fighting qualities of these Missouri soldiers from another journalist, who paid a sincere tribute to these exiled Rebels of the West, "who are fighting for Mississippi and the Confederacy, a thousand miles from their own desolated homes in Missouri, and who pour out their blood like water." The Missourians' performance at Corinth reconfirmed General Van Dorn's appraisal of the Missouri Brigade, "the Old Guard of Napoleon was not composed of braver men," and "I have never in battle seen their equals." General Maury also praised the Missouri Brigade, after witnessing Colonel Gates's attack at Corinth: "I mean no disparagement to any troops of the Southern Confederacy when I say that Missouri troops of the Army of the West were not surpassed by any troops in the world." Another Rebel general, John B. Villepigue, who witnessed the Missourians' tenacity at Corinth proclaimed: "Magnificent! Magnificent! With a hundred thousand such men I could fight my way across Europe!" These glowing contemporary tributes to the Missouri Brigade spread both across the South and even in the North after the blood bath of Corinth.

Indeed, the legend of Colonel Gates's Missouri Brigade had spread north into the Unionists' home territory. For example, one Northern journalist warned his readers of the fierce determination and the iron mettle of the Johnny Rebs from Missouri: "When men march barefooted miles after miles over rough and filthy roads their feet exuding blood, at every step; when their rations consist of a single ear of corn, and when their clothing hangs in rags about them [then] it is time to know that these [veteran Missouri soldiers] believe in the cause they have espoused. When men thus so, fight with a desperation unparalelled [sic] in history, as instanced by that terrific charge on our batteries at Corinth, it is time for us to understand that only an active and vigorous war will end the rebellion with honor to the Federal cause."[31]

CHAPTER SEVEN

Withdrawal and Reorganization

The Confederate withdrawal from Corinth began around noon. Retiring northwest the way they had come, the survivors of the Army of West Tennessee limped away from the bitter defeat at bloody Corinth. If Rosecrans had immediately pursued, the Rebel army might have been destroyed. On the next day, October 5, the ever-aggressive Van Dorn wanted to strike Union-held Rienzi, Mississippi, on the Mobile & Charleston Railroad south of Corinth, before launching an attack on Corinth from the south. Wisely, however, the general's lieutenants convinced Van Dorn otherwise. Unknown to the Confederates, more trouble was now brewing. Rosecrans finally began his pursuit from the southeast, while Ord's forces swung down from Bolivar, Tennessee, to the northwest of Corinth. The two Federal commands planned to crush the trapped Confederates between them and the Hatchie River, on the west, and the Tuscumbia River, on the east.[1]

The entrapment of the Confederate Army nearly became complete on October 5. Making a speedy escape for Van Dorn less likely was tough terrain, hot weather, recent rains, and the flooded Hatchie and Tuscumbia Rivers. The Yankee vise closed tighter, when General Ord's forces marched in from the west, racing for Davis's Bridge on the Hatchie to close the door on the Confederate retreat. With Rosecrans pressing west toward the Tuscumbia and Ord advancing east for the Hatchie, the Rebel army seemed doomed. But, to the east, the Army of West Tennessee received invaluable assistance throughout the withdrawal from the rear-guard defenders commanded by General Bowen. At the Tuscumbia River, General Bowen masterminded a brilliant defense at Young's Bridge. By employing desperate tactics, Bowen thwarted Rosecrans's pursuit from Corinth. In holding firm on October 5, Bowen proved to be one of Van Dorn's best officers.

To the west, Van Dorn's advance units barely won the race to Davis's Bridge, securing the west bank of the muddy Hatchie. But the Rebel toe-hold on the vital crossing was precarious, since the Confederate army was strewn out for miles east along the road. Before more Southerners could bolster the beachhead, the Unionists attacked. Smashed by the blue onslaught, the thin gray line buckled, then shattered. Those Rebels not killed, wounded, or captured were simply pushed into the Hatchie by the assault's momentum. Maury's arriving troops quickly took position along high ground on the Hatchie's east side and held firm. Van Dorn's disorganized army was trapped between two strong Union forces and two overflowing rivers, facing destruction. To one Missouri officer, "it seemed as if the gods and the fates were against us."[2]

With the charging Yankees flooding over the bridge, Green's cheering troops arrived just in time. Helping to stem the tide, the breathless and sweat-stained

Missourians rushed into positions in the weak Rebel battle-line around noon, after double-quicking past the debris of a Confederate army in serious trouble. There amid the chaos of a rout, Colonel Gates's ranks were shaken briefly, when a throng of defeated Southerners fled through the Missouri Brigade's alignment. Colonel Gates's Rebels were angry at being confronted with yet another disaster not of their making. Tempers had flared earlier, a fight broke out in column, and one Missouri soldier shot down a comrade. When not fighting Yankees, this "Damned Hard Set" of Missouri Rebels were often fighting themselves, even with battle imminent.

In the confusion, Colonel Cockrell took charge of the potentially disastrous situation. Among the bursting shells and noisy panic, the Warrensburg attorney rode among the demoralized Southerners, imploring them to stand firm. After solidifying his own Second Missouri, Cockrell rallied other buckling Rebel formations. Cockrell's leadership at the critical moment helped to stabilize a defense which halted the Federal attacks. For his vital role on October 5, Colonel Cockrell won fame throughout the Confederate army and the South as "the hero of Hatchie Bridge."[3]

Nevertheless, the Unionists continued to hold Davis's Bridge, blocking Van Dorn's escape. Just when it appeared that the Army of West Tennessee would be crushed, an unexpected discovery saved the day. Southern horse soldiers found a little-known crossing of the Hatchie, six miles south and below Davis's Bridge, which could be reached via the Boneyard Road. This obscure Crum's Mill crossing was the only escape route open for the boxed-in Army of West Tennessee. Soon the Rebel army's wagons and artillery pushed south in the blackness. A full moon and few clouds facilitated the nighttime withdrawal through Mississippi's dark forests.

In guardian fashion, Gates's troops held an advanced position to repel any attack, while the Army of West Tennessee's survivors departed from the front and stealthily moved off during the night. The Missouri Brigade was the last infantry unit to leave the line. Captain Canniff's skirmishers, meanwhile, held the advanced position before the main line, while their comrades disappeared into the somber woodlands. During the withdrawal south to the crossing, Colonel Gates once more rejoined his old regiment of ex-horsemen to skillfully protect the Missouri Brigade's rear. Later that night, the Missouri Brigade quietly slipped across the Hatchie River to rejoin the rest of the army.[4]

After the Corinth debacle, Van Dorn's forces pushed southwest to the Tupelo, Mississippi, area to recuperate. There, six miles below Holly Springs and near Waterford Station, the Missouri Brigade rested, attempting to heal from the slaughter of Corinth. That encampment around Lumpkin's Mill was designated Camp Pritchard in honor of the Third Missouri's fallen colonel. Initially Pritchard's wound did not seem to be mortal, but his condition rapidly worsened, and he died on October 20. The news of the popular colonel's death came as a severe blow to the entire Missouri Brigade. As one Missouri Brigade member lamented, "What a sad and irreparable loss to us!" Colonel Pritchard was buried near his own property at Coffeeville, Mississippi, where he had planned to start a new life once the war ended.

In Federal-occupied Carroll County, Missouri, Mrs. Pritchard was brought the news of her husband's wounding in far-away Mississippi weeks after the battle. Matilda Pritchard immediately left home and headed southeast to join her injured husband before it was too late. She journeyed through the Union lines and the no-man's-land of war-ravished Mississippi and reached the Missourians' camp in late

October. But she was "to receive suddenly upon arriving at Gen. Price's head-quarters the heartbreaking intelligence that her loved one was gone!"

Like so many other widows of Missouri Brigade soldiers, Mrs. Pritchard also became a casualty of war, emotionally traumatized by the loss of her dashing colonel-husband. For the rest of her life she believed that her husband had died because he had failed to heed the warning of the psychic African American slave from Carroll County. She had long ago told Matilda to warn Colonel Pritchard that to ride a sorrel horse into battle meant death. Evidently he had galloped forward on a reddish-brown horse during the charge on Corinth. For many years after the war "the sight of any horse of reddish color made her scream and sometimes faint."[5]

The Missouri Brigade's decimated officer corps had to be replenished after Corinth. Colonels Pritchard and Maupin, commanders of the Third Missouri and the First Missouri Cavalry (Dismounted) had been fatally cut down at Corinth. And the leaders of the Second Missouri, Colonel Cockrell, and Fifth Missouri, Colonel McCown, were wounded. Every regimental infantry commander of the Missouri Brigade had been hit on that fateful October 4.

After the death of Colonel Pritchard, Major Hubbell won promotion to lieutenant colonel and took command of the Third Missouri. The former merchant of Richmond, Missouri, had shown much initiative in private life and in Missouri State Guard service. Kind-hearted, scholarly, and analytical, Hubbell had demonstrated leadership ability on battlefields across Missouri, Arkansas, and Mississippi. He was a bachelor, as were many of the Missouri Brigade's younger officers. However, since arriving in Mississippi, Hubbell had become engaged to a Southern girl. Also he had bought Magnolia State property, investing in the future of a new nation like Colonel Pritchard.

By the fall of 1862, the thirty-one-year-old Hubbell had begun to grow tired of the killing and brutality, but still considered the struggle almost a holy crusade. Colonel Hubbell prevented his younger brother Richard, who had ridden under Colonel Rives during the war's early days, from joining the Third Missouri, anticipating the bloody fighting that made active service in Mississippi a living nightmare.[6]

Taking command of the First Missouri Cavalry (Dismounted) after Colonel Maupin's death was Major George Washington Law. The thirty-three-year-old Law had been a successful tobacco grower in the Boone's Lick country of central Missouri. Unlike the vast majority of his soldiers, he was a member of the frontier planter class.[7]

The decisive autumn of 1862 brought irreversible Confederate defeats in both the West and East. As in Missouri, the people of Kentucky and Maryland refused to rise up in revolt, taking a good deal of the steam out of both Bragg's and Lee's invasions, sabotaging the goal of "liberation," and denying the Confederacy what she needed most of all in a war of attrition, manpower. Sacrificing more men for no gain, General Bragg was forced to withdraw not long after a bloody engagement at Perryville, Kentucky. The South had once again won nothing for her three desperate efforts to secure victory, losing thousands of soldiers, irreplaceable amounts of materiel, and confidence.

In the East, the Army of Northern Virginia's invasion of the North ended with the war's bloodiest day along a small, clear creek named Antietam in northwestern Maryland. Thousands of Americans were slaughtered in the grain fields and green pastures of frugal German farmers, along the Sunken Road, and at the Burnside

Bridge. With the stunning losses and the triple reversals at Sharpsburg, Corinth and Perryville during the fall of 1862, the Confederacy reached its high-water mark. Never again would the South simultaneously launch three offensives from the Piedmont in the East to the Mississippi Valley in the West. After the Battle of Antietam, Lincoln issued the Emancipation Proclamation, which deflated hopes of the Confederacy winning foreign recognition. The dream of an independent Southern nation was fading away in the dark oak forests of Perryville, the brown cornfields around Sharpsburg, and the dusty streets of Corinth.[8]

That fall the Missouri troops recuperated in their encampments, drilled endlessly, and benefited from unexpected good fortune. Some barefoot soldiers received an issuance of shoes for the first time since joining Confederate service. Ragged, soiled, and lice-covered uniforms were replaced by donations of clothing from the Dixie Daughters' Society on October 20. Despite looking more like civilians than "the South's Finest," the Third Missouri boys, including Lieutenant Mothershead, published their "Thanks to the Ladies of Panola County" in a major Southern newspaper. However, the Missouri Brigade still needed clothing with winter and, perhaps, a Yankee offensive fast approaching.

On the same October day, a general reorganization occurred within the army. Then the First Missouri Brigade again became an all-Missouri unit with the departure of the Sixteenth Arkansas Infantry, which had provided splendid service for the previous eight months. Gray-bearded and capable General Green replaced Colonel Gates as the Missouri Brigade commander. Summarizing the Missourians' struggle in ideological terms, Green explained to the people of Mississippi, "We are now battling for the weeping goddess of Liberty upon your soil, and the banner of Missouri shall never trail in the dust."

Increasing unit pride and making a concession to states rights, the Confederacy adopted the policy of uniting regiments from the same state together in brigades. The First Missouri Brigade, of General Bowen's division, now consisted of the First, Second, Third, Fourth, Fifth, and Sixth Missouri Confederate Infantry, and the First Missouri Cavalry (Dismounted). In addition, the Third Missouri Confederate Cavalry Battalion (Dismounted) was assigned to the Missouri Brigade. Like the First Missouri Cavalry, the Third Missouri Cavalry Battalion had lost its mounted status upon crossing the Mississippi River with General Price. Representing every section of western Missouri from the Iowa border to the Arkansas border, this unit consisted of soldiers from Greene, Nodaway, Andrews, Moniteau, Clay, Polk and Cass Counties, Missouri. The consolidation of the Missouri units improved morale and bolstered esprit de corps. One jubilant St. Louis Rebel wrote in a letter, "The St. Louis boys are now all near together."[9]

One of the finest of the new units was the First Missouri Confederate Infantry. General Bowen had been the organizer and father of this excellent unit, which had begun organizing in Memphis during the summer of 1861. On the first day at Shiloh, the attacking First Missouri Regiment had helped overrun the Peach Orchard and then assisted in overpowering the Hornet's Nest, losing 133 men during the charges through the captured Federal encampments and the gory fields and forests along the Tennessee River.

At that time Kentucky-born Colonel Amos Camden Riley, known as "Cam," commanded the troops. One Missouri Brigade soldier wrote about Colonel Riley, "None possessed higher or more sterling qualities, and the stubborness [sic] with which he fought, and the dash and impetuosity that characterized his every movement, rendered him a model of chivalry, and won for him a wide and extended reputation." When the regiment's colonel was killed on the first day at Shiloh, Riley had taken command, and led the unit during most of the brutal two-day contest. He survived the battle unscathed despite bullets cutting through his uniform.

Riley, a slave-owning farmer before the war, was a young, well-educated bachelor. Colonel Riley was highly motivated, writing to his father that October of 1862 that, "God grant that our army may be able to wipe the stain of Corinth from their banners [now] our brigade is composed entirely of Missouri troops and [is one of the best] brigades I ever saw. I have got to believe that if there was ever a brigade that could whip a federal division ours surely can do it, so you can look out for squalls." A splendid education from the Kentucky Military Institute [Class of 1855] made the auburn-haired, twenty-five-year-old Riley a valuable addition to the Missouri Brigade.[10]

The First Missouri contained a diverse socioeconomic mixture, which combined incongruous urban and rural elements to a degree unlike any other of the Missouri Brigade's units. The following companies consisted of St. Louisans: Company B, the Wade Guards; Company D, the St. Louis Greys; Company E, the St. Louis Minute Men; and Company F, the St. Louis Southern Guards. In Company C were the Guards of Carondelet, Bowen's hometown just south of St. Louis. Hardy natives of the Bootheel region of southeast Missouri were members of Company G, the New Madrid Guards; Company H, the Pemiscot Rifles; Company I, the Missouri Guards, and Company K, the Missouri Greys. New Madrid County was the most heavily represented area among the Bootheel region Confederates.

An exiled company from the wharves and streets of New Orleans, Louisiana, Company A, the Suchet Guards, further added variety to the First Missouri regiment. Indeed, many of those Louisiana men were Irish, for Louisiana had the largest Irish population in the Confederacy after Missouri. In addition, Company C contained many Irishmen from Memphis, including Ireland-born Private James Burns, age sixty-five and a grizzled stone mason. Those Irish soldiers, young and old, were ready to fight to the end. They included a cabinet maker and widower, born in Ireland, Private Frank Flanigan, who was the oldest regimental member at age seventy-one. In the words of Colonel Riley that applied to most of the Rebels of this regiment, "I am now preparing myself for a 7 years war [,] death or independence is all the rank hear now."[11]

A group of high ranking officers, including Colonel Riley, had learned the art of war at the Kentucky Military Institute near Louisville, Kentucky, which was one of the oldest and best private military schools in the country. Also, a sturdy foundation that bolstered the regiment's quality came from vigorous young officers, who had perfected their skills on the parade grounds of West Point and the Virginia Military Institute. Many sons of the leading families of both St. Louis and the Bootheel region served in the First Missouri.

A large number of St. Louisans in that crack unit were "young men in the professions or in business—lawyers, doctors, bank officers, bookkeepers in some of the principal business houses, steamboat clerks [and] many of them were descendants of pioneer families of St. Louis." Quite a few of those veterans of the First Missouri Regiment had been ante-bellum Missouri militiamen, who were captured at Camp Jackson. One such reliable leader with valuable militia experience was

Major Hugh Alfred Garland, a St. Louis lawyer who had been the Jackson Grays' captain in Bowen's militia regiment when captured at Camp Jackson. Among the St. Louisans, Colonel Bowen's Confederate regiment became known as "the Camp Jackson Regiment": a designation that the large number of southeast Missourians of the regiment would have disputed. Many St. Louis parolees of Camp Jackson had fled to Memphis in the summer of 1861 to join Colonel Bowen.[12]

Father Bannon and other Emerald Islanders of the Missouri Brigade warmly welcomed the many Irishmen of Bowen's regiment. They were not poor immigrants and the unemployed, but included many who had fulfilled the New World dream of success in America by hard work and determination. Many of these sons of Erin had gained middle-class and lower upper-class status with service in the volunteer fire companies and militia of St. Louis. This means of social mobility had benefited no one more than Major Martin Burke, former captain of the St. Louis Greys [Company D], which contained many Irish Rebels. A strict Catholic, Ireland native, and brother of a priest, Burke had been a successful merchant in St. Louis. Captain Burke's St. Louis Greys were an elite militia company in prewar St. Louis, especially proficient in skirmish and drill tactics under the captain's expert instruction. Captain Burke had led his company during the Southwest Expedition before his capture at Camp Jackson. As a top officer in Bowen's regiment, he had taken a severe wound at Shiloh.

One of Major Burke's most important contributions to the Missouri Brigade was to have bugles abolished from the skirmish companies. Because armies on both sides used identical calls, Burke cleverly substituted whistles for bugles. The innovative concept proved effective on the battlefield. That substitution gave the Missouri skirmishers "the advantage of knowing [the Federals'] movements by the bugle calls, [while] he could not anticipate our moves," a key advantage in the confusion of battle.[13]

Fueled by the bigotries and hatreds of the 1850's Know-Nothingism, native Americans had clashed violently with foreign-born Irish citizens, resulting in urban strife which helped to strip away the immigrants' loyalties to the United States before the sectional conflict. More than any other Missouri Brigade members, the Irish of St. Louis in large part had joined the South's struggle to fight the Germans, who were Republican, pro-centralized government, anti-Catholic, and pro-Union. After having already felt the wrath of another centralized authority with British oppression of Ireland, these Celtic Rebels no longer wanted strong government control in their lives.

A careful study of more than 8,000 individual service records reveals that more Ireland-born soldiers of the Missouri Brigade's units hailed from the rural areas and small towns of Missouri than from the large urban centers of Missouri. In the Fifth Missouri which contained most Ireland-born members, for instance, the majority of these Rebels came from the rural areas outside St. Louis. Only the First Missouri Regiment, with the second highest number of Ireland-born soldiers in the Missouri Brigade, had more Irishmen from St. Louis than any other area. But in this regiment, the Ireland-born Rebels from Memphis, Tennessee, almost equaled the total number of Ireland-born St. Louisans.

Compared with the rural American-born counterparts of the Missouri Brigade, a higher percentage of those Ireland-born soldiers from outside of St. Louis were engaged in the more skilled occupations, such as shoemaker, stone cutter, bricklayer,

Captain Henry Guibor
Courtesy Missouri Historical Society,
St. Louis
(Unpublished Photo)

**Captain William H. Inge,
1st Missouri Infantry,
C.S.A., captured February
10, 1862, Imprisoned
Johnson's Island**
Courtesy Robert L. Hawkins III
Collection, Jefferson City, Mo.

Captain Martin Burke
Courtesy Missouri Historical
Society, St. Louis

**Lieutenant Colonel
Waldo P. Johnson**
Courtesy State Historical Society
of Missouri, Columbia

tailor, boiler maker, etc. Despite many skilled artisans being represented among the St. Louis Irish, more Ireland-born Missouri Brigade members were employed in menial positions as common laborers in St. Louis, such as loading and unloading steamboats at the busy levee on the Mississippi, than those Irish from the rural areas. As with the American-born of the Missouri Brigade, that social clash with the Germans caused more eastern Missouri Irish to become Rebels, while the threat of the Kansas Jayhawkers caused more Irish of western Missouri to fight for the South.

Representing St. Louis's upper-class in the First Missouri's ranks were members of the Kennerly family. Among the social, cultural and intellectual elite of the city were Lieutenants James Amadee Kennerly and Samuel Augustin Kennerly, and Captain Lewis Hancock Kennerly. One officer wrote that "the Kennerly brothers, Sam, Jim and Lew, [were] among the finest officers of the line we had in the brigade." These hard-fighting urbanites also were the brothers-in-law of General Bowen. The Kennerly family hailed from the pioneer stock of Virginia and had a proud Revolutionary War heritage.

The Kennerly boys' mother was the daughter of the French governor of the Illinois Territory. A cousin, Captain William Clark Kennerly, who had served on Colonel Little's staff at the Missouri Brigade's organization and at the Battle of Pea Ridge, fought in Clark's Battery. In 1861 Colonel Little chose Captain Kennerly who had served as Bowen's top lieutenant during the Southwest Expedition on the western border in 1860-61.

William, Samuel, Louis, and James Kennerly had been captured at Camp Jackson. A sister, Mary Lucretia Preston Bowen, no less devoted than her brothers, likewise had been trapped at the militia encampment. But she had slipped through the Federal net with the battle-flag of Bowen's regiment wrapped around her waist.

The Kennerly clan had suffered at Shiloh, so Mrs. Bowen had left Carondelet alone to assist her husband and brothers, wounded at that battle, and journeyed south. At a field hospital in northeast Mississippi, the Kennerly boys and General Bowen became "indebted for their lives, saved by [Mrs. Bowen's] careful and untiring care and devotion. Can a more singular...incident be found in the Confederate army, or can the country furnish a nobler record of heroism than this?," asked a *Mobile Register and Advertiser* journalist after describing the Kennerly story.

But Mrs. Bowen's feats of heroism had only begun. In passing through the Union armies, Mary had brought an invaluable supply of scarce and precious medicines, such as quinine and penicillin, for the Missouri troops. Additionally, "Mittie" had smuggled through the lines the same banner she rescued from Camp Jackson. Thereafter, Mrs. Bowen became "a mother" to the regiment and the boys in the ranks, working in the hospitals and serving on the battlefields as a nurse. In a tribute to her sacrifice and devotion, grateful Missouri cannoneers affectionately named one of their best guns the "Lady Bowen."[14]

Commanding the Sixth Missouri was the gifted grandson of Henry Clay, handsome and chivalric Colonel Eugene Erwin. At age twenty-seven, he was described by one soldier as "a brave officer, and a gentleman of talent and genius." His mother, an intelligent and lively woman, was the daughter of Henry Clay. The Clay property, Ashland, was located near the Erwin home. Both families were part of the pro-Southern planter class of the Bluegrass, modeled after the Virginia aristocracy of the Tidewater. Erwin's hometown of Independence, Missouri was a thriving commercial town and the departure point for the Santa Fe and Oregon

Trails. After leaving an attractive wife and three young girls to serve his state and country, Erwin had proved to be an outstanding natural leader.

One of Colonel Erwin's finest days had come at Pea Ridge. As a lieutenant in the Second Missouri Brigade, Erwin had employed skill and initiative to help carry the field on March 7. When an Iowa gun unlimbered on a knoll to sweep the right flank of the Confederate advance up Cross Timber Hollow, the young officer had spied an opportunity to capture the cannon. The Yankee artillery piece had to be taken quickly before the Confederates could gain the key higher ground at the southwestern edge of Pea Ridge. In a wild attack, Erwin had led the charge that captured the gun. Lieutenant Erwin's timely exploit helped to pave the way for the Missouri Brigade's successful charge on the first day. Somehow he had survived the day with a uniform cut by canister and minie balls.

With long black hair and mustache, Colonel Erwin looked like a Southern gentleman-turned-warrior. When an enraged Mississippi farmer complained to Erwin that the Sixth Missourians had burned all his fence rails for fuel and presented a bill of $600.00, the colonel felt the irony of the underpaid and ill-clothed defenders of the farmer's home state being saddled with such a heavy economic burden. Without informing his men, however, Erwin decided that, "the bill is unjust but I will pay it out of my own funds." Although he had just joined the Missouri Brigade, still limping from a bad Corinth wound, Colonel Erwin would shortly be the foremost candidate as the Missouri Brigade's next commander, and for a brigadier generalship, after Colonel Gates's transfer.[15]

Colonel Erwin's reputation in part reflected the superior quality of the rank and file of the Sixth Missouri, known as the "Bloody Sixth." That crack unit had been organized in the first week of September, when Erwin's Confederate Battalion was united with Colonel Isaac N. Hedgpeth's Confederate Battalion of southeast Missouri boys, with the addition of two recently organized companies not long after the Fifth Missouri's formation on September 1, 1862. The Sixth Missouri, wrote one Rebel, consisted "principabily [sic] of Young men of the best families of Missouri and were surpassed by none in either gallant or gentlemanly bearing."

Most regimental members hailed from the sprawling prairies of western Missouri where the raids of the Kansas Jayhawkers years before the Civil War had convinced them that they had to take up arms for self-defense. Half of the Sixth Missouri's five companies were represented primarily by counties that bordered the Missouri River, from mid-Missouri westward to the Kansas border. The demographic background of the majority of soldiers in these companies was as follows: Jackson and Cass Counties [Company A]; Lafayette, Jackson, and Saline Counties [Company B]; Howard and Boone Counties [Company C]; Jackson and Johnson Counties, [Company E]; and Howard and Chariton Counties, [Company H]. The Rebels of Company G hailed mostly from the north Missouri county of Platte, barely 20 miles south of the Iowa border. Company F was primarily a St. Clair and Cass County unit of western Missouri.

Like the First Missouri Regiment, the Sixth Missouri had a high percentage of southeast Missouri soldiers, helping to disprove the myth that the contribution from this region was insignificant. For example, Company I was represented by Cape Girardeau and Scott Counties, and Company K consisted primarily of Arkansas Rebels from Randolph County, and Missouri Confederates from Cape Girardeau County and Ripley County. Company D consisted mostly of St. Genevieve County soldiers and Rebels from the narrow band of southeast Missouri counties farther south bordering the Mississippi River. This distinctive region area of rich farm lands skirted the "Father of Water," which separated the area from Illinois.

Those Rebels of French ancestry from the St. Genevieve area added yet another culturally diverse element to the Missouri Brigade's composition, which enhanced its overall quality. Some of those Gallic Rebels included Privates John W. Barbour, Lewis Girard, born in Paris, France, Eli Labrarier, brothers Felix and Leon Thomure, Corporal Charles E. Proffitt and Musician Adrien Lalamondiere.

The best cook of French descent in the Sixth Missouri ranks, a former chef from New Orleans, was Private Emile Richeau. But the Epicurean found it difficult to adjust to stale beans, rock-hard corn-bread, and rancid bacon. A disgruntled Richeau stole a fast horse and evidently rode back to his fancy Creole restaurant in Louisiana. Other soldiers' names, such as Corporal Daniel Boone Caveny, reflected the intermingling of American and French cultures on the western frontier.

The Sixth Missouri's performance at Corinth had enhanced the regiment's reputation, but at a cost. Not only had Colonel Erwin been wounded, but also 57 of 75 Sixth Missouri noncommissioned and commissioned officers had been shot down during the fierce attack upon Corinth. The regiment took the third highest casualties of any Confederate unit at Corinth, with 31 killed, 130 wounded and 53 missing, a loss of 214 soldiers. But the terrible losses hardly diminished the Sixth Missouri's effectiveness.

However, some of the best officers had been cut down in the hell of Corinth. For example, Lieutenant Colonel Isaac N. Hedgpeth, age forty and Tennessee-born like a high percentage of his southeast Missourians, had been shot and captured at Corinth. Hedgpeth compiled a distinguished State Guard record in battles across southeast Missouri in 1861. Nestled in the picturesque valley of Current River, his hometown of Doniphan, named after the Mexican War hero and leader of the famous expedition, would lose seven of her Sixth Missouri sons in the South.

The Sixth Missouri contained the largest number of Arkansas soldiers of any unit in the Missouri Brigade. These out-of-state Rebels of Company K hailed from around Pittman's Ferry [where during late October, Colonel Burbridge, the Second Missouri's former commander, was battling an old Pea Ridge antagonist, the Twenty-Fourth Missouri and other Federals in the struggle for Missouri] and Pocahontas, south of Doniphan and down Current River. The Missouri Brigade had the good fortune to welcome such a fine regiment into its ranks.[16]

Another excellent addition to the Missouri Brigade came with the Fourth Missouri Confederate Infantry. This regiment had been organized on May 15, 1862, with the uniting of two veteran Confederate battalions under Lieutenant Colonels Archibald A. MacFarlane and Waldo P. Johnson and a company of mostly Marion County Rebels under Captain Jeptha D. Feagan. The Fourth Missouri also had been shot to pieces at Corinth. Commanding this regiment was hard-fighting Colonel Archibald A. MacFarlane, age twenty-six. More of an international flavor was fused into the Missouri Brigade with the addition of "Archie" MacFarlane, a fiery Scotsman. Colonel MacFarlane had been severely injured with a head wound at Corinth, but now swore to his soldiers, "Boys, I am going to get well and give it to the Yankees again."

That hot-tempered Confederate Scot commanded the largest contingent of Scotch-Irishmen in the Missouri Brigade, hardy and self-reliant mountaineers from the picturesque Ozark hill country of southern Missouri. Six of the ten companies of the Fourth Missouri were drawn from these counties of the heavily-forested Ozark hills. But those frontiersmen became some of the State Guard's best troops. In 1861, these rugged soldiers from the hill country had been the most individualistic element among one of the best democratic of armies [Price's] in American history: "Like all frontiersmen, they were shrewd, quick-witted, wary, cunning, and ready for all emergencies, and like all backwoodsmen, their courage was serene, steady, unconscious."

The Helms clan exemplified quality in the ranks. From Taney County, sixty-eight-year-old Private Hiram C. Helms, Sr., fought beside his twenty-four-year-old son of the same name. The regimental chaplain was W. A. Helms, who was related to the regiment's oldest member. But probably a better example of the never-say-die qualities of Fourth Missouri soldiers can be seen in the case of nineteen-year-old Lieutenant John Henry White from Oregon County. Young White had somehow managed to survive some risky days as a color bearer in the State Guard, but had been badly "wounded in the Privates" at Corinth.

Of all the Missouri Brigade's units, the Fourth Missouri was the most homogeneous unit in terms of Anglo-Saxon roots. For instance, of the 986 Rebels who served in the Fourth Missouri, only four were Ireland-born. This statistic reflects the relative geographic isolation of the Ozark highlands of southern Missouri, another region that has been ignored as a contributor to the Missouri Brigade.

Single counties represented more soldiers in each company than in other regiments: Company A, Taney County; Company B, Howell County, Companies D and I, Oregon County; Company E, Henry County and Laclede Counties; Company F, Christian County; Company G, Dallas County; and Company H, Cass County. Company K was represented by Marion County of northeastern Missouri in the Mississippi River country. But the regiment's most unlikely group of Rebels were in Company C: exiled Arkansas volunteers from the wooded Ozark hills of Fulton County, in north central Arkansas and just south of the Missouri line. But almost as many soldiers from Ozark County, Missouri, were in Company C as Arkansians.

The lieutenant colonel of this veteran regiment was Waldo P. Johnson, who had been expelled in January 1862 from the United States Senate for his political beliefs. While with Price, he had learned that his hometown of Osceola had been burned by Kansas raiders. Born in Virginia, Johnson held a seat in the Confederate Congress to represent Missouri.[17]

Also the dismounted soldiers of the Third Missouri Cavalry Battalion became Missouri Brigade members. By this period, those former cavalrymen had made the transition to infantry service. Commanding the former cavalrymen from all sections of western Missouri was a young officer of promise, Lieutenant Colonel David Todd Samuel, age twenty-four. The intelligent young man had greatly impressed Price, earning command of the personal mounted escort for the general. The fates of the Missouri Brigade and Major Samuel's escort were initially thrown together at Pea Ridge. On the battle's first day, wrote Samuel, when "attacked by ten times my force, I was compelled to fall back some 150 yards, at which time Colonel Little's brigade timely came to our aid [then] to victory! to glory!!" Samuel's dismounted cavalrymen had charged with the Missouri Brigade in overrunning the Elkhorn Tavern area. During the charge on Corinth, the battalion took a beating, as if to reconfirm the faith that cavalry service was preferable to charging fortifications.[18]

Another organizational change for the Missouri Brigade came during the first week of November, when the First and Fourth Missouri combined because these units had been so thoroughly decimated by disease in the summer and by losses at

Corinth. The merger resulted in the formation of the First and Fourth Missouri Confederate Infantry (Consolidated). By mutual agreement between Colonel MacFarlane and Colonel Riley, "Archie" MacFarlane was given command of the regiment. Riley, meanwhile, was elected as lieutenant colonel of the newly consolidated unit. But because MacFarlane was still disabled from his Corinth wounds, Colonel Riley took charge of the regiment. Riley was most fortunate to have reliable subordinates in Lieutenant Colonel Garland and Major Burke, both St. Louisans with solid experience in the Missouri Volunteer Militia.

One variable that remained constant despite the Missouri Brigade's restructuring was the role of Company F, Fifth Missouri. Captain Canniff's company continued to be the best skirmishers in the Missouri Brigade and some of the most effective in the army.[19]

Before the beginning of the Vicksburg Campaign, the Missouri Brigade's prowess was increased with the addition of experienced Missouri Confederate Batteries assigned to Bowen's division. One of these was the veteran Confederate artillery unit under the leadership of Captain Henry Guibor. Organized on March 25, 1862 at Van Buren, Arkansas, Guibor's artillery command would become perhaps the best battery of Bowen's division. Guibor's First Missouri Light Artillery traced its lineage to one of the finest artillery units, Guibor's Battery, of General Price's Missouri State Guard. Captain Guibor, of French-Canadian antecedents, had served on the western expedition, and then remained on the Missouri-Kansas border with Colonel Bowen's Southwest Battalion throughout the winter of 1860-61. There Lieutenant Guibor, age forty, and the martinet Bowen had transformed their St. Louisans into highly-disciplined and expertly-drilled gunners of "the best volunteer company of artilery [sic] in this country," boasted Bowen.

Upon the Southwest Battalion's return to St. Louis, Guibor had taken command of the Missouri Volunteer Militia battery at Camp Jackson. When surrounded by thousands of Unionists, Guibor had his 6-pounder cannon loaded and ready for action on May 10, 1861, but orders came to surrender. Symbolically, the state artillery that Guibor sighted upon the bluecoats were those Mexican guns captured during Doniphan's Expedition. With his arrest by Federal authorities imminent, Guibor had fled St. Louis on an appropriately dark night. Concerned about Union reprisals against his family, he had told them only that he was "going to [the] country on [a] short trip," which would turn into a sojourn of four years.

Like a great artist creating a masterpiece, Guibor had carefully perfected both his State Guard and Confederate battery into finely-tuned and efficient instruments of war. During the Battle of Pea Ridge, Captain Guibor had audaciously advanced his guns forward and joined the Missourians' attack on Elkhorn Tavern. Clearly Captain Guibor, a savvy Mexican War veteran and St. Louis University graduate, was the ideal artillery commander to play a lengthy and vital role in the Missouri Brigade's history. In the ranks were Irishmen, Frenchmen, Italians, Scotsmen, Germans, Britons, Jews, and even an exiled group of New Orleans volunteers, who were as colorful as the St. Louisans. Those zealous Louisiana soldiers originally had formed the Hannibal Missouri Light Artillery Company, and linked with General Price in the struggle for Missouri, after New Orleans fell in April of 1862.

Most of the cannoneers of Guibor's First Missouri Light Artillery were St. Louisans, and many were veterans of the Missouri Volunteer Militia, the Southwest Expedition and the Southwest Battalion, and Missouri State Guard service, a record of solid experience unmatched by any artillery of the South during the ante-bellum period. The influence of European artillery axioms also came to those gunners from a hard-bitten German private named Samuel C. Lutzen. Captain Guibor's high-spirited command was mostly an urban unit, with the majority of the artillerymen being street-wise and often rowdy city boys. Like his adventurous ancestors who had migrated down the Mississippi from Canada to find life in a new land, Guibor was a dedicated and pious Catholic Rebel whose accomplishments would become almost legendary. From that point until nearly the war's end, the histories of Guibor's light artillery and the Missouri Brigade were closely intertwined and almost inseparable.[20]

Another artillery unit destined to provide key support for the Missouri Brigade during the upcoming struggle for Vicksburg was Captain John Christopher Landis's Missouri Artillery. Steady and cool under the hottest fire, Captain Landis created his own reputation with bravery and an iron nerve. Captain Landis was combative and possessed a "mean spirit," complained one of his men in a letter. While sometimes causing difficulties in personal affairs, these characteristics combined to make Landis an invaluable asset, for he could be depended upon to provide timely support, inspired leadership, and aggressive action whenever the Missouri Brigade was in a tight spot. Landis capably led the roughhewn cannoneers from western Missouri and the St. Louis men of eastern Missouri during some of the most severe engagements in the West.

Captain Landis, the eldest of ten, came from a wealthy and respected St. Joseph family. Ambitious and strong-willed as if to compensate for his short stature, John had entered West Point as a teen-ager in 1854. Landis evidently had trouble tolerating the institution's strict discipline, and left the military life to take advantage of lucrative opportunities offered by his father's business. Only two years before his scheduled graduation in the Class of 1858, he had left the United States Military Academy and returned to St. Joseph.

Landis, however, had learned enough at West Point to play a key role in organizing resistance during the early days of the conflict. Despite a sizable Union force stationed in St. Joseph, Landis quietly enlisted Rebel volunteers as war clouds darkened over northwest Missouri. Weapons and munitions captured at Liberty Arsenal were hidden in a grove behind the Landis House. Captain Landis had not only brought critical supplies at an early date to Price's army, but also took a company of volunteers out of St. Joseph. But Landis's contribution to rebellion in western Missouri did not go unpunished. Federal authorities responded by throwing Landis's father in prison for his son's offenses. The nucleus of the Landis battery, organized in December of 1861, had fought at Pea Ridge in the Second Missouri Confederate Brigade.

With Guibor's and Landis's Batteries at their side, the Missouri Brigade's infantry was well-protected on the battlefield whenever artillery support was needed at the most critical moment. The reorganization of October 1862 was more than simply a bureaucratic reshuffling, forging a natural union that considerably enhanced the overall quality of the Missouri Brigade. Indeed, the Fourth and Sixth Missouri, the Third Missouri Battalion, and Captains Guibor's and Landis's batteries had fought together in Green's brigade on October 3-4, being the only Confederate troops to break through the Union lines and charge into the streets of Corinth alongside the Missouri Brigade's attackers. The reorganization of October 1862 made the Missouri Brigade even more formidable, creating a more lethal fighting machine in time for the Vicksburg Campaign.[21]

CHAPTER EIGHT

Winter Quarters

By late 1862, Confederate fortunes in the West had begun a downward spiral that would never be reversed. Indeed, "the war in the West has [been] from the outset, a constant and self-repeating failure [and] we have perpetually lost ground. We have [now] lost Kentucky, lost Missouri, lost half of Tennessee, lost in Louisiana, in Texas, in Arkansas, in Mississippi. Our lead mines, our wheat fields, our hog pens, our fatted herds are in the hands of the foe," complained one angry Southern journalist. Indeed, the Confederate nation was struggling for life during the late autumn of 1862.

After the Corinth success, General Grant turned his efforts toward Vicksburg to gain control of the Mississippi River and win a strangle-hold on the jugular vein of the Confederacy. Across the ever-impatient Union domestic front, much of the North and West "were now clamorous for the destruction of Vicksburg [for the city should be] razed to the ground...." To accomplish this objective Grant assembled a sizable force to push south down the Mississippi Central Railroad deeper into the Magnolia State. This offensive fit nicely into the Union's concept of simultaneous advances to exploit the numerical and logistical weaknesses of the South and deny the infant nation the foreign recognition that could ensure life. While Grant's forces swung down the railroad in northern Mississippi in an attempt to take Jackson and gain Vicksburg's rear, General William T. Sherman's corps and the Union Navy advanced south along the Mississippi River to hit Vicksburg from the north. In addition, Rosecrans's forces marched from Nashville to attack General Bragg's Army of Tennessee in middle Tennessee at Murfreesboro, which resulted in a bloody Union victory at Stones River on the last day of the year.[1]

Before the end of October the Confederacy replaced the much-lampooned General Van Dorn with Lieutenant General John C. Pemberton, a West Pointer [Class of 1837], Seminole War veteran, and Pennsylvania native. But in bowing to political pressure after the Corinth disaster, Confederate leadership made a critical mistake in bestowing the most important task in the West, the defense of Vicksburg, on an officer without the necessary field experience to handle this crucial assignment. Pemberton was simply not the kind of soldier that could stop the North's best general and save the Mississippi River for the Confederacy.

After enduring the carnage of Pea Ridge and Corinth, the Missouri Rebels welcomed the change of command before the beginning of another campaign. With considerable understatement, Lieutenant Warren wrote in a letter "the men had become very much dissatisfied with Van Dorn. They had tried him sufficiently, and found him wanting. It was no fault of the men, that the Battle of Elk Horn [and] Corinth were lost. Men never fought under as many disadvantages, with more courage." Van Dorn had been denounced across the South for "this [recent] disgrace" and defeat at Corinth. One of his chief subordinates, General Bowen, formally charged Van Dorn with a long list of organizational and tactical errors that he felt had led to disaster. Bowen's bold accusations resulted in a court of inquiry. The Confederacy, meanwhile, looked with hopeful eyes upon the latest savior in the West, General Pemberton, whose highly-touted arrival "cheers us with the hope that there will dawn a happier day for the army of the Mississippi," said one Southerner.

Before Grant could strike a blow, however, Pemberton's forces retired south from the Holly Springs area to a better defensive position behind the Tallahatchie River. Covered with dust and sweat after another long march, the Missourians established camp near Wyatt's Ferry, west of Abbeville, and about twenty-five miles below Holly Springs. A Southern journalist reported that "much attention has been given to the earthwork defenses, and in addition to the negro labor, a brigade of stalwart Missourians have been industriously employed. It is to be presumed that it is no pleasant labor for these fighting heroes," a correct assumption for the Missouri Rebels despised this type of work.[2]

After a Federal cavalry raid had slashed the Confederate logistical line in Pemberton's rear and with Grant ready to attack the Tallahatchie position in front, Pemberton ordered his out-numbered troops south once more. In early December the Missouri Confederates trudged through the cold rain during another cheerless withdrawal. After marching in the mud for more than fifty miles, the Rebels halted behind good defensive positions behind the Yalobusha River, north of Grenada, Mississippi. There Pemberton's army built fortifications and set up winter quarters. By the end of December, Grant's drive through northern Mississippi would be aborted by Van Dorn's cavalry raid on the supply depot at Holly Springs, Mississippi, and by Nathan B. Forrest's destruction of the Mobile & Ohio Railroad from Jackson, Tennessee to beyond Union City, Tennessee. Likewise, Sherman's effort to take Vicksburg from the north and via the Yazoo River would be doomed to failure.[3]

The Rebels' many weaknesses in the face of Grant's offensive underscored how the West continued to be considered of secondary importance to the Virginia theater by the Davis Government. Not even Vicksburg's defense with the entire Mississippi River Valley at stake convinced the Davis Administration to concentrate enough troops to save Vicksburg. As analyzed one Southerner, "The danger now threatening Mississippi is greatly underrated by [our] Confederate government [and] unless our army has been or will be reinforced by the Confederate government, it will be destroyed." Other Confederates also understood the high stakes at risk in the strategic Mississippi Valley. One Rebel realized that all-important Vicksburg "is fated to be the scene of [the most] decisive conflict in the second war of independence [and] upon the gallant defense of Vicksburg [now] the success of our revolution has turned." Unlike the Confederacy, the North had neatly combined military and political objectives in targeting Vicksburg, knowing that the winning of the Mississippi would prove of immense symbolic and political importance. Indeed, Union victory at Vicksburg would demonstrate that the Southern nation was not the legitimate heir of America's historic destiny as the possessor of the greatest waterway on the North American continent.[4]

In preparation for their first winter in the Deep South, the Missourians' encampments took shape about a dozen miles southwest of Grenada on the army's left. There in north central Mississippi, the frontier exiles protected the Tuscahoma crossing of the brown Yalobusha River. Relative quiet returned to war-torn

Mississippi. Then the only crisis within the winter encampment was the outbreak of measles. The chaplain of the First and Fourth Missouri, D. J. Harris, who had already buried a good many of his comrades, died of the disease in December. Colonel Gates fell victim to the smallpox but shortly recovered. During this medical emergency Missouri Brigade members were quickly vaccinated under the towering oaks and cypress lining the Yalobusha.

The winter respite was a period of rejuvenation. Decent food was abundant, better health returned, and wounds from past battles healed with rest and the advent of colder weather. After the devastating losses of the first two major battles of the Missouri Brigade, Lieutenant Warren wrote to his father, and explained that, "our numbers have been terribly reduced. Regments [sic] that numbered last spring when we entered Miss 7 or 800 men can scarely [sic] muster 2 & 300 men. What are left, are Veterans." Indeed, the Missouri Brigade had lost almost two-thirds of its strength since beginning duty in Mississippi.

At that time the never-ending routine of drill for those veterans continued along the Yalobusha as intensely as if they were still State Guard rookies, while the Missouri Brigade fine-tuned its precision maneuvers and tightened discipline for future battles. In the process, the Missouri Brigade further enhanced its reputation as the best disciplined and most thoroughly-drilled unit in the West. From the first day of viewing the Missouri Brigade, General Pemberton, with a gift for understatement, stated that he was "very much pleased" with his Missouri troops.[5]

One of Colonel Riley's soldiers, twenty-year-old Private William E. Nichols, a farmer from Marion County, wrote his last letter home and described that tranquil period along the sleepy Yalobusha: "We are laying in Camp having chicken fights and having a good time, generally [and] should I live to see this war over I expect to return to Marion [County, Missouri] and live there for the rest of my days. I think it is the best country and the best people that I have ever seen in the Confederacy."[6]

The Missourians' long-standing goal of liberating the home state from occupied Union control seemed to take a step forward on December 24. President Davis reviewed the army at Grenada. "He has seen no better soldiers, than the 1st Mo Brigade," proudly wrote Lieutenant Warren in a letter to his father. The tall, grave-looking president, wrote twenty-year-old Private William T. H. Snyder in a letter, promised that the Missouri Brigade would be "sent to Mo in the spring. Dear Parents when I think of fighting on Mo soil it makes me feel as big as Burks dog [an analogy indicating elation]. all the Boys are in the biggest spirits imaginable and are as determined sett [sic] of fellows as ever you saw. Victory is perched on our banners and God grant it many still continued so [and] if I could march in front of New Madrid [Missouri] with 'Bowen's gallant Brigade' I think I could do 'double duty' in killing Yanks. It would seem as if I was avenging my dear down trodden friends. God grant that I may yet see that day." Missouri soldiers like Private Snyder, a farmer from New Madrid County, would continue to die east of the Mississippi.

According to Dr. Albert Castel, "Pemberton felt that the Missouri Brigade was absolutely essential to the safety of the [most strategic] fortress," in the West, Vicksburg. The significance of the role a single unit of that size could have in a major campaign cannot be duplicated in the annals of Civil War historiography.

Ironically, the high quality performance of the Missourians during the Grenada review ensured that they would continue to serve east of the Mississippi for years.

In one Southern journalist's words, the frontier exiles "were acknowledged by all to be the best disciplined [troops in] the field." Upon viewing the Missouri Rebels, General Joseph E. Johnston, the department commander who like Pemberton had been transferred from the East, exclaimed to General Price how he had "never [seen] better discipline, or men march more regularly." General Bowen readily agreed, saying, "Nor I, even in the old [United States] service."

One newspaperman's column, read widely throughout Dixie, perhaps presented the most appropriate tribute to the Missouri Brigade: "No troops in the West, or in the East, in the provisional army, or in the old United States regular service, have ever exhibited more perfect and beautiful drill and military order than the Missouri troops. These veteran soldiers never falter in battle. They are never whipped! They do not seek sick furloughs. They do not straggle. When batteries are to be taken, they take them! When an enemy is [to] be routed, they charge him with a shout of defiance. They have met the foe on fifty battle-fields! They may be killed, but they cannot be conquered!"[7]

Heightened by the false promise of being unleashed to reclaim Missouri in the near future, the soldiers made Christmas especially festive. As Lieutenant Simpson wrote in his diary, "Many of the soldiers drunk on whisky [sic] [and] at night much confusion in camp [with the] firing of guns & pistols. Some making speeches [,] some swearing & fighting & some gambling." One of Colonel Riley's soldiers, Private John T. Appler, recorded in his diary that the Missouri "officers had a big dinner, all got drunk [and] had a fight and a merry Christmas with all." The fatal year of 1862 ended on a positive note for the Missouri Brigade members. However, the year 1863 would bring almost unbelievable hardships and suffering for the Missouri boys.

Had these somewhat naive and trusting Missourians known the future, they might well have followed the threat made by one more realistic Missouri Brigade member: "...being as we are used to seceding, I'd secede the second time, take this [First Missouri] brigade, go over into Missouri, and I be durned if I didn't fight anything that came to me, Yankee or secesh"; a typically defiant frontier attitude that grew more prevalent among the Missouri exiles as the war lengthened.[8]

Already by January of 1863, the fates of many of the Missouri Confederates were described in a desperate appeal published in a Mississippi newspaper that winter: "Wherever the lurid fires of battle have burned, there sleep the sons of Missouri. Long they guarded the gate of this [Mississippi] valley and withstood the advance of the foe: now they fight the battles of the Confederacy on the soil of Mississippi. Brave men! One day we shall have our homes! We battle for the South—the whole South; and all we ask is the boon of independence" and adequate supplies of clothing to ward off winter's cold.

Indeed, by the time of the first light snowfall in north central Mississippi, the Missourians' butternut-hued uniforms hung in shreds and many soldiers were barefoot. Clothing taken from the Yankees was not enough to fill the void, and nothing was forthcoming from either the Union-occupied home state or the Confederate government. The Missouri Rebels now looked more like scarecrows than the elite troops of the Confederacy.

Efforts to obtain supplies of clothing were sporadic and infrequent at best. For instance, Lieutenant Warren reached the Missouri Brigade's encampment on January 1, with 120 pairs of shoes and other articles of clothing that he had purchased in Mobile. But such attempts were never enough to meet the demand. In desperation, therefore, more advertisements were placed in Southern newspapers, pitifully begging for donations of clothes and shoes for "the naked and destitute soldiers in the army of Gen. Price." Unlike Confederate troops from other states, the Missourians could not use the resources of their Federal-controlled state. A Mobile journalist reported with dismay, "Those [Rebels] from Missouri are cut off from all such aid. They depend upon us, in whose midst they are fighting and suffering." But an inadequate supply of socks, shirts, and pants was forthcoming from the materiel-short South.[9]

By that time, Major Hubbell had relinquished command of the Third Missouri to Colonel William R. Gause. Born in Ohio, Gause held the distinction of being the Missouri Brigade's only Northern-born regimental commander. Defying the odds, he had recovered from a bad wound suffered at Corinth and returned in high spirits to take command. In the charge upon Corinth's fortifications, the attorney had been knocked unconscious by an exploding shell. Colonel Gause, age twenty-four, was a natural leader in battle, and had won the respect of all. Among the Missouri Brigade's ranks, Gause was considered to be a young officer of much promise and, best of all, a fighter.[10]

Also by the beginning of 1863, William Wade's star was on the rise. Wade had been promoted to lieutenant colonel, serving as the chief of the Missouri artillery battalion assigned to Bowen's division. Colonel Wade had declined a comparable position as Price's Chief of Artillery during the summer of 1862. The Marylander decided to remain only a captain of his artillery unit because "since my election to command this battery I have tried to the best of my ability to perfect it & make it servicable [sic] in the great cause in which we are engaged [and] the battery has won a very flattering name [and] hence it is I feel an insurmountable objection on seperating [sic] Myself from the Command." Captain Wade's unflinching loyalty to his Confederate battery had made it one of the most reliable Southern artillery units in the West.[11]

Another reorganization came in Bowen's division on January 21. Bowen took command of only the Missouri Brigade, while General Green assumed leadership over the division's other brigade of veteran Missouri and Arkansas boys. General Price then commanded the division, but General Bowen soon resumed charge of the best division in Pemberton's army. The most drastic change involved the transfer of one of the most experienced and popular commanders in the Missouri Brigade, the hard-fighting Colonel Gates. Both the First Missouri Cavalry (Dismounted), and the Third Missouri Cavalry Battalion (Dismounted) were transferred into the division's other brigade, the second brigade.[12]

As if to compensate for the loss of a leader of Colonel Gates's caliber, the Missouri Brigade now gained a commander in General Bowen, who was one of the best Confederate tacticians in the West. Bowen had been a cadet at West Point and an experienced officer in United States service. More than ever before, those superior fighting men needed a stern West Pointer to command them so that the Missouri Brigade could continue to evolve and mature to reach its fullest potential. The Missouri Brigade's development had begun and advanced to impressive heights under the leadership of General Little. General Bowen continued that tradition of excellence, completing the work left unfinished by General Little and making "the South's Finest" even better.

Brigadier General John Stevens Bowen, died of disease

Courtesy Missouri Historical Society, St. Louis
(Unpublished Painting)

The native Georgian's potential had been evident at West Point, where he excelled in the toughest courses that the academy offered. In 1853, he had graduated high [13th of 52] in his West Point class. After two years of training United States cavalry recruits at Carlisle Barracks in south-central Pennsylvania and then fighting Comanches on the Texas frontier, he had altered his life's course by suddenly retiring from the military in May of 1856. Bowen soon settled down in Carondelet, Missouri, with his young wife Mary Lucretia Preston Kennerly. He then had pursued his life's dream, putting his military education to good use by becoming an architect. There, just south of St. Louis he built a stately mansion atop a ridge overlooking the Mississippi. Business fortunes soared when the ex-army officer from the Deep South became a partner in a newly-formed architectural firm in St. Louis, Bowen and Miller.

Eager to uphold Southern interests in the West, Bowen had wanted to participate in the 1850's sectional conflict in "Bleeding Kansas." But community, business, and familial commitments kept the restless Bowen firmly anchored in St. Louis. By that time he had become a captain of a Missouri Volunteer Militia unit from Carondelet, the City Guards. Bowen's chance for direct participation in the sectional conflict finally came when Kansas Jayhawkers struck the Missouri border during the fall of 1860. The Kansas Red Leg attacks caused the governor of Missouri to call out the state militia in the Southwest Expedition. Since the raiders vanished before the expedition reached the western border, the militia brigade returned to St. Louis after two weeks of duty. But a reliable deterrent force had to be left on the border to protect the people of western Missouri throughout the winter from future Jayhawker attacks. Therefore, more than 300 miles west of Carondelet, Colonel Bowen and his Southwest Battalion remained on the border for almost six months.

One of Bowen's early contributions to the Southern war effort had been to put sections of western Missouri on a war-footing months before Fort Sumter. As if realizing that civil war was inevitable, the far-sighted Georgian had issued rifled-muskets to local militia companies and drilled them with an urgency seldom seen at such an early date.

In early May of 1861, the Southwest Battalion returned to St. Louis to be captured at Camp Jackson along with the pro-Southern militia. Bowen had intercepted the marching Federal columns with General Frost's letter, which acknowledged no wrongdoing, and attempted to present it to General Lyon. The letter from the militia brigade commander had been instantly refused, and Bowen galloped back to the doomed encampment west of St. Louis.

After his capture and parole, and a visit to President Davis to secure a colonel's commission, Bowen had begun organizing the First Missouri Regiment at Memphis during the summer of 1861. The new Confederate colonel showed much passion not only for the Southern cause, but also for his adopted western border state, composing a popular song entitled, "Missouri." One of Bowen's emotional verses reminded the Missouri exiles that:

> "They've invaded your soil, insulted your Press
> Mowed down your Citizens and shown no redress
> Then swear by our honor your chains shall be never
> And add your bright star to the flag of eleven."

General Bowen had seen distinguished service in Tennessee, Missouri, and Kentucky before the holocaust of Shiloh. As a colonel commanding a brigade, he had bullets clip off strands of his hair before being knocked out of action with a bad shoulder wound at the bloody Peach Orchard on April 6. But his greatest day had been on October 5 at Young's Bridge on the Tuscumbia River. Then, General Bowen thwarted Rosecrans's pursuit with skillful delaying tactics to help ensure that the Army of West Tennessee would live to fight another day.

A Mississippi newspaper reporter in the winter of 1862-63 introduced General Bowen to the Southern people: "Gen. Bowen was one of the Camp Jackson prisoners taken by Lincoln's Red Republican forces precipitated upon St. Louis, before the secession of Missouri. Well have those bandits attoned [sic] for the outrage at Camp Jackson. Some of those brutes were met by Bowen at Shiloh. Some of them will shed no more innocent blood. Gen. Bowen is a gallant man—a skillful officer—a true patriot—and a gentleman in his private and personal character. May he live to see his country free, and once more repose securely in his pretty mansion at Carondelet!"[13]

The tranquillity of winter quarters along the Yalobusha River was abruptly shattered during January of 1862 by the largest display of ill discipline in the Missouri Brigade's history. General Bowen issued an order forbidding those individualistic frontiersmen to leave camp without signed passes. A mutiny broke out when the boys of Company I, Fifth Missouri, expressed their disapproval by refusing to appear on dress parade. A heavy guard was sent to arrest the mutineers, but the Company I soldiers grabbed their muskets, assembled in line, and held the enforcers at bay with fixed bayonets. Therefore, Colonel McCown ordered Company E, Fifth Missouri, to assist the guards. But Company E's Lieutenant Warren recorded in his diary, "The mutineers refused to be taken alive!" Then the mutiny was on the verge of erupting into a full-scale battle, for other Fifth Missouri companies and hundreds of other Missouri Brigade members rallied to the support of those defiant Rebels, who were rebelling against their own rebellion. Warren described the frustration of quelling the escalating revolt, for "we could do nothing with them without causing Bloodshed." A tense standoff that pitted Missouri Confederates against Missouri Confederates lasted the entire day.

Finally, after tempers cooled during the night, General Green talked some sense into the mutineers on the following morning. At last the feisty Rebels who were rebelling simultaneously against both the United States and the Confederacy voluntarily laid down their rifles and marched off to the guardhouse. Clearly, at least on two cold days in January, those angry warriors failed to live up to their hard-earned reputation as "the South's Finest."

During that January in Mississippi, the Missourians finally received genuine Confederate uniforms for the first time more than a year and half after leaving home and more than a year of Confederate service! In one proud Rebel's words: "There was a suit of uniform issued to every man in the Briggade [sic]. Grey Pants, grey Jackets & grey Caps. The collars & cuffs of the Jackets are trimed [sic] with light blue. The men feel very proud of them being the first uniforms that they have recieved [sic]." Much of the free time of winter was spent in playing a popular card game of colonial antecedents known as "seven-up," drinking apple brandy, writing letters, and reading the Bible.

But the fun ended when the Missouri Rebels received orders to depart from their quiet village of winter cabins. During January dozens of Confederate units entrained south for Jackson, Mississippi, as most of Pemberton's forces shifted southwest, closer to Vicksburg. There thousands of Southern troops concentrated to resist the Unionists' threat to Vicksburg from the north and the Mississippi River, where the Union Navy operated at will. At the end of January, General Bowen's orders to prepare to move south immediately caused much rejoicing. In one Missourian's words: "There were several train loads [of troops] and a jolly good time we had. After being cooped up all winter it was a great relief to get out of camp and go somewhere, although we were shipped like a lot of cattle. Our boys would always get gay after a few months in camp and want to fight, and if there were no enemy handy, we would fight amoung [sic] ourselves."

By early February the Missouri Brigade was being transported by rail closer to Vicksburg to reinforce the citadel on the Mississippi if necessary. Some discipline broke down on the cold, rainy journey, after the Rebels had purchased rot-gut whiskey and "Louisiana Rum" at Grenada, and "the boys have plenty of Whiskey and there a great many of them tight," wrote Lieutenant Warren in his diary. Then the long trip through the dense forests of Mississippi continued south to Jackson. After a week's stay at the state capital of Mississippi, they then traveled west to protect the bridge on Big Black River, just east of Vicksburg on the Southern Railroad. During the second week of February the Missouri troops were encamped in the mud and swamps along the Big Black River, for "it was thought the Yankees may attack the City [Vicksburg] in rear," wrote Lieutenant Warren in his diary.

That was a lonely period for the young men from Missouri, far from families and with no female company available. A stoic Private Appler lamented in his diary, "St. Valentines day but they are *played out* and no place to send them. Our sporting times are over with valentines till the war ends, ..." In waiting for Grant's next move during this anxious period of cold rains and oceans of mud, death could strike quickly and unexpectedly. On February 22, for instance, two officers of the First and Fourth Missouri were killed in a railroad accident, proving that the daily existence of the average Confederate soldier was not without risks.

Several days later when the rains finally stopped, the Missouri "boys amuse themselves at games of ball," wrote one officer, who watched the enthusiastic games of baseball. Those were the last carefree celebrations of early spring before one of the bloodiest campaigns of the war. During that period General Price reviewed the Missouri troops for one last time and then said good-bye, before he returned for the Trans-Mississippi to continue the struggle for Missouri. General Bowen was guaranteed command of the Missouri-Arkansas division during the Vicksburg Campaign after Price's departure.[14]

Yet another crisis in the Confederacy's short lifetime occurred. General Grant was determined that Vicksburg had to fall during the spring of 1863. As if anticipating the crucial role the Missourians would play in the unfolding drama for Vicksburg, General Bowen and the Missouri Brigade received a new assignment on the Mississippi River at Grand Gulf, about twenty-five miles south of Vicksburg. The Missouri Rebel soldiers were optimistic and cocky about meeting with battlefield successes in the coming campaign, envisioning a bright future for an independent Southern nation. "Vicksburg is a worse snag than Fredericksburg," predicted Sergeant Robbins in a letter to his St. Louis family.

At that time the Missouri Brigade had never been in better shape. Private Dyson, for example, wrote in a letter, "The men are all in better health than they have been since they have ben [sic] in the service." Many of the sick and wounded had recovered during the winter. On March 9 the Missouri soldiers swung out of their western Mississippi encampment in perfect step, with flags flying and drums beating, heading for an obscure location called Grand Gulf. Those hardened veterans would soon make that town on the Mississippi River a household word across the South.

Few Missourians would ever forget the march southwest to their new assignment below Vicksburg. Cheering crowds lined the roads and expressed their gratitude to those westerners from the frontier. In one Southerner's words: "Such imperishable renown have the Missouri troops gained in the late battle of Corinth, that all are anxious to witness and cheer the brave fellows who have suffered so much [for which] the Southern people will never forget." As one Fifth Missouri soldier observed in his journal, "the First Brigade had acquired a great reputation with the citizens."

With the excuse of looking for stragglers, a few high-ranking officers themselves straggled behind the column and hunted for future wives or a lover for that night. Some enlisted men likewise slipped out of ranks to conduct lightning-swift raids on nearby farmhouses for food, while the owners watched and cheered the Missouri Brigade's passing formations. Clearly, such patriotic demonstrations by civilians often had its price, whenever the Missourians were nearby.[15]

Upon reaching the beautiful Grand Gulf area in the second week of March, the Missouri boys discovered that the once prosperous cotton port had been torched by the Union Navy and Army in June 1862. The river bluffs above the charred ruins urgently needed to be fortified to protect Vicksburg's southern flank and the mouth of Big Black River, just north of the town, before Grant struck with his characteristic ferocity. With only the Confederate strong-points of Vicksburg and Port Hudson left on the Mississippi, another powerful defensive position had to be established on the river between these two fortresses. With typical energy and skill, Bowen immediately had his troops and local slaves working around-the-clock on an extensive network of fortifications.

Despite the hard, sweaty work, spirits remained high in anticipation of the inevitable clash with Grant. In the opinion of the optimistic Colonel Hubbell, "Our future looks dark, but surely freedom's battles once begun, can but end in victory." Private Dyson wrote to his wife, telling her with pride of his determination to fight to the end: "You may not expect me home until peace is made or we gain a footing in Mo." Dyson's defiance was a representative attitude among the Missouri soldiery before the Vicksburg Campaign, which in part would explain their superior fighting performances in the hard days ahead.[16]

By the time two Union warships that had passed Port Hudson and ascended the Mississippi tested the new defenses at Grand Gulf on March 19, they were greeted by the imposing spectacle of two forts, a complex network of defenses, and the field pieces of Guibor's and Wade's Batteries lining the commanding bluffs. Indeed, in remarkably short time Bowen had skillfully transformed the high ground into a formidable bastion, known to the Federals as the "Little Gibraltar" of the Mississippi. During March the defenders were vigilant, expecting the Union Navy to continue to probe the strength of the Grand Gulf fortifications, just below the "key to the Mississippi and the Gibralter [sic] of the Southern Confederacy," fortress Vicksburg.[17]

Several Union ships reappeared to test the new defenses early on the night of March 31. Father Bannon wrote in his diary that, "the Fed Boats surprised us." Stationed in Grand Gulf's fortifications, the Missouri artillery and the gunners of Company A, First Louisiana Heavy Artillery, recovered from the surprise and blazed away with an accurate return fire. According to a Sixth Missourian, "there was a pretty brisk fire kept up for fifteen or twenty minutes [the shells] made a crashing noise amongst their vessels, but they all passed by, we received no damage from their guns, but one of our own guns bursted, killing two men and wounding eight others." That disaster at Fort Wade wrecked havoc among Guibor's battery.

Captain Guibor was one of the unlucky casualties. The France-born battery commander fell with severe stomach and arm wounds. Guibor never entirely healed from his life-threatening injuries, but he continued to serve during the war. The following morning, April 1, at Port Gibson, Father Bannon and comrades buried the two St. Louis boys killed by the cannon's accidental explosion. The thick Irish brogue and the inspiring words of the Missouri Brigade's chaplain emotionally affected the mourners at the heavily-attended funeral service. Later the Missourians began to sense that their isolated and under-manned position on the Mississippi was square in the path of Grant's fast-approaching army.[18]

At Grand Gulf the Missouri Rebels were visited by the governor of Confederate Missouri, Thomas C. Reynolds. That was the first time that the governor viewed the exiles, but he soon realized that they were "the best [of] the state, ..." Governor Reynolds discovered to his surprise that those veterans "by long service under good regimental officers, had become well disciplined, and almost considered their camps their homes [and already] they were favorites of the people of Mississippi..." Private Ruyle agreed, writing that the "Brigade had acquired a great reputation with the citizens, particularly the female portion, ..." Governor Reynolds spoke to the assembled soldiers, and confirmed what they already knew was true: "that the road to [Missouri] lay [through and] over the wrecks of the Federal gunboats in sight of their fortifications." Indeed, General Grant's immense army had to be defeated somehow that spring and summer in Mississippi if the Missouri Confederates ever had any hope of crossing to the west side of the Mississippi in a belated attempt to reclaim the homeland that they had not seen in almost two years.[19]

CHAPTER NINE

Louisiana Expedition

To reduce the Confederacy's greatest fortress in the West, Grant understood that he had to strike Vicksburg at its weakest point, from the rear on the east. The first step in launching his strategy to bypass Vicksburg and the commanding bluffs lined with Rebel cannon called for sending the Federal army south from Milliken's Bend, Louisiana, on the west bank of the Mississippi and northwest of Vicksburg, on a march through eastern Louisiana. Then the Union army would cross to the east side of the Mississippi below Vicksburg, linking with the Federal Navy after the fleet steamed south past the Vicksburg batteries.

After learning a valuable lesson about the vulnerability of a lengthy logistical rail line because of the destruction of Holly Springs, Grant based his Vicksburg Campaign on the waterways of the Mississippi Valley. Previous efforts to capture Vicksburg had failed, and discontent in the North was rising, forcing Grant to make one last gamble to bring the Union a decisive victory in the West that spring and summer of 1863.[1]

The initial phase of Grant's plan looked deceptively simple on paper, but the lack of decent roads, the swampy terrain of eastern Louisiana and logistical difficulties greatly complicated the strategy. Grant's army would have to push south into the swampy bayou country of eastern Louisiana, moving parallel to the Mississippi through Madison and Tensas Parishes, Louisiana. To secure a key staging port from which his army could be transported across the "Father of Waters," Grant wanted to capture New Carthage, Louisiana, about thirty miles below Milliken's Bend and, most important, well below Vicksburg.

By the spring of 1863, much of the fate of the Northern war effort hinged upon Grant's risky plan of establishing a passable waterway from Milliken's Bend to New Carthage, via an extensive series of former Mississippi River ox-bows: Walnut Bayou and Roundaway Bayou, Bayou Vidal, and Lake St. Joseph, from north to south. If these former channels of the Mississippi could be linked together, then Grant would have a shallow, natural waterway which stretched roughly south and bypassed Vicksburg: a logistical support system for the invasion of Mississippi. Grant's audacious plan was a strategic turning movement to out-flank Vicksburg on the south.[2]

Major General John A. McClernand, an ambitious political general from Illinois who commanded the Thirteenth Corps, Army of the Tennessee, would lead the Union advance south into Louisiana's flat wetlands along the west bank of the Mississippi. Anxious for a spring campaign, those veteran Yankees from Ohio, Kentucky, Illinois, Wisconsin, Indiana, Missouri [including those Missouri Federals who had faced the Missouri Brigade at both Pea Ridge and Corinth], were "inspired by an eager desire to prove [their] usefulness, and impatiently awaited an opportunity to do so.''[3]

As this fertile land bordering the Mississippi warmed toward the end of March, McClernand's advance elements pushed south in the bright sunshine. As if promising that that movement heralded the initial steps of a strategy which would hasten the downfall of Vicksburg and the Confederacy, the Unionists easily captured the seat of Madison Parish, Richmond, Louisiana, and gained Roundaway Bayou after a light skirmish on the last day of March.[4]

Two unexpected forces slowed the Federals' advance. First, the sole guardians of that section of Louisiana were a few hundred Rebels of Major Isaac F. Harrison's Fifteenth Louisiana Cavalry Battalion.[5] Adept at waging partisan warfare, Harrison's horse soldiers were the only available Confederate troops in eastern Louisiana to protect Madison and Tensas Parishes. After being driven out of Richmond, the Louisianians retired slowly before the relentless Union advance, employing harassing tactics that proved effective.[6] As if by an act of God, another element impeded the Union surge through the rich Mississippi alluvial plain of eastern Louisiana: rising flood waters and a break in the levee of Roundaway Bayou. The Mississippi River's swelling with the winter run-off from the north and the hit-and-run strategies of the elusive planters of the Tensas Louisiana Cavalry became "obstacles [that] opposed our advance," wrote a frustrated McClernand.[7]

Firm resolve inspired Major Harrison's defenders in the struggle for Tensas Parish. The defenders' motivations were also fueled by their interpretation of the Federals' designs. For the common Rebel soldier without the benefit of strategic insights, the long blue columns snaking through Madison and Tensas Parishes amounted to just another example of evil Yankee activity. One Missouri Confederate, for instance, described in a letter to St. Louis how the Federal incursion through Louisiana's agriculturally-rich Tensas Basin was nothing more than "a thieving expedition from Milliken's Bend.''[8] Neither Rebel generals or enlisted men had yet fathomed Grant's scheme for placing his army in a prime position for launching an invasion that would deliver the Confederacy a death blow.

As expected, the heavily-outnumbered Louisiana horsemen could not stem the blue tide. Therefore, in early April desperate appeals for help from vulnerable eastern Louisiana went to the nearest Southern garrison, Grand Gulf. Although in another department and on the east side of the Mississippi, General Bowen immediately ordered Colonel Cockrell to the rescue. But more important, Bowen instructed Cockrell to ascertain the locations, dispositions, and intentions of the Unionists. Fortunately for Major Harrison's troopers, they could not have requested assistance from a better or more aggressive commander in Pemberton's Army than General Bowen.[9]

But General Bowen had to take a considerable risk in further weakening his already diminutive command at Grand Gulf. In addition, Bowen initially was hampered by having no boats to transfer his Confederates across the Mississippi and into Louisiana for the hazardous mission: a bad sign in case they would have to suddenly recross during an emergency.[10] General Bowen chose some of his finest troops for the all-important reconnaissance in Louisiana. Bowen ordered the First Missouri, the Fifth Missouri, the Second Missouri, and the Third Missouri into Louisiana during early April. Also General Bowen called up a section of Captain Guibor's artillery under Lieutenant William C. Corkery, a former militiaman of St. Louis, to support the Missouri swamp rats in the wilds of Louisiana. Reliable Colonel Cockrell commanded that crack task force, causing Lieutenant Colonel Senteny to take charge of the Second Missouri. Even though Cockrell had never previously led an independent command of that size on his own, he was Bowen's top lieutenant and the right man for a dangerous assignment on the other side of the Mississippi which called for a good deal of sound judgment, common sense, and tactical ability.[11]

On April 4 the initial wave of the Missouri reinforcements were finally ready to cross the mile-wide Mississippi, swollen by the high water.[12] Rebels of the First Missouri and the Second Missouri, along with two of Guibor's field pieces, boarded two steamboats for the short journey across the swirling river to Hard Times Landing, Louisiana, which was slightly northwest of Grand Gulf.[13] That long-ignored Missouri expedition was crucial at the time, since the primary purpose consisted of gathering intelligence for Pemberton in an attempted try to ascertain Grant's strategy before it was too late. No Confederate yet knew what the ever-unpredictable Grant was thinking or planning during that rainy April in Louisiana. But a perceptive and analytical officer like General Bowen suspected that the sudden flurry of Union activity in eastern Louisiana might be much more than simply another "thieving expedition."

Federal units, meanwhile, steadily crawled south through the wet bayou country between the Tensas and Mississippi Rivers, inching closer to New Carthage, more than thirty river miles above Grand Gulf. The Union advance was led by Brigadier General Peter J. Osterhaus, one of McClernand's division commanders, a St. Louis German officer who had helped capture Bowen and his Missouri militia boys at Camp Jackson and who had fought against the Missouri Brigade at Pea Ridge.

As no other single Rebel source in the spring of 1863, intelligence gathered by Cockrell's scouting parties could prove invaluable in alerting General Pemberton as soon as possible to the full extent of the danger, and supplying clues as to the time and place of Grant's invasion of Mississippi. For the most decisive campaign in the West to date, Pemberton's greatest weakness was the lack of accurate information and intelligence, especially on the mysterious west side of the Mississippi.

General Bowen learned on April 7 that Richmond had fallen, but at this time he only thought McClernand's Corps was "en-route to Natchez," which was more than another thirty miles south down the Mississippi.[14] The key mission of the Missouri Rebels, therefore, was to solve the riddle. With darkness masking the crossing of the Mississippi, the steamboats full of Cockrell's troops churned upstream against the current, making for the wooded Louisiana shore. Hundreds of Missouri Confederates, with three days' rations in haversacks and full cartridge-boxes, disembarked at the muddy landing just before daylight on April 4.

Then on Louisiana soil for the first time, Cockrell's veterans made preparations for a circular march northwest, roughly in the direction of New Carthage, after the sun dropped in the west. The Southern formations swung under the Spanish moss-draped oaks and towering cypress at 5:00 p.m., trudging along the narrow dirt road bordering Lake St. Joseph, past sprawling cotton plantations of a scale unseen in Missouri. The westerners in gray encamped at some unknown location among the fertile fields, after skirting the curvature of ribbon-like Lake St. Joseph for hours. Sunday April 5 dawned clear and bright, providing more good weather for pushing further north to reach Bayou Vidal, a former bend of the Mississippi that was a flooded expanse of water, above Lake St. Joseph and adjacent to the Mississippi.[15]

After marching a grueling twenty-five miles from Hard Times Landing, the Missourians arrived at Harrison's hidden encampment in some thick woods along a slight ridge cutting across the extensive cotton plantation of Judge John Perkins. A Confederate congressman later exiled to Mexico, Perkins had lived in luxury on one of the finest plantations in Louisiana, Somerset. Here, on Bayou Vidal's south bank, about six miles below New Carthage, Cockrell established his base camp on good defensive terrain with the brown bayou between him and the Yankees.[16]

Exhausted after marching the entire day and sometimes wading through the flooded road, the worn Rebels shivered in the coolness without fires, so as not to betray their location. Soldiers devoured their meager pork and corn bread rations from haversacks like hungry wolves. Uniforms were wet, and no tents had been brought along. The ill-clad soldiers went to "sleep under the immense live oaks that were between his dwelling and the river." But Cockrell's men were well-suited for duty in the vastness of eastern Louisiana, and could easily adapt to the new challenges of this important assignment, benefiting from years of the frontier experience, guerrilla fighting in Missouri, and the campaigns of the Missouri State Guard. On the south, where Negro Bayou intersected Bayou Vidal, the Missouri boys took a position southwest of New Carthage, close enough to see the twinkling campfires and to hear the beating Union drums in the hostile encampments.[17]

The Louisiana Rebels looked upon those hardened Missouri soldiers as saviors. One Louisianian felt elation with the timely reinforcement, writing for a Southern newspaper that, "Gen. Bowen, although situated in another department, promptly sent forward a portion of his brave Missouri boys, under command of the gallant Col. Cockrill [sic], to our relief. With these noble and veteran troops, under command of their brave and determined leaders, we feel confident of being able to hold the enemy in check—more at present, we cannot attempt. Too much praise cannot be awarded to the chivalrous Bowen, and the gallant [Missourians], for their promptness in coming to the relief of our little command. They deserve, and will receive, the lasting gratitude of the people of this section."

Besides attempting to ascertain the strategic situation, General Bowen felt that his reconnaissance into Louisiana might also present an opportunity to punish a careless and confident Union advance. Indeed, the Unionists were dispersed and becoming increasingly bold after capturing New Carthage on April 6. Therefore, Bowen would soon eagerly ask General Pemberton that "if rumors of a heavy advance of the enemy's column into Tensas Parish prove true, shall I endeavor to prevent it with my entire command?" Fundamentally Pemberton responded in the negative, but that failed to diminish Bowen's ardor to strike a blow at the first good opportunity.[18]

Wanting to take immediate advantage of the Federals' haphazard advance through difficult and flooded country, Bowen had bolstered Cockrell's force with two more regiments, the Fifth Missouri and the Third Missouri, not long after the initial wave of Missouri Rebels arrived.[19] These reinforcements almost doubled Cockrell's numbers to about 1,800 men, who were stationed at one of the most "magnificent plantations of Louisiana." Middle-class yeomen from Missouri prepared to defend a land of cotton, the property of a slave-owning aristocracy and one of "the highest and wealthiest sections" in Louisiana.[20]

Colonel Cockrell, meanwhile, almost immediately found the Yankees. Skirmishing with the lead elements of Osterhaus's division continued on April 6-7, after the bluecoats had converged in overwhelming numbers to capture New Carthage.[21] At Pliney Smith's plantation, two miles north of the village where Roundaway and Vidal Bayous intersect, Osterhaus established his headquarters at the mansion house.[22] The Missouri Rebels at first only anxiously listened to the sound of fighting on April 7, but responded with enthusiasm when they were finally ordered "out in line of battle, [taking up positions and] waiting for them." Cockrell's eager foot-soldiers, however, saw no action during this reserve duty behind the Louisiana troopers, who had been chased out of New Carthage and off Joshua James's Ione Plantation.[23] At that time the confident Unionists had no idea that hundreds of veteran Confederate infantrymen from Missouri were hidden before them in the forests and plantations of Tensas Parish.

At James's Plantation below New Carthage along the Mississippi and the levee, the Federals had secured one of the area's few solid pieces of dry ground, which then resembled an island. That position of approximately twenty acres was soon turned into a Yankee fortified base camp amid a flooded wilderness.[24] In the contest for Tensas Parish, the high ground at James's Plantation and the cluster of buildings—gin house, saw mills, mansion, slave cabins—suddenly became the region's most strategic point.

Colonel Cockrell fully understood the urgency of recapturing James's Plantation, which was "now in a tolerable state of defense." Consequently, on the Perkins's Plantation, Cockrell's encampment stirred with activity in preparation for an immediate strike northeast to capture the all-important dry ground of the James's Plantation, which bordered the Mississippi.[25]

Guibor's veteran gunners from St. Louis and their 12-pounder cannon might prove decisive during such a completely unexpected offensive by the Confederates from Grand Gulf. Somehow negotiating the flood waters, deep sand, and belts of forest with their cannon, Guibor's St. Louisans boldly "went up to the feds out post [at the James's Plantation]" to initiate the engagement just before noon on April 8. Along with a section of 6-pounder field pieces from Captain Archibald J. Cameron's Louisiana Battery, the Southern guns bombarded the base camp that General Grant had to have to achieve his objectives during the campaign.

Captain Guibor's 12-pounders inflicted more damage than the lighter field pieces of the Louisiana gunners in the cannonade that echoed eerily through the marshlands. The surprised Unionists quickly rallied and responded, blasting away with two mountain howitzers. In addition, the Yankees of the Sixty-Ninth Indiana Volunteer Infantry were positioned in trenches behind barricades, standing firm with the determination "to hold [the position] at all hazards."[26]

The accurate fire of those veteran Rebel cannoneers continued to pound the defenders, and eventually the rain of shells proved too much for the Indiana soldiers. One Confederate projectile exploded in the Federals' midst, "causing great consternation." Some of Cockrell's swamp foxes grew irritated with their passive role as spectators. Wrote one amazed Southerner, "While the artillery duel was in progress, a few of the Missouri boys waded through the water some distance, and exchanged shots with the Yankee sharpshooters. But for the timely and peremptory order our boys would have charged the enemy inside of their fortifications." Several hundred Indiana soldiers were driven off, when Cockrell's troops ended the three-hour contest with a chorus of Rebel Yells, closed in for the kill, and tipped the balance of power, resulting in the capture of the Union position and the first Missouri success in Louisiana.[27]

So far, April 8 had been an action-packed day, resulting in a small but significant Confederate success. The Missourians and Louisianans had won a surprising victory in the swamps by capturing the Unionists' advance outpost, which was a staging area for conducting raids on the surrounding countryside and a potential port for the Union's fleet of warships and transports. But Colonel Cockrell had wanted to do more on April 8 than overrun a single fortified Yankee outpost. The ever-aggressive colonel had placed most of his troops under cover behind Bayou Vidal south of James's Plantation, in well-concealed ambush positions to annihilate any counterattacking Federals who thought they had clashed with only rag-tag Southern militia. Then after wiping out the overly aggressive Unionists with this classic guerrilla strategy, Cockrell planned to take the offensive and attack north to exploit his gains.[28]

The Confederate scheme for victory in Tensas Parish was working as planned. Rebel battle-flags waving over the James's Plantation dangled temptingly before the Unionists, providing the irresistible bait. However, darkness fell early and quickly on that early spring day, and thwarted Cockrell's well-conceived ambush. Near nightfall the Indiana regiment, bolstered by reinforcements, counterattacked to regain the key high ground as expected but halted with the setting of the sun. The Union strike had been launched about an hour too late to continue pursuit of the withdrawing Rebels as Cockrell had envisioned. With the Yankees suddenly charging out of the dark woodlands by the hundreds, the advanced contingent of Confederates, the bait, adroitly retired south toward the main force as planned.

The fading light and the lateness of the attack left Cockrell's concealed troops waiting in vain. In one frustrated Confederate's words, the Federals "advanced and took their former out post, burnt the house & still remain there."[29] On the cool night, the one-time conquerors of the James's Plantation splashed back through the cold standing water to their camps in the forests along muddy Bayou Vidal.[30]

Then the Tensas Parish battles temporarily ceased. Both sides retired to their high ground sanctuaries amid the flooded countryside. In the days ahead, skirmishing flared as blue and gray parties reconnoitered and stumbled into one another in the thickets, wetlands, and cane-brakes. Acclimating quickly to this strange Deep South wilderness, the versatile Missourians scouted the bayous and flooded countryside in dugout canoes and skiffs, pinpointing Yankee dispositions, mapping the area, and ambushing Union scouting parties. Point-blank brushes with the blueclad pickets and scouts in boats resulted in dueling "mosquito fleet" engagements on the water. One Missouri Brigade member recalled that these "many miniature naval battles were stoutly contested" along the bayous and lakes of Tensas Parish.[31]

When not on picket duty, the Missouri expeditioners found recreation along the coffee-colored Bayou Vidal in their spare time. On one Sunday, for example, some of Cockrell's enlisted men enjoyed a "Grand fishing excursion to-day, but no fish caught," wrote one soldier in his diary. But there was much more to worry about in Tensas Parish than fat catfish and buffalo fish in frying pans. Seemingly endless rains poured down on April 11, adding more water to the already badly-flooded countryside along the Mississippi.[32] The level of the Mississippi rose, which could strand Cockrell's isolated task force on the west side of the river.

Both General Bowen and Colonel Cockrell refused to relinquish the idea of regaining the crucial high ground around the James's Plantation. Hence, they wanted to resume the offensive once they spied an opportunity.[33] Aggressive action might upset Grant's plan of invading Mississippi via the Louisiana bayou country. The Union forces were widely dispersed to protect the thirty-mile-long logistical and communication line from Milliken's Bend, the levee, and roads. And most important, the bulk of McClernand's Thirteenth Corps had not yet arrived in the area. If the Yankees could not be stopped, then perhaps a Rebel cut in the Mississippi levee might submerge more of the whole country in water, especially because of the recent deluge.[34]

Since the James's Plantation had been reinforced and more heavily fortified, Cockrell wisely ruled out a frontal assault. The best target now seemed to be the Dunbar Plantation, on Bayou Vidal, adjacent to and west of James's lone Plantation. There, on the right of the Federal line, they could inflict considerable damage if the Yankees could be caught by surprise. The Dunbar Plantation base camp, situated on a thin neck of dry land a quarter mile west of the James's Plantation, had been a thorn in Cockrell's side from the beginning. From that encampment Union cavalry had often raided the country as far west as the Tensas River. Those Yankee strikes had deprived the Louisiana and Missouri soldiers of resources, a blow to an isolated band of Rebels existing on a precarious supply line to Grand Gulf. In addition, that westernmost Federal position had to be knocked out because it threatened Cockrell's left flank.[35]

Therefore, the Confederates planned to loosen the Yankee grip on the Dunbar Plantation. In addition to security concerns, Bowen and Cockrell wanted most of all to upset Grant's plan for using a Louisiana staging area on the river as a launching pad for the invasion of Mississippi. By mid-April, General Bowen was beginning to decipher Grant's plan. As early as April 11, thanks to a steady trickle of intelligence flowing to Grand Gulf from the Missouri Rebels, Bowen began to understand that Grant's mysterious movements along the chain of bayous were calculated to gain a point of the west bank of the Mississippi, realized that the Union strategy "looks practicable," and even correctly predicted that Grant's objective was New Carthage.

Therefore, after receiving Bowen's April 11 evaluation by telegram, General Pemberton actually had more time, by more than half a month, to marshal an effective counter-strategy and defense to attempt to stop Grant than historians have previously realized. Clearly the Missouri Rebels had already succeeded in their mission by providing the early intelligence to enlighten Pemberton, handing him precious advance warnings of Grant's intentions before mid-April.

Sensing that he was correct about Grant's strategy, Bowen had informed Cockrell to further evaluate the situation and prepare for offensive action. Rebel informants learned from the Yankees that Grant's forces were attempting to ease below Vicksburg. All the while more accurate intelligence about the Unionists' dispositions and movements was continuously being gathered daily by the Missouri scouts and carefully analyzed by Bowen and Cockrell.

Soon new information spurred General Bowen to definite action. He was also concerned that Union gunboats would link with the James's Plantation Federals and cut Cockrell's task force off from Hard Times Landing and his supply line. Consequently, the dynamic team of Bowen and Cockrell began an audacious attempt to capture New Carthage. The Rebel plan called for a difficult night march and a surprise attack at dawn to capture Dunbar's Plantation, smashing into the right and rear of the Unionists in one stroke. Then Cockrell's troops would roll east, hitting the Yankee force at the James's Plantation from behind and in the rear of their strong defenses. Simultaneously, to the east the Confederate double envelopment would be completed by a task force of Missourians and Major Harrison's revenge-seeking Louisiana Rebels, who would swarm north up the levee to attack the James's Plantation base camp in front, while its garrison would be facing Cockrell's assault from the west and rear.

Then the serious fighting would begin. After wiping out both the Dunbar's and James's Plantations strongholds, the Missouri Confederates planned to unite, charge east to capture New Carthage and plant battle-flags on the bank of the Mississippi. Bowen and Cockrell planned not only to destroy the advance elements of McClernand's corps with barely 2,000 Rebels, but also sought, in one Unionist's words, to "capture the whole of us" in a desperate bid to frustrate Grant's plan.[36]

With feverish activity, the eager Missouri Confederates made preparations all day on April 14, while the cold rains continued to pour down.[37] The veterans of the Fifth and First Missouri, Second Missouri, Third Missouri, and the battalion of Harrison's Louisiana cavalrymen, dismounted, quietly moved out from Perkins's Plantation in the chilly early hours of the night of April 15. Colonel Riley's First Missouri, the Second Missouri, and some Fifth and Third Missouri companies, under Colonel Cockrell, initially swung west, while the bulk of the Fifth and Third Missouri and the Louisiana horse soldiers, under Colonel Gause, simultaneously headed east, before both forces shortly turned north toward their respective objectives. Colonel Gause's command soon took up concealed positions below the James's Plantation.

Concealed by the darkness and dense woodlands, meanwhile, Colonel Cockrell led his Missourians north up Bayou Vidal's west bank as it curved toward Dunbar's Plantation, after crossing Negro Bayou. Most of the country remained flooded with the Mississippi continuing to rise. As rapidly as possible, Colonels Cockrell and Riley hurried their troops onward, hoping to launch the dawn flank attack.[38] Soldiers held cartridge-boxes and rifled-muskets high in the dark woods and fields that had become sprawling lakes, while the countryside lay bathed in moonlight.[39] The splashing, cursing, and slipping in the mud and water continued throughout the night. In one officer's words, "We waded from knee to waist deep, floundering along as best we could" for nearly eight miles in the darkness.[40] Soaked Missourians swatted insects and tried to keep their balance, while toiling north to beat the sunrise as they had done more than a year before at Pea Ridge. The hard march in the blackness, wote one Rebel in his diary, was over a seemingly never ending "vast sheet of water."

Intersecting Bayou Vidal from the west, an overflowing Mill Bayou stood as the most formidable obstacle between Colonel Cockrell's advancing forces and their objective, Dunbar's Plantation. There, just southwest of Dunbar's Plantation on Bayou Vidal, the veteran skirmishers of Company F, Fifth Missouri, and Company G, Second Missouri, waded forward in advance and fanned out, taking up skirmish positions in the cold standing water before the final push to launch the western phase of the pincer movement. No orders were spoken and hand signals were used.

**Captain
Archer Christian Bankhead**
Courtesy L. Carey Bankhead,
Jefferson City, Mo.

**Lieutenant
Benjamin Looney Mitchell,
Fifth Missouri, C.S.A.**
Courtesy William F. Moore,
Redstone, Ala. (Unpublished Photo)

Colonel Cockrell hurriedly deployed his troops for battle within sight of the quiet Yankee encampment and the Dunbar mansion, silhouetted by the faint glow on the eastern horizon. Shivering, with wet uniforms but dry ammunition, the Confederates once again waded forward through the water and mud.[41] Hundreds of veteran Rebels churned steadily northeast amid the murky sea of Mill Bayou.

While Colonel Cockrell's flank and rear attack converged on Dunbar's Plantation, Colonel Gause's Missourians and Major Harrison's several hundred Louisiana partisans were poised behind the Mississippi's levee to the south of James's Plantation ready to strike the Sixty-Ninth Indiana and exploit any success won by Colonels Cockrell and Riley.[42] Silent Missourians under Colonel Cockrell, meanwhile, labored onward with orders not to fire first, so they would not warn the Yankees of the attack. But just after 4:00 a.m. on April 15, the graycoat skirmishers smashed into the Second Illinois Cavalry's pickets, and the fight was on.[43] The blue troopers shot first, but then, according to one attacker's diary entry, "our skirmishers fired, killed one, wounded one," during the fight.[44]

After surrounding and cutting off the Union pickets, hundreds of onrushing Confederates overran the Dunbar Plantation with a cheer that rang across Bayou Vidal. The gray waves struck the Unionists' flank and rear, and easily brushed aside all opposition, swiftly pushing the Yankees rearward, capturing four Prairie Staters in the cool, half-light. With a shout, the water-soaked Rebels continued forward "with the expectation of surprising and capturing a regiment of the enemy."

In spite of the success, Colonel Cockrell was not able to destroy the garrison, which was a necessary objective for the overall plan. Upsetting Cockrell's delicate strategy and the all-night march, most of the base's garrison, the Forty-Ninth Indiana and the One Hundred and Twentieth Ohio Volunteer Infantry, had retired to a reserve position during the night.[45] The frustrated Private Appler wrote in his diary at Dunbar's Plantation, "To our great surprise [the] federals left during the night...."[46] Thanks to the Unionists' withdrawal, a probable Rebel success had vanished with the dawn.

The mud-splattered Confederates, nevertheless, had captured one of the Northern army's base camps necessary to support Grant's army upon its eventual arrival. Colonel Cockrell ordered a squad of Second Missouri soldiers to check Dunbar's mansion for Unionists. The western Rebels bounded up stairs with cocked rifled-muskets and in one bedroom discovered "a very ludicrous and amusing scene [for] a tall, spare, grave-looking personage, accompanied by a young, full-grown, athletic and very black negress, was marched down." More laughter erupted among the Confederates with the knowledge that the Yankee of exotic tastes was none other than the Protestant chaplain of the Second Illinois Cavalry![47]

With no time to waste, the dripping-wet Missourians hastily gathered captured supplies, a boon for soldiers who had subsisted off a shaky logistical line for nearly two weeks. Meanwhile, Cockrell surveyed the tactical situation and the extent of his success. Still full of fight, the colonel prepared to send his troops sweeping east over the strong point of James's Plantation where Colonel Gause's forces were waiting, before attacking New Carthage. But then the Federal units that had retired earlier and escaped the daylight attack "were rapidly assembling in arms" and within sight.[48] Clearly the advantages of surprise and momentum had slipped away. Hundreds of Ohio and Indiana soldiers rallied to assist the Second Illinois Cavalry. In that way Cockrell's strategy was thwarted. The colonel, therefore, was forced to cancel the attack east that would have unleashed Colonel Gause's forces at the levee below James's Plantation.[49]

Colonel Cockrell's Rebels, meanwhile, rested and remained in a defensive stance and collected booty around the Dunbar mansion "till daylight [when seeing] the fed cavalry coming across the field, ordered to fall back, fell back to where we crossed [Mill] bayou, in double quick, made a narrow escape," Appler wrote.[50] Soaked and cold Missourians labored south, melting like ghosts into the flooded cypress forests still hazy with morning mists. Another opportunity had been missed. While splashing through muddy waters, the Rebel raiders brought with them loads of bacon, cavalry horses, 100 slaves and new blankets.[51] But far from being the meaningful success it could have been, Bowen's and Cockrell's promising strategy only "proved to be an unsuccessful trip throughout," lamented Private Appler.[52]

In retaking their base camp, the Federals captured at least two Missouri soldiers.[53] And another one of Cockrell's Rebels was left behind, Private David Presley Woodruff. The young man had been cut off in the watery thickets during the fight. In a belt of woodlands on the Dunbar property, Woodruff suddenly found himself in a dilemma: "separated from my [Company A, Fifth Missouri] squad [and] surrounded by the enemy on three sides and a lake [Mill Bayou] 2 mi[les] wide on the other." But the lone Confederate grabbed a Unionist's loose horse. With the Yankees within a stone's throw, the soldier decided to make a run for it across the open water. "Taking my reins in my mouth, a revolver in each [hand], I spurred my mare and she dashed off like a grey hound. Heedless of bullets I fired as fast as I could." Nearly forty Yankee cavalrymen lined up along the shore, blasting away with carbines. In running the gauntlet, Woodruff had his "hat riddled" with bullets and his horse killed, but he safely reached the Perkins's Plantation hide-out without a scratch.[54]

The danger had only begun for Cockrell's isolated troops. Federal gunboats had run past the Vicksburg citadel on the night of April 16 and headed south downriver for New Carthage. The following day the entire Union fleet reached New Carthage. Then more vulnerable than ever before, Cockrell's task force and General Bowen himself, who had recently arrived in Louisiana to ascertain developments and to exploit any success, seemed destined to be cut off from Mississippi and their Grand Gulf base.[55]

Fearing a counterattack, Colonel Cockrell quickly shifted his camp closer to the Mississippi in partisan fashion and erected a ring of light defenses, after the April 15 missed opportunity. Unaware of the danger of prowling Yankee naval vessels on the Mississippi, the Missouri expeditioners were collecting firewood and cooking breakfast on the morning of April 17. From a Rebel look-out atop a tree or from the roof of a house on the Perkins's plantation, the cry of "a gunboat! a gunboat!" echoed over the base nestled amid the Louisiana forests.[56]

According to one Missourian, "We looked out on and up the river and the gunboats were in sight about five miles away, then there was great excitement in camp. Everybody was trying to get out of camp first."[57] Other Confederates then saw the columns of black smoke billowing up from the Union gunboats on the river. Half-cooked strips of Uncle Sam's bacon and biscuits were taken from skillets and tossed in haversacks. Frantic Missourians collected gear and hustled into column in record time, ten minutes.[58]

At the last moment a busy Colonel Cockrell remembered to dispatch a courier to recall the patrolling grayclad sailors of the "mosquito fleet," for they now had to be left behind. The abandoned Second Missouri soldiers of Captain Wilson's

Company G and Company B, under twenty-three-year-old Captain John S. Wells, a Virginia-born farmer from Lincoln County, later crossed the Mississippi on their own during a daring escape. Finally Cockrell's regiments moved out on the double-quick along the road toward Hard Times Landing on the Mississippi River in a race that they could not afford to lose. The departure was timely, for a Union gunboat steamed down the Mississippi and shelled Cockrell's deserted encampment not long after the Rebels had slipped away.[59]

Major Harrison's Louisiana troops would have to resume defending their land by themselves against impossible odds. One Missouri infantryman never forgot the hard-fighting Rebels of the Fifteenth Louisiana Cavalry Battalion, whose war had only begun in Tensas Parish: "This command, which was familiar with every nook and corner, with every pass and stronghold in that locality, was not to return with us. It was left behind [and] it was a fine battalion of men."[60] The Louisiana cavalrymen continued to oppose the Unionists' powerful advance in defending their homes and families against the invaders. Those partisans were shortly driven into the refuge of the Tensas River swamp.

The Missourians' desperate race for the Mississippi left no time to rest, while the swiftly-moving column of graycoats followed the full loop of Lake St. Joseph as it curved around to Hard Times Landing. Marching almost at a trot along the lake's south shoreline and wading through the flooded road, the Missourians continued the marathon competition between themselves and the Federal gunboats during the race for the landing.[61] They needed to cover twenty-five long miles to gain the landing during the sprint in which "not a soldier broke ranks, not one lagged behind."[62]

While pushing onward, Rebel eyes anxiously scanned the distant horizon to the east, hunting for "the first sign of that fatal smoke which was to cut us off from the east side of the Mississippi and make us prisoners."[63] The day was scorching hot and typically Louisiana humid, but the brisk pace continued mile after mile over the flat terrain dominated by the bright green of spring. The race to reach the river "was the fastest time for that distance infantry ever made in our part of the army."[64]

Against the odds, Cockrell's men finally gained the west bank of the Mississippi before dark. Soldiers fell to the ground of Hard Times Landing in exhaustion. The rest was brief, for Cockrell's infantrymen shortly scrambled aboard the steamboat *Charm*. But the danger was far from over. Federal vessels suddenly appeared on the river. For what seemed like an eternity, the steamboat struggled against the current, but finally gained Mississippi soil, while "in sight of some of the fleet." The Missourians' true, good luck *Charm* safely gained the Mississippi shore and safety.[65]

The Missouri Brigade's service, a dangerous and exciting thirteen-day period, in soggy Louisiana ended. The outnumbered Confederates had won no significant success during a rain-soaked April in the vastness of the Louisiana bayou country. But during their reconnaissance on the west side of the Mississippi, the Missourians had not only made the Unionists more cautious and slowed Grant's advance to buy General Pemberton more precious time to respond to the Yankee build-up and eventual Mississippi invasion if he chose, but they also had gained something that could not be priced: valuable intelligence from the mysterious west side of the Mississippi. The critical information and strategic insights gained by the Missourians amid the obscurity of the Louisiana's swamps and bayous helped convince General Bowen of the details of Grant's plan to subjugate Vicksburg by pushing his army south through Louisiana and crossing the river below the South's greatest stronghold in the West.

Bowen was able to predict that Grant's powerful Federal army would cross the Mississippi not only below Vicksburg, but also below Grand Gulf to land in Claiborne County, Mississippi. That was the bold Union strategy that would result in the winning of the Mississippi before the end of the summer of 1863.

Unfortunately for the South, however, high-ranking Rebel commanders, including General Pemberton, continued to think differently from General Bowen. Indeed, week after week, Confederate leadership ignored the critical information that Cockrell's soldiers continued to uncover in Louisiana and deliver to the highest levels of military leadership in Mississippi until it was too late. That was the most reliable and best information that General Pemberton received about the details of Grant's strategy, which Bowen understood earlier than previously thought.[66]

In addition, Grant needed to be checked in Louisiana for another reason. Thousands of Yankees swarming unchecked through eastern Louisiana meant that the resource-rich Tensas and Madison Parishes could no longer supply Vicksburg with foodstuffs. That shortage of foodstuffs would be keenly felt by the Rebel garrison of Vicksburg in only a few months.[67]

But, more important, had General Pemberton and others of the Confederate high command reacted quickly to Bowen's prophetic warnings about the strategic implications of the Union threat in Tensas Parish, Louisiana, during April of 1863, then perhaps an adequate defense of Mississippi could have been galvanized, and Vicksburg might have been saved. In embarking upon his bold but risky strategy, Grant had gambled that the Confederates would not be able to respond in time to adequately meet the challenge and deliver a counterattack that might destroy both his plan and his army. In making this decision and betting on the inability of Southern leadership to respond to the greatest threat to the life of the Confederacy in the spring of 1863, the general from Galena, Illinois, had won his first great success of the Vicksburg Campaign without firing a shot, which helped to pave the way to decisive victory.

At the last moment, General Bowen and his crack Missouri soldiers had given the Confederacy one final chance to reverse fate in the decisive Western theater. The inability of Southern leadership to exploit the intelligence derived from the Missourians' reconnaissance during the Tensas Parish expedition provided another classic example of a missed opportunity that helped lead to the failure of the Confederate experiment in nationhood.

Brigadier General Francis Marion Cockrell
Courtesy State Historical Society of Missouri, Columbia, Mo.

CHAPTER TEN

Fatal Spring in Claiborne County

General Bowen's repeated warnings about the accelerated Union activity across the Mississippi River in Louisiana continued to cause little alarm at Pemberton's head-quarters at Jackson, but at least General Green's brigade had been ordered to bolster the Missouri Brigade at Grand Gulf. After that timely reinforcement during the third week of April, General Bowen's entire division was at Grand Gulf. Bowen's garrison at Grand Gulf, however, remained too weak for the challenges ahead. Experienced officers, like the Missouri Brigade's commander, Colonel Cockrell, who was still in his twenties, continued to draw attention and admiration. One Rebel, for example, wrote that "when I first saw [Cockrell], he was an unusually hand-some man in appearance, worthy to command that splendid band of Missourians whom Jefferson Davis pronounced [as] the finest body of soldiers he ever grazed upon."

That spring the Southern people were praying for deliverance from the Yankee invader, placing their faith in the much-acclaimed Missouri Confederates to hold the strategic southern flank of Vicksburg at Grand Gulf. As a Mississippi newspaper-man reported:

> It may interest our readers to know that we have at [Grand Gulf] some of the best troops in the Confederacy [and] these veteran bands who stood the shock at Elkhorn, at Shiloh, at Iuka, at Corinth, are there. We know those troops of old. With Bowen a General, and other veteran officers in command; with such soldiers to fight; with equal conditions, and with equal numbers; with God on our side; we have a strong confidence that the invader will be [cut] in two the day he met these men in battle! They might be overpowered—they might all be killed, but they will not be conquered! If they are sacrificed by any unlooked for combination of numbers, it will be to the foe a most costly triumph! Such a disaster, however, we do not anticipate. Our brave men are ready for the fray. They would move in battle with such a shout as only they can give. Memorable will be the field when they are encountered by the Yankees. It is almost certain "somebody will be hurt."[1]

The Missouri Rebels shortly would face the initial phase of Grant's invasion largely on their own. General Grant planned to land his immense army on the Mississippi River's east bank at Grand Gulf, and launch his invasion of the Magnolia State to gain Vicksburg's rear. Grant was already a master of combined army-naval operations and expertly utilized his superior resources to create the necessary diver-sions to keep Pemberton baffled. As if knowing that all hell was about to break loose at Grand Gulf, a Vicksburg journalist wrote a final prayer for Bowen's isolated troops: "All honor to our noble band at the Gulf! May the Angel of Justice guard and protect them."[2]

Only a few more days of relative calm remained at Grand Gulf. Young Corporal Mike Casey, a St. Louis Irishman of Landis's Battery, wrote home saying "We are having a dull time here [and] have absolutely sunk to such a degree of laziness that the little gunboat fights &c, which we have don't even amuse us." The lull before the storm was a busy period, nevertheless. Captains Wade's and Guibor's Missouri cannoneers prepared for the upcoming fight, strengthening the earthworks and drilling to sharpen skills on Fort Wade's big guns: a 20-pounder Parrott, an 8-inch naval gun, two rifled 32-pounders, and a 100-pounder Blakely rifle, an English import which had been run through the Federal blockade.

Enlisted men slipped out of camp at night and made attempts to get "acquainted with some of the damsels of Port Gibson," knowing that they might never have another chance. Other Missouri Rebels became intimately acquainted with the slave women of a nearby plantation. At least one such offender was an older and highly-respected officer, but obviously no gentleman, and a dignified church leader in Missouri. When Captain Canniff's Irish Catholics rounded him up with about 60 other Missourians, who were drinking and carousing among the slave cabins with the "comely saddle-colored girls" during a single late night raid, the arrested Fifth Missouri officer swore that he "only went there to keep the boys straight." Much laughter greeted the flimsy excuse of the defrocked captain.

Life had almost returned to normal for high-ranking officers, such as General Bowen, after he was once more reunited with his attractive, high-spirited wife, Mary. In addition, Mrs. Erwin and her infant daughter had reached the Rebel community of white tents near the brown Mississippi in mid-April to rejoin Colonel Erwin. She had been banished by the Federal authorities from her fine home in Independence, Missouri, in early 1863. Mrs. Senteny likewise joined her young husband, Colonel Senteny, who led the Second Missouri. Near the end of April, one Missouri soldier saw "all three [wives, Mrs. Bowen, Erwin and Senteny] at General Bowen's headquarters, chatting gayly with one another [and] their faces were bright and cheerful, and in a reunion with their husbands and friends they seemed perfectly satisfied and happy."

Many of the inexpensive tintypes taken of those young Rebels by a Port Gibson photographer would never be seen by wives, lovers, and children in far-away Missouri. Those last images of stern-faced Rebel warriors were lost forever, when scores of bodies would be tossed in narrow burial trenches or solitary graves at Port Gibson, Champion Hill, Big Black River, and Vicksburg.

Not long before the killing began in earnest, the exiles of the Missouri Brigade received a psychological boost from the issuance of distinctive battle-flags. Those banners had been sewn and earlier presented to General Price by the ladies of New Orleans. For the Missouri troops who had recently been swept by a wave of religious revivalism in timely preparation for the upcoming slaughter, the battle-flags decorated with large white Latin crosses on a blue field reminded them of their idealized role as crusaders in gray.

Such powerful symbolism that indicated a distinctive Christian heritage was especially encouraging to Father Bannon and other chaplains. The imagery of those battle-flags reinforced the chaplain's fusing of religion and Southern nationalism, strengthening bonds of righteousness and commitment.

The fateful day when Grand Gulf was targeted for destruction fell on April 29. General Grant needed to capture Grand Gulf, because the town's old steamboat

Banner of First Missouri Cavalry, C.S.A.
Captured by Roswell M. Clarke, Co. F, 11th Wisconsin infantry, at Black River Bridge, May 17, 1863; presented by Lieut. R. E. Jackson. Blue bunting, with red border; Roman cross of white muslin in left of field.

Courtesy Wisconsin Historical Society

landing and road leading southeast to strategic Port Gibson were perfect for quickly pouring thousands of troops inland. The early morning sunshine of April 29 shone over the springtime forests near the dark earthen fortifications of Grand Gulf, contrasting with the severity of the approaching showdown. A powerful fleet of Union gunboats steamed down the Mississippi and toward Grand Gulf to wipe the stronghold off the map. Behind the armada of warships came transports crammed with 10,000 Yankees.

Believing that Grand Gulf could be eliminated with one swift knock-out punch, Grant was optimistic, writing that he expected "soon to be able to report our possession of Grand Gulf [and] once there, I do not feel a doubt of success in the entire cleaning out of the enemy from the banks of the river." However, General Bowen and his obstinate Missourians, Arkansans, Mississippians, and Louisianians were supremely motivated that day. Northern victory at Grand Gulf would relieve much political and domestic pressure that was mounting against Grant and the Lincoln Administration, especially after Union setbacks in the East. Much was at stake at Grand Gulf.[3]

In employing three clever diversions, Grant correctly estimated that a cautious and indecisive Pemberton had not adequately reinforced the Grand Gulf garrison. At that time only one small Rebel division stood against the might of the Union Navy and eventually more than 20,000 Federals. Too few Rebel reinforcements would belatedly be ordered south and these would be only a small percentage of the total available around Vicksburg, because the defenders anticipated Sherman's attack at

Snyder's Bluff, north of Vicksburg. Besides this diversion, Colonel Benjamin H. Grierson's raid through the length of Mississippi and another Union thrust near Greenville, Mississippi, served as effective diversions to mask Grant's strike upon vulnerable Grand Gulf.

Pemberton finally ordered a division south from Vicksburg but only after the April 29 fight for Grand Gulf had ended. Drastically short on numbers, cannon, and supplies, Bowen and his division were left on their own to confront Grant's massive invasion into Mississippi. When the fleet of ironclads appeared at 8 o'clock on the morning of April 29, Bowen's division faced one of the most one-sided challenges of the war.[4]

The Federal armada struck Grand Gulf with everything it had. Under a fierce bombardment, Wade's and Guibor's artillery pieces, in the lower defensive bastion at Fort Wade, roared as never before and blasted away at the sinister-looking ironclads. General Bowen had placed the Third and Sixth Missouri in the trenches fronting the river, while the rest of the Missouri Brigade was massed in the woods on top of the bluffs: a hidden force which would swarm downhill like an avalanche, whenever the Unionists poured ashore. Four "pook turtles" and three newer ironclads steamed along the Mississippi's east bank, firing rapidly on the Rebel guns outnumbered more than ten to one. Almost every Yankee expected Grand Gulf to be reduced quickly.

After dueling for hours, the Union Navy gradually gained the advantage, although it received severe punishment from the accurate fire of the veteran Confederate gunners. During one of the war's most intense artillery cannonades, the Rebel defenses took a pounding of unprecedented proportions. According to a Fifth Missouri Irishman, who avoided exaggeration in his letter, the contest "for desperation, has not been equaled in the Mississippi." As if hunting game back home, keen-eyed Missouri riflemen picked off Union sailors, unleashing a sheet of flame from the lengthy network of rifle-pits.[5]

Much of the Union firepower was concentrated on Fort Wade, which held out defiantly against the naval onslaught. There Colonel Wade inspired his hard-working artillerymen to do their best, for much of the Confederacy's future hinged upon repelling Grant's invasion.

While four gunboats punished Fort Wade, Guibor's battery flag waved amid the exploding shells, which hurled immense showers of earth 50 foot high and deadly shrapnel in all directions. The Confederate artillery continued to roar in return, despite much of the parapet being leveled, and soaring casualties. Rebel gunners frantically shoveled away the dirt and debris and pulled aside bodies to permit the cannon to resume firing. After several hours, Fort Wade was bombarded until "all our guns [were] injured," wrote Lieutenant Richard C. Walsh, and eventually all were silenced. Fort Cobun held out longer, while being "hit again and again, but its pieces had not been disabled" during the most furious naval bombardment of the war to date.[6]

From a nearby boat on the Mississippi, General Grant watched the raging contest in awe, hardly believing that Grand Gulf and a band of Rebels could not be whipped that day. He gained more respect for his former neighbor from Carondelet, General Bowen, and his graycoat defenders, who had thwarted his invasion. Against impossible odds, Grand Gulf withstood the storm, forcing the Union Navy to break off the contest. After cheering their surprising victory, the worn Missouri and Louisiana cannoneers, black with dirt and powder, slumped down beside their big guns and many shortly fell asleep. According to one St. Louis artilleryman, "never before or after were they so thoroughly exhausted."[7]

Grant's invasion had been stopped after a five-hour engagement. Protected by a brilliantly-engineered and well-constructed network of fortifications, in large part due to Bowen's engineering talents, Wade's and Guibor's Batteries and the Missouri infantry took few losses. One shell had exploded in the trenches with a blinding flash, wounding 11 men of the Third Missouri. However, the greatest loss on April 29 was the death of Colonel Wade, who was hit by one of the last shots fired at Fort Wade. The shell struck the popular St. Louisan in the head, bringing death almost instantly.

To bolster public morale and broadcast the unexpected victory at Grand Gulf, a Southern newspaper encouraged the Confederacy with the promise that, "Colonel Wade has fallen, and others of

Colonel William Wade, killed at Grand Gulf
Courtesy Vicksburg National Military Park, Vicksburg, Miss.
(Unpublished Photo)

his command; but others take their places! Wade 'died at his post,' and the post is now held by his brave comrades!" In a jubilant Vicksburg, Bowen's firm defense was celebrated by a relieved populace, who cheered the "Glorious Victory!" But the hard fighting for Vicksburg had only begun. Unfortunately the surprising Rebel victory at Grand Gulf would be mostly forgotten because it was only a temporary success.[8]

Demonstrating typical flexibility, General Grant quickly readjusted his strategy to compensate for the setback. Grand Gulf's defenders prepared for another attack that would never come, and Father Bannon made preparations to bury Colonel Wade and other defenders at Port Gibson on April 30. Meanwhile, after the Unionists marched a short distance down the river's west bank to board their vessels below Grand Gulf, the Union armada of warships and infantry-filled transports continued south down the Mississippi, heading for a good landing site without Bowen's defenders.

Grant quickly negated Bowen's improbable victory at Grand Gulf by landing his troops farther south at Bruinsburg on April 30. The divisions poured inland like a blue flood toward Port Gibson, about a dozen miles east of the landing site, without meeting opposition during the largest and most successful amphibious landing of the war.

Disembarking hour after hour from transports below Grand Gulf and below the mouth of Bayou Pierre, the Yankee tide rolled east through the low-lying cotton lands along the Mississippi on April 30. A long, winding column followed an obscure dirt artery, the Rodney Road, which led east to the timbered high ground that Grant had to have to secure his grip on Mississippi soil and toward Port Gibson, where key roads led to Vicksburg, Raymond, Natchez, and Jackson. Eventually, more than 20,000 Federals swarmed deeper into Mississippi without encountering even Southern militia, while most of Pemberton's forces around Vicksburg awaited attacks which would not be launched. The complex chess game for the possession of "the key to the Mississippi and the Gibraltar of the Southern Confederacy" next resumed in the forests of Claiborne County, Mississippi.[9]

Initially, only Bowen's small division at Grand Gulf was close enough to the landing site, about a dozen miles south, to oppose Grant's invasion. To ascertain the Unionists' locations and movements amid the dense Mississippi woodlands, General Bowen had dispatched a small force from Green's brigade several miles west of Port Gibson.

The Missouri Brigade, meanwhile, stood in readiness for another attack upon Grand Gulf. From the imposing bluffs of Grand Gulf, the Missouri soldiers viewed the unnerving spectacle to the south throughout an anxious April 30: Grant's transports ferrying thousands of veteran troops down river for the crossing from the west to the east bank of the Mississippi. One prophetic Southern journalist predicted that "the experiment on the part of the enemy of taking Vicksburg by flank movements and investment has fairly been inaugurated [and] the ball has been fairly opened, and one or two weeks at farthest will test the fate of the Hill City [and] verily, the crisis is a most critical one." Again General Bowen and his men were mostly on their own to face the greatest threat to the Confederacy in the spring of 1863.[10]

General Bowen's only hope was that Pemberton might send enough reinforcements south from Vicksburg in time. In desperation, the native Georgian attempted to muster as many available troops as possible to resist the invasion, after having again bought Pemberton more time to respond to the threat with his successful defense of Grand Gulf. General Bowen reinforced 1,000 of Green's soldiers with General Edward D. Tracy's 1,500-man brigade of Alabama troops and a Virginia battery late on April 30. But Bowen realized that he needed "from 15 to 20 thousand men to insure our success." Not even the later addition of a Vicksburg brigade of Mississippi and Louisiana troops, under General William E. Baldwin, could encourage General Bowen about the Confederate prospects for success at Port Gibson.

Indeed, it seemed that nothing could stop 23,000 Unionists from pouring through the grain fields of the Mississippi's bottoms and the forests covering the higher ground of Claiborne County. Amid the dark woodlands, General Green and his Arkansas boys clashed with the Federal vanguard in a hot, noisy skirmish during the pitch-black early morning hours of May 1, a sure sign to the Missouri defenders at Grand Gulf that all hell would shortly break loose.[11]

With the first pale light of May 1, the skirmishing began immediately, and then heavy fighting intensified along the timbered, rugged terrain of Port Gibson as the sun rose higher. Without adequate support or luck, Bowen understood that his outnumbered Confederates would be easily overrun by the blue juggernaut. Consequently, General Bowen ordered more than a thousand of his Missourians to leave Grand Gulf and hurry south to assist in the defense of Port Gibson before it was too late. At that time, however, the entire Missouri Brigade could not be used as a reinforcement, for it was widely dispersed. Bowen feared another attack on Grand Gulf. He stationed Colonel Senteny's Second Missouri on the Grand Gulf river front; the Fifth, Third, and Sixth Missouri, and Guibor's battery and a section of

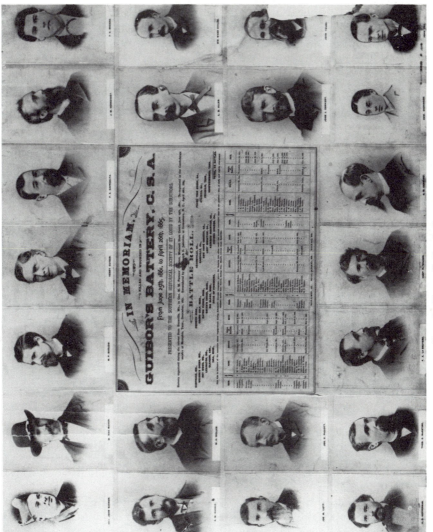

Captain Henry Guibor's Battery

Captain Landis's Battery atop the bluffs of Grand Gulf as a reserve force; Colonel Riley and his First and Fourth Missouri and Wade's Battery, now under the Ireland-born Lieutenant Walsh, as guards for a crossing on Bayou Pierre to Port Gibson's northwest. Colonel Riley's task force acted as a deterrent to stop Federal gunboats from steaming up the bayou, which flowed northeast between Bruinsburg and Grand Gulf, and cutting off Bowen's forces to the bayou's south.

By 10:00, a long gray column of 1,259 Missouri Confederates pushed southeast through the sweltering heat toward Port Gibson, while firing swelled higher and Bowen's already slim chances for stemming the Yankee tide diminished with each passing hour. Cockrell's reinforcements embarking on the long race to bolster Bowen's command around Port Gibson were the Third, Fifth, and Sixth Missouri, and two field pieces of Landis's battery and Guibor's battery of four guns.

Commanding Guibor's artillerymen was Lieutenant Corkery, a capable St. Louis officer who had been lately charged with "ungentlemanly conduct," for gambling with the enlisted men. Corkery, a native of Ireland and "a giant in strength," had first demonstrated his leadership qualities at Pea Ridge. And in the recent defense of Grand Gulf, the Irish officer had boldly led a squad of cannoneers on his own initiative, running a field piece by hand to almost the river bank to rake the gunboats from an advantageous position.

Those reinforcing Missouri Rebels were hardly fresh, for the Vicksburg Campaign had begun for them earlier than for most of Pemberton's troops. Unfortunately for the South, the Missouri Brigade's units were the last reinforcements to reach General Bowen, who had about 6,800 troops to stop almost 23,000 bluecoats in the forests west of Port Gibson on May 1.[12]

After covering eight miles in two and a half hours through the summer-like heat, past hills colored with the whites of flowering dogwoods and the flaming red-buds, the panting Missourians reached the field of strife about noon. There, about two miles west of Port Gibson at the vital junction of the Bruinsburg and Rodney Roads, which allowed Bowen to shift his troops more effectively than his opponent, the worn Missouri soldiers aligned as a strategic reserve to meet the advancing Federals, who were fighting furiously, achieving gains, and advancing east up both roads.

The arrival of the Missouri reinforcements could not have been more timely, for the over-extended Rebel lines were buckling under tremendous pressure. General Bowen quickly positioned his dependable Missourians at the key road junction to help stabilize the defense after the collapse of Green's position. Shortly, Green's battered units fell back from their shattered first line, astride the Rodney Road, and rallied upon Baldwin's and Cockrell's steadfast troops.

Then after a second defensive line was established closer to Port Gibson and the situation stabilized, the Sixth Missouri troops raced northwest to reinforce Bowen's mauled right wing just below Bayou Pierre. Colonel Erwin's hardened soldiers were about to be hurled into the midst of the Federal onslaught, then pouring east along both sides of the Bruinsburg Road.[13]

On Bowen's right wing to the north in the Buinsburg Road sector, Tracy's Alabama brigade had been roughly handled and was in serious trouble. An attorney and politician, Tracy was the first general killed in Vicksburg's defense and his hard-pressed defenders were low on ammunition, but not fighting spirit. In addition, the Botetourt Artillery, Virginia Volunteers lost two cannon to the victorious Unionists.

To stem that crisis, General Green's and Colonel Erwin's troops reinforced Bowen's right on the north. Upon reaching the Bruinsburg Road defensive line, Erwin's troops were directed by General Green to the left of Tracy's heavily-pressed brigade. Sweat-drenched and dirty, Erwin's troops immediately advanced at the double-quick through a field of young corn atop a narrow ridge. Meanwhile, a long line of blue skirmishers attacked the fast-moving column of Rebels, who made fine targets on the high ground. In running this gauntlet, occasionally a Missouri soldier dropped wounded.

Colonel Erwin halted and deployed his 400 Sixth Missourians on Tracy's left and just below the brow of a wooded ridge, extending the Alabamians' battle-line south. After the Missouri soldiers shifted a short distance to the right, or north, Green's regiments shortly aligned on Erwin's left, and completed dispositions south before the inevitable clash. To slow the onslaught from the west, the Sixth Missouri's colonel quickly threw out his best skirmishers, and soon a hot fire-fight blazed across the ridge. For about an hour, the Sixth Missouri maintained its elevated defensive position in the timber on the left of the Alabama brigade and southwest of the William Andrews House, which stood near the Bruinsburg Road. Always eager for action, Colonel Erwin was already half-mad that the day was already going against the Confederates. Even worse, the defenders in this sector had lost the initiative and were now "doing nothing."

But then suddenly, a critical situation developed on the right of the Alabama brigade at a vulnerable moment when the Alabama Rebels were redeploying. The powerful Federal line smashed into the Alabamians' right. If the attacking Unionists gained Bowen's right flank, then the Rebel line would be rolled up and shattered. A successful Yankee advance in this northern sector would result in the capture of the Bayou Pierre bridges, cutting the Southerners off from Pemberton and Vicksburg, and perhaps destroying Bowen's right wing, or even his entire command.

Colonel Erwin rose to the challenge. Quickly sizing up the situation, Erwin realized that "it was apparent that unless some assistance was afforded them they [the Alabama brigade] would be driven from their position. I therefore felt that a prompt action was necessary..." There, in the early afternoon, Colonel Erwin understood that the best strategy to reverse the tide at that critical moment was to strike quickly and as hard as possible. Without orders to advance and with young boys in gray beating their drums, Erwin hurriedly deployed his regiment for the attack. The sound of metal clanging upon metal rang across the wooded ridge, while Confederates fixed bayonets in the sunshine of another hot day in Mississippi. Mounted on a fine horse before his neat formations, a resplendent Colonel Erwin drew his saber, then roared, "Forward!"[14]

High-pitched Rebel Yells split the air, echoing over the forests of Port Gibson. The Sixth Missouri's assault poured off the ridge, catching the Federals' advancing legions by surprise. Heavily-wooded hillsides and rough terrain partly screened the Sixth Missouri's attack, allowing the onrushing Rebels to arrive almost before the Federals knew what had hit them. Erwin's charge rolled over everything in its path, smashing through the Union skirmish line before tearing into Grant's left wing.

The captured Virginia cannon, manned by Yankees, fired point-blank, but failed to stop Erwin's onslaught. Union infantrymen frantically worked those captured field pieces, mowing down groups of attackers. One soldier falling mortally wounded was Private Barbour, the sixteen-year-old of French descent from the Bootheel region, when a point-blank load of canister crushed both hips. Eagerly Missouri sharpshooters slaughtered the battery's horses, ensuring that those guns could not escape. Angered Missouri Confederates clubbed down Federal gunners with musket-butts or ran them through with bayonets. Then victorious, Colonel Erwin's Rebels raised a cheer as they recaptured the two 12-pounder howitzers of the "Old Dominion" battery.

But Colonel Erwin was far from finished on this blistering afternoon, having only begun to fight. Thinking that the Alabama regiments on his right had followed on his heels to exploit the success, Erwin led his cheering troops onward through the tangles of underbrush, clinging vines and suffocating humidity, for the reeling Unionists could not be allowed time to rally. Carrying the Sixth Missouri's colors forward after the flag bearer had been shot down was Private William E. Franklin, age twenty-seven. Franklin would shortly exchange battle-flag for scalpel and saw, becoming the regimental assistant surgeon.

Although he was forced to leave behind the two disabled cannon, Erwin decided to relentlessly press the attack. Consequently, Erwin's Rebels continued to charge forward, pushing gradually southwest, before General Green's stationary battle-line to the east. The drive penetrated deeper into the dark, tangled woodland with a will of its own. In total, the bold advance of the lone Confederate regiment covered more than a quarter mile, slicing further into Grant's left wing. "With one regiment I charged the whole left wing of the Federal army," proudly wrote Colonel Erwin of his most audacious gamble.

The Missourians continued pushing in a southerly direction, advancing under the tall magnolias and cypress draped with Spanish moss. Shortly, the regiment fragmented upon encountering a twisting maze of ravines, and cane and briar patches amid the blinding jungle of forest and the rougher and lower-lying terrain drained by Centers Creek. Seemingly the near-tropical woodlands and the deep ravines of the environs of Centers Creek had swallowed up the Sixth Missouri.

The regiment's right-wing of several companies under Major Stephen Cooper, a farmer of twenty-six who had lost his left arm at Corinth, veered away from Colonel Erwin's section. Meanwhile Colonel Erwin's regiment continued forward in the tangled wilderness, leaving Major Cooper's companies even further behind. Numerous attempts to reunite the regiment were in vain, only resulting in hours being lost amid the steaming woodlands of Port Gibson.

Knowing the danger of a small party stranded and unsupported in unmapped woodlands teeming with blueclads, a frustrated Cooper eventually turned his troops and eventually led them eastward out of the creek bottoms. Major Cooper's contingent successfully reached the higher ground and apparently linked with either Green's or Tracy's battle-line.

Undeterred by the difficulties, Colonel Erwin was inclined to keep moving. Despite losing more than half of the Sixth Missouri to Yankee marksmenship and the fragmentation of his regiment, and without being certain of his exact location or the tactical situation, Erwin pushed onward, apparently attempting to further exploit his advantage or to escape the tangled valley of Centers Creek and gain the Bruinsburg Road. But much time had been wasted, and it was late afternoon.

After veering southeast out of the creek's environs to strike higher and less brushy terrain, emerging from a timbered ravine into the sunlight, the Sixth Missourians finally escaped from the woodlands and entered an open field, which led uphill to the Wheeless House. There, just south of the Bruinsburg Road, Erwin's troops confronted a large number of Yankees once again, after having slipped through a wide gap between the brigades of Green and Tracy.

On the hill's other side was the advancing Forty-Ninth Indiana Volunteer Infantry, a tested regiment composed of rawboned westerners, who had recently clashed with the Missouri Rebels in the Louisiana bayou country. Those Federals were surging forward through a deep ravine. Instantly, Sixth Missouri skirmishers darted through the field and up the slope, taking possession of the house. Shortly the gray wave of sharpshooters, in and around the Wheeless House, peppered the Federals' lower position. But the accurate Rebel fire only stirred up a hornet's nest. Commanding the Indiana regiment, hard-fighting Colonel James Keigwin decided that he was going to take that house and ordered a charge.

On the house's opposite side, meanwhile, Colonel Erwin now realized that he had stumbled into a heavy Union force. He, consequently, instantly sent his troops charging up the hill to secure the high ground before it was too late. Both the northern and southern colonels understood that the commanding terrain around the Wheeless House had to be taken immediately. Then the Sixth Missouri and Forty-Ninth Indiana simultaneously charged forward to gain the same objective. Hundreds of westerners in blue won the life-and-death race uphill with the westerners in gray, capturing the house and driving off the outnumbered Missouri skirmishers.

Not stopping to catch their breath, the Unionists continued charging past the building and through the yard, while firing on the run. The contest for the high ground hinged upon which side first gained the split-rail fence behind the house. That fence, which spanned across the field at the highest point, became the bone of contention. But the race was one-sided, for the downhill sprint was easier for the Federals than the charge uphill for the thoroughly-exhausted Sixth Missouri. Again the spunky Indiana troops won the competition, dropping behind the fence with the onrushing Sixth Missouri only 30 yards distant. In Colonel Keigwin's words: "We were about one minute too fast for them."

About to be hit with a point-blank volley, Colonel Erwin ordered his soldiers to halt and fire, beating the Unionists to the punch. A close Rebel volley swept the fence, knocking down some startled blueclads behind the bullet-splintered rails. But the Confederates' fire mostly sailed high with few out-of-breath Missourians having time to compensate for elevation by aiming muskets lower than usual in firing uphill. In return, a scorching Yankee volley poured from the fence-line, exploding into the graycoats' faces. Casualties were high, for the Sixth Missourians were badly exposed and caught at close range in an open field on high ground without cover. To escape the death-trap, Colonel Erwin ordered his command to fall back, leaving behind many dead and wounded young men from Missouri scattered across the hillside in Claiborne County. Slow deaths from disease, months in filthy hospitals, and the nightmare of Yankee prisons awaited those injured Rebels abandoned around the Wheeless House.

After his hard-hit command retired downhill and across a deep ravine with the cheering Federals in hot pursuit, Colonel Erwin hurriedly reformed his survivors along the crest of an adjacent ridge, evidently west of the house and even farther away from the Bruinsburg Road and safety. There, south of the road in the path of the general Union advance, and still a good distance from the main Confederate battle-line, Erwin's Sixth Missouri continued to function as an organized unit, despite the shock of a point-blank volley, close Federal pursuit, the absence of Cooper's companies, and high losses. Additionally, some of Erwin's soldiers were cut off, captured, or missing during the confused retrograde movement. Perhaps at that point one Indiana infantryman captured his own brother, a Missourian in gray. After quickly rallying, the Sixth Missouri boys maintained a tenacious defense along the ridge-top, making a stand and returning fire. Wrote Lieutenant George R. Elliott in his diary, "We held them in check for an hour and a half, they on one side of a verry [sic] narrow ridge and we on the other, within 10 or 20 yards of each other."

Worn out and low on ammunition but still full of fight, the Confederates rested rifled-muskets on logs and trees, while delivering punishment. Private Matthew J. Moore, age twenty-two, found a good, but dangerous, perch from which to pick off blueclads. Although exposed in the open, Moore refused to leave his commanding spot from which he shot down Federals only fifteen paces away. Other soldiers of Company G passed an assembly line of loaded rifled-muskets up to the busy marksman from Platte County. Moore inflicted considerable damage, targeting officers and color bearers until felled by a serious wound. With the Yankees within a stone's throw, Missouri defenders cursed and taunted their adversaries, while loading and firing from the underbrush.

Colonel Erwin dispatched another messenger rearward to hurry up any reinforcements that should have advanced to exploit the Sixth Missouri's hard won gains. The aggressive colonel refused to give up the hope of success, no matter how slim. There, along the ridge-line, the Missouri Confederates kept blasting away into the swarms of Federals. But more and more Unionists began to converge upon the foremost Rebel position of Bowen's command. Cut-off and alone, the band of Sixth Missourians continued to fight from the protection of the ridge-top.

The forty rounds in Rebel cartridge-boxes, however, were dwindling fast. And after Erwin's advance so far in front of the main line, there would be no resupply of rounds forthcoming. Worst of all, no other Confederate troops had advanced with Erwin's counterattack. Nevertheless, the uneven struggle continued. Playing a key role on May 1, the Sixth Missouri's attack bought precious time, slowing Grant's relentless drive upon Port Gibson, and helping to save Bowen's right from being turned.

With the day going against him, Colonel Erwin felt a mixture of frustration and rage. With Rebel troops no longer advancing anywhere at Port Gibson, the isolated Sixth Missourians were in serious trouble. With some bitterness, Erwin lamented that if only the Alabama "brigade [had] joined me in the charge, instead of withdrawing at that time, we would have completely routed their left wing." But if Colonel Erwin had fully understood his regiment's quandary, he would have been much more upset: while the Sixth Missouri's location was unknown to Southern leaders, its vulnerable position was becoming well known to the advancing Unionists. Therefore, not only would no Confederate reinforcements or supplies of ammunition arrive, but also there would be no orders for the Sixth Missouri to withdraw. In his own words, Erwin refused to retire and forsake his "position which had been so gallantly won and perseveringly maintained."[15]

To the southeast of the Sixth Missouri's private war, Cockrell's two other regiments, the Fifth and Third Missouri, also made a dramatic impact on the engagement's outcome. In fact, their challenge was even greater than that of Colonel

Erwin's struggle. While Sixth Missourians fought and died, the Fifth Missouri, under Lieutenant Colonel Robert S. Bevier, and the Third Missouri, led by Colonel Gause, directed their efforts to save Bowen's hard-pressed left wing.

Shortly after arriving on the field with Cockrell's reinforcements, the Fifth and Third Missourians were dispatched south to bolster the left of the Rodney Road sector in the early afternoon. There, the sweaty Missouri boys rested and gulped down water from canteens, after taking a concealed reserve position behind Baldwin's heavily-pressured brigade on Bowen's left flank. While the battle raged furiously around them, the Missouri exiles, Bowen's last and only remaining strategic reserve, stayed there so long that some veterans thought that they would see no action that day.

Working miracles with what little he had available on May 1, General Bowen had skillfully divided his Missouri reserves, and deployed them most efficiently that afternoon to cover the two primary Union thrusts along the two roads leading toward Port Gibson. While the Sixth Missouri fought tenaciously to stop the Federal attacks on the north in the Bruinsburg Road sector, a final attempt to relieve the mounting pressure of Union assaults in the Rodney Road sector to the south was delegated to the Fifth and Third Missouri. In both sectors, a key mission goal of those elite Missouri reserves had been the same: win precious time for the arrival of Pemberton's reinforcements from Vicksburg.

All day General Bowen had made judicious dispositions in covering the two avenues east toward Port Gibson. Then Bowen correctly anticipated that the Federals would mount a great effort to turn his left flank, after the Yankee advances based upon the two roads had been barred by his well-positioned defenders. In a hot stubbled cornfield and a wooded ravine, the Fifth and Third Missouri, under Colonels Bevier and Gause, quietly awaited one of the toughest assignments of the war.

Meanwhile, the fighting escalated to levels seldom seen in the West, with Grant throwing thousands of troops forward in the fiery cauldron. Unleashing firepower to help keep the Unionists at bay, both Captain Landis's and Guibor's artillery pieces roared along the defensive line in the Rodney Road sector, growling angrily over the eerie landscape of Port Gibson.

Indeed, unlike any region ever seen by the Missouri farm boys, this haunting Deep South battleground in Claiborne County appeared foreboding and sinister, with the soft loose soil deeply cut in odd angles by water erosion from time immemorial. Drained by Centers Creek and its tributaries, that strange land was covered with a maze of branches, ravines, and gullies, which ran in every direction. The alien thickets, valleys, and cane-brakes of Port Gibson were part of a primeval world, almost impassable for both armies.[16]

As General Bowen had feared, the Rodney Road sector was strained to the limit by early afternoon. There, Southern resistance wavered under the unceasing pounding of Union artillery and infantry assaults. Without a suitable logistical link snaking down through the woods and across the rough terrain, Confederate fire sputtered as ammunition supplies ran low. A huge Yankee build-up prepared to smash through Bowen's center.

But the most danger of all existed farther south on Bowen's left flank. There, the right of Grant's line steadily grew and extended down a long narrow ridge, like a blue tidal wave. The day's greatest crisis was brewing with General McClernand's Corps attempting to turn Baldwin's left flank, the southernmost end of the Rebel

battle-line, with a powerful surge down the vital ridge that led straight to the Natchez Road and a decisive Union victory. If those Federals could not be stopped,
then Bowen's force would be captured or destroyed.[17]

Fortunately, the game of maneuver for Port Gibson was not yet over, and would
continue, because General Bowen held his last two aces in his hand to deal with
just such an emergency: the hardened veterans of the Fifth and Third Missouri,
Bowen's last reserves, were ready for the challenge. Bowen galloped over to the
Missourians' reserve position near Baldwin's left just before 1 o'clock.

About 700 Missouri Confederates quickly assembled in line and stood in neat
ranks, while battle-flags flapped in the faint breeze. Having been saved for just
such a critical situation, the Fifth and Third Missouri were to be sacrificed to reverse
the day's fortunes and save Bowen's army from destruction.[18]

One of the war's most desperate strategies now began to unfold. With the fate
of the Rebel forces and the battle hinging upon this audacious gamble, General
Bowen and Colonel Cockrell immediately led the two regiments down into the brushy
depths of Irwin Branch of Centers Creek. That branch paralleled the distant ridge
to the west, upon which hundreds of Union troops rapidly pushed south toward
the all-important Natchez Road, and the adjacent White Branch of Centers Creek,
which flowed in the same direction in front of the Union-held ridge. Accompany-
ing those crack Rebel infantrymen on their mission was at least one section of
Missouri artillery, most likely Captain Guibor's ever-reliable battery.

CHAPTER ELEVEN

A Desperate Gamble

On few occasions in the Civil War had so few troops on either side been given a more desperate assignment than Colonel Cockrell's two regiments. General Bowen realized that probably neither he nor many of his Missourians would survive the gamble to win time and salvage an improbable victory from the jaws of defeat. The target of those Missouri Confederates was the right flank of the Yankee army, which had never known defeat, and was led by the North's best general. High morale, nevertheless, had those veteran Rebels from the western frontier thinking that "we could do this with ease."[1]

The long, difficult march south through the thick woodlands and along underbrush-choked Irwin Branch marked the beginning of the Missourians' most daring undertaking to date. But before the march was completed, a glimmer of sunlight reflected off bayonets, rifled-muskets, and cannon, betraying the stealthy Rebel movement. In that way, General Alvin Peterson Hovey, commanding one of McClernand's divisions, caught sight of the Missouri column laboring south, because the intervening ridge dipped slightly and allowed visibility from the commanding ridge that pointed toward the Natchez Road. The skillful Union general, an experienced Mexican War veteran, quickly marshaled a solid defense to meet the threat. More than two dozen Union field pieces shortly unlimbered along the ridge, while the two Missouri regiments turned west, struggled out of the shadowy woodlands choking Irwin Branch, and pushed toward the heaviest concentration of Yankee field pieces seen in this campaign.

As Union artillery aligned in rows along the ridge-top and prepared to greet "the South's Finest," the fast-moving Rebels surged across the watershed between Irwin Branch and White Branch, the watercourse at the foot of the ridge overflowing with Yankee batteries and McClernand's masses. So rugged and brushy was the terrain that the Confederate artillery was evidently left in the environs of Irwin Branch. Apparently from this low point, the Rebel field pieces lobbed shells west that smashed into the Federal-held ridge. But by the time that Union artillery replied and projectiles exploded along Irwin Branch from a fire directed by Hovey, the shells did not reach the Southern infantry column. Shells smacking into the trees along the branch was indication that the Unionists failed to detect that the Missourians had already swung west out of the branch's depths and were heading directly toward them.[2]

Finally, after more difficult marching, the Missouri Rebels neared White Branch without being detected. West and just ahead in the tangled forests of hardwoods and blooming magnolias was Bowen's target, Grant's vulnerable right flank. But after leaving the high ground of the watershed and entering into the lower-lying, rougher land drained by White Branch, Bowen's trekkers encountered a dilemma: the thicker and summer-like vegetation and the canopy of virgin timber that had screened much of the march well that far, made it impossible for General Bowen to pinpoint the location of Grant's right flank. On a day that seemed hotter than any that year, the Missouri Confederates groped onward amid the dense woodlands.

Greatly complicating Bowen's situation and the task of discovering the southern end of the blue battle-line in the twisted green labyrinth was that McClernand's right flank extended much farther south down the ridge than expected or had previously been the case. Hundreds more Union troops and additional artillery bolstered the increasingly-formidable line, further upsetting Bowen's strategy. Consequently, General Bowen and his followers, unaware of those startling new developments, steadily pushed more in the direction of Grant's right-center instead of the Unionists' vulnerable right flank.[3]

Confident that he was at last near Grant's right flank, General Bowen ordered his two regiments forward atop the last ridge before, or east of, White Branch. The trail-blazers in gray labored up the brushy elevation, probably cursing a great deal and wondering where in the hell they were going. Once on the high ground, an unbelievable sight met their eyes. On the open ridge directly west and above White Branch stood lengthy blue formations and clumps of artillery, waiting for the Missouri Rebels. The element of surprise had vanished, but the Yankees did not know exactly where to expect Bowen's attack. The Confederates had pushed too far northwest, swinging past and missing Grant's right flank, which had continuously expanded and eased steadily south toward the Natchez Road. As if mocking Bowen's failed strategy, the Federal cannon instantly raked the position of the tired Johnny Rebs before they could rest for a few minutes atop the ridge.[4]

Although his battle plan was going awry, General Bowen knew that he had to strike quickly. After carefully assessing the tactical situation, Bowen found a splendid opportunity to strike a hard blow and do considerable damage. General Bowen discovered that the fine brigade of Colonel James Richard Slack, a judge and attorney, was isolated and vulnerable on a spur, just off the main Union-held ridge that led to the Natchez Road. Slack's exposed position stood before, or east of, the main ridge, upon which most of the Yankee forces were poised. There, was a weakness in an otherwise powerful Federal line that an opportunistic commander like General Bowen would exploit immediately.

With the Fifth Missouri leading the way and the Third Missouri close behind, the Confederates pushed forward to redeem the day. Remaining as silent as possible, the Rebels swarmed northwest off the high ground and into the heavily-timbered valley of White Branch, after swinging across a hollow and a slight elevation, about 300 yards southeast of Slack's flank. Even though, they missed a chance to hit the extreme right flank of Grant's army, the Missourians rapidly approached the extreme right flank of Colonel Slack's brigade of veteran Midwesterners.[5]

Upon reaching a thick cane-brake bordering the branch southeast of Slack's knoll, Bowen and Cockrell halted and deployed their troops in preparation for an attack. Worn soldiers at last had a chance to catch their breath in the stifling heat and humidity. The Third Missouri hurriedly shifted to the left of the Fifth Missouri, forming a near-perfect attack formation of steadfast veterans. About to lead the Third Missouri for the first time in battle as the regiment's third commander within one year, Colonel Gause had reason to be apprehensive. Indeed, the first two regimental leaders, Colonels Rives and Pritchard had been killed as first-time regimental commanders in action during the Missouri Brigade's first two major engagements.

Meanwhile, General George Francis McGinnis's brigade, of Hovey's division, had descended the ridge to deploy at the edge of the bottoms of White Branch to protect Slack's brigade, which likewise had swung further downhill and into the valley during its advance. General McGinnis, a hard-fighting Irishman of much ability, was another savvy Mexican War veteran. He was always eager for a challenge such as the one suddenly presented by General Bowen.

With a clatter of gear, Colonel Gause's 275-350 Rebels turned to the west to face the heavy force of McGinnis's brigade, forming for action and preparing to confront massed artillery on the high ground. The Fifth Missouri, meanwhile, was coiled to strike northwest toward White Branch and deliver a crushing blow to Slack's flank. After demonstrating flexibility by quickly adopting a new strategy to meet an ever-changing tactical situation, Bowen had succeeded in placing the Fifth Missouri in a position to perhaps deliver a knock-out punch by the early afternoon of May 1. Indeed, Colonel McCown's regiment was perpendicular to Slack's right flank. Demonstrating their mettle, the Unionists waved hats and tauntingly dared the Missouri Confederates to come and get them.

The most disturbing aspect, however, was the numerical advantage of the Federals along the bottoms, on the slopes, and on the ridge-top, and the unnerving sight of almost five full Union batteries commanding the high ground. Clearly, those two small regiments of the Missouri Brigade were about to pay a stiff price for the long list of mistakes and miscalculations of the Confederate leadership, both civilian and military, since the beginning of the Vicksburg Campaign.[6]

Now Bowen and Cockrell prepared to lead their veterans through a 100-yard wide cane-brake in the valley's lowest point during "one of the most desperate charges of the war," as Sergeant Hogan recalled in a letter. Bayonets were fixed, causing a metallic ringing of steel hitting steel to echo over the quiet valley. The Fifth and Third Missouri faced a formidable challenge. About 700 Missouri Confederates were about to hurl themselves against impossible odds and into hell itself, so that General Bowen's forces would survive on May 1.

At least one black Rebel stood in the Fifth Missouri's ranks. Shad, an enthusiastic and bright young man in his twenties, was the slave servant of Lieutenant Colonel Bevier. After years of brutal servitude on the plantations of the Deep South, the young African American was eager to tangle with the Yankees, much like the graycoats beside him when they had faced their first Unionists in 1861.

At last the Missouri leaders screamed, "Charge!" The deep valley of White Branch suddenly exploded with spine-tingling Rebel screams. In their first charge in more than six months, the Missourians surged forward as well as they had done at Corinth. With business-like efficiency, the charging Fifth Missouri initially achieved the most substantial gains, smashing into the rear and flank of Slack's two Indiana regiments bunched up in the narrow wooded valley. Crushed by Pemberton's "Old Guard" Rebels who had seemingly appeared from nowhere, Slack's Yankees from the small towns and middle-class farms of Indiana were swept aside by the onrushing gray tide.[7]

Quickly responding to the threat, Colonel Slack adroitly adjusted his troops to counter the attack, shifting his two remaining regiments off the knoll to replace the battered Indiana units on the low ground. Likewise, McGinnis's soldiers maneuvered to meet the threat more effectively. Then a more solid Union line quickly took shape at the base of the ridge as the Yankee regiments braced to meet at close quarters the howling Rebels roaring through the valley. Meanwhile, the momentum of the Fifth Missouri's charge barely slowed upon encountering a deep, eroded fork of White Branch, which was clogged with underbrush, cane, and saplings. Not even the leaden storm of shell from thirty Federal artillery pieces on the heights could stop the desperate bid for victory by those resolute exiles.

The two Missouri regiments poured out of the brush-clogged bottom ground, and charged into the extensive cane-brake with war-cries, colorful battle-flags waving. In addition to the murderous artillery salvos decimating the onrushing gray ranks, the sea of cane stalks, rising from the rich bottoms to heights above a man's head, hindered the advance. The Missourians' assault no longer looked like a parade ground maneuver, with wide gaps being blown into the Rebels' midst by exploding shells.

But the cane-brake also provided some protection, screening the charging Confederates from the worst of the infantry fire of the defenders. The anxious Unionists could only wait, while 700 Missouri Rebels swarmed through the tall stalks of cane in a wild "charge, with terrific yells, and could not be seen because of a very thick growth of cane," wrote one Yankee officer. At a range of only 90 paces from the blue formations, the gray soldiers suddenly burst out of the cane. The Unionists unleashed one ragged volley, before the screaming Confederates were almost amongst them.[8]

Unchecked, the Missourians' ferocious charge continued, slowed only momentarily by the bodies of the dead and wounded. On horseback, waving sabers or carrying flags, General Bowen, Colonels Cockrell, Bevier, Gause, and Hubbell, and other experienced officers encouraged their men forward.

And so often in the past, Bowen ignored the danger, having four horses shot from under him on that bloody day. At such close range, those mounted Confederate officers presented fine targets. Some Missouri leaders were toppled off horses by well-placed shots. Colonel Cockrell narrowly escaped death, when one Federal directed his fire exclusively upon "a gallant rider on a clay bank horse with white mane and tail." Incredibly, Cockrell escaped harm when his wounded horse "managed to carry him back into the brush."[9]

The blue wall of defenders began to crumble. With tremendous force, the Fifth Missouri slammed savagely into the right flank of the Twenty-Ninth Wisconsin Volunteer Infantry, a green regiment, and closed in on two exposed Ohio cannon, which had little support. In their first battle the raw Yankee soldiers from the land of clear blue lakes and hardwood forests of Wisconsin paid the heavy price of tangling with the best troops that the Confederacy could throw at them. During this brutal contest with the Missouri Rebels, the Twenty-Ninth Wisconsin suffered the second highest regimental loss in Grant's army at Port Gibson.[10]

But the opportunity to achieve significant gains on McGinnis's right flank was fleeting. More Union reinforcements spilled down from the ridge-top to bolster the hard-hit Federal regiments at the ridge's base until half a dozen Yankee regiments stood firm. Rejuvenated by the timely support, once badly shaken units, such as the Twenty-Ninth Wisconsin, held their own against the Missourians' hardest blows. The added Union firepower and the rough and brushy terrain forced the bloodied Fifth Missouri back into the ravine, which ran parallel to White Branch. There, Colonel MCown's Rebels made their stand. After fanning out along the ravine's bank, the Fifth Missouri returned fire from an ideal defensive position—a natural trench—amid the undergrowth choking the lowlands.[11]

The Third Missouri, to the Fifth Missouri's left, suffered a comparable fate in its westward charge. Colonel Gause's attackers ran straight into the massive firepower of a closer and much heavier artillery concentration from the ridge-top above them than that which had punished the Fifth Missouri. In addition, Federal reserve infantry also bolstered the defenders' position to help hurl back the Third Missouri's attacks. Colonel Gause and his survivors took position throughout the wooded ravine and returned fire with spirit. Both the pinned-down Fifth and Third Missouri held their ground either along the deeply-gorged main creek-bed of White Branch or one of its parallel tributaries, while more fresh Union regiments prepared to advance downhill to increase the odds against the already badly-outnumbered Rebels.[12]

Recoiling in the face of the murderous fire actually paid dividends, for the Confederates could take full advantage of those fine natural defensive positions. That was fortunate, for Cockrell's attackers had plowed headlong into the concentrated firepower of a vastly superior force, which would eventually swell to the strength of nearly two divisions. General Bowen, never one to exaggerate, estimated that his two small regiments had fought at least twelve Union regiments that day. So many Federal units had swung downhill that "the slope on their side was soon covered, it seemed about as thick as they could stand," wrote one soldier.

Despite the uneven contest, Colonel Cockrell's advanced position had to be held at all costs to buy more time. Thanks to the Missourians' assault, Bowen's center along the Rodney Road was not overrun on May 1. General Grant was thrown on the defensive by the unexpected strike of 700 Missouri Confederates.

In the words of an amazed Rebel journalist to the Southern people, "The gallant charge of two regiments of this [Missouri] brigade upon three brigades of the enemy [and] their success in preventing a further advance, or a flank movement of the enemy, I witnessed, and regard as one of the most daring deeds of the war. Although not a Missourian, I cheerfully 'render unto Caesar the things that are Caesar's.' " Indeed, the effort of the Fifth and Third Missouri that day was one of the most audacious and one of the "most daring deeds of the [Civil] war."[13]

The vicious fighting along White Branch was at close quarters. Casualties on both sides soared on that bloody afternoon. In the Fifth Missouri's sector, the dug-in defenders behind the creek bank blasted away at targets only ten feet distant. Likewise the Third Missouri was in a bad fix, pinned down in the brush-choked creek-bed and hammered incessantly by the rows of Yankee cannon and the multiple lines of infantry. Colonel Gause's troops once again clashed with the Eighth and Eighteenth Indiana Volunteer Infantry, veteran commands which had fought well at Pea Ridge and were fresh from occupation duty in Missouri. Unlike the fatal second day around Elkhorn Tavern, the Missouri Rebels, in the heavily wooded ravine, now held the most advantageous ground, while some Union regiments fought on open terrain along the hillsides, and suffered severely.[14]

The thirty massed field pieces of Company A, Second Illinois Light Artillery, Company A, First Missouri Light Artillery, Second Ohio Light Artillery Battery, the Sixteenth Ohio Light Artillery Battery, and other artillery units continued hurling death and destruction from the heights to the west and northwest. The punishment delivered by the First Missouri Light Artillery was another case of Missourians again killing Missourians five hundred miles from their home state.

More Rebels fell as salvos of shot and shell raked the ravine's length, turning the woodlands into an area that looked like a tornado-hit landscape. Fresh units began to replace those regiments most devastated by the Missourians' point-blank fires. The Federals seemed to have a limitless supply of reserves and ammunition. Struggling against the worst odds that he would ever face, Bowen was astounded to see how the Unionists' "first line, four regiments, was routed, the second [line] wavered & gradually gave way, the third held its place." There were so many Federal reserves because the Missourians had plowed into Grant's formations closer to the right-center than to the extreme right flank.[15]

Nevertheless, that day at White Branch, the Missouri Rebels could best measure success in the heavy concentration of Federal regiments converging on them and the accumulating heaps of blue bodies, which would neither be punching holes through the weak Confederate center or gaining Bowen's left flank and rear.

The Missouri Confederates wanted to accomplish much more. Aggressive, young, but experienced, officers led a force of Fifth Missouri soldiers in an effort to turn the Twenty-Ninth Wisconsin's right and encircle the regiment. The charging Missouri Confederates again ripped into the lines of the Wisconsin regiment, "which was being hotly pressed with great slaughter," wrote one Yankee officer. But the Union reinforcements and another deep gully blunted the attack and sabotaged the desperate strategy. After taking higher casualties, those Fifth Missourians fell back to resume firing from the brush-filled natural shelter of the gully. Although they did not hit the extreme right end of McClernand's line, and suffered heavy losses, the charge of the Fifth and Third Missouri had come close to rolling up the right of Grant's battle-line on the south.[16]

For more than two hours the savage fury along White Branch raged unceasingly without breaking the thin Missouri defensive line. Thirty Union cannon bellowed above the smoke-drenched valley, causing a deafening roar to reverberate over the hills, which became blanketed in sulfurous clouds. Instead of rolling up Grant's right flank, Cockrell's band was being annihilated in an obscure ravine in Claiborne County, and there was little glory in dying in the mud of White Branch.

However, each minute that the Missouri soldiers held their positions increased the odds that they might save Bowen's army. Thrown off-balance by the impact of that hard-hitting tactical offensive strike led by his former neighbor, General Grant was being cheated out of a complete victory that day.

But the situation grew even more critical when most Rebel cartridge-boxes were emptied during the duel. In frantic haste those Confederates without ammunition searched the cartridge-boxes of dead and dying comrades, piled-up ever-higher throughout the ravine. Some prepared to hold their position with the only weapons available, the bayonet and musket-butt. The defenders did not have to be told that there would be no reinforcements or ammunition sent their way on May 1.[17]

Finally in the late afternoon, a messenger from Bowen, who had left to rally the defenders in other sectors with the time won by the Fifth and Third Missouri, arrived with orders to withdraw. After the long duel between Cockrell's frontiersmen and the Yankees at extremely close range, General Bowen understood that the Fifth and Third Missouri already had accomplished their mission. He knew better than anyone how the Missourians' "desperate [charge had been] carried out with a determination characteristic of the regiments making it, saved us from being flanked and captured, and gave us until sunset to prepare for our retreat."

At that time General Bowen wanted to save what little remained of his best troops. The order to retire arrived at the last possible moment, for fallen graycoats blanketed the ground, the Rebel return fire dwindled further, and even more Federal units were "rapidly closing around us," wrote one survivor.[18]

The Fifth and Third Missouri survivors wasted no time in leaving the ravine-turned-graveyard. While Cockrell's soldiers began to dash east without order and not by the way they had come, a few Confederates volunteered for the dangerous mission of staying behind as a rear-guard. In the Fifth Missouri's sector, a delaying party of seven volunteers maintained a bold front in a risky game of bluff, firing rapidly, shouting orders in the hope of camouflaging the withdrawal and keeping the Yankee hordes in a fixed position. Gun-smoke and the thickly wooded environs of White Branch helped screen the Missourians' hasty exit, enhancing chances for a successful ruse by only a few Rebels.

The northeast Missouri volunteers of Company I, Fifth Missouri who remained behind were some of the Missouri Brigade's best soldiers. Included in that party of volunteers were brothers Corporal Stephen Allen Barton, a twenty-three-year-old farmer and regimental color bearer, and Private Elias Taylor Barton, age twenty-eight. They were the last survivors of six Barton brothers. The Barton boys had personal scores to settle with the Yankees: a younger brother had been dragged from their Woodville, Macon County home and brutally executed by Union militia; a diseased Private George Washington Barton, of Company I, struggled in vain for life in a filthy Mississippi hospital; another brother later died amid the squalor of the infamous Alton, Illinois prison, and another brother would be killed by Federal bullets before the war's end.

Also included among the rear-guard defenders of Company I were a father and son team from Macon County, Privates Allen Marion Edgar, age fifty-two, and John Henry Edgar, a twenty-two-year-old. Two battle-hardened sergeants, Charles B. Leathers, a farmer from Macon County, and Thomas D. Moore, were the leaders of that small group of Fifth Missouri soldiers. The surgeon of the Fifth Missouri, Benjamin Givens Dysart, described Sergeant Leathers in a letter as "one of the best soldiers I ever saw."

Young Sergeant Moore, a McGee College student, who had recently recovered from a wound suffered at Corinth, commanded the men. Always a fighter and a never-say-die type, Private John D. Dale, one of the main driving forces behind Company I, completed that distinguished group of rear-guard volunteers.[19]

While the Fifth and Third Missouri escaped, the last stand defenders kept the Union lines from immediately launching a vigorous pursuit. In one of the war's most daring exploits, the seven Confederates in the Fifth Missouri's sector "held in check the advance of a whole Fed Div[ision] after their Regt had fallen back [and until] expending all their ammunition," wrote an amazed Confederate officer shortly after the feat.

With their mission accomplished and cartridge-boxes empty, the last handful of Missouri Confederates fled east, just before their position was overrun by two Federal regiments. Surprisingly, the seven rear-guard defenders of Company I, Fifth Missouri, escaped without a scratch.

The Unionists at last claimed the hard-won ravine as their own, taking possession of an unnamed ditch in western Mississippi. Capturing the ravine had cost Grant a long casualty list, much time, and a complete victory, and ensured the escape of Bowen's forces that day. Offering the best explanation as to why Grant had not won a greater success on May 1, Colonel Slack stated simply that his veteran troops had clashed with the crack Missouri Confederates, the "flower of the Southern Army."[20]

At least 200 Fifth and Third Missourians were killed or wounded at Port Gibson, but probably more fell that day. But Cockrell's headlong assault "in gallant, reckless, Missouri style," wrote a Memphis reporter, was what General Bowen required to save the day at Port Gibson. After the Fifth and Third Missouri reassambled at their former reserve position at the cornfield near Baldwin's left, General Bowen paid an emotional tribute to the survivors, "for I did not expect that any of you would get away, but the charge had to be made, or my little army was lost."

With the Confederate lines on the verge of total collapse, General Bowen handed another risky assignment to the two badly cut-up Missouri regiments, rear-guard duty. Colonel Cockrell's troops covered the difficult withdrawal of Bowen's forces north along the dirt road, following the open ridges to the bridges across Bayou Pierre. Again Colonel Cockrell played another valuable role at Port Gibson. Despite the high losses, the Missouri guardians protected the precarious "move off the field [and] in a masterly way," complimented one Southern journalist.[21]

Colonel Erwin, meanwhile, had stubbornly maintained his advanced and isolated position amid the steep ridges and tributaries drained by Centers Creek below the Bruinsburg Road, refusing to relinquish gains and awaiting reinforcements in vain. Without support, Erwin continued the battle along the wooded ridge-top. But like their Missouri Brigade comrades in the struggle around White Branch to the southeast, the Sixth Missouri soldiers also expended most of their ammunition. Simultaneously more Federals converged on the lone Rebel command, which continued to hold out probably west of the Wheeless House. To the north, meanwhile, fresh units bolstered the Union advance near the Bruinsburg Road and "just before sunset [they launched] a desperate attack," wrote Bowen of the final drive to separate the Confederates from Bayou Pierre.

Finally admitting to himself that the day had been lost, Colonel Erwin approached his company captains, including trusted leaders like Jeptha Duncan and John Henry Cooper, the younger brother of Major Cooper. In spite of the loss of an eye at Corinth, Captain Cooper retained command and continued to lead Company C, consisting mostly of tried veterans from Howard and Clay Counties. As bullets zipped past and with the Unionists hovering nearby at point-blank range, Colonel Erwin spoke to the assembled group: "Gentlemen, it is necessary to fall back out of this. We are being surrounded and are in danger of being captured. We must fall back."[22]

The situation of the decimated Sixth Missouri was critical. It was then around 5:30 p.m. and Southern resistance on the Bruinsburg Road sector on the extreme north had all but ended. As if yet trying to win the day, the Sixth Missouri continued its personal fight, after General Bowen had ordered General Green to disengage and to withdraw his Confederate regiments, the nearest Rebels to the Sixth Missouri, across Bayou Pierre. While the Fifth and Third Missouri covered the rear, the final withdrawal of the beaten Rebels had begun around 5:00 p.m. Because no Southern officers or couriers had discovered the Sixth Missouri's position, no orders to retire were forthcoming. While Bowen's forces hastily retired north toward Bayou Pierre's bridges and the Union legions advanced to carry the field, the Sixth Missouri continued to defend its ridge-top.

Then the Sixth Missouri was the last Rebel unit remaining in a fixed position and not withdrawing. On Bowen's right where the Alabamians had fallen back, Union regiments had advanced east far beyond the Sixth Missouri's position. After having surged east through the gap between General Green's right and the left of Tracy's Alabama troops, the bluecoats gained Erwin's immediate rear. Thousands of victorious Yankees, including the Sixth Missouri's old adversary, the Forty-Ninth Indiana, pushed forward toward Port Gibson in the last great advance of the day.

The dilemma for Colonel Erwin was how to withdraw the Sixth Missouri immediately with strong northern forces on the right flank, in the rear, and only a few yards in front. Colonel Erwin was no ordinary regimental commander as he would prove repeatedly during the Vicksburg Campaign.[23]

The quick-thinking Erwin developed a strategy to extricate his survivors, which he hurriedly explained to his company captains. Putting his plan swiftly into action, Colonel Erwin bellowed, "Attention, battalion! Fix Bayonets! Forward double quick, march!" at the top of his lungs. This directive caused the Rebels to deploy, bluffing a frontal attack. While Unionists only 10-20 yards in front of the Sixth Missouri braced for the expected charge, the Confederates filed to the left flank at a brisk pace. All the while, the Yankees continued blasting away. At a designated point on the left, each Sixth Missouri company discharged a volley with their few remaining rounds, before retiring rearward through the timber and underbrush. That point-blank discharge of musketry provided another screen, helping the Rebels to slip away.

Fooled by Erwin's maneuver, the Federals hurriedly adjusted to meet the expected attack on their right flank. In an understatement, a young Missouri lieutenant wrote in his diary how "our regiment made a verry [sic] narrow escape [for] we had to extricate ourselves by takeing [sic] to our heels, and moving off by the left flank, under a severe fire." Quickly, the Missourians retired down a narrow ravine discovered by twenty-eight-year-old Captain William Henry Oldham, the Kentucky-born commander of Company A, a farmer and woodsman familiar with life in the forests. The deep ravine ran east, providing a sheltered escape route. Down that briar-laced and brushy avenue, Colonel Erwin and his survivors fled from the trap and quickly escaped, but only momentarily.

Indeed, the danger for the isolated Sixth Missouri was not yet over. By that time, even more Federals had gained additional ground in the regiment's rear, forming a battle-line only about 75 yards distant. That new danger threatened to block Erwin's route of withdrawal. The colonel quickly halted and aligned his troops in an open cornfield to face the Yankees, who had poured farther east, closer to the Bruinsburg Road. Hurriedly, the gray ranks adjusted to meet the next crisis. Somehow untouched by a bullet that day, Private Franklin held the flag high for the Yankees to see, as if to signify a charge. The aggressive front again threw the Federals into a defensive stance, buying the boxed-in Sixth Missouri a new lease on life and another opportunity to escape. A hasty volley erupted from the Yankee formations, the minie balls sailing high over the Confederates.

Union forces hovering on three sides now attempted to encircle the cut-off Rebel command. Colonel Erwin, therefore, ordered an about-face and retirement by the rear rank at the double-quick. Without order but intact, the Sixth Missouri barely evaded being surrounded at the last moment. At last free from the woodlands, the

Confederates raced 300 yards through the cornfield lining the ridge, upon which the Bruinsburg Road ran toward Port Gibson, while swept by a heavy fire. Additional Missouri soldiers fell in running the gauntlet, finding a final resting place beside the young shoots of corn on the black loam soil of Claiborne County. Among the pursuers tormenting the Sixth Missouri were once again the Forty-Ninth Indiana. While the sprinting Rebels on the high ground were nicely silhouetted against the sky, those Unionists shot down the fleeing graycoats from behind, cutting off and capturing about 50 of Colonel Erwin's men.[24]

After reaching the Bruinsburg Road, Erwin's survivors dashed northwestward until they reached the farm road below the Andrews House that followed a barren ridge northeastward toward Centers Creek and led to the Bayou Pierre bridge. The Yankees kept up the chase, following the Rebels on the run, and cutting down those who lingered behind. Quite a few Missourians never survived the wild scramble across Centers Creek, the final natural obstacle blocking their path to Bowen's withdrawing command and safety.

One Rebel who fell with a bullet through the leg at the muddy creek was Private Enoch A. Gill. There, at the creek crossing, more of Erwin's Rebels were shot down by their pursuers. One Confederate officer stayed mounted too long near the crossing, hurrying stragglers onward. The Missouri leader was toppled off his horse by a good shot. Rushing forward to inspect his kill, the Federal stripped the dying officer of his sword, and took his horse with a fine saddle and bridle as trophies of the nightmarish contest of "Magnolia Hills," or the Battle of Port Gibson.

Badly wounded and losing blood, meanwhile, Private Gill crawled into the underbrush along the creek with a broken leg, not relishing the idea of spending the winter in a Yankee prison. He found good cover and rested his back against a tree, nursing his injury as best he could, applying a makeshift tourniquet. One Rebel-hating Federal eased down the creek-bank, dispatching wounded Missouri Confederates by bludgeoning them to death with blows to the head. After performing those acts, the opportunistic bluecoat stole the valuables from the victim's body. As the vengeful Yankee approached Gill, the wounded Rebel private raised his rifle and screamed: "Halt right there,—Come another step, and I'll blow your brains out." The Northerner backed off. Resisting temptation, Gill smartly refused to fire in order not to draw the attention of nearby Federals.

Not long afterward, a Union officer suddenly emerged from the woods bordering the creek, saying, "As I live, that is the voice of a Gill." That Federal, an old classmate from Oberlin College in Ohio, assisted the wounded Private Gill as much as he could. Generally, Union soldiers took decent care of their captive and injured Missouri Confederate prisoners at Port Gibson as much as circumstances permitted.[25]

In praising the role of the Sixth Missouri that day, a Southern journalist told the people of the Confederacy only days after the Battle of Port Gibson: "Col. Eugene Erwin's regiment covered itself with glory, cutting through the enemy who at one time surrounded it..." Indeed, after each new challenge and sacrifice in a major battle in the South, the Missouri Brigade's reputation grew to greater heights across the Confederacy, and the Battle of Port Gibson was no exception to the rule.

Miraculously escaping to fight another day, the Sixth Missouri had added more laurels to its reputation with the loss of 82 soldiers. As the sun dropped over the dark forests to the west, Erwin led his exhausted troops north toward the Bayou Pierre bridges, although he was wounded. Colonel Erwin and his survivors were the last Confederates from Bowen's right wing to leave the battlefield on May 1.[26]

A couple of miles northwest of Port Gibson, General Bowen made a stand on the north bank of Bayou Pierre, and awaited the Yankees. While the reflection of a red sunset shimmered off the bayou's dark waters, the Missouri Confederates rapidly entrenched in the flat, bottom lands along the watercourse in anticipation of the inevitable clash. Spirits lifted with the arrival of Colonel Gates and his First Missouri Cavalry (Dismounted), now of another brigade, and the dependable First Missouri under Colonel Riley. In addition, Captain Guibor's battery unlimbered to protect the Missouri Brigade. And as if now assisting the Missourians in return for the Sixth Missouri's earlier capture of its two disabled cannon which had to be left behind, the Virginia cannoneers, with two guns of the Botetourt Artillery, were poised for action at Bayou Pierre. Those recently arrived Missouri Brigade soldiers helped cover the withdrawal across the bayou.

Colonel Cockrell feared that he had lost most of the Sixth Missouri and one of this top officers, Colonel Erwin. One-armed Major Cooper and his companies of the Sixth Missouri had already safely rejoined the Missouri Brigade. As night began to fall over the bayou, there was still no sign of Colonel Erwin and his missing command. But Bowen kept faith, for the Confederates had not yet burned the suspension bridge over the bayou: another risk taken by the young Confederate general of so much ability and promise, who had proved at Port Gibson that he could beat the odds and out-gamble the greatest gambler of them all, General Grant.

Suddenly they heard noises from the south bank of the bayou, which sounded like advancing Federals and another fight on the way. The mysterious troops, however, were those of the "lost" command of Colonel Erwin and his Sixth Missouri survivors, appearing from the pitch-black night like ghosts from the grave. With a clatter of accouterments, Colonel Erwin's late comers quickly passed over the bayou to safety. Surely a resounding cheer echoed in the night and over Bayou Pierre upon the reuniting of the Sixth Missouri.[27]

The last Missouri Rebel to cross the bayou on May 1 was James Synnamon, senior lieutenant of Company G, Sixth Missouri. The carpenter of Platte County had been knocked senseless by an exploding shell during the attack and recapture of the two Virginia artillery pieces, and left for dead. Lieutenant Synnamon, age twenty-four and the only Sixth Missouri member born in Philadelphia, Pennsylvania, had lain in the hot woodlands for hours before recovering consciousness. Then he found himself alone, except for his dead and wounded comrades scattered around him. Splattered with blood and half-stunned, the lieutenant struggled to his feet. Synnamon did not know his regiment's location, but managed to push north through the woods toward Bayou Pierre. Synnamon would be wounded seven other times by 1865, earning him the nickname, "Ball Catcher Captain." After more narrow escapes from advancing Yankees, Synnamon swam the bayou and rejoined the Sixth Missouri late that night.

Effectively preventing pursuit, the Missourians burned the suspension bridge over Bayou Pierre after Colonel Erwin and his men crossed over to the bayou's safe, or north, side. Knowing the Sixth Missouri had been through hell and back today, General Bowen allowed Colonel Erwin's soldiers to leave the Bayou Pierre line. Partially taking away the sting of another bitter defeat and a long list of more dead comrades, one of Erwin's lieutenants wrote in his diary, "We marched back that night to camp [near Grand Gulf] and felt thankful that we had escaped as well as we had."

General Green perhaps best summarized the key role played by the Sixth Missouri at Port Gibson: "I cannot refrain from mentioning the conduct of the Sixth Missouri Infantry. It has been my fortune to be with this regiment in every engagement in which it has participated since we crossed the Mississippi River, and on each occasion have I been struck by their gallant conduct, and in this engagement, though I expected much of them, they more than came up to my expectations." But without orders to advance, Colonel Erwin had been overly-aggressive in launching an unsupported attack by one small regiment that had plowed headlong into Grant's entire left wing. But such aggressiveness and boldness was actually an asset at Port Gibson, where only desperate tactics could have held off both General Grant and certain disaster, as General Bowen proved repeatedly on May 1. In the bid to save Vicksburg, General Pemberton and the Confederacy needed a good many more such hard-hitting and high-spirited young leaders as Colonel Erwin.

Only the exploits of the Fifth and Third Missouri were comparable to those of the Sixth Missouri at Port Gibson, where the battle had raged as fiercely as any in the West. As one Rebel journalist, who watched the Fifth and Third Missouri's attack, reported across the Confederacy in another Missouri Brigade tribute, which were becoming almost regular features in the South's leading newspapers: "The 1st Missouri brigade, of course, fought well [and] to acting Brigadier General Cockrell, commanding the brigade...the highest praise is due for gallantry on the field, in that daring charge, as also to Colonels Gause, Bevier, [Lieutenant Colonel Finley Lewis] Hubbell and other officers [and] the officers and men of the line deserve special mention for coolness and courage [but the] best blood of the land has been again poured out to water afresh the tree of liberty."

With only belated and insufficient support from his superiors, Bowen had held almost 24,000 Federal troops at bay for almost an entire day with less than 7,000 men. Unleashed in desperate offensive thrusts at just the right time and at the right place and then standing firm for hours, Colonel Cockrell's Missourians played a crucial role in saving the day at Port Gibson. The Sixth Missouri veterans were instrumental in not only stabilizing resistance in the Rodney Road sector during a crisis, but also in keeping the attacking Federals off balance, slowing a portion of the Union advance in a key sector by delivering a crushing assault without orders.

But the sweeping attack of the Fifth and Third Missouri was the most important offensive strike at a critical moment at Port Gibson. The timely charge of those two small regiments that slashed into Grant's right did the extensive damage necessary to slow the Federal juggernaut that was well on its way to achieving a complete Union victory at Port Gibson. The Missouri Confederates had come amazingly close to rolling up the right flank of Grant's battle-line. By guaranteeing the escape of Bowen's forces, the almost suicidal attack of the Fifth and Third Missouri also won for General Pemberton a better possibility of later defeating Grant in one final decisive battle for Vicksburg.

If enough reinforcements had been available [Colonel Cockrell suggested 10,000 men] to exploit the tactical advantage won on the right by the Vicksburg army's finest troops, the Missourians, and by the Vicksburg army's best commander, General Bowen, then perhaps that had been the best opportunity in the Vicksburg Campaign to stop Grant and yet "drive the enemy back to the river," wrote one Southerner, "and [cut] off his retreat and captur[e] the whole force."

Or, in much less ambitious terms, General Bowen and his Fifth and Third Missouri veterans surely could have rolled up the right of Grant's battle-line with the assistance of only one veteran brigade of Vicksburg's reinforcements.[28]

All the Rebel valor in the world at Port Gibson could not turn defeat into victory. The same tragic results had once again resurfaced at Port Gibson: more of the best officers and enlisted men had been sacrificed in another Confederate defeat. At Pea Ridge, Corinth, and Port Gibson, the soldiers of the Missouri Brigade had fought longer and harder, sacrificed more and struggled against heavier odds than any other Confederate troops. In addition, the "Old Guard" Missouri

Colonel Robert S. Bevier
From his book (1879)

troops were the last Rebels to leave the battlefields of Pea Ridge, Iuka, Hatchie Bridge, and Port Gibson, providing vital rear-guard protection after that dismal string of Confederate reversals.

The same disastrous Pea Ridge and Corinth pattern had been repeated at Port Gibson: not enough ammunition or reinforcements, incompetent Southern leadership at the highest levels, and an opportunity for victory slipping away. Consequently, the somber thickets, cane-brakes, and deep ravines of Claiborne County became the unmarked final resting places for many idealistic, young Missouri Confederates in dirty gray uniforms.

CHAPTER TWELVE

To the Hill of No Return

Dawn on May 2 revealed the horrors of the Port Gibson battlefield. The dug-in Missouri Rebels held their positions along Bayou Pierre, barring Grant's most direct route to Grand Gulf. There, they lay in the muck and dirt behind earthworks, swatting mosquitoes and awaiting Grant's advance. In a short time Missouri Unionists swarmed forward through the forests on the bayou's south bank. While more Federals advanced toward Bowen's weak defensive line on Bayou Pierre, no substantial Confederate reinforcements from Vicksburg arrived. Therefore, Bowen's isolated defenders again risked being surrounded and annihilated.

To delay the attackers, the Irish Rebels from Company F, Fifth Missouri, skirmished out in front, peppering the bluecoats of the Seventh Missouri Volunteer Infantry. The infantrymen of the First, Third and Fifth Missouri were cheered by the arrival of the Sixth Missouri before noon to bolster their weak position. To raise spirits in a gloomy situation, Colonel Erwin went up to seventeen-year-old Private Duke S. Lipscomb, and said, "Duke, I've got a race horse." The young private from Jackson County asked his colonel why he thought so. Colonel Erwin replied with the punch line, saying "because he kept up with you all the way across that field yesterday." The joke raised a laugh among the Sixth Missourians.[1]

The irrepressible Bowen was ready to fight, knowing that if Pemberton would advance enough troops from Vicksburg to support him, then this might be the last chance to contain Grant's beachhead. With both Grand Gulf, the potential base to support Grant's invasion, and Vicksburg out-flanked by the capture of Port Gibson, General Bowen understood the urgency of making another attempt to dislodge the Unionists. But when Bowen learned that Federal troops were about to ford Bayou Pierre to the east, another withdrawal north toward Vicksburg was inevitable.

An angry Father Bannon described the dilemma of the outnumbered Missouri defenders: "because no reinforcements were sent to check [the] Feds who flanked us on both wings—fell into the line of march at midnight." Late on the night of May 2, the Missouri Rebels again were the last troops to depart from the Unionists' presence, leaving Bayou Pierre and heading for Big Black River, seventeen miles north, protecting Bowen's rear amid the black cypress and magnolia forests.[2]

Reflecting silently upon the many comrades lost at Port Gibson, the Missouri boys pushed north, trekking deeper into the darkness. In an emotional letter written to the Lafayette County mother of handsome, twenty-four-year-old Private Isaac M. Lewis of the Sixth Missouri, whom she was to marry, a distraught Port Gibson girl wrote with pride: "Though he fought and died [the young farm boy and Company B soldier had been mortally wounded at Port Gibson] in a stranger land yet he died amoung [sic] friends as many more of the brave and noble and the true

148

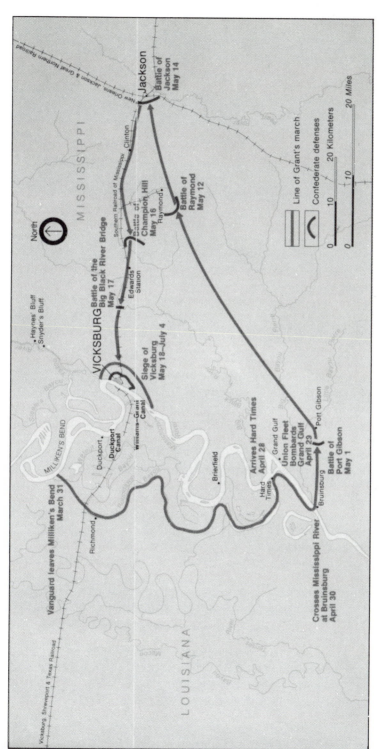

Campaign for Vicksburg

Courtesy National Park Service

Missourians have done. Long will there [sic] name be remembered by us'': a pledge kept faithful by Port Gibson's citizens for almost 130 years.[3]

Despite the heavy losses and recent defeat, the Missouri troops retained surprisingly high morale, praying for another opportunity to avenge comrades' deaths and to beat the wily Grant. Never ceasing to be impressed by the quality of his soldiers, Colonel Hubbell wrote during this dark period of trials: "The boys keep up their spirits though, through all difficulties. Noble fellows, they deserve to be made famous in all time to come."

The Missourians became increasingly concerned about preserving their own historic record, forming historical societies in the Missouri Brigade. The frightful attrition rate emphasized the need to preserve the Missouri Brigade's history before it was too late. "With [the deaths of] Rives, Little, Pritchard, and many others, officers and privates—much of our unwritten history and historical incidents, perished for want of a record," worried a Missouri soldier in a newspaper appeal. They feared that "the future historian must draw his material, in no small part, from Yankee sources, which have so misrepresented and falsified our history." But, ironically, later-day Northern historians would be less guilty of obscuring the rightful role of the Missouri Brigade in the annals of Civil War historiography as Southern historians who glorified the histories of their pet brigades after the war.

The Missourians meanwhile continued to plod north along the dusty road with sore feet and empty haversacks. But perhaps the most consolation came from the unshakable faith that Vicksburg was impregnable, and that the campaign had only begun.[4]

Danger was ever-present during the May 2-3 withdrawal north from Bayou Pierre to the Big Black River, despite the addition of a brigade of Major General William W. Loring's division to reinforce Bowen's command. If Grant gained the vital Big Black River crossing at Hankinson's Ferry to the north, then the Confederates would be cut off from Pemberton and Vicksburg, trapped between Bayou Pierre and Big Black. A frantic race with the bluecoat pursuers to reach the boat-bridge at Hankinson's Ferry occurred. The hard marching continued hour after hour, with few rest breaks and no relief for blistered feet. Again providing invaluable service, Captain Canniff and his Irish wharf workers and rural Emerald Islanders covered the rear of the withdrawing Rebel forces. The relentless Unionists continued to pursue closely, nipping at the heels of Bowen's battle-weary, but still dangerous, force.

With Bowen's troops racing north for Vicksburg, out-flanked Grand Gulf to the west had to be abandoned. "Little Gibraltar" was another prize that fell to Grant during this decisive campaign. Exploding magazines in the early morning hours of May 3 announced the end of a Confederate Grand Gulf. Under Colonel Senteny's direction, parties of Second Missourians had spiked those siege pieces which had recently stopped the Union Navy. But more disturbing than the echo of Grand Gulf's exploding magazines was that in the Missouri Brigade's immediate rear, "we could hear their drums all day."[5]

To ensure Bowen's escape across Big Black at Hankinson's Ferry, Cockrell quickly formed the Missouri Brigade for action at Hardscrabble Crossroads. Another difficult assignment for the Missourians on the morning of May 3 called for holding Grant's forces at bay. Captain Canniff's skirmishers set up a clever ambush for pursuing Federal cavalry. The Missouri Brigade's stand and a blistering volley from Company F thwarted the mounted force's effort to deliver the Missouri Brigade, Bowen's division, and other Confederate units a knock-out punch south of Big Black River.[6]

The Missouri Brigade's other principal skirmish unit, Company G, Second Missouri, also fought well beside Company F, providing reliable service. There, just below the suddenly strategic Hardscrabble Crossroads, the majority of Missouri Brigade members awaited an attack, but the Union pursuit had lost momentum. Nevertheless, the risk still existed of being trapped between Big Black and Big Bayou Pierre, and Cockrell's guardians would shortly be the only Confederates south of Big Black.

Protecting Cockrell's defenders were the busy guns of Landis's battery. Those bronze field pieces were commanded by one of the Missouri Brigade's top artillery officers, Lieutenant John M. Langan, age twenty-four. Often serving with the rear-most skirmishers during the withdrawal, those Missouri cannon had repeatedly unlimbered and turned to blast those opponents who approached too near. On May 3, the South Carolina-born Langan proved to be an excellent replacement for Captain Landis. Captain Landis had taken over as the commander of all the artillery in Bowen's division after Colonel Wade's death at Grand Gulf.

After swinging north several miles, the rear-guard Missouri Rebels made another stand to guarantee that all Confederates escaped to the north side of Big Black River on May 3. Colonel Cockrell quickly aligned his regiments and Landis's artillery in fine defensive positions along a commanding ridge. Here, on the last high ground before Big Black and north of Kennison Creek, the Missourians fanned out across the timbered crest.

Once again, the Missouri Brigade was employed for the most hazardous duty. That guardian role would continue uninterrupted throughout the Vicksburg Campaign. Shouting Federals suddenly spilled from the forests and charged into an open field in the late afternoon light. The attacking Yankees made one final effort to destroy the last isolated Confederate forces remaining on the south side of Big Black.

Upon knocking out targets with an accurate shell-fire, Landis's artillerymen cheered and waved hats. Yankee formations spanning across a cornfield were a Confederate gunner's dream-come-true. The Missouri cannon boomed hoarsely over the landscape of Claiborne County, blowing holes in the blue lines and driving the Unionists back into the forests. One Second Missouri Rebel marveled at "the rapid and skilful [sic] management of this battery, and the style in which the boys handled their pieces, were certainly splendid. Covered with black stains of powder, and almost enveloped in smoke, ...the men who fought each piece seemed to vie with the others in driving [the Unionists] back as quickly as possible." Indeed, Bowen's Missouri artillerymen were among the most experienced Confederate gunners in the West.[7]

The solid defense of the rear-guard Missouri Rebels slowed the Yankees' pursuit. While two other Southern brigades also provided key rear-guard support, the Missouri Brigade played the most important role during the risky withdrawal. After the Confederate units safely crossed Big Black, the Missourians trotted over the boat-bridge. As Cockrell's exiles pushed farther north on the river's opposite side, Union artillery pounded the woodlands filled with withdrawing Rebels.

With Bowen's forces continuing north, the bridge at Hankinson's Ferry had to be destroyed to ensure escape. The reliable Second Missouri skirmishers of Company G, under Captain Wilson, and some Alabama pioneers began their destructive work. But the demolition was interrupted by attacking Federals on the south bank. Because the Confederates were driven off before finishing the job the Unionists won a repairable bridge across the Big Black River. Therefore, General Grant could advance north more rapidly to hit Vicksburg from the south if he chose.[8]

After passing through Vicksburg, the fatigued Missouri Confederates pushed east for Bovina, Mississippi. There, at the small railroad town a couple of miles west of Big Black and about ten miles east of the Mississippi River fortress, the defensive-minded Pemberton concentrated his forces along the high ground west of Big Black to protect Vicksburg's rear. At that point between Vicksburg and Jackson, Pemberton wanted a wide river between him and the brilliant Grant, but he failed to use the reservoir of troops left around Vicksburg effectively.

Retaining the initiative and exploiting Pemberton's bewilderment, Grant had swung northeast into the interior of Mississippi and farther away from his Grand Gulf base. He wanted to cut the Southern Railroad of Mississippi, which supplied Vicksburg with life, by striking the state capital of Jackson, the vital communications center and depot for the citadel.

Knowing that flexibility and speed were essential for success, General Grant again gambled. By utilizing a mobile supply-line of wagon trains rolling overland from the Mississippi River, Grant violated standard logistical axioms, giving him greater freedom to maneuver. Unlike Pemberton, Grant would be able to concentrate more troops for the decisive clash at Champion Hill, instead of having to establish large garrisons to guard and occupy territory along an extensive, static communications and supply line. In addition, the cavalry-short Pemberton would be less able to cut such a flexible support system. Hence, the key logistical support system for the invasion was kept rolling forward to keep pace with Grant's rapid advance through Mississippi.[9]

In the oak and pine woodlands bordering Clear Creek, the Missourians' ordeal ended when they finally encamped, after trudging more than fifty miles. During the uplifting services given by their faithful chaplains, Cockrell's Rebels gave thanks for their recent escapes, and said prayers for the many dead comrades. From the Bovina encampment, one Southern journalist paid a fitting tribute to the Missouri Brigade: "There has been no more desperate fighting during the war than was done by Gen. Bowen's men during the two or thee days' engagement at Grand Gulf [and Port Gibson], and the slaughter of Yankees was appalling. Bowen's Missourians are now at Big Black, absolutely used up with fatigue and want of rest. The poor fellows have thrown away their shoes [or simply had none at the campaign's onset] and stockings to relieve their blistered feet." Colonel Cockrell's troops had garnered more laurels for their role at Port Gibson and for their rear-guard duty during Bowen's risky withdrawal.[10]

After shifting east and closer to the Big Black River on May 6, the Missourians prepared for the killing to resume. "We expect to have to fight them in one or two days," wrote one soldier. The previous day's news of General Thomas Jonathan "Stonewall" Jackson's death during another pyrrhic Confederate victory at Chancellorsville, Virginia, came as a shock. Anticipating the imminent bloody contest to decide Vicksburg's fate, the Missouri Rebels now drilled even longer and harder than usual.

One of Captain Landis's cannoneers, for instance, described the representative attitude among Missouri Brigade members in a letter: "You must not think that I often get homesick, thinking about home, so far, far away. Not a bit of it. I have become so used to think of it as something to fight for, that it is to me like a prize for [which] one exerts all his energies." Indeed, all of the Missouri Brigade's pent-up energies would shortly be released on an obscure, heavily timbered elevation in Hinds County, Mississippi, known as Champion Hill.

Many urgent reasons existed for a march to reclaim their home state. For example, the most barbarous guerrilla war in American history was raging fiercely across Missouri. An Iowa soldier stationed amid the sectional storm of Missouri probably best summarized the nightmare: "Missouri was neither North nor South; she was simply hell, for her people were cutting one another's throats." The horror of Missouri's agony beckoned, and, the all-consuming desire of Cockrell's soldiers was that they "should all water their horses in the Missouri River." As one exile stated the feeling among Missouri Brigade members: "Our hearts are all overshadowed with the sorrows of Missouri, but we pray the God of battles that [we will be led] back to the homes not yet consumed by fire."

Colonel Cockrell's Rebels who had returned to Missouri were often executed by vengeful Union Home Guards not for guerrilla activity, but simply for being members of the famous Missouri Brigade. For example, Fifth Missouri Lieutenants Isaac Templeton Davis, a Tennessee-born farmer who had gone home to recover from a dangerous wound, and Virginia-born Hamilton E. Kelley, age thirty and cursed with syphilis, were taken from their Missouri homes and brutally executed by Unionists. Recruiting assignments to fill the Missouri Brigade's decimated ranks could also prove fatal. Among others, Captain Aurelius E. Samuel, age twenty-five, was killed by Unionists while seeking volunteers for the Third Missouri.

Few Southerners could fully understand the extent of the destruction wrought upon Missouri. "We have no idea of what Missouri has suffered [but] still the spirit of Missouri is undaunted, her sons cling to the cause," proclaimed the editor of the *Vicksburg Daily Whig*. The Missouri Rebels wondered why "the Confederate government seems to have forgotten that Missouri exists [and] when will the Missourians now in arms in the Confederacy be permitted to bring joy and aid to those who await them with outstretched arms and bleeding hearts [and these] wrongs appeal to the chivalric sons of the South for swift and terrible retribution. The blood of her murdered sons, the tears of her daughters made widows and orphans by bayonets of the bloody legalized butchers, call upon us for a redress."

Other developments came for the Missouri troops during that quiet period. Causing the most complaint was an assignment to erect fortifications across the cotton fields on Big Black River's east side. The Missouri Brigade's prowess increased with the arrival of 400 exchanged Missouri prisoners—the first reinforcements in almost a year and a half—and the issuance of Enfield rifles. The .577 caliber rifled-muskets from England had been run through the Union naval blockade, and were the Confederacy's best firearms. If caught in another bad fix with empty cartridge-boxes as at Pea Ridge and Corinth, the Missouri boys could use the rounds from Union dead. Bullets for the Yankees' .58 caliber Springfield rifled-muskets would fit into the .577 Enfields.[11]

Health among the Missouri Brigade was much improved, after a relatively mild winter and before the intense heat of summer. With the Missouri wounded at Port Gibson under the care of both Federal and Rebel surgeons, such as the Fifth Missouri's Surgeon Dysart, the workload of the regimental surgeons and the Missouri Brigade's surgeon, John Marshall Allen, eased briefly before the slaughter of the Vicksburg Campaign continued. Surgeon Allen, formerly the Third Missouri's surgeon, held the highest reputation and the most seniority among all the Missouri Brigade's medical personnel.

Surgeon John Marshall Allen
Courtesy Dr. Thomas P. Sweeney, Springfield, Mo.
(Unpublished Photo)

"Marsh" Allen, age thirty-three, had been among the first volunteers to join Confederate service, enlisting with Colonel Rives. An alumnus of St. Louis University's College of Medicine, surgeon Allen met his future wife in the Port Gibson community.

The physician of Colonel Riley's First and Fourth Missouri, Surgeon John Henry Britts, also obtained a fine medical education from St. Louis University, the first medical school west of the Mississippi. He had won much acclaim "for his mechanical skill in adopting the limited means within his reach to the requirements of his patients; would cut unsparingly when necessary, but was always conservative in the practice of his profession, and was the means of saving many a wounded soldier his limbs, which others less conservative might have sacrificed."

No institution of higher learning had a greater influence on the overall quality of the Missouri Brigade than St. Louis University. Discipline and maturity gained at the university during formative years resulted in quality leadership throughout the Missouri Brigade. Among the university's alumni had been such leaders as Captain Samuel Churchill Clark and Colonel Burbridge. Also among the Missouri Brigade's best officers were the Kennerly brothers, Lieutenant Colonel Garland [promoted on May 1, 1863], Captain Guibor, and other fine leaders who owed much to St. Louis University.

In addition many former St. Louis University students were in the Missouri Brigade's enlisted ranks, especially among the Irish Catholic Rebels from St. Louis. The Spartan-like discipline and high standards learned by the young students from both Catholic and Protestant families at the Jesuit university were reincarnated into the superior performance of those Missouri soldiers on the battlefields of Pea Ridge, Corinth, and Port Gibson. Other St. Louis University graduates wore the blue and now fought in Union armies, and were especially eager to kill their fellow alumni in the Missouri Brigade and vice versa.[12]

While Pemberton's army remained inactive in protective fashion around fortress Vicksburg, Grant maneuvered to take Vicksburg from the rear. After slashing northeast and getting between the forces of Generals Pemberton and Joseph E. Johnston, elements of Grant's army won an engagement and possession of Raymond, Mississippi, on May 12.

The Missouri Rebels remained in the fortifications of Big Black River, about half-way between Jackson and Vicksburg. Then vital Jackson swiftly fell two days later, as Grant broke the rail line leading to Vicksburg to keep reinforcements and supplies from reaching Pemberton. The fruits of Grant's blitzkrieg were impressive: Vicksburg lost its supply base, and its communications link to the outside world, and Johnston's defending forces were scattered in one lightning stroke.

While two Union corps caused havoc in Vicksburg's rear and chased off Johnston's Rebels, a third corps before Pemberton gave him second thoughts about advancing beyond the Big Black River line. After pushing aside General Johnston's forces behind Vicksburg, Grant turned west to concentrate on Pemberton: a classic example of eliminating an opponent in the field who would have reinforced the primary objective, Vicksburg, had not an indirect strategy been employed. President Davis's policy of protecting almost every section of the sprawling Southern nation instead of employing a wise concentration of force at key strategic locations, such as Vicksburg, and Pemberton's similar obsession with closely guarding Vicksburg instead of concentrating his forces against the Federals east of Vicksburg were masterfully exploited by Grant's lightning-quick, modern tactics. By that time, Pemberton's lack of aggressiveness and command inexperience made the saving of Vicksburg almost impossible, no matter how valiantly Vicksburg's defenders fought during the misguided campaign.[13]

In a belated effort to strike Grant while he knocked the all-important Jackson out of the war, troops from Pemberton's army tentatively ventured east from Big Black River. But the conservative Pemberton left two divisions of about 10,000 men close to Vicksburg; approximately 23,000 Rebels would hardly be the most effective concentration necessary to beat almost 33,000 Federals. Ever-cautious, the general attempted to swing southeast toward Raymond and cut the invader's supply line near the W. F. Dillon Plantation. But Grant had hurriedly concentrated his forces and pushed west toward Vicksburg to deal with Pemberton, before an off-balance Confederate leadership realized what was happening in the vastness of Mississippi. During the chaotic march toward Raymond, spring rains, muddy roads, traffic jams, flooded Baker's Creek, and logistical breakdowns caused the Confederate army to bog down on May 15 amid the rough terrain of Hinds County, southeast of Edwards Station.[14]

Grant's objective was to catch Vicksburg's main protective army exhausted and half-confused. Therefore, Grant's forces now moved swiftly west toward Edwards Station, on the Southern Railroad of Mississippi, to hit Pemberton's command before it could recover. A golden opportunity for Grant's seven advancing divisions to pounce on an unwary Rebel army had been handed to the resourceful Union general.[15]

Both the day and night of May 15 were hard for the worn Missouri Rebels, consisting of a grueling fifteen-hour ordeal of delays, and slipping along in the mud, which did not end until an hour before midnight. A worn soldiery suffered from a cold rain pelting down, lying on arms all night without fires or blankets in the wet blackness around the J. W. Ratliff Plantation Road. Father Bannon spent much of the night walking the bivouac, waking Rebels, listening to confessions, and trying to save as many souls as possible, as if knowing that so many of these young men would shortly be united with their God. "Many a gallant heart slept that night his last sleep in this world," wrote Sergeant Hogan in a letter. On this eerie night in Mississippi's pitch-black forests, Missouri boys prayed that they might survive the impending confrontation and win the long-awaited decisive victory which might unleash them to reclaim the Union-occupied homeland.[16]

Sunrise of May 16 found neither army fully prepared for the decisive confrontation to decide Vicksburg's, and perhaps the nation's fate. As so often in this war, two American armies were about to collide and fight with a tenacity seldom seen. But Grant had the advantages of greater maneuverability, and knowledge of Pemberton's intentions from a captured dispatch. In addition, Grant wanted badly to smash Vicksburg's guardian army, so that it could never unite with Johnston's army. Three powerful Federal corps, therefore, poured west down three parallel roads, the Jackson, Middle and Raymond, from north to south. To ensure that Pemberton and Johnston would never link, thousands of Unionists rapidly closed upon Pemberton's forces, which were anything but ready for a major battle on May 16.[17]

CHAPTER THIRTEEN

Champion Hill

Obeying orders to unite with Johnston that overruled the strike toward Raymond, southeast of Edwards Station, Pemberton reversed his army's course to return to Edwards. The directional shift from southeast to north wasted more time and caused a reversal of march, which was another factor keeping the befuddled Rebel army in a relatively fixed position and vulnerable amid rugged terrain. Like a giant gray snake, the Confederate army turned north to crawl back to the Jackson Road, from which they could gain the railroad at Edwards Station. Then, if all went well, Pemberton could unite with General Johnston's forces to confront Grant on more equal terms.[1]

But the Southerners never completed their confused march, for skirmishing suddenly erupted in the woodlands along the Raymond Road. General Grant had caught his opponent by surprise and in mid-march, without a plan of battle, much fatigued, and scattered in a rough countryside. One of the most battle-tested Union generals was about to match tactical wits with an inexperienced Confederate general during a decisive battle.

Crackling musketry warned the Missourians of the Yankees' proximity and the beginning of the most important engagement of their lives. Shortly, it seemed as if the forests were alive with bluecoats. Pemberton responded quickly to the challenge, forming an ad hoc battle-line on high and good defensive ground above Jackson Creek facing east. Three Rebel divisions hastily aligned along the north-south Plantation Road, which served as an interior line to hurry reinforcements to meet the Yankee threats along the three east-west roads: General Carter L. Stevenson on the north around the east-west Jackson Road, General Bowen on the center and General Loring south on the right, near the east-west Raymond Road.[2]

Federal batteries hammered the Missouri Brigade's position in an open field. To protect Colonel Cockrell's infantrymen and to punish the advancing Unionists in the broad valley below, Captains Wade's and Guibor's guns unlimbered just behind the prone exiles. With pressure mounting in front, Bowen feared that Grant's whole army might suddenly spill out of the dark valley of Jackson Creek. Colonel Cockrell galloped down the lines and encouraged his grayclads to stand firm under the pounding. Cockrell reminded his troops "that he expected the brigade to give a good account of itself during the day. The men were in fine spirits, animated, gay and buoyant, and in good condition for the field."[3]

To allow final dispositions and slow any Union advance surging west out of the valley, General Bowen ordered Colonel Cockrell to form a detail of his five best companies for a skirmish battalion. This battalion included Captain Canniff's experienced Company F, Fifth Missouri. In addition, the skirmish battalion consisted of Captain Wilson's Company G, Second Missouri; Captain Martin Burke's Company D, First and Fourth Missouri; Captain Jepthah Duncan's Company E, Sixth Missouri, and Company G, Third Missouri, under twenty-five-year-old Captain William C. Adams, a farmer and former commander of the "Independence [Missouri] Blues." Two of these five companies, those of Captains Canniff and Burke, had their origin in the prewar militia of St. Louis.[4]

Chosen to command the skirmish battalion was Lieutenant Colonel Hubbell, the handsome bachelor and scholar of the Third Missouri. About 10:00 a.m. Hubbell led his skirmishers east through the grain fields, mid-way between the Middle and Raymond Roads, on the double, while the battle escalated. As Rebel whistles sent shrill directives cutting through the humidity of the year's hottest day, the Missouri skirmishers deployed 400 yards in front of the Missouri Brigade. The Missouri cannon, meanwhile, continued roaring behind Cockrell's long gray lines. As the Union threat from the environs of Jackson Creek intensified, the skirmish battalion members hustled back to a deep gully. There, the skirmishers found some shelter from the brewing storm. The unnerving sight of the head of Private William H. H. Sparks, age twenty-five, rolling across the ground after a shell had decapitated the Monroe County farmer convinced the skirmishers to keep their heads down without being told.[5]

For most of an hour, the artillery duel continued and escalated to a deafening roar, warning of the hot work ahead for the infantrymen. Even a veteran officer like Colonel Riley marveled with a soldier's wit at the "lively time [of] exchanging compliments (such as Twenty pound Parrot [sic] shell &c.)." Unable to resist the temptation, Colonel Cockrell dismounted and personally directed the fire of one of Wade's field pieces, resulting in the explosion of a Federal artillery caisson. Then Captain Landis, wrote one cannoneer in his diary, "sat up on his horse, while the shells flew thick & fast around him, one shell from the enemy's battery burst under his horse, which only seemed to make him more erect in the saddle, & he continued to direct" an accurate fire from the cannon of Bowen's division. Captain Landis was "one of the best officers in the army." Such defiance from the Missouri artillery, in spite of the fact that two of Lieutenant Langan's cannon were disabled, and another spirited advance of Hubbell's skirmish battalion east made Bowen's position on Pemberton's center more secure, helping to discourage Union assaults from ripping into this sector.[6]

However, ominous developments occurred elsewhere. With a heavy concentration of his forces on the north via the Jackson Road, Grant had an opportunity to deliver a devastating blow because Pemberton had anticipated the main attack from the Raymond Road sector on the south. Grant had other advantages that day. First, Pemberton's front was much too long, with the thin gray lines strung out for about three miles. And General Stevenson's Rebels, the northern-most and the weakest of Pemberton's three divisions, were again in motion. Prematurely concluding that no battle would occur, Pemberton had ordered the march resumed to link with Johnston.

Despite the last-minute efforts of Brigadier General Stephen D. Lee in galvanizing an east-west defensive line in Stevenson's sector, Pemberton's left was still at Grant's mercy, and there he massed an overpowering force of three divisions on the northeast. Without enough cavalry to reconnoiter and supply timely information, Pemberton was not convinced of the massive build-up on his left flank.

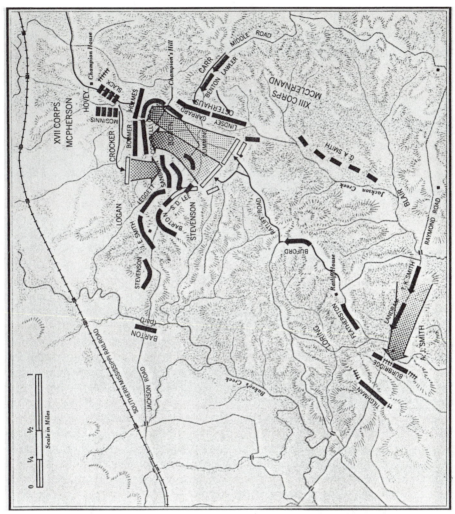

On the morning of May 16, Alvin Hovey's Federals seized Champion Hill, only to be repulsed about 1:30 p.m. by John Bowen's Confederate division. When William Loring's division failed to advance in support of Bowen, Federal reinforcements from John Logan's and Marcellus Crocker's divisions were able to move into the breach. By late afternoon the Confederates were in full retreat southwestward toward the lower bridge over Baker's Creek.

Courtesy *Time-Life Books*, Alexandria, Va.

Consequently, the bulk of Pemberton's force continued looking in the wrong direction, expecting an attack from the east and southeast instead of from the north. Also a Federal advance on Pemberton's left might gain control of the bridge over Baker's Creek, cutting the Rebels off from Edwards Station and Vicksburg. "We had only three Divisions to meet Grant's entire army," lamented an Atlanta, Georgia correspondent. A disaster of unprecedented proportions seemed as inevitable as it was imminent by the late morning of May 16.[7]

Indeed, thousands of Federals shortly tore savagely into Pemberton's left, mauling the outnumbered defenders. Hovey's veteran division, the Missouri Brigade's Port Gibson antagonists, spearheaded the assault. The Union drive from the northeast steamrolled down the Plantation Road and smashed through Pemberton's line, crumpling up and crushing Rebel units with relative ease. Most important, the highest ground in the area—Champion Hill on the Sid Champion Plantation—the key to the battlefield was captured by the Unionists. The powerful onslaught of the victorious Federals steadily gained impetus, tearing through everything in its path.

Then Hovey's division, with Colonel Slack on the left and General McGinnis on the right, overran the strategic Crossroads, the intersection of the Jackson, Middle, and Plantation, or Ratliff Roads. There, 400 yards southwest of Champion Hill, the Confederates lost still another key position, after another round of vicious fighting. Swooping up more prisoners and artillery at the Crossroads, the cheering Unionists continued southwest down both sides of the Plantation Road, swarming toward Pemberton's headquarters and the vulnerable left flank of Bowen's idle division.[8]

Few Southern armies were closer to destruction than Pemberton's command by 1 o'clock. The entire Rebel left had disintegrated, shattered by the Yankee onslaught. A half-mile of Pemberton's line had been chewed up and spit out by Grant's ferocious attack, leaving only the shattered debris of what had been a fine division only a short time before. Thousands of Confederates were dead, wounded, or captives, and thousands more were fleeing down the road and through the grain fields in panic before the long formations of advancing Unionists. Several Rebel batteries were taken in the attack that already demolished a third of Pemberton's army. Pemberton's army had not only been whipped by early afternoon, but seemingly might be split and destroyed within the next few hours. It appeared that only divine intervention could now save the Southern army, fortress Vicksburg, and the Confederacy.[9]

With Pemberton's left nonexistent, Bowen's division, in the center, was the next in line. The Federal attack threatened to finish the destruction of the badly mauled Southern Army and completely roll up Pemberton's battle-line, which still faced east instead of north. But before the Union flank attack did more damage, Pemberton ordered Bowen's Division to turn and race northwest to support the battered remains of Stevenson's left west of the Crossroads, where General Lee was patching together a defense with his brigade.

On Bowen's left, the crack Missouri veterans were the first troops to turn to meet the serious threat. Cockrell's buglers signaled the gray ranks to shift to the northwest and into echelon. Then, within seconds, the Missourians raced forward with loud cheers and flags waving. But Pemberton soon redirected them in mid-stride, sending the Missouri Brigade swiftly northeast for an attempt to recapture the Crossroads. Without halting to rest, the Missouri Rebels double-quicked onward through farmers' fields to save the day in another Port Gibson-like assignment. The Missouri artillery, limbers, and caissons bounced through the rows of corn and rye plants behind the fast-moving gray infantry.[10]

Upon nearing the holocaust, the cheering Missouri Rebels encountered the throng of demoralized Southerners, fleeing from the Crossroads disaster. Around 300-400 yards south of the Crossroads, Pemberton had rallied two tough Georgia regiments across the Plantation Road. It had been no small accomplishment for the Georgia troops of General Alfred Cumming's brigade to rally against the odds and after the beating they had taken.[11]

Union pressure was intense, with Hovey's troops on the verge of breaking the last thin line of graycoats during what appeared to be one of the most successful Union assaults of the war. Missouri Brigade Bugler Samuel B. Lyons, age twenty-four, sounded the call to align and prepare to meet the rapidly attacking blue legions. As the clear notes cut across the wide fields and bullets made the air sing, the Fifth Missouri, the first unit to reach the scene of disaster, quickly formed on the left of the Fifty-Sixth Georgia, an already mauled unit which had gamely rallied.

Drenched in sweat from the long run in the blistering heat, Cockrell's Rebels were completely worn-out but eager for the fray. Those Confederate troops had no time to catch their breaths before being thrown into the vortex of the storm. But the first phase of a most difficult task was completed: the anchoring of the Missouri Brigade's right, while under heavy attack.[12]

But it would still take some time for the rest of the Missouri Brigade to arrive and deploy farther west on the Fifth Missouri's left. The terrific momentum of Hovey's attack would not allow a respite for those Confederates attempting to make a stand below the Crossroads, however. Suddenly the Georgia troops on the right of the Fifth Missouri were swept aside by the blue tide. Nothing stood on the Fifth Missouri's, the Missouri Brigade's, right but hundreds of charging Unionists.

Unable to see the Georgians' rout amid the clouds of battle-smoke, Colonel McCown's men were suddenly astounded to see advancing Federal soldiers only ten feet distant! A Union volley rippled through the Fifth Missouri from the right flank, dropping many. Some Unionists even gained the regiment's rear and banged away, cutting down Fifth Missourians from behind. To escape the trap, Colonel McCown's soldiers retired a short distance in reasonable order through the layers of smoke, loading and firing on the move. The hardened Fifth Missouri veterans refused to break in a situation that would have severely tested the mettle of even the most reliable soldiers. So far, the Missouri Brigade was the only unit of that size to stand firm before the Yankee onslaught at Champion Hill.[13]

As the Missouri Brigade's position was being enfiladed by bluecoats on Cockrell's exposed right flank, a disastrous chain reaction began. Because the Fifth Missouri retired a short distance, the right flank of Colonel Gause's Third Missouri, the second regiment in line to the Fifth Missouri's left, was exposed to an unmerciful flank fire. After taking severe punishment and losing more good men, the Third Missouri likewise was forced to fall back. Perhaps there regimental bugler George Perry Major, age twenty-two, was killed. This punishment was simply too much for some Third Missouri soldiers, including officers. Despite the inspiration of his Revolutionary War namesake, Lieutenant John Paul Jones, age twenty-three and a Jackson County farmer, gave a new meaning to Commodore Jones's famous battle-cry, "I have not yet begun to fight," when he bolted from the ranks of Company G and ran off.

Farther west, meanwhile, only the natural cover of the sunken Middle Road, high rail fences, and much stubbornness kept the Sixth and Second Missouri from folding at such a critical moment. Those two regiments were able to deploy and sustain their positions to the left despite taking a heavy fire.[14]

At the same time the Fifth Missouri and much of the Third Missouri were maintaining their new positions along a fence behind the original line, after retiring a short distance and then rallying. There, McCown's and Gause's troops made their stand, firing from behind the fence-rail shelter upon the charging Yankees. Perhaps the most sensible action called for joining the throng of Confederates fleeing the field, especially with almost all hope gone. Some of Cockrell's faint-hearted soldiers, indeed, threw down muskets and took to their heels, but not many. As at Port Gibson, General Hovey had again clashed with Pemberton's elite troops, who did not break on May 16.[15]

Within the next few minutes the Missouri Brigade had to be reunited and alignment completed before a counterattack could be launched. Private John D. Dale, who had been among the Port Gibson delaying party, took the initiative. Before the stationary ranks of Company I, Fifth Missouri, Dale suddenly bounded over the rail fence and charged forward through the open field. Issuing a bold challenge, the ragged enlisted man screamed, "Come on Company I, we can whip the God Damn Yankee sons-of-bitches!" Colonel Cockrell's Rebels were rejuvenated by the example of the seemingly half-crazed private from Randolph County.

Catching the spirit, the soldiers of Company I cheered and advanced from the fence-line in the face of the Union charge and a withering fire. Then like magic, the rest of the Fifth Missouri likewise joined the charge of the handful of the regiment's color company. Also Colonel Gause's troops shortly followed the Fifth Missouri's example and surged forward from the rail fence shelter with colorful battle-flags waving through the drifting smoke.

On their own, the enlisted men in dirty uniforms, not resplendent generals or colonels, turned the tide that day: appropriate because that struggle with so much at stake would largely be a privates' battle. The fighting spirit that had hurled men against Corinth's fortifications and thrown Grant off balance at Port Gibson had returned at the last moment. The Missouri soldiers advanced to push back the foremost attackers.

Finally, the Fifth Missouri and Third Missouri regained their former positions. Despite the odds and heavy losses, the Missouri Brigade now stood firm just west of the Plantation Road, and was ready to strike back. The Missouri Brigade had accomplished the two most difficult tasks for any combat unit to perform while under heavy attack. First, iron discipline and a thorough mastery of drill routines enabled them to perform the complicated and intricate maneuver necessary to move more than 2,000 men from a marching column to an attack formation in record time in spite of routed Confederates fleeing through the ranks. Second, the Missouri Brigade's formations had fallen back on the key flank position, but eventually rallied without assistance to regain its advanced position, while being attacked with tremendous force.[16]

Three developments at this crucial juncture ensured that the Missouri Brigade would maintain its solid stance, after having weathered the worst of the storm. After being recalled, Hubbell's battalion of five skirmish companies rejoined the Missouri Brigade after a long run, adding invaluable reinforcements. Next, Cockrell hurried Colonel Riley's First and Fourth Missouri from the line's left to reinforce the right, after a young staff officer, twenty-three-year-old Captain Robert L. Maupin, had excitedly informed Colonel Cockrell that the Missouri Brigade's right flank was in serious trouble. Not long afterward, Captain Maupin was knocked off his horse with a dangerous wound, resulting in the loss of an arm. The cheering soldiers of the First and Fourth Missouri arrived to stem the crisis, after double-quicking some distance. To stabilize the situation, General Bowen was in the midst of the action, helping to position his old regiment on the mauled right flank of the Fifth Missouri, while Hovey's victorious troops continued to roll forward.

After quickly forming in line under a heavy fire, the reliable veterans of the First and Fourth Missouri unleashed a point-blank volley into the Yankees, who had charged to within 10 paces. The blistering fire shocked the attackers and relieved the heavily-pressured right of the Fifth Missouri. The Union onslaught, however, continued and the situation remained critical, for the Missouri Brigade was the largest force of Confederates which stood between Hovey's juggernaut and the annihilation of Pemberton's army.

Indeed, the Confederates of the First and Fourth Missouri suddenly found themselves in a bad fix, taking an enfilade fire and discovering that the Federals were attempting to turn the regiment's right flank. More of Riley's soldiers were hit while standing firm. One casualty was a twenty-five-year-old drummer boy, Musician Charles A. Miller. He was killed while beating his drum in attempting to rally his hard-hit unit. To parry the serious threat, Colonel Riley ordered his two right companies to shift and align at right angles to the Missouri Brigade's line. That complicated maneuver for the two companies to face east was extremely difficult under fire, but it was completed swiftly and efficiently and prevented the First and Fourth Missouri from being enfiladed.

To further solidify the Missouri Brigade's tenuous position, General Bowen ordered his old regiment to charge with the bayonet, as on the first day at Shiloh. The First and Fourth Missouri Rebels surged forward with shouts of defiance, gaining more ground and winning additional precious time for the last-minute solidification of the Missouri Brigade's alignment. Despite the short charge of this lone Confederate regiment, the crisis was far from over. Colonel Riley's St. Louisans and Bootheelers kept dropping because of the unceasing flank fire from the advancing Yankees only 30-40 yards distant.[17]

The odds for success increased with the arrival of Bowen's other brigade. Arriving in timely fashion, General Green's veterans deployed on the First and Fourth Missouri's right. Then the alignment of Bowen's division was complete. The familiar battle-cries of the Missouri and Arkansas Rebels to the right told Missouri Brigade members of a successful union. At last, Bowen's 5,000 soldiers were ready to come to grips with the best of Grant's Army that afternoon.[18]

A sense of invincibility raced through the Missourians' ranks upon viewing the inspiring sight of Colonel Cockrell coolly shaking hands with Colonel Gates, whose First Missouri Cavalry (Dismounted) held the left of Green's brigade, while bullets whizzed by and the Yankees charged closer. The meeting of those two aggressive leaders brought back memories of the fleeting moments of victory at Pea Ridge and Corinth. Equally encouraging was the arrival of the Missouri Brigade's three batteries, which dashed into position behind the sprawling gray battle-lines. Quickly unlimbering amid a heavy fire, those Missouri cannon roared in reply. General Bowen and his eager Confederates were encouraged by the bellowing of the field piece christened the "Lady Bowen."[19]

Barely 2,000 Missouri Rebels were ready to strike a powerful blow, feeling that the chance to hit Grant harder than at any other time in the Vicksburg Campaign was imminent. Indeed, that was the first and last time that the entire Missouri Brigade—Pemberton's "Grenadier Guard"—would have an opportunity to take the tactical offensive against Grant. Each soldier also seemed to realize that the path to Missouri lay straight through the heart of Grant's victorious army.

"At this time our Brigade was in fine fettle," concluded Private Kavanaugh. Colonel Cockrell's veterans were hardened and tough, being "lithe, sinewy, ragged, and bronzed, the very type of our Missouri rebels," wrote one Macon County officer. Every soldier able to shoulder a musket was standing in the assault formations, including Privates Thomas Doyle, William Henry Hicks, and John T. Tipton, one-armed Rebels of the Fifth Missouri.

Never had motivation been so high as on May 16. Recent letters from Union-held Missouri had told of fathers, brothers and other family members robbed, beaten, or executed by Union militia. Others had learned that their homes and even entire towns had been burned to the ground. In addition, Colonel Cockrell had recently promised his soldiers that "by our acts we will avenge" the deaths of the many comrades slain at Port Gibson barely two weeks before. In terms of morale and fighting spirit, therefore, the normally unsettling reality that "it was [now primarily] the Missouri Confederates against Grant's army" was not quite the unequal equation as it looked on paper.[20]

The resolve of the individual soldier could be viewed in the Sixth Missouri's color bearer, New York City-born Lieutenant William Henry Huff, a twenty-six-year-old farmer of Jackson County. In leading the charge upon Corinth's fortifications, Huff was hit by five bullets before he was convinced to hand over the banner to another soldier. After miraculously recovering from wounds in both arms, both thighs, and a leg, he returned to fight at Champion Hill.[21] The distinctive battle-flag of the "Bloody Sixth" that Huff held proudly, and other Missouri banners gave the advancing Yankees notice of another bloody reunion with "the South's Finest." One Federal who later reflected upon the Sixth Missouri's flag said: "I dreaded the sight of it [for] it meant the hardest fighting we ever had to do."[22]

More minie balls whistled by and additional Confederates became casualties, while the Federals intensified their efforts to hurl Bowen's obstinate Rebels off the field. As Colonel Cockrell wrote, "The heavy, strong lines of the enemy [were] rapidly advancing and cheering, flushed with their success and the capture of our guns." Finally, it was now the Confederates' turn to strike back.[23]

About 2:30 p.m. the blistering sun of May 16 beat down upon the gray formations, reflecting off the rows of bayonets. Graycoats falling out of line dead or wounded only resulted in the closing up of ranks. General Bowen and Colonels Cockrell, McCown, Gause, Riley and Senteny and Major Stephen Cooper—leading the Sixth Missouri because Colonel Erwin was sick and wounded—made final preparations for the charge. Shouting encouragement before the double lines of Confederates, these experienced leaders rode along their lenghty formations, which extended across the sun-baked fields of the Isaac Roberts's Plantation. To clear the way for the counterattack, enlisted men darted before the line and hurriedly dismantled a rail fence. The opportunity for which the Missourians had waited so long had arrived.[24]

Brightly-colored battle-flags waved above the Missourians' lengthy lines, snapping in the afternoon sunlight. Colonel Cockrell galloped down his formations with a sword in one hand and a colorful magnolia flower in the other. The flower's symbolism represented both the vibrance of that beautiful Mississippi spring and the springtime of the infant Southern nation to the soldiers in the ranks. In a neat line that spanned hundreds of yards across the hot fields, the entire Missouri Brigade was finally intact and ready to launch an attack. As the Yankee onslaught roared ever-closer, confident Rebel officers drew sabers and at last screamed, "Charge!"[25]

More than 2,000 Missouri Confederates rushed forward, unleashing their distinctive, unearthly-sounding "Missouri Yells." McGinnis's seasoned Federals realized that they were once more about to tangle with the shock troops of Pemberton's army. Advancing side by side Cockrell's soldiers assaulted the enemy west of the Ratliff Plantation road, while Green's Confederates charged to the road's east.[26]

The onrushing Missouri Rebels slammed into the Unionists in the Roberts's orchard, just south of the Crossroads. Murderous volleys were exchanged at point-blank range and bodies began piling up under the blooming fruit trees. In the afternoon heat and humidity, young soldiers in blue and gray slugged with rifle-butts and lunged with bayonets. Stunned by the Missourians' accurate fire and reckless abandon, the reeling Indiana and Wisconsin soldiers retired through the orchard. Raising another cheer, Cockrell's Rebels continued charging through the orchard and past the dead and wounded bluecoats lying amid the dust and fallen blossoms. One elated St. Louis Irishman in gray perhaps here implored, "At them boys! at them! for the honour of old Ireland." The Missouri Brigade surged toward the next target, the strategic Crossroads.[27]

After fighting north on the run for several hundred yards, the howling Missourians converged on the Crossroads. There, the Unionists had rallied and marshaled a desperate defense around the captured Southern artillery. Without pausing or counting the cost, Cockrell's grayclads poured over the Crossroads, sensing victory. Covered in dirt and sweat, the attacking Confederates killed and drove out Hovey's soldiers with bayonets, rocks, fists, and musket-butts. In overrunning the Crossroads, they had taken the first difficult step to reverse the day's fortunes. In the first Rebel success of the day, Cockrell's troops recaptured four pieces of Captain James F. Waddell's Alabama Battery and continued forward, pushing the fiercely resisting Federals toward Champion Hill.

Ugly clumps of dead and injured Confederates outlined the path of the Missouri Brigade's charge through the grain fields, the orchard, and belts of forest. Around the captured artillery, Missouri dead were lying in sickening piles, where blasts of canister had cut them down. The deep, sunken roads were splashed red with the gore from blue and gray, wrote a horrified Private Smith, until "the blood ran in a stream, as water would have done, after a hard rain."[28]

The slashing charge of the Missourians rolled onward, surging up through the heavily timbered lands that gradually rose to Champion Hill, the most important objective that had to be captured to save the day. In a letter to his father, Sergeant Hogan wrote that the cheering Missouri Confederates tore savagely "through the enemy's lines, the ground strewn with their dead."

The close-range and often no-quarter struggle for Champion Hill, still another 600 yards north, was being decided in the jungle-like forests, deep ravines, and hilltops of the Sid Champion Plantation. The near-perfect formations of Cockrell's

Brigade were no more, having dissolved into fragments as the contest degenerated into a savage fight between isolated groups of antagonists. Bitter hand-to-hand fighting swirled under the towering oaks, pines, and magnolias, amid the drifting smoke of battle. Bullets smacked into trees and sent bark flying, while cutting down long strands of Spanish moss. With ear-piercing screams, bands of Missouri attackers often charged down into deep gullies choked with underbrush and up the other side only to have volleys explode in their faces.

That day Cockrell's Rebels struggled with the Yankees for possession of white oak thickets, ravines, and clumps of pines on slight elevations which suddenly had to be taken before the advance could continue. The wild, hand-to-hand fighting continued for what seemed like an eternity, with the attackers leap-frogging onward to the next series of ravines held by the Yankees.[29]

Steadily retiring Unionists maintained a scorching fire, dropping more Rebels in Cockrell's relentless drive to secure the all-important crest of Champion Hill. Leading Company E, First and Fourth Missouri, Captain Norval Spangler fell mortally wounded. He had rejoined his command only the day before, after recovering from a nasty Iuka wound. Splashed in blood, Captain Spangler, a twenty-six-year-old poetry lover and promising writer from the once-picturesque St. Clair County town of Osceola, spoke his last words in a soldier's arms only seconds before expiring: "I guess I'll take supper with Stonewall Jackson tonight." An old friend from an Illinois regiment would later recognize Captain Spangler's body and give him a decent burial. Torn to pieces by an artillery shell, Private William E. Nichols, a twenty-year-old soldier from Marion County, was so badly mangled that he could only be identified by the tintypes of his relatives found in his pocket.[30] Practically all of the Missouri Brigade's dead would be unceremoniously piled like cordwood in a shallow burial trench by the Unionists after the battle.

On the strategic crest of Champion Hill, meanwhile, McGinnis tried frantically to patch together a defense to halt the seemingly unstoppable Missouri Rebels, who continued screaming like crazy and kept coming as if there were no tomorrow. As at Port Gibson, McGinnis's Indiana brigade was cut to pieces by Cockrell's ferocious counterattack. Success was also gained to the east on the Missouri Brigade's right, where Slack's brigade of tough Iowa, Ohio, and Indiana troops took a terrific beating from Green's advance. The tables were finally turned by Bowen's counterattack, with the vanquished becoming the victors. With machine-like efficiency, Bowen's division destroyed Hovey's division, turning the tide and obtaining a measure of revenge for being whipped by that fine command at Port Gibson.

General McGinnis had one last hope. With a new sense of urgency, he brought up as much artillery as possible in a desperate attempt to blunt Cockrell's attack. In a short time a couple of Sixteenth Ohio Light Artillery cannon hurriedly unlimbered along the commanding terrain and then literally blew apart the foremost groups of Missouri soldiers. The best and brightest of the Missouri Brigade were mowed down by double loads of canister, but "yet, though the slaughter was appalling, still on they came," wrote one unbelieving Ohio cannoneer, "they were determined to break our line at this point at any cost."

Meanwhile, the Missouri Yells grew louder and more unnerving to Champion Hill's defenders. And those waving blue battle-flags, with the white Latin crosses reminiscent of the Crusades, pointed the way to decisive victory for Cockrell's troops. Heavy losses only intensified Rebel efforts to carry the wooded hill lined with blue formations and United States flags. Formidable Champion Hill, the area's highest elevation, was the key to the battle ground.[31]

Lieutenant Colonel Finley Lewis Hubbell, mortally wounded at Champion Hill
Courtesy Mrs. Leon Rice Taylor, Richmond, Mo.
(Unpublished Painting)

The Tragic Fate of Three Brothers

Private David Henderson Duvall, killed at Champion Hill
Courtesy Dr. Thomas P. Sweeney, Springfield, Mo.
(Unpublished Photo)

Private Thomas Isaac Duvall (left), killed at Champion Hill. Lieutenant William Russell Duvall (right), killed at Corinth as color-bearer of the Third Missouri Confederate Infantry
Courtesy Dr. Thomas P. Sweeney, Springfield, Mo.
(Unpublished Photo)

More and more attackers dropped in the fields and woodlands like fallen autumn leaves. Lieutenant Colonel Hubbell was leading his Third Missourians forward with his saber raised high, shouting encouragement, when a bullet whistled through his arm. By today's standards it was a minor flesh wound but was a fatal injury during that scorching May afternooon in Mississippi.

The lieutenant colonel had eagerly accepted one of the most dangerous assignments on May 16, leading the Missouri Brigade's skirmish battalion. But for the Hubbell family in Ray County, only the three gold stars of "Fin's" colonel's rank from his uniform collar would be brought back from Champion Hill for the grieving relatives. Ironically, the final entry that the ever-optimistic Colonel Hubbell had written in his diary emphasized a reality that would never come true for either the Missouri Brigade or the Confederacy: "Our future looks dark, but surely freedom's battles once begun, can but end in victory."[32]

In the Third Missouri's ranks, among those mortally wounded were two of the regiment's best soldiers, the two youngest brothers of the four-man Duvall clan, Lieutenant Thomas Isaac and Private David Henderson Duvall, age nineteen. Both died in the smoky forests of Champion Hill hundreds of miles from their home along the placid Crooked River. The young brothers found a final resting place in Mississippi soil, like another brother who had been killed at Corinth, Lieutenant William R. Duvall. The last surviving brother, Private Joseph F. Duvall, continued attacking through the tangled woodlands and up the bloody hill of no return.[33]

Fueled by a fanatical desperation, the Missourians' desire to win the day at Champion Hill almost bordered on madness. Many of the wounded refused to retire, advancing onward through the thick layers of smoke as best they could in a last grasp for victory. Hobbling forward from tree to tree with make-shift bloody bandages hastily tied together, injured soldiers continued to ram minie balls down muskets and blast away. Battle-toughened Colonel Riley could hardly believe "some of the men receiving two wounds before quiting [sic] the field" and seeking medical treatment.

One such Confederate was Private David M. Gill, who continued to charge with the First and Fourth Missouri's colors, despite a serious wound. Six color bearers of Colonel Riley's unit were shot down while carrying the regimental banner at Champion Hill. On May 16 the representative attitude of the Missourians was to "do or die."

Another determined soldier was Private Daniel Monahan, a St. Louis laborer of the Fifth Missouri. Monahan waged his own private war amid the blooming magnolias and tall pines, attacking a squad of Yankees, who were firing from behind a large log. Bounding over the log, the twenty-two-year-old Irish Rebel "commenced striking right and left, with mad energy [and] his long hair streaming in the wind, the Herculean blows he made, and the [curses] with which he accompanied each one, gave him the appearance of being some avenging angel," wrote one Missouri officer.[34]

With battle-flags falling repeatedly and then being quickly picked up again, Cockrell's Rebels poured up the southern slope of Champion Hill, loading and firing rapidly during the push through the snarled brush and timber. Powder-stained Missourians bayoneted or clubbed down their opponents in the surge toward the crest. Countless savage individual battles between small groups of antagonists swirled in the suffocating thickets and brushy ravines, for which more young men of each side died. Those Missouri Rebels without rounds frantically searched through the cartridge-boxes of friend and foe, gaining an invaluable resupply amid the smoke-laced woodlands.[35]

Private David F. Lenox, age twenty-four, grabbed a special bullet from his pocket, having saved this memento of Corinth for such a moment. A Confederate surgeon had recently removed the lead ball from his arm, where it had been embedded for months. The vengeful First and Fourth Missouri Rebel evened the score, loading the ball into his Enfield and taking a carefully-aimed shot at the nearest Yankee.

Few survivors of the struggle for Champion Hill would ever forget the horror of the "hill of death" deep in Mississippi's forests. The day's most bitter fighting lay in the path of the Missouri Brigade's onslaught. In the words of Colonel Slack, whose veteran brigade was simply torn apart by the Missouri Confederates that was a most "terrible, and most sanguinary conflict, which, in point of terrific fierceness and stubborn persistency, finds but few parallels in the history of civilized warfare."[36]

Finally the Missourians charged within close enough range to punish the Ohio cannoneers atop the bald crest of Champion Hill. Spilling into the last ravine before the crest, Cockrell's marksmen picked off Yankee gunners, battery horses, and officers. Amid an open field around some rustic slave cabins, the withering fires of those expert sharpshooters decimated the Union defenders. Then the yelling Confederates sprinted forward to bayonet and bludgeon Federal cannoneers to death around their field pieces, after McGinnis's mauled infantrymen were hurled off the crest by the Missouri Brigade.

At last the victorious Rebels raised a cheer across the hilltop, drowning out the rattle of musketry and the groans of the fallen. Hundreds of Missouri Confederates overran Champion Hill's crest, capturing two Ohio cannon and two Rebel guns lost earlier. Laying a solid claim to the body-littered hilltop, the Missouri artillery unlimbered in the barren cotton patch along the crest.

Incredibly, Cockrell's troops had accomplished what was practically impossible: defeating a victorious and more numerous opponent, retaking the two most strategic points on the battlefield—the Crossroads and Champion Hill's crest—, capturing prisoners, reversing the day's fortunes, reclaiming captured Confederate batteries, and earning Grant's respect, while "the farthest the enemy was away from us during that time was not over 25 yards," wrote Sergeant Hogan in a letter.[37]

Also on the road's right, or east, the charge of Green's brigade achieved significant gains, pushing resistance rearward. Unleashing tremendous striking power, Bowen's attackers had smashed the crack brigades of Slack and McGinnis. Bowen's division had not only saved the day, but also had regained and handed the initiative to Pemberton for the first time during that all-important campaign.

With the capture of Champion Hill, the hard-hitting team of Bowen, Cockrell, and Green had punctured Grant's center. Continuing the attack north to the next elevation might result in the destruction of Grant's army by splitting it in half, and putting an abrupt end to the invasion of Mississippi. Not only were no bluecoats except the dead and wounded in sight before the Missouri Brigade, but the Union army's supply train was in plain sight, ready for the taking.[38]

Those experienced soldiers instinctively knew when to keep pushing forward. The Missourians' charge, therefore, continued downhill off Champion Hill, for only a few more yards needed to be gained to achieve a complete victory. It almost seemed as if Missouri Brigade members would hurl the last resisting "Yankees clear into Alabama," swore one soldier. As at no other time in their history, the Missouri Confederates seemed on the verge of achieving an unparalleled success in the West during their most decisive battle of the war.

Cockrell's attackers took additional ground, inflicting more damage, and tearing further into Grant's dissolved center. According to a Sergeant Hogan letter which recorded the extent of the Missouri Brigade's amazing success, the feeling of victory was high, "for one mile [we had] advanced through the enemy's lines." Grant's never previously defeated army was on the verge of being split in half. Lieutenant George Elliott scribbled in his diary that the day had appeared lost and the fate of Vicksburg sealed, "but we turned the tide, and drove the enemy back a mile," during one of the most successful counterattacks of the war.[39]

To Cockrell's right, General Green's brigade continued its devastating attack. By that time, two of Lee's reliable Alabama regiments, of Stevenson's division, had rallied "as if by magic" on the Missouri Brigade's left and advanced, after being inspired by Cockrell's charge. Unexpected help also came from a couple of good Georgia regiments which plugged a dangerous gap between Cockrell's and Green's brigades, fueling the attack's momentum. Consequently, the two brigades of Bowen's division now remained intact and continued to advance as a cohesive fighting machine, while spilling onward through the fields and forests of Hinds County.

As in the past, the spectacle of the Missouri Rebels attacking recklessly inspired resolve in other Confederates. A Rebel surgeon could not believe the extent of the Missouri Brigade's success but counted the high cost, writing in his diary: "Oh God! how many brave and gallant soldiers [were lost and] the ground is covered with the dead and wounded federals whom, our division [,] Bowens [,] has driven two miles, breaking through several lines of battle."[40]

The Missouri Brigade held the primary key to the battlefield, Champion Hill. One Second Missouri soldier never forgot how the defeated and fleeing Unionists left "us almost in possession of their ammunition train [and] the drivers were whipping up their mules and making every effort to escape [and] we had broken Grant's centre and felt the day ours." General Pemberton learned that day how a total disaster could be suddenly turned into victory by his crack "Old Guard" troops. Additionally, General Pemberton also began to realize how "if I had 10,000 more Missourians [such as these] I would have won and carried the war."[41]

But victory was suddenly snatched away. At almost the last moment, General Marcellus M. Crocker's division of 4,000 fresh Union troops poured from the thick woods of the adjacent hill to the north, where the Champion House stood. Colonel Cockrell's charge was being transformed into the brutal reality that the elated "Missourians [were only blindly] going to their deaths," lamented one Southerner.[42]

Their drive was blunted by the initial mass of blue reserves south of the Champion House. Cockrell's survivors stubbornly retired a short distance to the belt of timber along Champion Hill's northern slope. There, they would make their stand, despite having suffered hundreds of casualties and with few rounds left in cartridge-boxes. Sergeant Hogan told of the crisis that had befallen the outnumbered Missouri Brigade soldiers, writing that he had already "fired forty-five rounds during the [more than a mile] charge, which was about the hardest one hour's work that I ever done." The Missouri Rebels could now load their rifles with Springfield rounds taken from the cartridge-boxes of Union dead and wounded. Consequently, Cockrell's soldiers tenaciously held their positions and poured a steady stream of fire from their new Enfields.

Hundreds of Federals of Colonel George B. Boomer's brigade aligned in dense formations before the survivors of the Missouri Brigade and halted to blast away at close range. Then more slaughter occurred among the already decimated Missouri

The Missouri Brigade is depicted in position along the woodline during the final stages of the Battle of Champion Hill
Courtesy Frank Wood's Picture Bank, Alexandria, Va.

regiments, as both sides traded volleys in the sweltering heat and dense smoke of battle. One Unionist knew that Boomer's brigade had encountered the South's finest troops, when the attack of his regiment was stopped by "a solid wall of men in gray, their muskets at their shoulders roaring as if it were the end of the world. Bravely they stood there [and now we] killed each other as fast as we could." Those Federal reserves of Boomer's veteran brigade, which included one Missouri regiment, had smashed hard into Cockrell's brigade, but they had met their match. However, the gap of opportunity leading to decisive victory, which had been opened wide only minutes before, was slowly being closed forever as more units of Crocker's fresh division reached the field.[43]

With most ammunition expended among the powder-stained Missouri infantrymen after some soldiers had fired almost 100 rounds, the roles of Wade's, Guibor's, and Landis's batteries became more crucial than ever before. In the assessment of St. Louisan Lieutenant Joseph Boyce, age twenty-one: "Had it not been for the quick movements of Guibor and Landis [and Wade's battery] we were lost [but] it was the artillery saving the infantry."

Led by aggressive, experienced officers who advocated the mobile and flexible tactics of the "flying artillery" of the Mexican War, the Missouri guns were rolled downhill through the timber and off the bald crest of Champion Hill to take position beside the Missouri Brigade's ever-dwindling formations on the hill's northern slope. Such an advanced position for artillery was risky with a powerful Federal counterattack in the making.

Keeping pace with the Missouri Brigade's infantry, somehow the Missouri field pieces had been pushed forward by the hard-working artillerymen through tangles of underbrush, between trees, and over ravines filled with dead and wounded. Lieutenant Cockery's pieces of Guibor's unit roared on the Missouri Brigade's left. Farther east, meanwhile, the cannon under Lieutenant Walsh, of Wade's battery, and Lieutenant John M. Langan, of Landis's battery, bellowed from the right flank of the Missouri Brigade. Salvos of canister kept the hordes of Federals from turning both of Colonel Cockrell's flanks at that critical time. If Pemberton rushed reinforcements to the Missouri Brigade, then perhaps their gains could yet be exploited.[44]

Not all the Missourians were engaged in the brutal stand-up fight, exchanging volleys and killing each other as rapidly as possible. Colonel Riley's First and Fourth Missouri on Cockrell's right and companies of the Fifth Missouri, to Riley's left, continued attacking with almost suicidal abandon. That charge north centered on the narrow Plantation Road, the objective being the wooded hill upon which stood the Champion House. After the Union army's ordnance train had fled in the face of the Missouri Brigade's attack, those wagons raced north and took position north of the Champion House elevation. Colonel Riley was eager to overrun the hill and destroy Grant's bountiful supply train, the logistical support system for the invasion of Mississippi. Colonel Riley felt "a wagon train could be seen immediately over the hill, hence my desire to gain the hill."[45] The southeast Missouri colonel, well-trained at the Kentucky Military Institute and battle-tested since the inferno of Shiloh, knew that success equated to his regiment's torn battle-flag being firmly planted atop the hill to the north on this nightmarish afternoon in Mississippi.

Colonel Riley's charge through the timber and up the Plantation Road, rolled forward in a desperate bid to carry the field. Cheering Rebels of Riley's regiment tore into the Union reinforcements, striking and almost turning the left of Boomer's brigade. If Colonel Riley could roll up Boomer's flank, then the Missouri Brigade might continue the advance. With his fighting blood up, Colonel Riley was determined to achieve victory on May 16.

Despite the odds, twice the First and Fourth Missouri charged forward to redeem the day. After ripping through the one blue line, an isolated band of Missouri Rebels engaged in a grisly contest with musket-butts and bayonets beside the wagons of a Union ambulance train in the rear. Also another lone party of Cockrell's foremost soldiers had set some Yankee supply wagons on fire, before being driven off. Those two determined thrusts by the First and Fourth Missouri only brought the same results: a lengthening casualty list, a bloody repulse, and a near victory.[46]

In achieving the deepest Confederate penetration of the day, Colonel Riley's regiment was devastated, probably suffering the highest loss of any Southern regiment at Champion Hill. The First and Fourth Missouri's desperate bid to carry the hill and capture Grant's supply wagons cost the regiment many of its best officers. For example, two fine captains, William C. P. Carrington and Spangler, leading Companies A and E, were killed on the field. Also among the fallen were steadfast regimental leaders such as Captain Burke, who suffered shell wounds.

Other First and Fourth Missouri officers cut down by Yankee bullets were Lieutenant Colonel Garland, Lieutenant Samuel Kennerly, and Captain Charles L. Edmondson, who had all served in the Missouri Volunteer Militia of St. Louis before the war. In addition, many of the regiment's finest enlisted personnel were killed, such as the Irishman "Wild Pat Doolan," who fought as hard as he raised hell.[47]

The Missouri troops came surprisingly close to turning Boomer's left and sweeping Grant's initial reinforcements off the field. But, as at Port Gibson, General Hovey proved to be the Missouri Brigade's nemesis. Hovey had learned his lesson well at Port Gibson, where a heavy concentration of artillery had smashed the Missourians' attacks. In a repeat performance, he ordered the First Missouri, Company A, and Sixth Wisconsin batteries and surviving Sixteenth Ohio cannon to unlimber on high ground southeast of the Champion House. Those same Wisconsin guns had helped to stop the Missouri Brigade's attack upon Corinth. Hovey's timely actions resulted in the same disastrous consequences for Confederate fortunes, with Green's brigade and Colonel Riley's regiment taking the brunt of the punishment from the massed firepower.

In addition to the arrival of Crocker's division and Hovey's rallied units, the rows of Federal cannon ensured Union victory at Champion Hill. The fury unleashed by the Yankee artillery pieces again proved Hovey's wisdom. In short order, the attacking Confederates were decimated by the concentrated firepower. Among those fresh units thrown into the fray were Colonel Samuel A. Holmes's regiments, of Crocker's third brigade, which included Missouri units that had clashed with the Missouri Brigade at Pea Ridge and Corinth.

Another vicious exchange of swinging muskets, lunging bayonets, and thrown punches erupted, when still another charge by the First and Fourth Missouri clashed head-on with the arriving blue reinforcements in the barren cotton fields between the two hills. In addition to being punished by the artillery salvos, Colonel Riley's regiment received no urgently needed assistance from Green's brigade, to the right, in helping to turn the left flank of Boomer's brigade because those units had been enfiladed and smashed by the cannonade. That was the third time that the First and Fourth Missouri tried to overrun the hill, turn Boomer's flank, capture Grant's munitions train, and snatch victory from the jaws of defeat.[48]

The concentrated artillery fire forced the battered Missouri and Arkansas regiments to fall back. That collapse of the forward progress of the Missouri Brigade's right flank placed Cockrell's main line in an even more precarious position. A flank fire shortly erupted from the east, raking the Missouri Brigade's rightmost units. Heavy blue formations hovered around each flank, and prepared to strike a blow from which the Missouri Brigade would never recover.

Captain Wade's, Guibor's and Landis's guns again rescued Cockrell's hard-pressed infantrymen from destruction. Anchoring each flank, the Missouri cannon roared across the body-strewn fields and woodlands, keeping the advancing Federals at bay. Many Unionists, however, came within close range and shot down Rebel cannoneers, who refused to desert their positions before the Yankee onslaught.

Taking the place of a fallen gunner was Father Bannon, who had previously assisted the artillerymen during desperate emergencies. Captains Landis's and Wade's batteries on the Missouri Brigade's right faced the greatest challenge, for hundreds of Federals attempted to turn Cockrell's flank and gain the rear.

And on the left, Guibor's cannon faced a similar crisis. Father Bannon worked an artillery piece of Guibor's battery like a seasoned veteran. The Confederacys' "Fighting Chaplain" was again in action, providing inspiration to the troops by deeds and not simply words. Every Missouri Rebel was needed on Champion Hill. But as during the crucial moments at the Battles of Pea Ridge, Corinth, and Port Gibson, Colonel Cockrell's Rebels would receive no support or breaks in their bid for success.[49]

While the blazing cannon kept the Yankees at a distance, around 4 o'clock orders to withdraw were received from General Bowen. No reinforcements or ammunition and impossible odds left the Missourians with no choice but to retire or die. Colonel Cockrell, nevertheless, refused to obey the withdrawal order immediately for the Missouri Confederates felt that Loring's troops "might still arrive in time to push forward the successes and advantages so gallantly and dearly won." Making the right move, Pemberton had ordered Loring forward to exploit the dramatic gains won by Bowen. However, General Loring had balked, refusing to support Bowen's soldiers, who continued to be slaughtered while fighting almost alone at Champion Hill. Grant's troops pressed both flanks, swarming forward on three sides, almost surrounding the Missouri Brigade.

Bowen's division, mangled but not beaten, finally retired through the war-torn lands of the Champion Plantation. The day's impressive gains were suddenly void: pushing the Unionists back more than a mile, almost splitting Grant's army in two, capturing two Union cannon, retaking six Rebel guns, struggling for more than two and a half hours, and nearly saving both Vicksburg and perhaps the Confederacy with one great charge during one of the war's most decisive contests.[50]

During the confusion and deafening noise of battle, Colonel Riley, however, never received orders to withdraw. A breathless officer at last reported to the colonel that the rest of the Missouri Brigade had retired. Colonel Riley's survivors quickly turned and rejoined the Missouri Brigade, swinging across Champion Hill and through a torrent of bullets on the double.

Other Missourians also never heard the command to withdraw. Thick gunsmoke, a large percentage of officers already killed or wounded, the noise of battle, and the heavy timber and underbrush guaranteed a breakdown of communication. Sergeant Claudius Marcellus Bonaparte Thurmond, age twenty and a law student from Louisiana, Missouri, was rapidly loading and firing in the thickets with another sergeant, "confident the day was ours, ..." The "beardless, handsome boy" heard a shout, turned rearward and learned that he and his comrade were the foremost Rebels confronting the counterattacking Federals. Sergeant Thurmond shortly escaped through the forests, later continuing to compile a distinguished record as the "boy captain" of the Second Missouri.[51]

A desperate race for the Crossroads began with a strong Yankee column pushing toward the intersection from the east via the Middle Road. Bowen's troops could only escape by reaching the Crossroads before the Federals. They had fought their way northeast beyond Champion Hill and then had to contest the same terrain during the withdrawal southwest out of the woodlands.

That blood-stained avenue was a graveyard where a staggering total of 600 Missouri Brigade members were killed, wounded, or captured. The First and Fourth Missouri suffered the highest casualties with the loss of 175 soldiers. Other units also suffered high losses: the Sixth Missouri, 121; the Third Missouri, 120; the Fifth Missouri, 90; and the Second Missouri, 83. Captains Wade's, Guibor's, and Landis's Batteries lost at least 22 artillerymen. Almost a third of the Missouri Brigade had been destroyed in less than three hours.

The withdrawal continued to be dangerous because the Missourians had "to pass between two lines of the enemy, which were not far apart and receive a fire from both lines, one on either side of us," recalled one of Cockrell's survivors. Also Union artillery zeroed in and shelled Colonel Cockrell's retiring units. Occasionally, the last straggling Confederates with a few remaining rounds in cartridge-boxes banded together to unleash the Missouri Brigade's final volleys of the day. The possibility existed that the Missouri Brigade might be cut off and destroyed, for strong Union forces continued to push west for the Crossroads. But only a few of Cockrell's veterans threw down muskets and raised hands to surrender.[52]

Beating the Yankees in the race, the Missouri Rebels finally neared the strategic Crossroads, where other Confederate troops were holding the key position. Much of Pemberton's army pushed for the crossing over Baker's Creek before heading toward Vicksburg. Around the Crossroads, the Missouri batteries again unlimbered to provide timely service. Amid a wide cornfield, Captain Guibor's, Wade's, and Landis's trusty cannon spat fire at a frantic pace, keeping the blue formations at a distance. That was another good example of the Missouri Brigade's artillery and infantry working closely together and fighting to survive each new crisis on May 16.

Apparently about that time, an enraged Captain Landis ordered a shell fired close to the rear of a wavering Southern regiment, which needed to hold the line to avert a rout. The resulting explosion just behind the shaky regiment kept more of its members from fleeing, steadying the command in an unusual example of artillery assisting an infantry unit in a crisis. Perhaps that was the last shot fired by Landis's battery, which expended every round. Swore one Missouri infantryman, "The thunder of [Captain Landis's] guns was glorious music to us." Such inspiration helped some of the most decimated Missouri units to rally around the Roberts's House, barn and cotton gin, which were part of a vast field hospital complex and an island amid a sea of suffering humanity. At Champion Hill, however, most Missouri Brigade soldiers would lay for two or three days on the field before receiving medical attention.[53]

After pushing southwest down the Plantation Road to strike the Raymond Road, Cockrell's units swung west and finally crossed Baker's Creek. As often in this campaign, the Missourians were ordered to provide rear-guard service. General Pemberton used the Missouri Brigade once again in the role as the army's most reliable troops. Despite their devastating losses, Colonel Cockrell's soldiers earned the key assignment to hold the vital Baker's Creek crossing to allow other Southerners, including those who had protected the Missouri Brigade's withdrawal, to reach safety.

Meanwhile, Green's brigade likewise completed dispositions on the west bank. Grant's army continued to pursue, intent on crushing Pemberton's command. Any Federal advance upon the fords of Baker's Creek had to be repulsed to allow Pemberton's army time to escape.[54]

With shell-fire raking the bank, bluecoats advancing and no additional Confederates coming across, Colonel Cockrell finally ordered his troops to the rear, after the successful stand at the Baker's Creek ford. Bowen was forced to abandon that position with his left out-flanked. Union cannon had crossed the creek to the north, enfilading the Rebel lines and commanding the road leading to safety.

Unfortunately, the Missouri Confederates had held their position on the west bank of Baker's Creek too long in waiting for Loring's division, which had earlier protected Bowen's withdrawal. Loring's units fell back by another route away from the main army to link with Johnston, and never rejoined Pemberton. The Missourians looked in vain for Loring both during their charge on Champion Hill and during the withdrawal. The absence of Loring's more than 7,800 troops had cost the lives of many Missouri Brigade members and brought about defeat at Champion Hill. Another crisis developed when the withdrawing Missouri Rebels discovered the main road to Edwards Station was blocked by Federal units. Cockrell's escape route and the road to Vicksburg was barred.[55]

Sunset and the absence of Union cavalry helped to save the Missouri Brigade from capture or annihilation. Cockrell led his regiments south off the main road, before marching west across the rough countryside of Hinds County. At last Colonel Cockrell's Rebels escaped into the night, after the Missouri Brigade had made a "grand old charge, in which it bored a hole through the Federal army, and finding itself unsupported turned around and bored its way back again," wrote one Confederate.[56]

After the nightmare of Champion Hill, surviving Missourians felt that they had been left to shoulder most of the responsibility for stopping Grant's invading army during the decisive battles for Vicksburg. First the Missouri Brigade played key roles and made significant sacrifices at Grand Gulf and Port Gibson without receiving adequate support. And on May 16, Bowen's command, the smallest Confederate division, had attacked Grant's army without support, after a third of Pemberton's army had been destroyed and the other third under Loring failed to help.

Perhaps worst of all, two fresh Rebel divisions of nearly 10,000 troops were farther west, protecting Vicksburg during the climactic clash at Champion Hill. Throughout that all-important campaign, the ugly reality had been the same for the Missouri Brigade: taking on impossible odds, losing hundreds of men, and never receiving support when needed to exploit a hard-won success.

Bowen's troops had suffered 44 percent of the killed and wounded in Pemberton's army during the first two great battles of the campaign, Port Gibson and Champion Hill. On May 16, "when the Missourians were called to the rescue they gallantly carried themselves this day, winning imperishable renown and saving the entire army by their valor. Had they been supported by Loring's divisions they could have cut [Grant's army] to pieces,'' wrote an embittered surgeon of Bowen's division in his diary.

Throughout the campaign, Grant had repeatedly struck blows against the Missouri Brigade, gradually chipping away at the real "stonewall" brigade of the war, sapping more of its strength and fighting ability.[57]

In solidifying his reputation as the North's best general, Grant achieved one of his most important battlefield successes at Champion Hill. Vicksburg's fate was sealed in the cornfields and woodlands of Sid Champion. Then Pemberton's forces headed west toward Vicksburg, which beckoned invitingly. However, Vicksburg loomed as a trap on the Mississippi not for Grant, but for Pemberton. Because of its strategic importance, fortress Vicksburg drew Pemberton like a fatal magnet toward a snare from which there would be no escape. After Champion Hill, both Pemberton's army and Vicksburg were doomed.

Nevertheless, Pemberton was fortunate to have had Bowen's division available on May 16. Without Bowen's counterattack, the Southern army would have been destroyed. Pemberton should have been thankful to have escaped Grant's clutches and to have lost only about 1,300 more soldiers than his opponent, who had come so close to annihilating the Confederate army at Champion Hill.[58]

The Missouri Rebels played the key role in almost winning it all for the beleaguered South at Champion Hill.

As at Pea Ridge, Corinth, Grand Gulf, and Port Gibson, the Missouri Brigade had once more had an impact far out of proportion to its numbers. In each of the first four major battles in which the Missourians fought they engaged in combat against superior odds without the benefit of any type of defensive works, and aggressively took the tactical offensive: a primary factor explaining the devastating losses at Pea Ridge, Corinth, Port Gibson, and Champion Hill in barely six months. The Confederacy was dealt a blow on May 16 from which she would never recover.

Perhaps the most appropriate assessment of the role of the Missouri Brigade at Champion Hill came from a Federal soldier, who had been among those who had stopped the fierce charge of Cockrell's troops. He wrote that the thwarting of the Missouri Brigade's attack "gave us Vicksburg, made Grant immortal as a soldier, and helped to save this country."[59]

CHAPTER FOURTEEN

Last Stand on the Mississippi

The Missouri Brigade's withdrawal concluded about midnight. Worn Missourians literally fell into the Big Black River trenches that blocked the main road leading to Vicksburg, after trekking ten miles through rough country during the night. One survivor straggling in late from Champion Hill was Lieutenant George Washington Bates, twenty-five. A Marion County farmer and former brigade inspector, Bates rejoined the Missouri Brigade after a long ordeal with an arm broken by a bullet. In the level flood-plain of the river below where the Jackson Road and railroad cut through the defense's center, the Missouri Brigade held the line's right. Pemberton ordered Bowen's Division into the north-south running fortifications about a mile east of Big Black without a rest, despite the unit's recent heavy losses. Facing disaster at every turn, General Pemberton could place his trust in at least one unit: "I knew that the Missouri troops, under their gallant leaders, could be depended upon."[1]

Pemberton made a stand at Big Black in the vain hope that Loring's "lost" division would rejoin the army. Green's brigade held the defenses on the left, or north. Holding the center between Bowen's two brigades was General John C. Vaughn's brigade from the Vicksburg garrison, and the Fourth Mississippi of Baldwin's brigade. Immediately to the Missouri Brigade's left and to Vaughn's right, the Fourth Mississippi defended the line.

General Vaughn, a solid commander with Mexican War experience and political aspirations, and his East Tennessee mountaineers held the ditches at a critical sector. But three key conditions worked to the Tennessee brigade's disadvantage and in Grant's favor at Big Black. First, Vaughn's men were inexperienced rookies and conscripts from the most Unionist region of the Confederacy. Secondly, the Volunteer State unit was small and relatively weak. But even worse, Vaughn's assigned sector was much too long for the number of defenders. Clearly, this was the most vulnerable point of the defensive line, an Achilles heel for Bowen's stalwarts.[2]

The Missouri artillerymen were unable to rest that night. Cannoneers of Wade's and Guibor's Batteries and a section of Landis's Battery unhitched their guns, then pushed them by hand into position in line. The Confederates dozed in the sleep of the exhausted behind cotton-bale and earthen fortifications. Cockrell's Rebels finally obtained some badly needed rest.

A disastrous scenario was developing. Loring's troops were pushing toward Johnston and not Pemberton. In addition, thousands of Grant's veteran troops were advancing through the night toward Big Black, hoping to smash the final Rebel defensive position and cross the last river between them and Vicksburg. Big Black's defenders also had a rain-swollen river behind them. That precarious situation was compounded by the fact that the defenses stretching across the river's bend were simply "on the wrong side of the river," as one Missouri cannoneer wrote in his diary.[3]

After burning away patches of an early morning fog, the first rays of the sun fell upon lenghty Union formations in front of the fortifications on May 17. Skirmishing opened immediately, alerting the defenders to a new danger. In a short time Union artillery hammered Bowen's outnumbered soldiers, who were again left on their own to face the might of Grant's army. As had happened throughout the arduous campaign, General Bowen and his division had once again garnered the difficult mission of trying to stop Grant.[4]

While the intense heat and musketry increased that morning,

Lieutenant George Washington Bates
Courtesy Lily Hazel Bates, Palmyra, Mo.

the Federals became more aggressive. The Missouri Confederates unleashed a volley from the muddy trenches, deterring a Yankee probe. But the Missouri Brigade did not face the greatest danger for the Federals were about to hit the vulnerable Confederate left-center. Slipping past the left of Green's troops on the north and down a hollow running parallel to the fortifications, hundreds of Unionists from General Michael Lawler's brigade eased within striking distance of Vaughn's unwary Volunteer Staters.

Suddenly Lawler's Iowa and Wisconsin infantrymen charged from the hollow in the late morning humidity. After angling past Green's front, the Union forces tore savagely into the Tennessee brigade's left flank, smashing through the thin gray line. Cheering Federals spilled over Vaughn's position and routed the raw Tennessee Mountain troops. In one of the shortest charges of the war, a gaping hole was ripped in the Confederate left-center, exploiting Bowen's weak link.[5]

Because of the flat terrain of the sprawling cotton fields, Cockrell's defenders failed to ascertain the disaster befalling Vaughn's brigade to their left. The Missouri Rebels, therefore, were shocked by a sudden order to fall back. As thousands of Unionists flooded through the wide gap to the north, the Missouri soldiers belatedly realized the danger. One of Cockrell's followers wrote with disgust in his diary that all other Southern troops had "deserted us [and] the Missourians were the last to leave." Without order, the Missouri Rebels sprinted for their lives during the "Big Black Races," lampooned a Second Missouri survivor.

A jumbled crowd of Southerners raced for the Big Black bridges nearly a mile distant. But, in a repetition of Port Gibson no withdrawal directive reached the

Sixth Missouri. When the First and Fourth Missouri left its position on the far right and swung north behind Erwin's regiment and toward the road, the Sixth Missouri defenders mistakenly thought that the command was only redeploying to another position. Unmindful of the danger, Colonel Erwin's troops, consequently, remained for some time in their trenches, lingering until they were almost surrounded. Upon learning of their predicament, those remaining Confederates in the trenches retired on their own accord.[6]

On the line's left, meanwhile, large numbers of Green's troops were quickly cut off and surrounded. The Missouri Brigade's former unit, the First Missouri Cavalry (Dismounted) met with disaster. Hundreds of Gates's dismounted cavalrymen were captured. The Eleventh Wisconsin Volunteer Infantry gained the regimental colors. Instead of fleeing after a horse was shot from under him, Colonel Gates stayed beside about 90 of his boys. Wrote Gates, "the officers and men who could not swim pleaded so hard for me to stay with them that I gave way to them, and we were all captured." About half of the dismounted Missouri cavalrymen would spend the upcoming winter in Northern prison camps. Irrepressible Colonel Gates soon escaped his captors.[7]

Cockrell's survivors continued to dash across the bottoms. The Missourians, wrote Sergeant Hogan in a letter, fled "in regular Bull Run style—the devil take the hindmost being the order of the day." Some exiles refused to run, however. Captain Wilson, commander of one of the Missouri Brigade's best skirmish units, Company G, Second Missouri, lay in the ditches to be captured. The Virginia-born officer had seen enough of the insanity of killing for one lifetime, and quietly awaited capture in the bottom of a trench.

In contrast, many of Bowen's Missouri cannoneers stayed behind, refusing to forsake their field pieces. A serious blunder made earlier came back to haunt Wade's and Guibor's batteries and a section of Landis's battery at the works. An unknown Confederate officer had ordered the artillery unit's horses to the river's west side. Consequently, Bowen's cannon could not be hauled to safety. Blue legions soon engulfed the artillerymen and their field pieces like a tidal wave. Alone at the fortifications, the defiant handful of Missouri cannoneers, said one soldier in his diary, "did some noble fighting—defending & firing their guns, until the enemy," were practically on top of them.[8]

At the river hundreds of Southerners crowded over a railroad and flat-boat bridge that spanned the swirling Big Black. In the panic to escape, Confederates pushed their way across amid the noise and confusion. The bridges were set ablaze by the Rebels despite wounded Southerners lying on the structure. Late-comers reaching the river bank had no avenue for escape across the wide, flooded river. Many who did not know how to swim capitulated. Other desperate men, including the late-arriving cannoneers, attempted to swim across and drowned. However, some of the Rebels escaped, swimming to the west bank while bullets splashed around them. Lieutenant Thompson Alford, a sturdy young blacksmith from Ralls County, swam to Big Black's safe side in his underclothes. Some Missouri soldiers were captured while they were taking off cartridge-boxes just before plunging into the muddy waters. Other Confederates retreated down the east bank, pushing through the woods along the river for a suitable fording point farther south.[9]

Most of the Confederate troops at Big Black escaped. No Rebels present at Big Black accomplished more to save the day than Colonel Riley and his First and Fourth Missouri. After Southern resistance had collapsed, Riley led his soldiers

Obediah Taylor, Captain, C.S.A. 3rd Infantry, Missouri Vols. Taken during the Siege of Vicksburg.
Courtesy Eleanor S. Brockenbrough Library, The Museum of the Confederacy, Richmond, Va.

on the double-quick north from their position on the Missouri Brigade's right near Gin Lake. The First and Fourth Missouri was the only intact and functioning Confederate regiment on the field.

Colonel Riley's route of withdrawal north along the east bank of Gin Lake led to the road. About half-way between the defenses and the river was the narrowest point of land in the bottoms, less than 500 yards wide. It was located between the river on the north and the lake on the south. There, without being ordered, Riley hurriedly formed his regiment astride the road. At the small end of a natural funnel as the land tapered west toward the bridges, the St. Louisans and the "Swamp Foxes" of the Bootheel region withstood the advancing Yankees.

Colonel Riley's stand before the surging blue forces closest to the bridges blocked the road to the bridges, protected the Rebel withdrawal, and slowed the pursuit. Holding their ground despite the stampede of thousands of panicked Confederates, the First and Fourth Missouri formed a thin defense between the fleeing Rebels and the onrushing Federals.

Slowly, the disciplined Missouri regiment retired west through the fields. Riley's soldiers held their own during the half-mile delaying action to the bridges. Those last withdrawing Missourians maintained their poise and bold front. Once near the river, Colonel Riley organized a small party of his most reliable soldiers before the bridges. That allowed the First and Fourth Missouri to escape, and to rejoin Pemberton on Big Black's west side.

A Rebel surgeon recorded in his diary the First and Fourth Missouri's important role at Big Black River: "and for the honor of Old Missouri this part [of the withdrawal] under Col. [Riley had been] effected at a leisurely soldierly pace [because] scarcely any preparation had been made for the protection of this bridge." May 17 was one of the First and Fourth Missouri's finest days.

Another key contribution to minimize the disaster came from the remaining Missouri artillery of Bowen's division, which had not been captured. Allowing countless Rebels to escape and repelling the attackers were two remaining cannon of Landis's Battery and one of Guibor's guns. Earlier positioned by General Bowen on the bluffs on the west bank beside strong infantry support, the Missouri cannon kept the Yankees away from the bridges. "Capt. Guibor who had only one gun with him at [this] point perform[ed] some excellent execution with this gun and held the enemy somewhat in check." On the west bank Colonel Cockrell organized his survivors. As so often in the past, the exhausted Missouri soldiers instinctively banded together around their battle-flags during another fiasco not of their making, but one that had cost them dearly.[10]

Big Black River was another catastrophe in a disastrous campaign. As at Grand Gulf, Port Gibson, and Champion Hill, Bowen's division suffered the greatest losses on May 17. Less than twenty-four hours after Champion Hill, the division lost about 1,000 additional soldiers at Big Black. More than a dozen Missouri cannon from Bowen's division were captured during the Big Black River retreat. Those were the Missouri Brigade's first guns lost in action since its formation almost a year and a half before.

General Grant had further crippled Pemberton's crack division while sustaining few casualties and capturing 1,700 prisoners on May 17. Perhaps during the battles for Vicksburg, the real turning point of the campaign came as a result of Grant's relentless pounding of Bowen's division during less than three weeks in bloody May. The elite fighting force of Pemberton's army, Bowen's division, had been reduced by nearly one-half.

For General Grant to capture Vicksburg that summer, those western soldiers, especially those of the Missouri Brigade, had to be beaten. And at Port Gibson, Champion Hill and Big Black River, the Union general had accomplished that difficult task of mauling Pemberton's "Old Guard" Missouri troops as never before.[11]

One Confederate shortly after the engagement described the Missouri Brigade's dilemma at Big Black River: "I'm a Missourian, and our boys stood it almost alone, not knowing what was wanted to be done; yet, fighting as long as possible, every one leaving us, and we were obliged to fall back [for] we Missourians always fight well, even if we have to retreat afterward." Indeed, during that brutal campaign, many newspapers throughout Dixie carried stories of "Bowen's gallant Missourians" and their exploits, which garnered more fame for the dwindling band of frontier exiles.[12]

After the disaster at Big Black River, the Missouri troops joined the Confederate withdrawal, trudging wearily west toward Vicksburg. Even though Grant's pursuit was slowed at Big Black, the price of thwarting the Union advance was not yet paid in full. Cut-off from the Missouri Brigade during the withdrawal, two of the remaining Missouri cannon were captured on May 18. One Unionist wrote how the Rebel guns were unceremoniously "surrendered, with horses, harness and ammunition complete without a shot." Now 15 cannon of Bowen's division had been captured as a result of the Big Black disaster including the Iowa field pieces taken by the Missouri Brigade at Pea Ridge. Only the two-gun section of Landis's Battery and one cannon of Captain Guibor's Battery survived to enter Vicksburg.[13]

The small port community, known for its fast pace, houses of prostitution, and rough river elements, was the Confederacy's most strategic city in the West. Vicksburg was located on the most important north-south river in America and on a vital east-west railroad by which men and materiel could be drawn from the Gulf region. Also, troops and resources could be received up the "Father of Waters" from the Trans-Mississippi via the Red River, which snaked through Louisiana and Texas.

One religious-minded soldier from rural Missouri had written to his mother, and mentioned the source of the city's popularity among the men, "Vicksburg is the fastest place I have been in." But a much hotter type of action was about to descend upon the river city in Warren County, as if retribution from God. The thriving commercial town, positioned upon the second highest terrain between Memphis and New Orleans, was the prize for which both sides competed. The Southern people across the nation eagerly watched developments at Vicksburg, praying for a miracle and a victory that might save a young republic.[14]

In one journalist's estimation, Vicksburg "is fated to be [now] the scene of [the most] decisive conflict in the second war of independence." If Vicksburg and the Mississippi could be held, Confederate strategists envisioned the waning of the Northern will to prosecute the war to the end, a bolstering of the Northern peace party, the failure of Union conscription, and the downfall of the Lincoln Administration: the recipe for the Confederacy's independence. Whichever side won the Mississippi would win an invaluable moral, strategic, and psychological victory.

An Atlanta, Georgia newspaperman described the life and death struggle on the Mississippi in stark terms, attempting to rally support for a greater effort to save Vicksburg: "Men of the South, one vigorous determined effort and we are free! This conflict decides it all, and forever!" Meanwhile, General Lee's invasion, launched in part to take pressure off Pemberton's defense of Mississippi, and later the climactic clash at Gettysburg, Pennsylvania, would continue to dominate newspaper headlines in both North and South, but Vicksburg was the key in the war.[15]

Northerners also believed that the future of the American nation was about to be decided at the small Mississippi town of Vicksburg. Deep South Confederates more readily comprehended the importance of Vicksburg in contrast to Southerners in the east. One newspaperman from Memphis, Tennessee, perhaps best explained the strategic importance of Vicksburg:

> Vicksburg must be held at all hazards. This done, the war may be brought to a speedy close [and] we have believed from the first, that the decisive battle of this war would be fought somewhere in the valley of the Mississippi. That valley is the backbone of the continent. Nature has designed it as the great focus of wealth and power in North America [and] should we gain the day in the West, ...that victory will make the Confederate States the ruling power in the new world. It will permanently establish our institutions, give us dominion over this great 'inland sea,' and the annexation of the Northwest to the Confederacy will be merely a question of time. It is our destiny [for] we are fighting [now] for liberty, for the right of self-government": shades of Manifest Destiny under the Confederate banner.[16]

But visions of grand destinies and future Southern empires faded when Grant's army arrived and encircled the isolated fortress dominating the Mississippi's imposing bluffs. Despite having fought longer and harder than any other Southern troops in Pemberton's army, the Missouri troops received no respite, for the first assignment of the siege came immediately. On the northern defensive sector during the evening of May 18, the Missouri Brigade swung outside the works to keep encroaching Unionists at bay, allowing the entry of General Martin Luther Smith's division into the city. Rushing through the fire of artillery and sharpshooters before the fortifications, the Missourians swarmed forward to make a stand, keeping the Federals from penetrating the unfinished weak defenses.

Occasionally a Confederate soldier fell from a sniper's bullet. Colonel Cockrell, in front as usual, was wounded when a shell exploded near him. But he stayed with his troops, ignoring the pain inflicted by iron fragments. After once more providing valuable service and the first Rebel resistance of the siege, the Missouri Brigade retired into the defenses. The Missouri Brigade's losses during its risky assignment before the defenses were 1 killed and 8 wounded.[17]

Arduous service for the Missourians was only beginning, however. General Pemberton knew that he had to have his most dependable soldiers for the toughest role at Vicksburg. In a pattern established since the campaign's first days, Cockrell's troops continued to receive a difficult assignment in Pemberton's army: duty as the strategic reserve. At Vicksburg reserve service meant rushing at a moment's notice to any threatened sector.

Defending an incomplete and much too lengthy defensive line, a 32,000-man Southern Army facing a total of 77,000 Federals guaranteed that weak and endangered sectors would be many. Vicksburg's defenses were built to accommodate the natural topography and rough terrain, following a series of ridges encircling the city. Those earthworks, atop the high ground, formed a nine-mile line which Grant could hit at any point and at any time. Consequently, General Bowen's entire division was placed on strategic reserve duty, wrote one soldier in his diary, since it had "acquired a reputation for steadfast reliability."

Many of the Missouri Brigade's best officers consisted of rising stars in the West, especially after proving their worth at Grand Gulf, Port Gibson, and

Champion Hill. Brigadier generalships were destined for both Colonels Erwin and Cockrell and a major general's rank for Bowen that summer.

As the strategic reserves of Vicksburg, the Missouri Brigade stood watch over the defenses on the north and east, above the Jackson Road, which was the most important arena. The Missouri troops were positioned close to the vital Stockade Redan, the key defensive bastion on the north, which guarded the Graveyard Road. Encamped in the cane-filled hollows behind General Baldwin's brigade on the left, the Missourians stood ready to meet the next crisis. Likewise Colonel Riley's First and Fourth Missouri was prepared to pour from a deep ravine behind General John C. Moore's brigade on the east and near the Jackson Road.[18]

Impatient for victory, Grant envisioned another Big Black River-like victory. Consequently, he ordered a massive assault to overrun Vicksburg in one stroke. Three Union corps advanced on May 19. The heaviest of Grant's blows fell on the northern sector of the Stockade Redan Complex, which Cockrell's reserves had to support.

Colonel Cockrell had correctly estimated that the most intense Federal attack would hit the Stockade Redan Complex. That key position, a defensive network protecting one of the two main entries into the city, the Graveyard Road, was held by General Francis Shoup's Louisiana troops. The Yankees also targeted the earthworks defended by General Louis Hebert's brigade near the Jackson Road. To meet the challenge, Cockrell directed his regiments to bolster those heavily threatened points, while musketry and artillery crashed like thunder. At the Stockade Redan Complex, the fate of Vicksburg was in jeopardy on May 19. Thousands of Unionists advanced on the north and east sides of the complex.

To the notes of blaring bugles, the columns of Missourians poured on the double from their reserve hollow, reaching out to help quell the multiple threats. Colonel Erwin led his Sixth Missouri soldiers to the left, or west, to shore up the defenses held by General Vaughn's brigade on Baldwin's left. The First and Fourth Missouri and the Fifth Missouri rushed forward to strengthen the Stockade Redan proper, sprinting through the dust, scorching heat, and exploding shells. Defenders from the Thirty-Sixth Mississippi in the Stockade were rejuvenated with the arrival of the Missouri Rebels.[19]

Colonel Riley's Confederates raced forward and reinforced the weak link between Hebert's left and Shoup's right. That was a crucial strengthening of a weak sector on the verge of breaking. The First and Fourth Missouri's "Tiger" flag soon flew from the bullet-swept parapets of the Stockade's defenses. Out-of-breath and drenched in sweat, Fifth Missouri Rebels dashed into position on the Thirty-Sixth Mississippi's left. The Fifth Missouri's arrival was timely, for the Magnolia Staters had just expended their last rounds, when Pemberton's exiles rushed beside them with "a rousing Missouri Yell" that drowned out the more hoarse cheers of the attackers.[20]

The Second Missouri, meanwhile, hustled into the earthworks of the lunette to the Stockade's west. There, Colonel Senteny's Rebels fell into place with the Twenty-Seventh Louisiana, bolstering Shoup's right. Before the Union forces scored a breakthrough, Cockrell's reserves swiftly reinforced these vital points along Vicksburg's defensive perimeter. Pemberton had wisely placed the Missouri Brigade in a reserve position on the north: one of the highest honors the commander could bestow upon any troops at Vicksburg.

And if the Unionists smashed through the lines of the Stockade Redan Complex, then Colonel Gause and his Third Missouri Rebels stood ready in the Stockade's rear with loaded muskets, drawn swords, and fixed bayonets. To save Vicksburg on May 19, Pemberton knew that the ideal defensive deployment in that crucial situation called for reserve Missourians behind another back-up reserve of Cockrell's troops.[21]

After their long run Cockrell's men took defensive positions at those threatened sectors and released volleys into the attackers. In some cases, entire regiments, with adequate ammunition and experience, moved aside to allow the Missouri Rebels to replace them. Those hard-pressed defenders were encouraged by the unexpected appearance of the army's shock troops to reinforce them.

One St. Louisan had written in a letter that Missouri Brigade members were "all anxious to have a tussle with [Brigadier General Clinton Bowen] Fisk, [Major General Francis] Blair & [Colonel Giles A.] Smith," who commanded the hated Missouri Federals and had helped to win Missouri for the Union in 1861. Colonel Smith led a brigade, with two Missouri Union regiments, in the attack of Blair's Second Division, Fifteenth Corps.

But best of all, the Missouri Yankees of Blair's division, including Smith's brigade, charged the Stockade Redan Complex. In a letter Sergeant Hogan wrote that the Federals launched "three desperate attempts to carry our works by assault, but [they were] driven back with great slaughter; they fought bravely and desperately [and] there was no running from them trenches, as every man intended to die rather than surrender." Rapidly loading and firing, Fifth Missouri defenders severely punished Blair's charging Sixth Missouri Volunteer Infantry on that sanguinary day in Mississippi. Yankee artillery, meanwhile, continued to pound the defenses, taking Confederates from the ranks at a steady rate.[22]

Grant's poorly synchronized attacks were repulsed at every point. Fighting, nevertheless, continued even after the sun began to set. After their last rounds were expended, some Missourians held the trenches at the point of the bayonet. Grant's forces had suffered an unexpected setback. More than 1,000 soldiers, most of them from Illinois, Ohio, and Iowa, fell during the reckless frontal assaults. The Missouri Brigade played an important role in ensuring that the defenses did not break on May 19.

Sergeant Hogan was elated, writing with pride, "we took five stands of colors and any amount of muskets," as well as shoes, revolvers, clothes, and accouterments from the dead Yankees that night. In a badly needed morale-booster, Pemberton lost only a couple hundred defenders. The Missouri Brigade suffered casualties of 8 killed and 62 wounded, which was more than a third of the total Southern losses on May 19.[23]

As usual, the unsung heroes of this day were many, such as the ordnance sergeant of the Second Missouri, William F. Luckett, twenty-one. Among the first volunteers from St. Charles County, Luckett fell mortally wounded while bringing ammunition. And Sergeant Elijah H. Reid, First and Fourth Missouri, had left a hospital bed with an unhealed Champion Hill wound upon learning that "every man would be needed at the breastworks." Reid hobbled to the trenches, grabbed a rifle, and fought all day with distinction.[24]

One more assignment remained after the attacks of May 19 had been hurled back. During the night Cockrell ordered Lieutenant Gillespie to lead a party of

The Brothers' War: A Sketch by a member of the Sixth Missouri Volunteer Infantry, U.S.A., depicting Missourians in blue attacking Missouri Brigade, C.S.A., positions on May 19, 1863

Courtesy Frank Wood's Picture Bank, Alexandria, Va. (Unpublished Sketch)

Second Missouri Rebels before the lines to burn the Adam Lynd House. That structure, a make-shift Union infirmary, needed to be destroyed, for it afforded the attacking Federals an advanced position close to the works. Gillespie's nighttime sortie was risky. After removing the injured and taking about a dozen prisoners at the house, Company G's raiders burned the structure to the ground. The handful of Rebels from northeast Missouri then high-tailed it back to their lines, escaping in the blackness.[25]

With the thin Southern lines once more secure, Cockrell's regiments withdrew to their reserve positions, after another job well done. But two units, the Fifth Missouri and the First and Fourth Missouri, remained in the fortifications. The Missouri Brigade then endured the worst of both worlds at Vicksburg: reserve and front-line duty at the trenches. Since losing their guns at Big Black, many of the artillerymen of Captains Wade's, Guibor's, and Landis's Missouri batteries manned cannon in various sectors. Other cannoneers took up rifles and became voluntary sharpshooters in the dusty trenches, and tried hard to kill artillerymen in blue. Ironically, the Missouri gunners' former artillery, lost at Big Black only two days before, turned against them.[26]

CHAPTER FIFTEEN

The Siege of Vicksburg

By the spring of 1863 Grant had proved to be a successful gambler. He had found winning ways by carefully calculating the risks that had to be taken to secure victory. Thinking the Rebels were still reeling from earlier setbacks, Grant scheduled "the heaviest and most desperate assault on a line of breastworks that had ever been attempted during this war" for May 22. That grand attack was projected to win it all with one throw of the dice.

Again demonstrating foresight, Pemberton kept the Missouri Brigade near the Stockade Redan Complex, as if definitely knowing that the greatest crisis would soon develop at that point. About 6:00 a.m. on May 22, Grant unleashed his wrath upon the land scarred by miles of trenches. Hundreds of cannon pounded the defenses unmercifully. With his reserves coiled and ready to spring forward, Colonel Cockrell wrote that, "the air was literally burdened with hissing missiles of death."[1]

The primary target was the Stockade Redan Complex. As on May 19, the Missouri Confederates rushed forward and bolstered the most important sectors: the Fifth Missouri on the Thirty-Sixth Mississippi's right; five Second Missouri companies with the Twenty-Seventh Louisiana in that unit's lunette on the Stockade's left, and the remaining five companies in reserve; the Sixth Missouri strengthened General John C. Moore's brigade on the east and south of the Stockade Redan Complex. Later, to face a more severe attack, the Sixth Missouri would shift to reinforce Hebert's brigade, which would be in serious trouble after suffering under the impact of five assaults.

In the Stockade Redan proper were positioned six First and Fourth Missouri companies with the Thirty-Sixth Mississippi on the redan's southeast side. Another of Colonel Riley's units, Company C, held a small redan to the Thirty-Sixth Mississippi's right. Riley's remaining three companies were dispatched to bolster Shoup's position. On the redan's north face and at other portions of the Stockade stood the reliable veterans of Colonel Gause's Third Missouri. Spared from the worst of the May 19, Gause's men were especially eager for action. The Fifth Missouri Rebels, meanwhile, held the trenches to the redan's south.[2]

Countless shells from rows of Yankee cannon battered the fortifications with a ferocity not yet seen at Vicksburg. Head-logs were knocked to pieces by explosions, which hurled chunks of timber that knocked defenders unconscious and broke limbs. Cutting like razors, wooden splinters caused more injuries among Cockrell's troops than iron shell fragments. Thousands of Federals rolled forward from the ridge-tops and into the deep valleys before the works. But the grand assaults of May 22 were a replay of May 19, only on a larger scale. Few examples in the war spoke higher of Federal courage than the furious assaults on May 22.

General "Bowen's gallant Missourians never fired a shot," wrote a newspaper correspondent, until the Yankees were almost on top of them. Then a solid gray wall of Rebels rose up to unleash a murderous volume of fire. Line after line of Unionists charged forward to be cut down like wheat before the scythe.

The horror of the brothers' war continued when Cockrell's defenders again shot down their old antagonists of Blair's division, the Sixth and Eighth Missouri Volunteer Infantry. Advancing Federals, eventually including the Missouri Brigade's Iuka adversary, the Eleventh Missouri, were devastated by the volleys of Colonel Gause's Third Missouri, while simultaneously hit with a cross-fire from the First and Fourth, and Fifth Missouri Regiments. Among the attackers cut down that day by the Second Missouri were Yankees of the Twelfth and Seventeenth Missouri Volunteer Infantry. Whenever the smoke cleared, wrote one Missouri Brigade Rebel, "the dead Yankees were lying in heaps as far as the eye could reach."[3]

The Missouri Confederates fulfilled their key role in repelling the onslaughts. Colonel Cockrell described, "Nobly did the officers and soldiers of this brigade greet every assault of the enemy with defiant shouts and a deliberately aimed fire, and hurled them back in disorder." Private James Calvin Brown, "a promising young man" with a passion for history, responded quickly when the Third Missouri's flag was shot off the parapet. Private Brown, age twenty, jumped atop the earthwork to replant the colors. He raised the flag, which brought a cheer from comrades and a minie ball through his stomach. Young Brown, a farmer from Ray County, suffered in agony until mercifully relieved of his pain the next day. Also some of Colonel Gause's soldiers were shot down in reckless attempts to capture a Union banner, which had been planted on the Stockade.[4]

Colonel Riley's St. Louisans at last avenged the capture of Camp Jackson more than two years before. Many of Cockrell's Rebels had been captured by the St. Louis Yankees of Blair's command. An enraged Private Robert W. Busch of St. Louis rose to the occasion. Amid whistling bullets, the young man of German descent leaped on top of the works and rushed for the colors of the Eighth Missouri. Cheering Union Missourians, meanwhile, continued to scramble forward to retrieve the banner. But Private Busch beat them to the trophy, after the Federal color guard was shot down. The twenty-three-year-old St. Louisan then flaunted the banner and yelled, "Come and get your flag! The Camp Jackson boys are here. Don't you want to take us to the arsenal again! It's our time now." Private Busch had to be pulled off the parapet by comrades. Busch exemplified the role of the Missouri Brigade members of German ancestry both from St. Louis and the rural counties, indicating that, like the Missouri Irish Rebels, the Germans were often also deeply divided by the sectional conflict. Indeed, on May 22, Private Busch captured the flag of a Missouri regiment composed largely of Germans.[5]

Another desperate defender was Captain Robert Napier, who had lost an arm in a previous battle. He could barely be kept from leaping the defenses in a rage to strike at the onrushing Federals on May 22. Only darkness ended Grant's most determined effort to take Vicksburg by storm. With protection of the night, the Unionists retired to their ridges. More than 3,000 Yankees were cut down for no gain. So many bodies were stacked before the Third Missouri's position that the area around the Stockade looked like a field of blue: Vicksburg's most extensive "slaughter pen."

The grim business of killing continued in the darkness. About fifty Federals, including a few Missourians in blue, remained pinned down in the redan's deep ditch. Those Federals were unable to escape from the Third Missouri's front. No one knew of the size of the Union force below the defenders. Therefore, Lieutenant King Hiram Faulkner of Company E, Third Missouri, investigated. He leaned over the parapet to appraise the situation until a bullet whistled past his head. Faulkner, a Kentucky-born farmer from Daviess County, was the wrong man to anger: a younger brother, fourteen and also of Company E, had died of disease only last winter. After receiving a negative response to a surrender demand, Faulkner threw a cannonball that hit one opponent in the face.

That threat so close to the fortifications had to be quickly eliminated. But surrender demands were greeted with the reply, "Poke your head up here and we will show you whether we came here to surrender or not!" Faulkner secured artillery shells from a nearby battery. He then hurled the lit projectiles into the crowded ditch with the taunt, "Damn you, will you surrender now?"

Colonel Gause shortly took action to bolster Faulkner's novel means of waging war, ordering cases of shells forward. The fuses of those projectiles were lit with cigars, then the shells were thrown into the ditch. Despite heavy losses, the Federals remained defiant. Additional calls for capitulation brought cries of "Go to hell!" To wipe out the remaining Yankee bands, more than forty shells were hurled down the parapet, killing more than twenty Unionists. Eventually that grim innovation of the Third Missouri eliminated the day's final threat. That brutal type of warfare became a regular feature of the siege. Missouri artillerymen without cannon were shortly organized into shell hurling details, which would throw more than 1,000 of these home-made "grenades" during the siege. May 22 was a costly day for Cockrell's reserves, for they again probably lost more than any other Rebel brigade at Vicksburg, with 28 killed and 95 wounded, a total of 123: a high percentage of Confederate losses which totaled less than 500.[6]

Long a special favorite of the Third Missouri, Private Henry Rives Allen was killed on May 22. A nephew of Colonel Rives, Allen was only seventeen. The bullet that killed him symbolically shattered the daguerreotype in his breast pocket of the girl that he had left behind, another sad example of more than one life being wrecked by a single minie ball. The Third Missouri took more punishment that day than any other Missouri Brigade regiment. Hit by an enfilade and rear fire, Colonel Gause's regiment suffered a loss of 12 killed and 52 wounded, the highest Confederate regimental loss suffered on May 22, for about half of the Third Missouri became casualties.[7]

On May 25 a truce to bury the piles of Union dead lying before the earthworks was declared. The odor of decaying bodies filled the trenches with a nauseating stench for days. Private Theodore Fisher complained in his diary that, the Yankee dead "were almost stinking us out of our works." With the truce, soldiers of both armies crawled out of their fortifications to fraternize. Many Missourians in blue met Missourians in gray before the lines, for the state was represented by 40 units at Vicksburg. Old friends, brothers, and relatives in different colored uniforms came together briefly during the truce that allowed these war-weary soldiers to forget momentarily the nightmare of civil war.

Johnny Rebs traded tobacco for coffee and newspapers. Ohio-born Colonel Gause met an old friend, a colonel of the Indiana regiment. And Colonel Cockrell conversed with General Blair, the two commanders who led the most Missouri troops at Vicksburg. Impressed by Lieutenant Faulkner's stratagem of May 22, Blair asked Cockrell the name of the daring officer, who had thrown the shells over the parapet.

One Rebel of the Sixth Missouri, C.S.A., met his brother of the Sixth Missouri, U.S.A. The Confederate asked, "John, have you heard from mother and sister lately?" The Federal responded, "Yes, I got a letter yesterday." News of the family and the letter were exchanged. After burying the dead, it was back to the dirty business of killing each other. The parting of two other Missouri brothers from opposing sides prompted one to promise to "blow the other's head off" on the next day.[8]

Then the Unionists settled down to conduct one of the longest sieges in American history. No Missouri Brigade soldier excelled more at trench warfare than Private William Walker Morrow, a teen-ager of Company I, Fifth Missouri. He was an expert sharpshooter and "killed more Yankees at Vicksburg than any other soldier there," wrote one comrade in a letter. But even as Morrow shot down more Federals each day, typhoid fever was already beginning its fatal work.

From May 22 to June 25, the Missouri Brigade's encampment was located in a deep wooded ravine, which descended into Glass Bayou behind the Stockade Redan Complex. Throughout that period of desultory shelling and sniping, the Missouri regiments took turns serving in multiple sectors of the nine-mile-long line. They spent much time and effort in marching to those widely-scattered assignments, strengthening defenses at night, simply trying to survive, and burying comrades who fell daily.[9]

As the Yankees dug closer and the siege lengthened, no spot in the whole of Vicksburg was immune to the constant shelling, night and day. Now "dig, dig, dig, is [the only] strategy [and] God will give us the victory in His own good time," prayed one Southerner. The close proximity of antagonists often led to quiet, informal meetings on dark nights between blue and gray. Early in the siege, for instance, Private Fisher wrote, "We are in hearing distance of the enemy and they often come across the works."

The Missouri Brigade encampment nestled in the ravine's depths proved to be as dangerous as the front lines. Often Cockrell's soldiers, recorded one Missouri Brigade Rebel in his diary, were "aroused from our slumber [in the] morning by the heavy firing of artillery and the bombs popping and bursting immediately above our heads." Before the end of May, most Missourians had already suffered some type of wound or injury. From May 18 to June 4, the Missouri Brigade lost 275 men killed and wounded, sapping more strength from the already depleted command. As one of Cockrell's bitter soldiers analyzed, "the Missouri Brigade suffered more than any troops around the lines." Also both the city hospitals and field infirmaries were hit by shells and bullets at all hours.[10]

Some of Cockrell's unit commanders refused to accept the fact that the new realities of siege warfare infringed upon traditional leadership roles. On one occasion, for example, Colonel Erwin sat on his horse during a heavy artillery bombardment and intense sniper fire. But the common-sense privates responded in time to the needless heroics of the popular colonel. Ragged enlisted men "dragged him from his horse and led both out of danger's way" during one of Vicksburg's unforgettable scenes.[11]

The Missourians' determination to fight to the bitter end remained strong despite the devastating losses of the campaign. At that time, Colonel Cockrell's "troops would die in the trenches before they would surrender." In his diary, Private Fisher caught the mood of Missouri Brigade members, offering a prayer of deliverance from the Yankees who are "endeavoring to despoil our homes and wrench from us those rights so dear to the human heart—freedom and independence." But an ever-escalating death rate, rapid spread of disease, and scorching weather gradually began to take a toll, deflating morale a bit more each day. By June 1, wrote Private Fisher, "the [Missouri Brigade's] men are weary and tired. The weather is extremely warm and a great many of the men are not well. I have been sick for several days, but continue with the regiment." Already meager rations were slashed in half, then by one-fourth before mid-June. Spirits and health suffered accordingly. Experiments with an unpalatable bean-bread by Pemberton's commissary and the soldiers' concoction of a bean-coffee failed to compensate. Ill-clad defenders standing day and night in cool downpours of rain and shivering in water-filled trenches, and subsisting on low-quality food lowered their bodies' resistance to the ravages of disease. Pneumonia, malaria, scurvy, and dysentery steadily committed more Missouri boys into permanent quarters in the yellow soil of the surrounded "Republic of Vicksburg."

Vicksburg's defenders never realized that their beleaguered city on a hill had been perhaps doomed from the start. Since the war's beginning, the strategic errors and the disproportionate priority placed upon the Eastern theater by the Davis administration had led to a series of reversals in the West that now resulted in thousands of Rebels being bottled up and forsaken in Vicksburg. "No one dreamed that the Government at Richmond would quietly contemplate our distress and refuse to render that assistance which the bravery of the troops" beckoned, fumed one Southerner. General Lee's invasion into Pennsylvania had failed to relieve pressure on the Western theater and Vicksburg. Long before Vicksburg was surrounded, the war for the Mississippi Valley and for possession of the Mississippi River had been lost by military mismanagement, strategic miscalculations, and the chain of Confederate defeats in 1861 and 1862, beginning with the loss of Missouri.[12]

Morale among the common soldier improved with the arrival of letters from Missouri at the end of May. Two daring mail couriers from Missouri, including Grimes, had floated south down the Mississippi to bring the exiles hundreds of letters. About half of these letters, however, could never be delivered to the young farm boys from across Missouri. Indeed, more than 1,000 Missouri Brigade members already had become casualties during the four weeks since the defense of Grand Gulf. Many of those men now filled unmarked graves at Grand Gulf, Port Gibson, Champion Hill, Big Black River, Vicksburg, and across the State of Mississippi.[13]

On June 2, Lieutenant Elliott wrote in his diary of the type of losses which were becoming common: "There was a family of four [five Holtzclaw] brothers come out in the army from [Fayette, Howard County], Mo, one of them was killed at the battle of Corinth, one was wounded at Bakers creek, the 3rd one was killed and the fourth wounded by the bursting of a shell to day." Like many other familial groups throughout the Missouri Brigade, the Holtzclaw clan of Captain Synnamon's Company G, Sixth Missouri, had compiled a distinguished record, including State Guard service.

Twenty-six-year-old Lieutenant William M. Holtzclaw, a physician, had been killed at Corinth, while Private Clifton D. Holtzclaw, age thirty-one, had been wounded and captured at Corinth. Private James P. Holtzclaw, a twenty-six-year-old student, received a serious wound at Champion Hill. After May 16, the Holtzclaw twins, James and William, had been knocked out of action. Both Privates Benjamin Franklin Holtzclaw, age twenty-three, and John W. Holtzclaw found final resting places at Vicksburg. But such sacrifices among family bands within the Missouri Brigade were so widespread as to go almost unnoticed.[14]

Despite the fading hope for the arrival of General Johnston's relief column and the daily diminishing of the ranks, Cockrell's defenders felt that the saving of Vicksburg was essential for any real chance of ever reclaiming Missouri. Such a belief fueled fighting spirit and resolve. The outnumbered Missouri Confederates, consequently, stood faithfully in the trenches and endured Vicksburg's hell, refusing to desert in large numbers as many other defenders had. Private John W. Sattenwhite, a twenty-four-year-old Cass County farmer of the Sixth Missouri, wrote in his diary of the determination of the Missouri Brigade: "A wetter, dirtier, muddier lot of rebels were never seen; but we kept our powder dry." Soldiers became accustomed to the everyday horror of Vicksburg. Without a trace of emotion, Lieutenant Elliott noted in his diary that he "saw a man today with both legs shot off close to his body [and] he talks cool and rational half an hour after it was done."[15]

Shelling continued both day and night. Even nature's wrath seemed to turn on the defenders. Private Fisher recorded that, "it rained very hard [and] the enemy's artillery, intermingling with the thunder, kept up a constant roar for hours [and] the 'Feds' have continued the old programme [sic] of sending unwelcome missiles into our little confederacy." The Missouri Brigade suffered an irreplaceable loss when a huge naval shell smashed into the City Hospital, to Vicksburg's northeast, on June 10. Surgeon Britts, the ex-First and Fourth Missouri's physician and now Missouri Brigade surgeon in Surgeon "Marsh" Allen's absence, lost his leg in the explosion. The giant 200-pound shell from a 13-inch mortar barely missed Father Bannon, who also worked occasionally in the infirmary. Amid the chaos, Father Bannon saved Surgeon Britts's life by applying a tourniquet just in time. Despite the loss of his right leg, Surgeon Britts continued duty on an artificial limb.

Long a favorite of officers and enlisted men, both Catholic and Protestant, Bannon served in the trenches daily and shared the dangers with the exiles. Often when a soldier fell, the St. Louis priest gave the last rites in his Irish brogue for the dying man, while shells exploded nearby and sharpshooters' bullets whizzed overhead. Father Bannon's courage, boundless energy, and good humor uplifted spirits and faith during Vicksburg's most severe trials.[16]

The steady toll of daily casualties further wreaked havoc among the Missouri Brigade's already decimated ranks, especially after Green's brigade was taken off reserve duty barely two weeks after the siege's beginning. As one soldier lamented in his diary: "Our division [Bowen's] now will make a respectable brigade." Therefore, the luxury of reserve troops at Vicksburg was becoming increasingly impractical. The Missouri Brigade was finally removed from reserve duty in late June. No longer would the Missouri Rebels be forced to sleep "with our accouterments on to be ready for any emergency," wrote a thankful Private Fisher. Now, Cockrell's defenders maintained regular duty at the fortifications.[17]

**Colonel Eugene Erwin,
killed at Vicksburg**
Courtesy State Historical Society
of Missouri, Columbia

**General Martin E. Green,
killed at Vicksburg**
Courtesy State Historical Society
of Missouri, Columbia

June 25 brought an innovation to Vicksburg's deadly routine: the nightmare of mine warfare. To parry that new threat to Vicksburg's life, Pemberton had his Missourians ready in the threatened Jackson Road sector. For some time, wrote fatalistic Private Sattenwhite in his diary, "we are looking for a blow-up every hour." Indeed, the principal bastion guarding the Jackson Road, the formidable Third Louisiana Redan on the north side of the dirt road that led to Vicksburg, was targeted by Grant for destruction. The Federal troops had dug a lengthy mine shaft under the redan, planting more than a ton of black powder beneath the powerful defensive position, known to the Yankees simply as "the Key fort." Colonel Cockrell's veterans of the Second, Fifth, and Sixth Missouri were expecting the worst, since "all was [too] quiet" for much too long.

Finally, the great explosion came about 3:00 in the afternoon of May 25. Much of the earthen structure was blown sky-high with the tremendous eruption that rocked Vicksburg like an earthquake. Wrote a Sixth Missouri boy in his diary: "The blast shocked the whole hill, they then commenced fireing [sic] [artillery] more rapidly, which created some excitement" among the defenders.[18]

As the attackers of the Forty-Fifth Illinois Volunteer Infantry led the charge to exploit the break, Colonel Erwin hurried his Sixth Missouri Rebels from the opposite direction to counter the threat. Northern artillery pounded the coveted area around the crater, impeding restoration of the line by the Third Louisiana soldiers, and raking the advancing Sixth Missouri reinforcements with a heavy barrage. Fortunately, a second defensive line behind the demolished redan had been erected for just such an emergency. There, a solid defense needed to be quickly patched together, if Vicksburg was to survive June 25.[19]

Colonel Erwin, meanwhile, continued encouraging his Confederates onward through the shell-fire and toward the point of contention. A sick and bed-ridden Erwin had forced himself to return to duty on the morning of June 25, after ignoring the sound advice of surgeons. The yip-yip of the Rebel Yell split the air when the Sixth Missouri soldiers gained the second line and fanned out to take up defensive positions with the Third Louisiana boys.

Now hundreds of cheering Federals were rapidly spilling into the crater and firing away "before the dirt and smoke was cleared away," wrote one defender. The crater was the attackers' body-littered avenue by which they could split Pemberton's army and capture Vicksburg. Like two locomotives about to crash head-on along the same narrow track, the Sixth Missouri and the Forty-Fifth Illinois charged forward on a collision course, arriving simultaneously at the crater.

With the crisis at hand, Colonel Erwin knew that only an immediate counterattack could throw the blue onslaught off-balance and plug the hole in the line. Waving his saber, Erwin urged his Confederates over the retrenchment line. After mounting the parapet near the crater's edge, the colonel stood erect amid the stream of bullets to inspire the Sixth Missouri counterattack onward. Seconds later, many Yankee muskets spat fire from the crater's depths, riddling and blowing Colonel Erwin off the parapet with a point-blank volley. As Erwin fell dead into the arms of his men with five bullets through his chest, a torrent of Ketchum hand grenades were tossed over the parapet by the Federals only a few feet away.

The position of the Sixth Missouri at the retrenchment was in danger of buckling at any moment, especially after Colonel Erwin's fall, which "of all the blows that the 6th Missouri had suffered, this was the worst." With Rebel infantry support

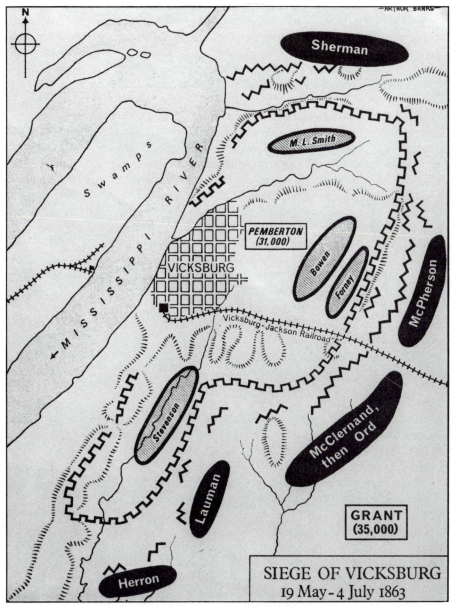

Siege of Vicksburg—19 May-4 July 1863

Courtesy *Grant As Military Commander General Sir James Marshall-Cornwall* 1970, Van Nostrand Reinhold Company, N.Y.

wavering, Vicksburg's most strategic point was now practically defenseless. The onrushing Federals shouted in victory and pushed forward "to mount our [second line] of works" and fight their way into Vicksburg itself.

Private Matthew J. Moore was the first Rebel to jump on top of the parapet to stand beside Colonel Erwin. After Erwin was fatally cut down, the Confederate private boldly held his ground on the exposed parapet in a repeat of his Port Gibson heroics. Like Colonel Erwin, Private Moore had left the hospital to meet the Yankees, leaving with an unhealed Port Gibson wound.

Like most regimental members, Moore was "enraged at his [colonel's] death." Wrote one Sixth Missouri soldier of the turning point "when the enemy first exploded his mine and blew up our breastworks, and was passing into our trenches a perfect shower of hand grenades—that burst as soon as they struck the ground—when the ditches were filled with the dead, wounded and dying, and the parapet was left almost defenseless, at the point where the gallant Col. Erwin [had] stood [Private Moore] [remained] undaunted [and] maintained his position and with the greatest coolness, catching the terrible hand grenades and hurling them back at the enemy." Moore's defiance and Colonel Erwin's example rallied and inspired the Sixth Missourians and Third Louisianians to hold their hard-hit positions at the second line, while suffering under a murderous cannonade and facing a heavy infantry assault.[20]

Gradually a solid defense of Missourians and Louisianians formed at the crater. More Federals, meanwhile, charged into the breach to exploit their advantage and attempt to widen the toe-hold gained in the Rebel line. Hand-to-hand combat raged fiercely on the lip of the crater, when the Unionists tried to storm the retrenchment. Musket-butts crushed skulls and steel bayonets plunged into bodies. The "Bloody Seventh" Missouri Volunteer Infantry, U.S.A., was among those troops ready to plow through the "Bloody Sixth" Missouri, C.S.A. Ironically, that Federal regiment of Irish Yankees from St. Louis had been organized by a veteran of Colonel Doniphan's Expedition. But the most ex-members of that Mexican War expedition were in Colonel Erwin's Sixth Missouri.[21]

Vicksburg was made secure after Sixth Missouri volleys exploded in the faces of the Unionists, hurling the attackers back. Solidifying the defense, the Sixth Missouri was reinforced by the timely arrival of the Fifth Missouri. The extra firepower delivered from Colonel McCown's newcomers helped to ensure that the Federals would not again attack the thin Rebel line. The Sixth and Fifth Missouri and the Third Louisiana soldiers maintained their forward positions, while more shells and hand grenades tumbled down into their midst. Exploding shells blew the Confederates out of formations, but the ranks were quickly closed in text-book fashion, despite the carnage.[22]

Having learned the lessons of May 22, Cockrell's men hurriedly distributed cases of shells—makeshift hand grenades—among the defenders. After fuses were lit by the Rebels, dozens of shells were thrown or rolled down into the crater. A stream of projectiles exploding among the Federals forced them to retire to the opposite side of the crater. Confederates rapidly fired their Enfield rifles and screamed "to the Yankees and begg[ed] them to come on." But the battered Unionists had enough of tangling with the Missouri Brigade for one day. No additional Federal infantry attacks were forthcoming. Both sides then exchanged an unceasing fire across the crater. Despite the intense bombardment continuing and more Confederates falling throughout the night, the strategic position of the Jackson Road was secure.

Knowing that his strategic and vulnerable sector had been saved by Colonel Cockrell's Missourians, a thankful General Hebert spoke highly of the timely rescue of his Third Louisiana by "the brave Missourians [who] have added laurels to their already glorious renown." In once again playing the key role in thwarting Grant, the Fifth and Sixth Missouri lost a total of 48 men on bloody June 25-26.[23]

On that day, Father Bannon added yet another page to his already impressive list of exploits during the siege. The Irish chaplain had been in the southern sector when he learned that a top Missouri officer had been mortally wounded and requested Bannon to prepare him to meet his Maker. Father Bannon, consequently, galloped north toward the Jackson Road sector, racing along the bullet-swept ridges. In front of both armies, "his commanding figure [now] enabled him to be recognized, and the troops on both sides, Federal and Confederate, struck by his heroism started up from their trenches, ceased firing, and cheered him loudly."[24]

Close exchanges of gun-fire continued at the crater past midnight and into the early morning hours of June 26. The Federals held their ground on the crater's opposite side, and could launch another attack at any moment. Lieutenant Elliott wrote in his diary, "the fireing [sic] continued fiercely all night, the enemy was within 30 feet of us fireing [sic] over breast works, passed the night without sleeping a wink." Death struck twice behind the crater on June 26, when a shell landed in a sleeping hole of two Second Missouri brothers from Lincoln County, Privates William B., age twenty-six, and Thomas A. Tuttle, age twenty-nine. When comrades found them, little remained of the two soldiers, after the shell's explosion.

Every Missouri regiment eventually took shifts in occupying the dangerous crater sector. Once more, the Yankees began to mine under the half-wrecked redan position of the Third Louisiana. Then the siege returned to its usual deadly routines. As July neared, surviving Missourians tasted Vicksburg cuisine more unorthodox than hard pea-bread and weak bean-coffee. Rates, snakes, mule steaks, and evidently even dogs were devoured by famished soldiers. Private Timothy E. Callahan, an Irishman of Guibor's Battery, wrote in a letter to his St. Louis wife how he survived on "a little Mule meat [but] even that has got scarce" before the siege's end. One critical shortage was the lack of fresh drinking water, as Private Robert C. Dunlap, a DeKalb County cannoneer of Landis's Battery, emphasized in his diary.[25]

General Green's death on June 27 dampened the spirits among Cockrell's "caged birds," as Private Fisher described the plight of Vicksburg's defenders. Shot through the head by a sniper, the Missouri Brigade's old commander was the only general to perish at Vicksburg. One Southerner at Vicksburg wrote an emotional tribute to Green: "Many noble sons of Missouri have fallen during this war; but none of her martyrs in our war of independence will be spoken of in more glowing terms, or more deserved praise than 'the old man' who fell in defence [sic] of Vicksburg. His wish was gratified—he lived not to see Vicksburg fall!"

Along with the death of General Green, a melancholy mood haunted the Sixth Missouri with the loss of Colonel Erwin. Colonel Erwin's death sent a wave of shock through every regiment, for the Missourians had lost a future Brigade commander and a friend. One of Riley's enlisted men captured the dark mood in his diary and wrote, "The 6th Missouri loses in him a gallant and efficient officer [and] his men all loved him as a brother." Colonel Erwin left behind a young exiled widow and three young daughters.

Having recovered from a wound received at Corinth and having been exchanged after his capture on October 4, 1862, capable Lieutenant Colonel Isaac N. Hedgpeth had rejoined the Sixth Missouri just in time to be trapped in Vicksburg. The hard-fighting native of Doniphan took command of the Sixth Missouri when Colonel Erwin was killed. Only two days later, Hedgpeth fell seriously wounded in the trenches. A worthy replacement, one-armed Major Cooper assumed charge of the Sixth Missouri, and prayed that he would not become the third regimental commander to be hit in three days.[26]

Father Bannon had another close brush with death on June 28. While the Missouri Brigade chaplain held Mass at St. Paul's Catholic Church, shells exploded around the beautiful house of worship perched atop Vicksburg's second highest hill. One projectile tore through the church, hurtling brick and plaster and passing over the altar only inches from Bannon's head. A veteran of combat, Father Bannon calmed the panicked congregation with his words and cool example. He then proceeded with his religious service in the smoke-filled church as if nothing had happened. During the noisy bombardment, Chaplain Bannon's Sunday Mass on the Mississippi continued as scheduled.[27]

The dangerous duty, meanwhile, continued for the Missourians along a new parapet erected across the gorge of the half-destroyed Third Louisiana Redan. Again Cockrell's Brigade received the most hazardous assignment, manning the defenses where a second mine could explode at any time. Each rotating shift of Missouri soldiers hoped that it would not be their turn to be blown to hell, while each minute of duty passed like an hour. The only question was which regiment—either the Fifth, Sixth, or First and Fourth Missouri—would be blown up when the inevitable explosion erupted. By the onset of July, the prospect for General Johnston's arrival became more remote. Defenders began to realize that they were definitely on their own.

As 3:00 p.m. of a scorching July 1 approached, Companies B and H of the Sixth Missouri occupied the defenses on top of the second great Union mine. The usual noise of digging immediately below Cockrell's Rebels suddenly stopped and the Unionists' firing died down: ominous signals to those perceptive veterans. Then, "an unusual calm prevailed," promising that 1,800 pounds of black powder directly beneath the Missouri boys were about to be ignited. Forty-two-year-old Lieutenant John T. Crenshaw felt as uneasy as his men. The mature and experienced Crenshaw, an attorney born in Tennessee, commented to a fellow officer, "I wouldn't be surprised if this whole hill is blown to hell in less than ten minutes."[28]

Suddenly the entire hill rumbled, and then shook as if by an earthquake, violently jolting what little remained of the Third Louisiana Redan. Then came the massive explosion. Much of the redan, the new parapet, and the retrenchment line vomited upward in a billowing black cloud of debris, men, earth, and cannon. To the stunned Missourians, "it seemed as if hell itself had joined the efforts of the enemy to dislodge us." Defenders such as Lieutenant John Roseberry, a twenty-four-year-old farmer from Howard County, were blown up, hurled high into the air, and killed in the eruption. Other Missouri soldiers, such as Lieutenant Crenshaw, were simply never seen again.

At least 20 Sixth Missouri Rebels were buried in a permanent tomb by the explosion. Not one soldier of the mostly Howard and Chariton County Company H survived unscathed on July 1. Company B was likewise devastated, losing 27 Rebels

St. Paul's Catholic Church, Vicksburg, Mississippi, built in 1849

Courtesy J. Mack Moore Collection, Old Courthouse Museum, Vicksburg, Miss.

in the explosion. One "poor Missouri boy [flew] up about a hundred feet and came down with a mass of earth and debris" in the Third Louisiana's sector. When some Louisiana soldiers finally dug out the blackened survivor, the angry Confederate wanted to resume fighting immediately and yelled, "Damn it boys, where is my gun!"

In addition, a work party of an overseer and eight African American slaves, who had been underground sinking a counter-mine to intersect the Yankees' mine, were likewise blown into another world. One black later recalled that upon descent, he saw a Sixth Missouri sergeant ascending. That victim was Sergeant Thomas Morris of Company H, one of the regiment's best men. Sergeant Morris, a twenty-one-year-old Howard County farmer, was buried alive. Half a dozen Missouri Rebels were catapulted east and into the Federal line, dropping among the bluecoats like dirty gray apples shaken from a tree.[29]

As on June 25, another wide hole had been ripped into Pemberton's line. It again appeared as if Vicksburg might be taken by assault. Once more Cockrell's troops were primarily responsible for stopping the attack. The terrific blast, however, left the reserves in bad shape, for many of those Sixth and Second Missouri boys at the retrenchment were knocked head-long into the deep ravine behind the redan. Whole companies of soldiers were tossed and thrown together like ten-pins.

Colonel Cockrell had another miraculous escape. The colonel had been called outside the redan only seconds before the destruction of the works and its defenders. Cockrell's uniform jacket had been twisted off his body by the force of the terrific blast during his skyward journey and then rough descent into the bottom of the ravine behind the redan.[30]

A Confederate surgeon from Bowen's division never forgot one of the most remarkable sights ever witnessed by any soldier in the war, recording in his diary: "I was going in that direction at the time and saw a number of men in the air; among them [was] general Frank Cockrell, who is an honor to his state; and more gallantry was there displayed in a marked manner. Landing on his feet he grasped a musket in his hand and led the reserve" forward into the raging storm. Cockrell hurried his old regiment onward, screaming, "Come on, Old Bloody Second Missouri; you have died once, and can die again!"[31]

Then Colonel Cockrell rallied the remainder of the Sixth Missouri, hurling them forward to avenge their many fallen comrades, who were either dead or buried alive and suffocating under tons of earth. As a giant cloud of black, billowing smoke rose higher in the summer sky, Cockrell dashed over to the First and Fourth Missouri. He ordered the command headlong into the fray with the battle-cry, "Victory or death!" The fiery lawyer from Warrensburg also encouraged Colonel McCown's Fifth Missouri onward into the tempest. Amid the confusion, tumult, and the rain of shells, the First and Fourth, Second, and Fifth Missouri, and the Third Louisiana rallied at the new crater to face the latest threat to Vicksburg's life.[32]

Before the gapping breach in the defenses, the Missouri Rebels deployed in neat formations. The Confederates hastily fixed bayonets, while shells from scores of cannon, including Missouri Federal artillery, fell among the defenders. Explosions repeatedly blew holes in formations, while Confederates braced to meet the expected attack. But Grant ordered no troops forward into the crater, having learned the bloody lessons of June 25.

A much excited Colonel Cockrell, black with dirt and "badly bruised" from his wild flight through the air and hard tumble, yelled above the noise of bursting projectiles: "All of us must die here before this point is carried. Men of Missouri, stand firm; the fate of Vicksburg depends on you." A rousing cheer echoed down the Missourians' gray line, as straight as on a parade ground. The spunky enlisted men of Colonel Riley's regiment responded to Cockrell's challenge with cries of, "Stand to your ground, colonel, the First Missouri will die with you too."[33]

After ascertaining that no Union assault was forthcoming, handfuls of Confederates left the ranks to assist the many injured friends and relatives scattered around them or half-buried in the yellow clay. Corporal George

Lieutenant Colonel Pembroke S. Senteny, killed at Vicksburg
Courtesy Vicksburg National Military Park, Vicksburg, Miss.

Washington Ferrill, a twenty-year-old farmer, had been hurled high into the air and came down in a huge shower of earth. He was buried up to his chin, when two Sixth Missouri comrades found and quickly dug him out of his grave.

Many others were not so fortunate. Corporal Robert Williams, a Sixth Missouri teen-ager, was uncovered already dead. The student from Keytesville, Chariton County, was laid in a blood-stained row of bodies, blackened and almost torn beyond recognition, which steadily grew longer as the frantic excavations continued.

But some soldiers blown up in the blast were still alive. Of the ill-fated Company H, Sixth Missouri, Lieutenant Robert A. Dickey, a Chariton County merchant of twenty-four, had been "buried alive." The Virginia-born Dickey was rescued too late, eventually dying from extensive internal and external injuries. And Private James J. Moore, an eighteen-year-old farmer of Chariton County, survived the fall to earth, landing in underbrush some distance behind the lines. Many unfortunate Missouri boys could not be saved from what had become their tombs.[34]

Still expecting an attack, the Missouri Brigade remained in position and continued to take heavy punishment. Rebel casualties steadily mounted. One defender from St. Louis wrote in his diary that "their artillery kept up the most terrific fire that ever grated upon the human ear [and] small [wooden] mortars of 6 and 12 pound[er] balls were unceasingly fired into the works, nearly every one taking some veteran from our ranks." Despite the pounding, the ever-thinning Confederate lines held firm. With bodies piling up around them, the Rebels withstood the incessant cannonade, while the slaughter continued and the tattered Missouri battle-flags waved in the drifting palls of dust and smoke.

With explosions erupting around them, desperate Confederates hastily threw up dirt and earth onto wagon and tent covers. Those were then dragged forward to partially reconstruct the battered retrenchment. But there was not enough protection to stop the deadly Federal mortars from taking more lives. Further making the defense entirely a Trans-Mississippi one, at least one gun of the Appeal Arkansas Battery roared beside the Louisiana and Missouri troops at the second line. As at Hatchie Bridge, this veteran artillery unit again provided timely service, and maintained its fine reputation with a rapid and accurate fire.[35]

Sunset failed to stop the killing. Grant's massed array of artillery, especially the destructive homemade wooden mortars, continuously raked the whole area. Anticipating an attack, Lieutenant Colonel Senteny, commanding the Second Missouri, reconnoitered the Unionists' advanced position in the fading light. Seconds later, a sharpshooter's bullet tore through Senteny's head. Wrote one defender, "With bitter tears of grief and sorrow the regiment beheld the body of this gallant officer [which was] now borne back a corpse. No more would we hear his calm and deliberate, though firm and quiet, commands, and be re-assured and stimulated."

The entire Missouri Brigade took the news of Colonel Senteny's death extremely hard. One Missouri Brigade member wrote in his diary: "In him we lose a friend and an efficient and gallant officer. He was beloved by all his men and many are the hearts that have been made sad by his death. A tender wife [Fannie] and children are left to mourn his loss. God comfort these in this their sore grief." Taking Senteny's place, Major Thomas M. Carter became the new commander of the Second Missouri, despite having suffered a wound during the attacks on May 19.[36]

Casualties on bloody July 1 were high. The Sixth Missouri suffered the worst, taking a loss of 8 killed and 48 wounded. Besides losing its commander, the Second Missouri had 3 killed and 35 wounded. The Fifth Missouri losses were comparable to the Second Missouri's casualties, about 40 soldiers. For the remainder of the siege, the Missouri Brigade maintained its precarious grip and forward position around the crater. The mine explosion of July 1 brought no strategic advantage for either side, only more death.[37]

The routine of the siege continued after the great mine explosion of July 1. Soaring losses from Yankee fire and disease steadily sent more of Cockrell's defenders to shallow graves among the hills of Vicksburg. Escaping death repeatedly during the siege was Colonel Flournoy, who led a charmed life. For instance, he had a bullet whiz through his hat upon stepping down from an embankment at the front. Flournoy won fame throughout the Confederacy for an act of heroism, which was published in Southern newspapers. At the unit's ravine encampment, a large shell landed in the middle of a group of Second Missouri soldiers, who were relaxing off duty or preparing supper. Without thinking, Flournoy instantly grabbed and threw the hissing shell away only seconds before it exploded. By employing his medical skills and by that act of bravery, the colonel-surgeon saved a number of Rebel lives during the siege.

Finally, one of the most stirring dramas in American history came to an end. White flags suddenly appeared on top of the Rebel fortifications on the morning of July 3, indicating that Vicksburg's demise had come at last. Die-hard veterans in the trenches felt sick in body and mind, for "every thing [was] as still as death [and] we all knew that the fatal hour had arrived," wrote an embittered Private Sattenwhite in his diary.

General Pemberton and his top lieutenants had decided to surrender fortress Vicksburg. About one third of Vicksburg's garrison of 32,000 men, and one third of Bowen's Division, had been killed or wounded or were sick in filthy and understaffed hospitals. But the fighting spirit remained strong with Colonel Cockrell and most of his soldiers, because the Missouri Brigade's war could not end with defeats or surrenders, as long as the home state remained under Federal control. Indeed, General Pemberton's top brigade commander, the ever-aggressive Colonel Cockrell, begged to be allowed to personally lead an attack through the Federal

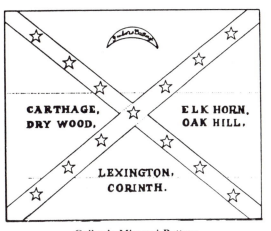

Guibor's Missouri Battery
Courtesy *The Battle Flags Of The Confederate Army Of Tennessee*, Howard M. Madaus and Robert D. Needham

lines in one final bid for freedom.

Among Cockrell's hardened veterans, "great excitement prevailed, and the troops desired to be led over the works and cut our way" out of Grant's strangle hold to win the opportunity to fight another day. However, Colonel Cockrell's desperate appeal was rejected. In his effort to save Vicksburg, Pemberton had gambled all and lost all in playing his weak hand against the master gambler, General Grant, saving neither his army or the mighty fortress on the Mississippi.[38]

The news that the surrender ceremony was scheduled for the morning of the great Union holiday, the Fourth of July, brought more anguish among Cockrell's Confederates. Cursing Missourians burned possessions and damned commanding generals. Other grayclads smashed Enfield rifles over logs or trees. A few infuriated soldiers left camp, leaving forever the east side of the Mississippi and the ill-fated army that never won battles. Those Missouri Confederates escaped across the Mississippi on wooden planks, for the risk of death was worth saying that one "never surrendered to the Yankees." The faint red glow of a fading sun setting over Vicksburg on July 3 foreshadowed the sunset of the Confederacy.[39]

Other Missouri Brigade soldiers made sure that their cherished battle-flags, "smoke-begrimed, blood-stained, shot full of holes, in tatters," were not handed over to the victors. Preparations were made to smuggle the Second Missouri's colors out under one soldier's shirt. Feisty Mrs. Mary Bowen arranged for the safekeeping of the "Camp Jackson" flag, when not attending to her disease stricken General Bowen. The resourceful "Mittie" hid the First Missouri banner and another Missouri battle-flag in the ambulance which took General Bowen from Vicksburg.

The optimistic dreams of the Confederacy holding onto the Mississippi River and surviving the war as an independent Southern nation were dying after Grant's triumph which forever guaranteed to split the Confederacy in half and secured a permanent Union grip on the entire length of the Mississippi. Father Bannon, in a Celtic rage over Vicksburg's capitulation, took the flag of Guibor's Battery to a Catholic merchant for concealment. Taken by the chaplain to a store in Vicksburg's business district near the river, the treasured emblem remained safely hidden until the war's conclusion. Then, during Reconstruction, the flag would be retrieved by Captain Guibor.

Doing her part despite the pain of losing her husband, the grieving Mrs. Erwin sewed the Sixth Missouri's colors inside her petticoat. That was an ideal hiding place that no self-respecting Billy Yank would venture to search in helping to preserve the Union. Such a defiant act that outfoxed the conquerors of Vicksburg would have made Colonel Erwin, dead less than two weeks, proud of his young wife.[40]

July 4 came only too soon for 29,500 Rebels about to surrender. At 10:00 a.m., the surviving Missourians embarked upon the most difficult duty of their lives, marching out of camp to stack arms just north of the Jackson Road. A mounted General Grant watched the diseased and ragged Confederates from Missouri, who had fought him more tenaciously than any other Rebel troops. In an understatement, a Sixth Missouri soldier described in his diary: "It is humiliating but we were driven to it by the want of rations and by overwhelming numbers."[41]

At that time the Missouri Brigade resembled little more than a skeleton command. The pitifully small number of those surrendering, including those in the hospitals, spoke eloquently of the decimation of General Pemberton's most lethal fighting machine of the Vicksburg Campaign: 344 First and Fourth Missouri men; 356 Second Missouri soldiers; 258 Rebels of the Third Missouri, under Major James K. McDowell with a sick Colonel Gause in the hospital; 276 exiles of the Fifth Missouri, and only 216 Sixth Missouri survivors. Those Missouri artillerymen who surrendered were 37 gunners of Landis's battery, 56 cannoneers of Guibor's unit, and 56 survivors in Wade's battery.[42]

The Missouri Brigade was cruelly devastated in sustaining its hard-won reputation as "the South's Finest." Just before the campaign's beginning, a Southern politician had "asked President Davis what he thought of the Mo. Troops, [and] his reply was [that] there is none better." That lofty appraisal was elevated even higher, after the Missouri Brigade's superior combat performances at Grand Gulf, Port Gibson, Champion Hill, Big Black River, and Vicksburg. Even in Union-occupied Missouri, "everyone here is speaking of how gallantly the 1st Mo brig fought at Port Gibson [and] Champion Hill. They have a good reputation, and most gallantly have they fought for it," recorded one Rebel in his diary. And another Confederate in a letter wrote "truly the 1st Mo Brigade covered itself with glory."

The Missouri Brigade suffered the second heaviest losses of any Confederate unit at Vicksburg: 98 casualties from the First and Fourth Missouri, 106 killed and wounded from the Second Missouri, 101 less soldiers in the Third Missouri's ranks, and 72 from the Fifth Missouri. These official figures fail to tell the full story of the sacrifice during the siege, for service records of individual soldiers indicate higher losses for each regiment.

A total of 166 killed and wounded men gained the Sixth Missouri the dubious fame of having suffered the greatest loss of any Confederate regiment during the siege of Vicksburg. It also had the highest rate of loss of any Southern regiment during the entire Vicksburg campaign from May 1 to July 4: a staggering total of 367 Sixth Missouri Rebels were killed, wounded or missing. During the 47-day siege, two regimental commanders of the Missouri Brigade were killed, Colonels Senteny and Erwin, of the Second and Sixth Missouri.

Like Colonel Cockrell's infantry units, the Missouri Brigade's artillery commands had been hurt, with at least 26 men killed or wounded among the three

Missouri batteries. More than two months after the siege, a few rare death notices appeared in a St. Louis newspaper, and listed Missouri Brigade members as having been "killed either in the battle of Champion's Hill, Big Black Bridge, or siege of Vicksburg."[43]

Colonel Cockrell bestowed upon his mangled Missouri Brigade a fitting tribute:

> This is a loss in killed and wounded of over a third of the whole brigade, and shows that this brigade was almost continuously during the entire siege exposed to the enemy's fire, and at no time during this eventful siege did these troops ever waver or fail to go to or occupy any point, regardless of its exposure, and frequently had to and did occupy points on the line so exposed that other troops, although on their own line, would give them up for these troops to occupy [the Missourians were] desirous of holding out and fighting as long as there was a cartridge or a ration of mule or horse, and when the garrison capitulated they felt, and were, disarmed, but in no wise whipped, conquered, or subjugated.

The Missouri Brigade served as the most dependable troops during the siege, acting as General Pemberton's Grenadier Guard of Vicksburg.

Indeed, the reputation for fighting quality, unparalleled sacrifice, and iron discipline applied to the Missourians' role throughout the entire Vicksburg Campaign. In barely two months, the Missouri Brigade had lost more than one half of its men, losing at least 1,382 of its best soldiers during the Vicksburg campaign. As in the past, those horrendous losses were in vain for Vicksburg's fate had been largely sealed before the campaign's beginning. Bowen's division took devastating losses of nearly 2,300, suffering the highest casualties of any division—North or South—during the Vicksburg campaign.

Morale ebbed to a new low because of the loss of Vicksburg. Survivors were dazed from the bitter months of hard fighting and the slaughter at Port Gibson, Champion Hill, and Vicksburg. Even the Confederacy's best troops began to grow war-weary and tired, sickened by the futile killing and the wasted efforts, no matter how valiant, which never produced victory.

A frustrated Private Dyson caught the representative mood in a pitiful letter to his wife, "Our [Fifth Missouri] suffers every fight we have. I hope we will not have to fight anymore. God speed the time when peace shall be made": a prayer that would be answered only by greater carnage in the years ahead. Consequently, after Vicksburg, hundreds of Cockrell's men simply deserted.

Those desertions were perhaps an inevitable result of the Missouri Brigade "cover[ing] itself with glory" for more than a year and a half, and long-overdue in the absence of victory, and with the high losses, with duty under some of the Confederacy's worst army commanders, and with their home state under Union control. A large percentage of Missouri Brigade members who departed returned to the Trans-Mississippi to resume the struggle for Missouri.

Those destined to remain east of the Mississippi felt like one Missouri soldier who wrote home, and declared that he preferred "to rise no more on the field of battle than to shamefully desert the cause..." Another Missouri Brigade officer reflected the resolve of the exiles, writing in a letter that, "I never was more determined than at present to see this matter to the bitter end, and fight the Yankees while my life lasts, or our independence."

The formidable fighting machine that had been so painstakingly built by Generals Little and Bowen, and Colonel Cockrell was practically no more. The strength of the Missouri Brigade filled burial trenches and lay in unmarked graves under magnolia trees, on scarred hills overlooking the Mississippi, in lonely pine thickets and brushy ravines, at Northern prison camps, and near field hospitals in almost too many places to count. Worst of all, not one significant victory—except Grand Gulf, and that was only temporary—could be counted for all the sacrifice.[44]

The home front never forgot the terrible word "Vicksburg" and all of its tragic implications. It would be months before families in Missouri learned that fathers and sons had met their end in the defense of the small town on the Mississippi. The pain of relatives was later expressed in the words of the middle-aged son of John T. Crenshaw, the Sixth Missouri officer who was buried alive during the July 1 mine blast, from an early Twentieth Century letter to one of his father's old comrades: "Any information concerning the Place where he was blown up or whether any remains were ever found...would be thankfully Received": almost 40 years after the great mine explosion near the Jackson Road.[45]

On July 11, 1863, the paroled Confederates marched out of the fallen citadel, and toward their Alabama parole camp. Colonel Cockrell's survivors led the army east down the Jackson Road, swinging past the haunted fortifications where so many comrades had died. The Missourians passed by the blue formations with heads held high, for those troops refused to be humbled in defeat. Sergeant Hogan of St. Louis caught the representative attitude of defiance among the survivors: "The city is now in the hands of the invaders, yet its fall adds not one single laurel to their wreath of victory [and] starvation succeeded in doing what the Federal army could never have done."[46]

Officers retained personal possessions—side arms, sabers, horses, etc.—as a condition of parole. Body servants were liberated, including 33 belonging to the Missouri Brigade. Most of the slaves eagerly embraced their freedom. But others broke down in tears at the separation from owners, who were like family after growing up together on Missouri farms and with ties to these white families that stretched back generations. One African American, Jefferson Patterson, refused to leave the Missouri Brigade, staying beside Colonel Riley to the war's end. Likewise, Jack Coats refused to desert "Marse Francis" Marion Cockrell. The father of both Colonels Riley and Cockrell had purchased those men and handed them on to their sons. Shad, the servant of Lieutenant Colonel Bevier, attended Union officers. But he eventually escaped and rejoined the Missouri Confederates.

Virginia-born Major Robert J. Williams, age thirty-six, a Ray County farmer, rode out of Vicksburg on his thin and weak mule, "Old Juley." That durable animal survived the siege unlike most other Missouri officers' mounts which died of starvation or direct hits. The Third Missouri officer, who had marched through northern Mexico with Colonel Doniphan and clashed with John Brown on the plains of Kansas, had somehow kept his mule alive during 47 days of siege. After the war, the lucky Rebel mule, perhaps a Missouri Brigade mascot, earned a final resting place in the Williams's family cemetery near the Missouri River and eventually beside its owner.[47]

Having left Vicksburg on July 6, an ambulance also steadily creaked east, moving slowly through the dust and scorching heat of a Mississippi summer. The dysentery-racked General Bowen was being carried toward Alabama at his own insistence. Along with two Missouri battle-flags, the vehicle carried Father Bannon and Mrs. Bowen, both of whom prayed for Bowen's survival. Typically, Bowen had continued to command his division at Vicksburg when he should have been admitted to an infirmary. After the surrender, he had refused the kind offers of hospitalization from Union officers whom he had known in prewar days. General Bowen was determined to leave the fallen city, for he felt "anxious to get away from here that they may breathe free air once more."

The long, tortuous journey down a narrow Mississippi road led the ambulance to a quiet farmhouse near Raymond. There, Bowen died quietly of dysentery far from his Carondelet home. But perhaps Bowen's inglorious demise was appropriate since so many of Vicksburg's defenders died in comparable obscurity. In losing General Bowen, the Confederacy in the West suffered yet another severe blow.[48]

The Missouri Brigade's "long, hard and tedious march" east led to parole camp, and also eventually to some of the most bloody and important battles in the West during the next twenty months. But in the future there would be much less hope for success, because Vicksburg's fall and the loss of the Mississippi had decided the struggle in the West and, therefore, in large part in the East as well. The Southern boast that "we could afford to lose fifty Vicksburgs" proved false.

Spirits among surviving Missourians lifted as they marched farther away from the city of death on the Mississippi. One Missouri Rebel expressed elation in his diary: "I am so happy to feel that we will soon be where we breathe once more the free air of the South, uncontaminated with the tyranny of those hirelings who are engaged to subjugate a free people and take from them their rights and privileges so dear to the human heart and without which life would be a barren waste."

During the spring and summer of 1863, Grant's swift Napoleonic tactics and then strategy of attrition in Mississippi had reaped a rich harvest for the victory-hungry Union, capturing Vicksburg and almost 30,000 soldiers, who were desperately needed by the South. A strategic, symbolic, and, most important, political victory for the North, the winning of Vicksburg bolstered the Northern will to prosecute the war to the end as much as it sapped the will of the Southern people, and loosened another pillar from under the shaky foundation of Confederate nationalism. After the fall of Port Hudson on July 9, all of the Mississippi River was once more under Union control. Beginning with the loss of Missouri, the Confederacy's left had been turned and most of the Mississippi Valley had been conquered.[49]

The battle-scarred survivors of Pea Ridge, Iuka, Corinth, Grand Gulf, Port Gibson, Champion Hill, Big Black River, and Vicksburg carried with them little more than the memories of the many fallen comrades and the fine leaders of the Missouri Brigade who were no more. They remembered the popular Captain Samuel Churchill Clark, age nineteen, who had his head taken off by a shell near an Arkansas tavern called Elkhorn, after helping to save a badly beaten army; a dying Colonel Benjamin Allen Rives, supported in the saddle during a final gallop down the wavering Confederate lines, ensuring that his hard-pressed soldiers would stand firm during a critical rear-guard stand at Pea Ridge. Some thought of the gifted General Henry Little shot off his horse at Iuka, after saving the day on a warm Indian summer afternoon in northeast Mississippi and handsome Colonel James Avery Pritchard cut down on Corinth's fortifications at the moment of victory.

Others recalled Colonel William Wade falling at Grand Gulf before he could celebrate the success of his steadfast artillery in thwarting Grant's mighty invasion of Mississippi; Colonel Finley Lewis Hubbell mortally wounded in the bloody, smoke-filled forests of Champion Hill, while leading his screaming Confederates onward in one of the most fierce charges of the war; Colonel Eugene Erwin killed on a hot June day amid a man-made hell, while encouraging his Rebels forward in a timely counterattack which eliminated one of the most serious threats to Vicksburg's life; and dashing Colonel Pembroke S. Senteny shot through the head by a sniper and falling beside his men in the trenches of Vicksburg. Perhaps the most serious loss of all was the brilliant General John Stevens Bowen who died unnoticed of dysentery at a lonely farmhouse deep in Mississippi and far from glory, after becoming the best Confederate division commander in the West.

From then until the war's end, the Missouri Confederates would be motivated to continue to fight so that such sacrifices would not have been in vain. While struggling hundreds of miles away from home and the center stage arenas of Antietam, Chancellorsville, and Gettysburg in the East, no troops in the Confederacy accomplished so much and on so many important Western battlefields and in more key combat situations than "the South's Finest." Indeed, during the first half of the war, the First Missouri Confederate Brigade covered itself in glory across Missouri, Arkansas, Louisiana, and Mississippi and compiled a combat record unsurpassed by any comparable unit, North or South.

ENDNOTES

Introduction: The Winter of Decision

1. Allan R. Millett and Peter Maslowski, *For the Common Defense: A Military History of the United States of America*, (New York, 1984), 154; *The Memphis, Tennessee, Daily Appeal*, 20 Dec. 1861; Robert S. Bevier, *History of the First and Second Missouri Confederate Brigades 1861-1865 and From Wakarusa to Appomattox, A Military Anagraph*, (St. Louis, 1879), 76-77; Robert K. Wright, Jr., *The Continental Army*, (Washington, D.C.; 1983), 43, 45, 65, 91-92, 119; *The Weekly, Jackson, Mississippian*, 8 Oct., and 5 Nov. 1861; Dunbar Rowland, ed., *Jefferson Davis, Constitutionalist: Letters, Papers and Speeches*, (Jackson, 1923), 5: 183-184; Albert Castel, *William Clarke Quantrill, His Life and Times*, (Marietta, 1992), 57.

2. Bevier, *History of the First and Second Missouri Confederate Brigades*, 76-77; Millet and Maslowski, *For the Common Defense*, 158; *The Memphis Daily Appeal*, 26 June, 24 July, 28 Aug. and 8 Sept. 1861; *The Weekly Mississippian*, 17 Sept. 1861; Richard M. McMurray, *Two Great Rebel Armies: An Essay in Confederate Military History*, (Chapel Hill, 1989), 10-14; Clement Eaton, *Jefferson Davis*, (New York, 1977), 187-188; *The Intelligencer, Atlanta, Georgia*, 14 May 1861 and 19 Mar. 1862; *The Memphis Daily Appeal*, 12 Nov. 1863; James A. Rawley, *Turning Points of the Civil War*, (Lincoln, 1989), 11-14; Anne J. Bailey, "The Abandoned Western Theater: Confederate National Policy toward the Trans-Mississippi Region," V, *Journal of Confederate History*, (1990), 35-37; Archer Jones, *Civil War Command And Strategy: The Process of Victory and Defeat*, (New York, 1992), 48-51, 143-144, 236-237; Christopher Phillips, *Damned Yankee: The Life of General Nathaniel Lyon*, (Columbia, 1990), 138.

3. *The History of Newton, Lawrence, Barry and McDonald Counties, Missouri*, (Chicago, 1888), 328-330; *The Memphis Daily Appeal*, 15, 19, 20, 28, 29 Nov. and 6 and 20 Dec. 1861; Eaton, *Jefferson Davis*, 187-189; Stanley F. Horn, *The Army of Tennessee*, (Wilmington, 1987), 15-16, 32-34; *The Richmond, Virginia, Enquirer*, 22 June 1861; *The Memphis Daily Appeal*, 12 Nov. 1863; *The Intelligencer*, 14 May 1861 and 19 Mar. 1862; Arthur Roy Kirkpatrick, "The Admission of Missouri to the Confederacy," *Missouri Historical Review*, 55: (1961), 366-386; Georgia Cook, "Neosho...Its Part in a Confederate Dream," *Gateway Magazine*, 2: (1981), 26-30; William Parrish, "Missouri," in W. Buck Yearns, ed., *The Confederate Governors*, (Athens, 1985), 130-139; Ephraim McDowell Anderson, *Memoirs: Historical and Personal; Including the Campaigns of the First Missouri Confederate Brigade*, (St. Louis, 1868), 94; "Sketch of Colonel B. A. Rives of Ray County, Missouri," Missouri Historical Society; Steven E. Woodworth, *Jefferson Davis and His Generals: The Failure of Confederate Command in the West*, (Lawrence, 1990), 93-94.

4. Anderson, *Memoirs*, 111; *The Mobile, Alabama, Register and Advertiser*, 11 Feb. 1862; *The Memphis Daily Appeal*, 22 Dec. 1861; Horn, *The Army of Tennessee*, 16; "Personal Memoirs of I.V. Smith," 13, Western Historical Manuscript Collection-State Historical Society of Missouri; Bevier, *History of the First and Second Missouri Confederate Brigades*, 14; Albert Castel, *General Sterling Price and the Civil War in the West*, (Baton Rouge, 1968), 38-39, 128, 131-134; George William Warren to Brother, 15 Jan. 1865, letters, diary, and Family Papers, Ellen R. Warren, Alexandria, Virginia.

5. Howard Wight Marshall, *Folk Architecture in Little Dixie: A Regional Culture in Missouri*, (Columbia, 1981), vii-11; Adjutant General of Service Records of Missouri Confederate Soldiers,

Adjutant General's Office, Jefferson City, Missouri; *Journal of the House of Representatives, Missouri 21st General Assembly, 1st Session*, Appendix, 762; Phillip Thomas Tucker, "A Perspective of Johnson County's Confederate Dead Who Served in the First Missouri Brigade, C.S.A., 1861-1865," 1978 Graduate School Study, Central Missouri State University, Warrensburg, Missouri; Duane G. Meyer, *The Heritage of Missouri*, (St. Louis, 1988), 240, 316, 322; Walter A. Roher, "Confederate Generals—the View from Below," *Civil War Times Illustrated*, (1979), 13; William A. Ruyle Memoir, 27, private collection of Dee Ruyle, Bolivar, Missouri; *The Mobile Register and Advertiser*, 27 Nov. 1862, 1 Nov. 1863 and 19 and 24 Jan. 1864; Various 1859 and 1860 issues of *The Bolivar, Missouri, Courier*; Edwin C. Bearss, *The Campaign For Vicksburg: Grant Strikes A Fatal Blow*, (Dayton, 1986), 2: 675; *The Atlanta, Georgia, Intelligencer*, 10 and 11 Apr. 1862 and 2 June 1863; John A. Leavy Journal, 58, 63, Vicksburg National Military Park Archives, Vicksburg, Mississippi; *The Savannah, Georgia, Republican*, 6 and 13 May, 1863; *The Mississippian*, 4 and 9 Jan. 1863 and 14 and 26 Nov., 1863; *The Memphis Daily Appeal*, 18 Oct. 1862 and 23 Mar., 8 Apr. and 6 and 8 Aug. 1863; Compiled Service Records of Confederate Soldiers Who Served in Organizations From the State of Missouri, Record Group 109, National Archives, Washington, D.C.; Anderson, *Memoirs*, 13, 116-123, 125; McMurry, *Two Great Rebel Armies*, 97-99; "Personal Memoirs of I. V. Smith," 1, WHMC-SHSM; Alfred N. Hunt, *Haiti's Influence on Antebellum America: Slumbering Volcano in the Caribbean*, (Baton Rouge: 1988), 137-146, 181-190; Samuel Dunlap Diary, Western Historical Manuscript Collection-State Historical Society of Missouri; Records of Pictoral Archives, Missouri Historical Society, St. Louis, Missouri; Joseph Boyce, "Military Organizations of St. Louis," Missouri Historical Society; Charles Royster, *A Revolutionary People at War: The Continental Army and American Character, 1775-1783*, (New York, 1979), 6-8; Absalom Roby Dyson to Wife, n.d., 11 Aug. 1863 and 23 Dec. 1863, Absalom Roby Dyson Collection, Western Historical Manuscript Collection-State Historical Society of Missouri; John T. Wickersham, *The Gray and the Blue*, (Berkeley, California, 1915), 3; Richard S. Brownlee, *Gray Ghosts of the Confederacy: Guerrilla Warfare in the West, 1861-1865*, (Baton Rouge, 1984), 5-6; Babcock Scrapbook, Missouri Historical Society; *Daily, St. Louis, Missouri Republican*, 3 Dec. 1860; Castel, *Quantrill*, 60.

6. *History of Southeast Missouri*, (Chicago, 1888), 909; Ellsworth Eliot, Jr., *West Point in the Confederacy*, (New York, 1941), 418-419; James E. Payne, "Early Days of War in Missouri," *Confederate Veteran*, 38: (1931), 58; *The St. Louis Missouri Republican*, 26, 27, and 29 Nov. 1861 and 1, 3, 5, 12, and 14 Dec. 1861; *The Daily St. Louis Missouri Democrat*, 26, 27, and 29 Nov. 1860 and 3, 8, 10, and 14 Dec. 1860; *The Courier*, 8 Dec. 1860; Bevier, *History of the First and Second Missouri Confederate Brigades*, 13, 76, 353-354, 406-407; Anderson, *Memoirs*, 12, 124, 131-132; William H. Kavanaugh Memoir, 2, 5, William H. Kavanaugh Papers, Western Historical Manuscript Collection-State Historical Society of Missouri, Columbia, Missouri; Asa M. Payne, "Story of the Battle of Pea Ridge," Manuscript, Pea Ridge National Military Park Archives, Pea Ridge, Arkansas; George Engelman Diary, Missouri Historical Society; Richard Barksdale Harwell, ed., *Kate: The Journal of a Confederate Nurse*, (Baton Rouge, 1959), 287; Compiled Missouri Confederate Service Records, RG 109, NA; David D. March, *The History of Missouri*, (New York, 1967), 186; *The Kansas City, Missouri, Times*, 5 Dec. 1941; Joseph Boyce to Smith Hawes, 18 Jan. 1864, Joseph Boyce Papers, Missouri Historical Society; *The Memphis Daily Appeal*, 20 Dec. 1861 and 2 Mar. 1862; *The Richmond Enquirer*, 22 June 1861; Floyd C. Shoemaker, "Missouri-Heir of Southern Tradition and Individuality," *Missouri Historical Review*, 36: (1942), 435-436; Judith Lee Hallock, " 'Lethal and Debilitating': The Southern Disease Environment as a Factor in Confederate Defeat," *Journal of Confederate History*, VII, (1991), 51-61; Bevier, *History of the First and Second Missouri Confederate Brigades*, 352, 406, 414; George William Warren Diaries and Family Papers, George William Warren, IV, Montpelier, Virginia; John Stevens Bowen Papers, Missouri Historical Society; Larry J. Daniel, *Soldiering in the Army of Tennessee: A Portrait of Life in a Confederate Army*, (Chapel Hill, 1991), 14-15.

7. Compiled Missouri Confederate Service Records, RG 109, NA; Kimball Clark, "The Epic March of Doniphan's Missourians," *Missouri Historical Review*, 80: (1986), 134-155; Alonzo H. Shelton, "Memoir of a Confederate Veteran," 2, Archives of William Jewell College, Liberty, Missouri; Castel, *Quantrill*, 3.

8. J. Glenn Gray, *The Warriors: Reflections on Men in Battle*, (New York, 1967), ix, 40; *The Missouri Army Argus*, 28 Oct. 1861; Kavanaugh Memoir, 9, WHMC-SHSM; Francis Marion

Cockrell to Samuel Cooper, 12 Sept. 1863, John S. Bowen Letter Book, Virginia Historical Society, Richmond, Virginia; John C. Moore, *Confederate Military History, Extended Edition, Missouri*, (Wilmington, 1988), 12: 446; *The War of the Rebellion: A Compilation of the Official Records of the Union and Confederate Armies* (128 vols., Washington, D.C., 1880-1901), 52: ser. 1, pt. 2, 524-526; Anderson, *Memoirs*, 13; Wickersham, *The Gray and the Blue*, 10-11; Avington Wayne Simpson Diary, Western Historical Manuscript Collection-State Historical Society of Missouri; Warren to Father, 21 June 1863; I. G. Brawner to William Skaggs, 16 May 1915, Skaggs Collection of Confederate Veteran Letters, Arkansas History Commission, Little Rock, Arkansas.

Chapter One: The First Missouri Brigade

1. Anderson, *Memoirs*, 111-113; Kavanaugh Memoir, 8-9, WHMC-SHSM; *The Memphis Daily Appeal*, 17 July 1861 and 12 Jan. 1862; Robert St. Peters, *Memorial Volume of the Diamond Jubilee of St. Louis University, 1829-1904*, (St. Louis, 1904), 229; *O.R.*, 8: 737: Samuel Dunlap Diary, 51, Western Historical Manuscript Collection-State Historical Society of Missouri; Compiled Missouri Confederate Service Records, RG 109, NA; *History of Pike County, Missouri*, (Des Moines, 1883), 1: 261, 274-276; Clayton Keith, *Military History of Pike County, Missouri*, (Louisiana, 1915); Gaylord O'Connor, Louisiana, Missouri, to author, 29 May 1989; *The St. Louis Missouri Republican*, 18 July 1885; Robert E. St. Peters, Alton, Illinois, to author, 30 June 1985; Joseph A. Mudd to William Skaggs, 7 Aug. 1909, Skaggs Collection, AHC; H. C. Burbridge, Jr., Jacksonville, Florida, Burbridge Family Papers; John Gerber, "Twain's 'Private Campaign'," *Civil War History*, 1: (1955), 40-41; Adjutant General of Missouri Service Records; Clinton Burbridge, Sr., to Clinton Burbridge, III, 1 June 1965, Henry C. Burbridge, Jr., Papers, Jacksonville, Florida.

2. Compiled Missouri Confederate Service Records, RG 109, NA; *The University Missourian*, 23 Dec. 1915; Kavanaugh Memoir, 5, WHMC-SHSM; Anderson, *Memoirs*, 114.

3. Compiled Missouri Confederate Service Records, RG 109, NA; Adjutant General of Missouri Service Records; *History of Ray County, Missouri*, (St. Louis, 1881), 756, 776-777; *The Mobile Register and Advertiser*, 18 Apr. 1862; L. Carey Bankhead Papers, private collection of L. Carey Bankhead, Moberly, Missouri; *The St. Louis Republican*, 30 Sept. 1900; *The Albany, Missouri, Ledger*, 9 Mar. 1906; Marjorie Evans, Troy, Missouri, interview with author, 20 Nov. 1987; *Missouri Partisan*, Sons of Confederate Veterans, Missouri Division, VII (Summer/Fall 1991).

4. Adjutant General of Missouri Service Records; Elizabeth Tunstall White, Rives Family History, Marie Oliver Watkins Papers, 1702-1962, Western Historical Manuscript Collection-State Historical Society of Missouri; Anderson, *Memoirs*, 137; Compiled Missouri Confederate Service Records, RG 109, NA.

5. Compiled Missouri Confederate Service Records, RG 109, NA; "Official Proceedings of Fifth Annual Reunion of Missouri Division, United Confederate Veterans, Springfield, Missouri, August 8, 9 and 10, 1901," Missouri Historical Society; Benjamin Allen Rives to Charles A. Watkins, 21 Apr. 1845 and miscellaneous papers, Marie Oliver Watkins Papers, 1702-1962, WHMC-SHSM; Bevier, *History of the First and Second Missouri Confederate Brigades*, 37, 55-56, 86, 109; Robert Underwood Johnson and Clarence Clough Buel, eds., *Battles and Leaders of the Civil War*, (New York, 1884-1888), 1: 277; "Sketch of Colonel B. A. Rives of Ray County, Missouri," MHS; Richard M. Hubbell, "Personal Reminiscences," 3, Missouri Historical Society; Adjutant General of Missouri Service Records; James Bradley, *The Confederate Mail Carrier*, (Mexico, 1894), 267; "Personal Memoirs of I. V. Smith," 3, WHMC-SHSM; Robert C. Dunlap Diary, private collection of John B. Sampson, DeKalb, Missouri; *Richmond, Missouri, Missourian*, 13 July 1933.

6. Compiled Missouri Confederate Service Records, RG 109, NA; Adjutant General of Missouri Service Records; *The St. Joseph, Missouri, Gazette*, 4 and 5 Mar. 1915; Edwin L. Miller Scrapbook, 1888-1897, Western Historical Manuscript Collection-State Historical Society of Missouri; *The St. Louis Missouri Republican*, 24 July 1876 and 5 Mar. 1915; *Portrait and Biographical Record of Buchanan and Clinton Counties, Missouri*, (Chicago, 1893), 127-131; 1860 Buchanan County, Missouri, Census Records; Walter Williams, ed., *History of Northwest Missouri*,

(Chicago, 1913), 3: 1923-1924; "Union and Confederate Annals: The Blue and Grey in Friendship Meet, and Heroic Deeds Recite," 1: (1884), Missouri Historical Society; *The United States Biographical Dictionary, Missouri Volume*, (Chicago, 1878), 522-523; *The St. Louis Post-Dispatch*, 26 Aug. 1910; Chris L. Rutt, *History of Buchanan County and the City of St. Joseph, Missouri, and Representative Citizens*, (Chicago, 1904), 282-283; Champ Clark Scrapbook, 15: Champ Clark Papers, Western Historical Manuscript Collection-State Historical Society of Missouri.

7. Adjutant General of Missouri Service Records; Bradley, *The Confederate Mail Carrier*, 267; *The St. Louis Post-Dispatch*, 26 Aug. 1910; Burbridge Family Papers; *The St. Louis Missouri Republican*, 18 July 1885; *Portrait and Biographical Record of Buchanan and Clinton Counties, Missouri*, 128; *The United States Biographical Dictionary*, 523; Rives Family History, Watkins Papers, WHMC-SHSM.

8. James I. Robertson, Jr., *The Stonewall Brigade*, (Baton Rouge, 1963), viii, 5-6, 10-16; Clark Family Papers, MHS; Compiled Missouri Confederate Service Records, RG 109, NA; Boyce, "Military Organizations of St. Louis," 65, 68-69, MHS; Anderson, *Memoirs*, 40, 99; Dabney H. Maury, "Recollections of the Elkhorn Campaign," *Southern Historical Society Papers*, 2: (1876), 192; *The St. Louis Daily Evening News*, 17 Dec. 1860; John M. Hopewell, *The History of Camp Jackson*, (St. Louis, 1861), 27; *The St. Louis Missouri Republican*, 24 and 27 Nov. 1860 and 12 Dec. 1860; "Partnership Agreement Between Wade, Stille, Osborne, and D. M. Frost as Trustee," 9 Apr. 1853, Fordyce Collection, Missouri Historical Society; *The Daily Missouri Democrat*, 18 Dec. 1860; Bevier, *History of the First and Second Missouri Confederate Brigades*, 111; *The St. Louis Missouri Democrat*, 7 May 1855, 7 Jul. 1855 and 18 Aug. 1857; Joseph Boyce to Messrs. Keogh and Dowell, 20 Jul. 1861, Boyce Papers, MHS; *The Memphis Daily Appeal*, 30 Jun. and 26 Oct. 1861; Samuel Churchill Clark to Aunt, 25 June 1861, Clark Papers, MHS; *St. Louis Daily Missourian*, 26 Nov. 1860.

9. St. Peters, *Diamond Jubilee of St. Louis University*, 236; Moore, *Confederate Military History, Missouri*, 12; 258-259; *The Missouri Republican*, 28 Nov. 1885; Bevier, *History of the First and Second Missouri Confederate Brigades*, 101; Samuel Churchill Clark to Aunt, 25 Jan. 1862 and miscellaneous papers, Clark Papers, MHS; Henry Howe, *The Times of the Rebellion in the West*, (Cincinnati, 1867), 219; Compiled Missouri Confederate Service Records, RG 109, NA; Meriwether Lewis Clark to Samuel Churchill Clark, 14 May 1860, Clark Papers, MHS; Francis Hurd Stadler, "Letters From Minoma," *The Missouri Historical Society Bulletin*, 16: (1960), 238-239; Frank Moore, ed., *The Rebellion Record*, (11 vols., New York, 1862-1868) IV, 266.

10. Compiled Missouri Confederate Service Records, RG 109, NA; *The Chattanooga Daily Rebel*, 4 Nov. 1862; Henry Little Diary, The United States Army Military Institute, Carlisle Barracks, Pennsylvania; Ray W. Irwin, "Missouri in Crisis: The Journal of Captain Albert Tracey, 1861," *Missouri Historical Review*, 51: (1956), 19; *The Richmond Enquirer*, 24 June 1861 and 10 Oct. 1861; Henry Little Biographical Sketch, Maryland Historical Society, Baltimore, Maryland; *The Memphis Daily Appeal*, 19 Apr. 1862; Anderson, *Memoirs*, 114; Grady McWhiney and Perry D. Jamieson, *Attack and Die: Civil War Military Tactics and the Southern Heritage*, (University, 1982), xiii-24.

11. Father John Bannon Diary, Yates Snowden Collection, South Caroliniana Library, University of South Carolina, Columbia, South Carolina; Father John Bannon Sketch, The Confederate Museum, Richmond, Virginia; "Rev. John Bannon," *Confederate Veteran*, 21: (1913), 451; Joseph Boyce, "Rev. John Bannon-Chaplain Price's Missouri Confederate Division," 8 Mar. 1914, Missouri Historical Society; Champ Clark Scrapbook, vol. 15, Champ Clark Papers, Western Historical Manuscript Collection-State Historical Society of Missouri; Compiled Missouri Confederate Service Records, RG 109, NA; Anderson, *Memoirs*, 131.

12. Brauckman Scrapbook, Missouri Historical Society; Buel and Johnson, eds., *Battles and Leaders*, 1: 275; *The Memphis Daily Appeal*, 30 May 1862; Dr. Thomas Sweeny, Springfield, Missouri, private collection of Civil War photographs; Anderson, *Memoirs*, 101, 129-141; Leslie Anders, *Confederate Roll of Honor: Missouri*, (Warrensburg, 1989), vi; Daniel, *Soldiering in the Army of Tennessee*, 13.

Chapter Two: Mr. Cox's Tavern

1. *O.R.*, 8: 58-59, 554, 756-757; *The Memphis Daily Appeal*, 14 Jan. 1862 and 11 Feb. 1862; Bevier, *History of the First and Second Missouri Confederate Brigades*, 87-88; Bannon Diary, SCL; Joseph Mothershead Journal, 1, Tennessee State Library and Archives, Nashville, Tennessee; "Personal Memoir of I. V. Smith," 13, WHMC-SHSM; Michael A. Mullins, *The Fremont Rifles: A History of the 37th Illinois Veteran Volunteer Infantry*, (Wilmington, 1990), 50-52; Alvin M. Josephy, Jr., *The Civil War in the American West*, (New York, 1991), 319-337; Glenn W. Sunderland, *Five Days to Glory*, (New York, 1970), 25-27.

2. Bevier, *History of the First and Second Missouri Confederate Brigades*, 86-92; Brauchman Scrapbook, MHS; Bannon Diary, SCL; "Personal Memoirs of I. V. Smith," 13-14, WHMC-SHSM; Mothershead Journal, 3-6, TSLA; *O.R.*, 8: 757; Anderson, *Memoirs*, 144-156; William L. Webb, *Battles and Biographies of Missourians*, (Kansas City, 1900), 114; *The St. Louis Missouri Republican*, 28 Nov. 1885; *The Memphis Daily Appeal*, 11 Feb. 1862 and 2 and 20 Mar. 1862; Josephy, *The Civil War in the American West*, 337.

3. "Personal Memoirs of I. V. Smith," 13, WHMC-SHSM; *The Memphis Daily Appeal*, 5 Dec. 1861; *History of Lafayette County, Missouri*, (St. Louis, 1881), 678-679; *O.R.*, 8: 757; Bevier, *History of the First and Second Missouri Confederate Brigades*, 88-91; Michael Fellman, *Inside War: The Guerrilla Conflict in Missouri During the American Civil War*, (New York, 1989), 142, 178; Compiled Missouri Confederate Service Records, RG 109, NA; Anderson, *Memoirs*, 144-148, 151-153; Brauckman Scrapbook, MHS; Mothershead Journal, 3-5, TSLA; Williams, ed., *History of Northwest Missouri*, 1: 380-381, 404 and 2: 605; *History of Andrew and DeKalb Counties, Missouri*, (Chicago, 1888), 538; Walter Williams, ed., *History of Northeast Missouri*, (Chicago, 1913), 1: 295; *History of Clay and Platte Counties, Missouri*, (St. Louis, 1885), 675-678; William M. Paxton, *Annals of Platte County, Missouri*, (Kansas City, 1897), 312-314, 319-320, 323, 358-359, 361, 372, 377; Homer L. Calkins, ed., "From Elk Horn to Vicksburg," James H. Fauntleroy's Diary of the Year 1862, *Civil War History*, 2: (1956), 12; Moore, ed., *The Rebellion Record*, 3: 462-463; Cora N. Barns Scrapbook, 2: Western Historical Manuscript Collection-State Historical Society of Missouri; Wilbur P. McDonald, St. Joseph, Missouri, to author, 12 Dec. 1988; Leslie Anders, *The Eighteenth Missouri*, (New York, 1968), 16; William E. Connelly, *Doniphan's Expedition*, (Topeka, 1907), 560-561; McWhiney and Jamieson, *Attack and Die*, 62-66; James E. Payne, "Fighting John Brown at Osawatomie," *Confederate Veteran*, 28: (1920), 460; J. W. Gibson, *Recollections of a Pioneer*, (St. Joseph, 1912), 129; Robert Dunlap Diary; Williams, ed., *History of Northwest Missouri*, 1: 604-605; Brownlee, *Gray Ghosts of the Confederacy*, 102-103, 254-255, 260.

4. Mothershead Journal, 4, TSLA; Anderson, *Memoirs*, 151; Bannon Diary, SCL; Brauckman Scrapbook, MHS; "Personal Memoir of I. V. Smith," 13-14, WHMC-SHSM; Gibson, *Recollections of a Pioneer*, 129; Warren Diary.

5. Bannon Diary, SCL; "Personal Memoirs of I. V. Smith," 15, WHMC-SHSM; William Clark Kennerly, *Persimmon Hill: A Narrative of Old St. Louis and the Far West*, (Norman, 1948), 238, 242; Samuel Churchill Clark to Aunt, 25 Jan. 1862, Clark Papers, MHS; St. Peters, *Memorial Volume of the Diamond Jubilee of St. Louis University*, 274; Bevier, *History of the First and Second Missouri Confederate Brigades*, 79; Brauckman Scrapbook, MHS; *The Memphis Daily Appeal*, 5 Jan. 1862 and 29 Mar. 1862; Mothershead Journal, 5-6, TSLA; Anderson, *Memoirs*, 161; Warren Diary.

6. Mothershead Journal, 7, TSLA; Walter Brown, "Pea Ridge: Gettysburg of the West," *Arkansas Historical Quarterly*, 15, (1956), 3-4; Compiled Missouri Confederate Service Records, RG 109, NA; *The Memphis Daily Appeal*, 21 Jan. 1862 and 8, 9, 11, 12, 20, 25, 26 and 28 Feb. and 4 and 19 Mar. 1862; Dabney H. Maury, "Recollections of the Elkhorn Campaign," *Southern Historical Society Papers*, 2: (1876), 180-181; *Mobile Register and Advertiser*, 13 and 14 Mar. 1862; Robert C. Dunlap Diary; Jones, *Civil War Command and Strategy*, 98-109; Thomas C. Reynolds, "Gen. Sterling Price and the Confederacy," 36, Missouri Historical Society; "Personal Memoirs of I. V. Smith," 15, WHMC-SHSM.

7. Henry Voelkner to Family, 18 Mar. 1862, Missouri Historical Society; Buel and Johnson, eds., *Battles and Leaders*, 1: 276; John Bannon Diary, SCL; Anderson, *Memoirs*, 163; *The St. Louis*

Missouri Republican, 21 Nov. 1885 and 19 Dec. 1885; Calkins, ed., "From Elk Horn to Vicksburg," *CWH*, 12-13; John McElroy, *The Struggle For Missouri*, (Washington, 1909), 320; "Personal Memoir of I. V. Smith," 15, WHMC-SHSM; Mothershead Journal, 7-8, TSLA; Wiley Britton, *The Civil War on the Border*, (New York, 1890), 218-219; Josephy, *The Civil War in the American West*, 338.

8. Buel and Johnson, eds., *Battles and Leaders*, 1: 276; *O.R.*, 8: 307; Bannon Diary, SCL; Castel, *General Sterling Price and the Civil War in the West*, 72-73; Jones, *Civil War Command and Strategy*, 50; Warren Diary.

9. Castel, *General Sterling Price and the Civil War in the West*, 72-73; Bannon Diary, SCL; *O.R.*, 8: 307.

10. Bannon Diary, SCL; *O.R.*, 8: 307; *The St. Louis Missouri Republican*, 19 Dec. 1885; Anderson, *Memoirs*, 167-168.

11. *O.R.*, 8: 307; Bannon Diary, SCL; Maury, "Recollections of the Elkhorn Campaign," *SHSP*, 186-187; Castel, *General Sterling Price and the Civil War in the West*, 73.

12. Anderson, *Memoirs*, 167-169; *O.R.*, 8: 272-273, 305, 307; Edwin C. Bearss, "The First Day at Pea Ridge, March 7, 1862," *Arkansas Historical Quarterly*, 17: (1958), 142-143, 263-265, 277-278; Buel and Johnson, eds., *Battles and Leaders*, 1: 323; Samuel Dunlap Diary, 69, WHMC-SHSM; Edwin C. Bearss, "The Battle of Pea Ridge," *Annals of Iowa*, 36: (1962), 587-589; Asa Payne, "Story of the Battle of Pea Ridge," Pea Ridge National Military Park Archives, Pea Ridge, Arkansas; *The St. Louis Missouri Republican*, 4 July 1885 and 28 Nov. 1885; "Personal Memoirs of I. V. Smith," 16, WHMC-SHSM; Adjutant General of Missouri Service Records.

13. *O.R.*, 8: 258, 263-265, 274-275; *The St. Louis Missouri Republican*, 7 Mar. 1885; Castel, *General Sterling Price and the Civil War in the West*, 73; Kennerly, *Persimmon Hill*, 242-243; Bearss, "The Battle of Pea Ridge," *Annals of Iowa*, 37: (1963), 9-10; Bearss, "The First Day at Pea Ridge, March 7, 1862," *AHQ*, 137; Compiled Missouri Confederate Service Records, RG 109, NA.

14. Steven R. Hayes, *A Headwaters Creek Trail*, (Pea Ridge National Military Park, n.d.), 14; Buel and Johnson, eds., *Battles and Leaders*, 1: 323; Bannon Diary, SCL; Adjutant General of Missouri Service Records; *O.R.*, 8: 259, 265, 307; Ninth Annual Reunion of the Ex-Confederate Association of Missouri, Aug. 19 and 20, 1891, 21, Missouri Historical Society, St. Louis, Missouri; Compiled Missouri Confederate Service Records, RG 109, NA.

15. *O.R.*, 8: 259-260, 263-269, 274-276; Buel and Johnson, eds., *Battles and Leaders*, 1: 323; Bearss, "The First Day at Pea Ridge, March 7, 1862," *AHQ*, 138-139; Compiled Missouri Confederate Service Records, RG 109, NA.

16. Mothershead Journal, 9-10, TSLA; Anderson, *Memoirs*, 170; Bearss, "The Battle of Pea Ridge," *AI*, 16-22; *O.R.*, 8: 258-261, 266-267; Jay Monaghan, *Civil War on the Western Border, 1854-1865*, (New York, n.d.), 157.

17. Bearss, "The First Day at Pea Ridge, March 7, 1862," *AHQ*, 139, 144; Anderson, *Memoirs*, 170; *O.R.*, 8: 260, 271-272, 307-308; Bannon Diary, SCL; Mothershead Journal, 10, TSLA; Vinson Holman Diary typescript, Pea Ridge National Military Park Archives, 36-37.

18. Payne, "Story of the Battle of Pea Ridge," PRNMPA; Bearss, "The First Day At Pea Ridge, March 7, 1862," *AHQ*, 139; Anderson, *Memoirs*, 170-171; *O.R.*, 8: 259-260.

19. Mothershead Journal, 10, TSLA; Bearss, "The First Day at Pea Ridge, March 7, 1862," *AHQ*, 139, 144; *O.R.*, 8: 260, 263, 271, 308; Anderson, *Memoirs*, 171; Bannon Diary, SCL; Holman Diary typescript, 36-37, PRNMPA.

20. James T. King, *A Life of General Eugene A. Carr*, (Lincoln, 1963), 46-49; *O.R.*, 8: 258-260, 263; Holman Diary typescript, 36-37, PRNMPA; *The St. Louis Missouri Republican*, 19 Dec. 1885.

21. Kennerly, *Persimmon Hill*, 242-243; *O.R.*, 8: 258-260, 263, 268-269, 308; Payne, "Story of the Battle of Pea Ridge," PRNMPA; Mothershead Journal, 10, TSLA; Anderson, *Memoirs*, 171; Bearss, "The First Day at Pea Ridge, March 7, 1862," *AHQ*, 139, 144-145; *The St. Louis Missouri Republican*, 19 Dec. 1885; Holman Diary typescript, 37, PRNMPA; Compiled Missouri Confederate Service Records, RG 109, NA.

22. *The St. Louis Missouri Republican*, 11 July 1885; Anderson, *Memoirs*, 171; Payne, "Story of the Battle of Pea Ridge," PRNMPA; Mothershead Journal, 10, TSLA; *O.R.*, 8: 260-261, 308; Bannon Diary, SCL.

23. Mothershead Journal, 10-11, TSLA; Anderson, *Memoirs*, 171; Bannon Diary, SCL; *The New York, New York, Herald*, 9 Mar. 1862; *O.R.*, 8: 260-261, 308; "Personal Memoir of I. V. Smith," 16, WHMC-SHSM; *The St. Louis Missouri Republican*, 4 July 1885.

24. Anderson, *Memoirs*, 171; Mothershead Journal, 10-11, TSLA; *O.R.*, 8: 260-261; Bannon Diary, SCL; "Personal Memoir of I. V. Smith," 16-17, WHMC-SHSM.

25. Compiled Missouri Confederate Service Records, RG 109, NA; *O.R.*, 8: 260-261, 308; *The St. Louis Post-Dispatch*, 26 Aug. 1910; *O.R.*, 8: 261; *Confederate Veteran*, 4: (1896), 255.

26. *The New York Herald*, 9 Mar. 1862; "Personal Memoir of I. V. Smith," 16-17, WHMC-SHSM; Robert G. Hartje, *Van Dorn: The Life and Times of a Confederate General*, (Nashville, 1967), 149; *O.R.*, 8: 260-261, 267, 269, 308; Mothershead Journal, 10-11, TSLA; *The St. Louis Missouri Republican*, 11 July 1885; Thomas W. Knox, *The Lost Army*, (New York, 1894), 187-188; Bearss, "The First Day at Pea Ridge, March 7, 1862," *AHQ*, 139; *History of Andrew and DeKalb Counties, Missouri*, 538; Moore, ed., *The Rebellion Record*, 4: 266; Bannon Diary, SCL.

27. Edwin C. Bearss, "The Battle of Pea Ridge," *Annals of Iowa*, 37: (1963), 36; Mothershead Journal, 11, TSLA; Compiled Missouri Confederate Service Records, RG 109, NA; *The Mobile Register and Advertiser*, 22 Mar. 1862; *O.R.*, 8: 261, 309; *History of Carroll County, Missouri*, (St. Louis, 1881), 502-503; John W. Bond, "The History of Elkhorn Tavern," *Arkansas Historical Quarterly*, 21: (1962), 4; *The Memphis Daily Appeal*, 19 and 21 Mar. 1862.

28. *The St. Louis Missouri Republican*, 5 May 1886 and 4 July 1885; Mothershead Journal, 11-12, TSLA; Bearss, "The Battle of Pea Ridge," 33, *AI*; Payne, "Story of the Battle of Pea Ridge," PRNMPA; Miscellaneous Clark Papers, MHS; Maury, "Recollections of the Elkhorn Campaign," 188, *SHSP*; *O.R.*, 8: 326; Bearss, "The Battle of Pea Ridge," 33, *AI*; *The Albany Ledger*, 9 Mar. 1906; "Personal Memoirs of I. V. Smith," 16, WHMC-SHSM.

29. Bannon Diary, SCL; Calkins, ed., "From Elk Horn to Vicksburg," 13, *CWH*; Maury, "Recollections of the Elkhorn Campaign," 189, *SHSP*; Moore, ed., *The Rebellion Record*, 4: 266; Compiled Missouri Confederate Service Records, RG 109, NA; "Personal Memoirs of I. V. Smith," 18, WHMC-SHSM.

30. *The St. Louis Missouri Republican*, 7 Mar. and 4 and 11 July 1885; Mothershead Journal, 11-12, TSLA; Castel, *General Sterling Price and the Civil War in the West*, 75-76; "Personal Memoir of I. V. Smith," 17, WHMC-SHSM; *The Mobile Register and Advertiser*, 27, 29 and 30 1862; Bannon Diary, SCL; *The Memphis Daily Appeal*, 12 and 29 Mar. and 4, 6 and 8 Apr. 1862; Payne, "Story of the Battle of Pea Ridge," PRNMPA; *The Intelligencer*, 23 Mar. 1862.

31. Bannon Diary, SCL; *O.R.*, 8: 309; Brauckman Scrapbook, Missouri Historical Society; Payne, "Story of the Battle of Pea Ridge," PRNMPA; Anderson, *Memoirs*, 172; "Personal Memoir of I. V. Smith," 18, WHMC-SHSM; *The St. Louis Missouri Republican*, 11 July 1885 and 28 Nov. 1885; *O.R.*, 8: 309; Breckenridge Scrapbook, 1: 1893, Missouri Historical Society.

Chapter Three: Counterattack

1. *O.R.*, 8: 309; Maury, "Recollections of the Elkhorn Campaign," 188, *SHSP*; Edwin C. Bearss, "The Battle of Pea Ridge," *Annals of Iowa*, 37: (1964), 217-218.

2. Knox, *The Lost Army*, 142; *The St. Louis Missouri Republican*, 11 Jul. 1885; Voelkner to Family, 18 Mar. 1862, MHS.

3. Bannon Diary, SCL; Bevier, *History of the First and Second Missouri Confederate Brigades*, 105; Maury, "Recollections of the Elk Horn Campaign," 188, *SHSP*; Alwyn Barr, "Confederate Artillery in Arkansas," *Arkansas Historical Quarterly*, 22: (1963), 243-244, 247-248.

4. Mothershead Journal, 12-13, TSLA; *O.R.*, 8: 220, 309-310; Voelkner to Family, 18 Mar. 1862, MHS; Bearss, "The Battle of Pea Ridge," 224, 227-230, *AI*; Anderson, *Memoirs*, 177; Compiled Missouri Confederate Service Records, RG 109, NA.

5. *O.R.*, 8: 222; Voelkner to Family, 18 Mar. 1862, MHS; Mothershead Journal, 13, TSLA; "Personal Memoirs of I. V. Smith," 18, WHMC-SHSM.

6. *O.R.*, 8: 309-310; Maury, "Recollections of the Elkhorn Campaign," 191-192, *SHSP*; Grenville M. Dodge, *The Battle of Atlanta and other Campaigns, Addresses, etc.*, (Council Bluffs, 1911), 27; *St. Louis Missouri Republican*, 26 Dec. 1885.

7. Mothershead Journal, 13, TSLA; *O.R.*, 8: 310; "Personal Memoir of I. V. Smith," 18, WHMC-SHSM; Calkins, ed., "From Elk Horn to Vicksburg," *CWH*, 13; Anderson, *Memoirs*, 149, 177; Payne, "Story of the Battle of Pea Ridge," PRNMPA.

8. *O.R.*, 8: 310; Mothershead Journal, 13, TSLA; "Personal Memoir of I. V. Smith," 18, WHMC-SHSM; Calkins, ed., "From Elk Horn to Vicksburg," *CWH*, 13; Albert W. Simpson Watch, Civil War Museum, Pea Ridge National Military Park; Compiled Missouri Confederate Service Records, RG 109, NA.

9. *The St. Louis Missouri Republican*, 11 July, and 28 Nov. 1885; "Personal Memoir of I. V. Smith," 18, WHMC-SHSM; Bannon Diary, SCL; Adjutant General of Missouri Service Records; Maury, "Recollections of the Elkhorn Campaign," 189, *SHSP*; *The Mobile Register and Advertiser*, 29 Mar. 1862; *O.R.*, 8: 310; Marie Oliver Watkins and Helan Watkins, *Tearin' Through the Wilderness: Missouri Pioneer Episodes and Genealogy of the Watkins Family of Virginia and Missouri*, (Charleston, 1957), 80; Champ Clark Scrapbook, vol. 15, Champ Clark Papers, WHMC-SHSM; Compiled Missouri Confederate Service Records, RG 109, NA.

10. Mothershead Journal, 13, TSLA; Watkins and Watkins, *Tearin' Through the Wilderness*, 80; Buel and Johnson, eds., *Battles and Leaders*, 1: 322; "Personal Memoir of I. V. Smith," 18, WHMC-SHSM; Moore, ed., *The Rebellion Record*, 4: 266; Moore, *Confederate Military History, Missouri*, 12: 230.

11. Kennerly, *Persimmon Hill*, 242; Bannon Diary, SCL; Buel and Johnson, eds., *Battles and Leaders*, 1: 322; Maury, "Recollections of the Elkhorn Campaign, 189, *SHSP*; Mothershead Journal, 13-14, TSLA; Watkins and Watkins, *Tearin' Through the Wilderness*, 80; *O.R.*, 8: 310; "Personal Memoir of I. V. Smith," 18, WHMC-SHSM; Adjutant General of Missouri Service Records.

12. Bannon Diary, SCL; Maury, "Recollections of the Elkhorn Campaign," *SHSP*, 189-190; L. V. Reavis, *Saint Louis the Future Great City*, (St. Louis, 1876), 475; *The St. Louis Missouri Republican*, 8 May 1886.

13. *O.R.*, 8: 310; *The Mobile Register and Advertiser*, 16 Mar. 1862; *The Richmond Enquirer*, 14 Mar. 1862; Mothershead Journal, 13, TSLA; Mary Loughborough, *My Cave Life at Vicksburg*, (New York, 1864), 152; William I. Truman, "The Battle of Elk Horn, or Pea Ridge, Arkansas," *Confederate Veteran*, 36, (1928), 170.

14. Reavis, *Saint Louis the Future Great City*, 475; Kennerly, *Persimmon Hill*, 243; *The Memphis Daily Appeal*, 19 Apr. 1862.

15. Anderson, *Memoirs*, 177; Miscellaneous Clark Papers, Clark Papers, MHS.

16. Compiled Missouri Confederate Service Records, RG 109, NA; *The St. Louis Missouri Republican*, 11 July 1885; Miscellaneous Clark Papers, Clark Family Papers, MHS; Anderson, *Memoirs*, 177; William H. Kavanaugh Memoir, 15, Western Historical Manuscript Collection-State Historical Society of Missouri; Bevier, *History of the First and Second Missouri Confederate Brigades*, 105; *O.R.*, 8: 310-311; Buel and Johnson, eds., *Battles and Leaders*, 1: 322.

17. Mothershead Journal, 14, TSLA; Milo M. Quaife, ed., *Absalom Grimes: Confederate Mail Runner*, (New Haven, 1926), 38; Bannon Diary, SCL; *O.R.*, 8: 310-311; Compiled Missouri Confederate Service Records, RG 109, NA; *The St. Louis Missouri Republican*, 11 July 1885; Mothershead Journal, 14, TSLA; *The Richmond Enquirer*, 14 Mar. 1862; Calkins, ed., "From Elkhorn to Vicksburg," *CWH*, 14; *History of Andrew and DeKalb Counties, Missouri*, 538; "Personal Memoirs of I. V. Smith," 18, WHMC-SHSM.

18. *O.R.*, 8: 310-311; Theodore T. Fisher Diary, typescript of diary of the Siege of Vicksburg, 8, Missouri Historical Society; Kavanaugh Memoir, 9, WHMC-SHSM; Compiled Missouri Confederate Service Records, RG 109, NA; *Confederate Veteran*, 17: (1909), 613; Gaylord P. O'Conner to author, 21 Nov. 1985; *History of Cole, Moniteau, Morgan, Benton, Miller, Maries, and Osage Counties, Missouri*, pt. 1, (Chicago, 1889), 420-422; William S. Bryan and Robert Rose, *A History of the Pioneer Families of Missouri*, (St. Louis, 1876), 140-141; David P. Dyer, *Autobiography and Reminiscences*, (St. Louis, 1922), 26-27, 32-33, 42; *History of Lincoln County, Missouri*, (Chicago, 1888), 517; *Moscow Mills Memories*, (n.p. 1976), 15-17; Marjorie Evans, Troy, Missouri interview with author, 20 Nov. 1987; Francis Marion Cockrell Scrapbook, 4: Western Historical Manuscript Collection-State Historical Society of Missouri; "The Tallest Confederate: Henry C. Thruston," *Civil War Times Illustrated*, (Nov. 1974), 42; Adjutant General of Missouri Service Records.

19. Mothershead Journal, 15, 17, TSLA; Buel and Johnson, eds., *Battles and Leaders*, 1: 337; Anderson, *Memoirs*, 180; W. A. Everman, "Bledsoe's Battery," *Confederate Veteran*, 28: (1928), 140; *The Mobile Register and Advertiser*, 30 Mar. 1862; "Personal Memoirs of I. V. Smith," 19, WHMC-SHSM; Compiled Missouri Confederate Service Records, RG 109, NA; James M. McPherson, *Battle Cry of Freedom: The Civil War Era*, (Oxford, 1988), 405.

20. Rives Family History, Marie Oliver Watkins Papers, 1702-1962, WHMC-SHSM; Faye L. Stewart, "Battle of Pea Ridge," *Missouri Historical Review*, 22: (1928), 190-191; Compiled Missouri Confederate Service Records, RG 109, NA; Anderson, *Memoirs*, 178; Buel and Johnson, eds., *Battles and Leaders*, 1: 337; Albert Castel, "A New View of the Battle of Pea Ridge," *Missouri Historical Review*, 62: (1968), 149-151; "Sketch of Colonel B. A. Rives of Ray County, Missouri," MHS; William H. Tunnard, *A Southern Record: The History of the Third Louisiana Infantry*, (Dayton, 1970), 151.

21. *O.R.*, 8: 311.

22. *Richmond, Missouri, Missourian*, 13 July 1933; Rives Family History, Marie Oliver Watkins Papers, 1702-1962, WHMC-SHSH; Miscellaneous Clark Papers, Clark Papers, MHS; Adjutant General of Missouri Service Records; *The St. Louis Missouri Republican*, 26. Dec. 1885; *History of Clay and Platte Counties, Missouri*, 937; Eaton, *Jefferson Davis*, 187-188; Brown, "Pea Ridge: Gettysburg of the West," *AHQ*, 15-16.

23. Compiled Missouri Confederate Service Records, RG 109, NA; *History of Carroll County*, 286, 502-505; Dale L. Morgan, ed., *The Overland Diary of James A. Pritchard from Kentucky to California in 1849*, (Denver, 1959), 37, 43-45.

24. Morgan, ed., *The Overland Diary of James A. Pritchard from Kentucky to California in 1849*, 46; Compiled Missouri Confederate Service Records, RG 109, NA; *History of Carroll County, Missouri*, 504; Hugh P. Williamson, *South of the Middle Border*, (Philadelphia, 1946), 113; Gray, *The Warriors*, 106; Bevier, *History of the First and Second Missouri Confederate Brigades*, 45-49, 156-157.

25. Williamson, *South of the Middle Border*, 101-102.

26. Compiled Missouri Confederate Service Records, RG 109, NA; *History of Ray County, Missouri*, 522-523; *Portrait and Biographical Record of Clay, Ray, Carroll, Chariton, and Linn Counties, Missouri*, (Chicago, 1893), 569-570.

27. Anderson, *Memoirs*, 195; Compiled Missouri Confederate Service Records, RG 109, NA.

28. Buel and Johnson, eds., *Battles and Leaders*, 2: 277, 717; *The Mobile Register and Advertiser*, 30 Mar. 1862; *The Memphis Daily Appeal*, 8, 9, 11, 12, 20, 25, 26, and 28 Feb. 1862 and 19. Mar. 1862.

29. Mothershead Journal, 17, TSLA; Warren Diary; *O.R.*, 8: 791; Calkins, ed., "From Elkhorn to Vicksburg," *CWH*, 14; Castel, "A New View of the Battle of Pea Ridge," *MHR*, 149-151.

30. Buel and Johnson, eds., *Battles and Leaders*, 2: 717; Warren Diary; Mothershead, 17-19, 21, TSLA; Jones, *Civil War Command and Strategy*, 51-52; Castel, "A New View of the Battle of Pea Ridge," *MHR*, 149-151.

31. Buel and Johnson, eds., *Battles and Leaders*, 1: 337; *O.R.*, 8: 309; John Harrell, *Confederate Military History, Arkansas*, 10: 314-315; John F. Walter, Capsule Histories of Arkansas Military Units, 273-275, Arkansas History Commission; *The Encyclopedia of the New West*, (Marshall, 1881), 113-115.

32. Compiled Missouri Confederate Service Records, RG 109, NA; Anderson, *Memoirs*, 190; Calkins, ed., "From Elkhorn to Vicksburg," *CWH*, 14, 15, 17, 23-24; *The Memphis Daily Appeal*, 16 Apr. 1862.

33. Compiled Missouri Confederate Service Records, RG 109, NA; Anders, *Confederate Roll of Honor: Missouri*, vi.

Chapter Four: Exiled East of the Mississippi River

1. Warren Diary; Mothershead Journal, 21-22, TSLA; "Personal Memoir of I. V. Smith," 20, WHMC-SHSM; Anderson, *Memoirs*, 152; Little Diary, USMHIA; Bannon Diary, SCL; Buel and Johnson, eds., *Battles and Leaders*, 2: 717; *The Atlanta, Georgia, Intelligencer*, 12 Apr. 1862; Edward C. Robbins to Brother, 17 May 1862, Edward C. Robbins, Letters, Mercentile Library, St. Louis, Missouri.

2. Buel and Johnson, eds., *Battles and Leaders*, 2: 717-718; *The Mobile Register and Advertiser*, 7 and 14 May 1862.

3. Buel and Johnson, eds., *Battles and Leaders*, 3: 717-719; *The Mississippian*, 5 Mar. 1862.

4. *The Mobile Register and Advertiser*, 20 and 31 May 1862 and 3 June 1862; Jones, *Civil War Command And Strategy*, 45, 54, 56.

5. Buel and Johnson, eds., *Battles and Leaders*, 2: 718-719; Warren Diary; Bannon Diary, SCL; Mothershead Journal, 25-26, TSLA; Anderson, *Memoirs*, 197-199; Calkins, eds., "From Elk Horn to Vicksburg," *CWH*, 18; *The Memphis Daily Appeal*, 10, 13, 24 and 28 May 1862; Compiled Missouri Service Records, RG 109, NA; Absalom R. Dyson to Wife, n.d., WHMC-SHSM; Jones, *Civil War Command And Strategy*, 57.

6. Compiled Missouri Confederate Service Records, RG 109, NA; Warren Diary; "Personal Memoir of I. V. Smith," 20, WHMC-SHSM; Little Diary, USMHIA; Buel and Johnson, eds., *Battles and Leaders*, 2: 719; Anderson, *Memoirs*, 194-195.

7. Buel and Johnson, eds., *Battles and Leaders*, 2: 719-720; Warren Diary; Bannon Diary, SCL; Little Diary, USMHIA; Mothershead Journal, 24-25, 27-30, 33-34; *The Mobile Register and Advertiser*, 24, 29 and 31 May 1862 and 3 and 12 June 1862; *The Memphis Daily Appeal*, 4 Apr., 29 May, 9 June, 17 and 18 Sept. 1862; Jones, *Civil War Command And Strategy*, 57.

8. Horn, *The Army of Tennessee*, 152; Buel and Johnson, eds., *Battles and Leaders*, 2: 720-722; Mothershead Journal, 34, TSLA; Little Diary, USMHIA; Calkins, ed., "From Elk Horn to Vicksburg," *CWH*, 22.

9. Buel and Johnson, eds., *Battles and Leaders*, 2: 722-723; *The Memphis Daily Appeal*, 19 July 1862; Calkins, ed., "From Elk Horn to Vicksburg," *CWH*, 24; Colonel Elijah Gates to Sterling Price, 12 July 1862, Henry E. Huntington Library and Art Gallery, Los Angeles, California; Dyson to wife, 29 Nov. 1862, WHMC-SHSM; Jones, *Civil War Command And Strategy*, 57-59, 81-82.

10. *O.R.*, 17: ser. 1, pt. 2, 634; Compiled Missouri Confederate Service Records, RG 109, NA; Gaylord P. O'Connor to author, 21 Nov. 1985; Little Diary, USMHIA; Francis Marion Cockrell Scrapbook, Missouri Historical Society; Bevier, *History of the First and Second Missouri Confederate Brigades*, 84; Moore, *Confederate Military History, Missouri*, 12: 398-399; Cockrell Scrapbook, 4: WHMC-SHSM; Warren Diary; Anderson, *Memoirs*, 208; Castel, *General Sterling Price and the Civil War in the West*, 87; Little Diary, USMHIA; Donald R. Hale, *We Rode With Quantrill: Quantrill and the Guerrilla War*, (Clinton, 1975), 40: *St. Louis Missouri Republican*, 14 Dec. 1915; *University Missourian*, 14 Dec. 1915; Edwin L. Miller Scrapbook, 1888-1897, Western Historical Manuscript Collection-State Historical Society of Missouri.

11. Quaife, ed., *Absalom Grimes*, 62-65; Calkins, ed., "From Elk Horn to Vicksburg," *CWH*, 27; Compiled Missouri Confederate Service Records, RG 109, NA; Anderson, *Memoirs*, 213-214; Warren Diary; W. A. Mitchell, "The Confederate Mail Carrier," *Confederate Veteran*, 22: (1914), 549; Warren to Sister, 22 May, 1864; Dyson to Wife, 22 Aug. 1863, WHMC-SHSM; Warren Diary.

12. Buel and Johnson, eds., *Battles and Leaders*, 2: 725-726; Compiled Missouri Confederate Service Records, RG 109, NA; *The Weekly Mississippian*, 17 Nov. 1862; *The Vicksburg, Mississippi, Daily Whig*, 14 Apr. 1863; *The Memphis Daily Appeal*, 15 Aug. 1861.

13. Thomas L. Connelly, *Civil War Tennessee: Battles and Leaders*, (Knoxville, 1979), 54-57; Buel and Johnson, eds., *Battles and Leaders*, 2: 726-727.

14. Anderson, *Memoirs*, 205-206; *The Mobile Register and Advertiser*, 30 July 1862; Buel and Johnson, eds., *Battles and Leaders*, 2: 728; Warren Diary.

15. *The United States Biographical Dictionary, Missouri Volume*, 723; Ewing Cockrell, *History of Johnson County, Missouri*, (Topeka, 1918), 220, 547; The Johnson County Historical Society, "The Johnson County Historical Society Bulletin," Aug. 1959; Compiled Missouri Confederate Service Records, RG 109, NA; Benjamin Whiteman Grover, "Civil War in Missouri," *Missouri Historical Review*, 8: (1913), 14; George S. Grover, "Col. Benjamin Whiteman Grover," *Missouri Historical Review*, 1: (1907), 133; *Portrait and Biographical Record of Johnson and Pettis Counties, Missouri*, (Chicago, 1895) 345-346; Warren Diary; Simpson Diary, WHMC-SHSM; *California, Missouri, Weekly Times*, 22 Apr. 1861; *California Weekly Times*, 27 Apr. 1861.

16. Warren Diary; J. C. McNamara, "An Historical Sketch of the Sixth Division-Missouri State Guard, from its organization in 1861 to its surrender to Shreveport, La., in 1865," 29, Missouri Historical Society; Camp Jackson Papers, Missouri Historical Society; Bevier, *History of the First and Second Missouri Confederate Brigades*, 330; Compiled Missouri Confederate Service Records RG 109, NA; *The St. Louis Missouri Republican*, 5 Dec. 1884; Albert Carey Danner, "Historical Memorandum," private collection of Dorothy Danner DaPonte Trabits, Mobile, Alabama.

17. Compiled Missouri Confederate Service Records, RG 109, NA; Camp Jackson Papers, MHS; Babcock Scrapbook, MHS; Warren Diary; *The Daily Missouri Democrat*, 14 Dec. 1860; J. B. Johnson, *History of Vernon County, Missouri*, (Chicago, 1911) 2: 258; *The Courier*, 22 Dec. 1860.

Chapter Five: The Battle of Iuka

1. Simpson Diary, WHMC-SHSM; Warren Diary; William T. H. Snyder to Parents, 25 Nov. 1862, private collection of H. Riley Bock, New Madrid, Missouri; *The Mobile Register and Advertiser*, 30 Oct. and 20 Nov. 1862; Little Diary, USMHIA; Buel and Johnson, eds., *Battles and Leaders*, 2: 726, 730-731; *The Memphis Daily Appeal*, 2 Mar. 1862, 28 May 1862, 22 July 1862 and 23 Mar. 1863.

2. Simpson Diary, WHMC-SHSM; Warren Diary; *The Memphis Daily Appeal*, 15, 27 and 30 Sept. 1862; Johnson and Buel, eds., *Battles and Leaders*, 2: 730-731; Castel, *General Sterling Price and the Civil War in the West*, 96-98; Horn, *The Army of Tennessee*, 172-174; *The Chattanooga, Tennessee, Daily Rebel*, 17 Sept. 1862 and 3 Oct. 1862; *The Mobile Register and Advertiser*, 17 and 23 Sept. 1862 and 5 Nov. 1862; *The Intelligencer*, 20 Sept. 1862; Kitchens, *Rosecrans Meets Price*, 32.

3. *The Chattanooga Daily Rebel*, 14 Oct. 1862; Warren Diary; Cockrell Scrapbook, 4: WHMC-SHSM; Compiled Missouri Confederate Service Records, RG 109, NA; Simpson Diary, WHMC-SHSM; *The Memphis Daily Appeal*, 30 Sept. 1862 and 23 Mar. 1863; *The Mobile Register and Advertiser*, 17 and 23 Sept. 1862 and 5 Nov. 1862.

4. Simpson Diary, WHMC-SHSM; Castel, *General Sterling Price and the Civil War in the West*, 97-100; Buel and Johnson, eds., *Battles and Leaders*, 2: 730-731; Warren Diary; *The Memphis Daily Appeal*, 7 Oct. 1862.

5. Buel and Johnson, eds., *Battles and Leaders*, 2: 731-732; Little Diary, USMHIA; Castel, *General Sterling Price and the Civil War in the West*, 99-101; Bannon Diary, SCL; Francis V. Greene, *The Mississippi*, (New York, 1883), 40-42; Warren Diary; Anderson, *Memoirs*, 221-222; *The Memphis Daily Appeal*, 30 Sept. 1862 and 7 Oct. 1862; Jack W. Gunn, "The Battle of Iuka," *Journal of Mississippi History*, 24; (1962), 154; *The Chattanooga Daily Rebel*, 24 Sept. 1862 and 3 Oct. 1862; *The Mobile Register and Advertiser*, 23 Sept. 1862 and 7 Oct. 1862. *The St. Louis Missouri Republican*, 5 June 1886.

6. John R. Cook, *The Border and the Buffalo: An Untold Story of the Southwest Plains*, (New York, 1967), 9; Warren Diary; Anderson, *Memoirs*, 222-225; Bradley, *The Confederate Mail Carrier*, 71; Bevier, *History of the First and Second Missouri Confederate Brigades*, 333-335; Johnson and Buel, eds., *Battles and Leaders*, 2: 736; *O.R.*, ser. 1, pt. 1, 126; Harvey L. Carter and Norma L. Peterson, "William S. Stewart Letters: January 13, 1861, to December 4, 1862," *Missouri Historical Review*, 61: (1967), 471-474; Compiled Missouri Confederate Service Records, RG 109, NA; Simpson Diary, WHMC-SHSM.

7. Little Diary, USMHIA: Ben Earl Kitchens, *Rosecrans Meets Price: The Battle of Iuka, Mississippi*, (Florence, 1985), 15, 152-153; *The New Orleans, Louisiana, Picayune*, 11 Aug. 1901; Bannon Diary, SCL; Dabney H. Maury, "Campaign Against Grant in North Mississippi," *Southern Historical Society Papers*, (1885), 13: 289; Warren Diary; Little Diary, USMHIA; Buel and Johnson, eds., *Battles and Leaders*, 2: 732-733; *The Memphis Daily Appeal*, 30 Sept. 1862 and 7 Oct. 1862; *The Daily Whig*, 14 Apr. 1863.

8. Buel and Johnson, eds., *Battles and Leaders*, 2: 733; Little Diary, USMHIA; Bannon Diary, SCL; *The New Orleans Picayune*, 11 Aug. 1901.

9. Warren Diary; Anderson, *Memoirs*, 225; *The Memphis Daily Appeal*, 7 Oct. 1862; Bevier, *History of the First and Second Missouri Confederate Brigades*, 335-336; Calkins, ed., "From Elk Horn to Vicksburg," *CWH*, 32.

Chapter Six: "Corinth Must & Shall Be Ours"

1. *The Richmond Enquirer*, 18 Oct. 1862; Johnson and Buel, eds., *Battles and Leaders*, 2: 730; John Tyler, Jr., to Hon. William L. Yancy, 15 Oct. 1862, Western Historical Manuscript Collection-State Historical Society of Missouri; Johnson and Buel, eds., *Battles and Leaders*, 2: 730; Warren Diary; *The Weekly Mississippian*, 25 Sept. 1861.

2. *The Richmond Enquirer*, 18 Oct. 1862; Tyler to Yancy, 15 Oct. 1862, WHMC-SHSM; Castel, *General Sterling Price and the Civil War in the West*, 106-107; *The Mobile Register and Advertiser*, 7 May 1862 and 30 Oct. 1862; *O.R.*, XVL, pt. 2, 782-783; Rawley, *Turning Points of the Civil War*, 100-101.

3. Compiled Missouri Confederate Service Records, RG 109, NA; Moore, *Confederate Military History, Missouri*, 12: 314-315; Gibson, "Recollections of a Pioneer," 108.

4. Calkins, ed., "From Elk Horn to Vicksburg," *CWH*, 34: Compiled Missouri Confederate Service Records, RG 109, NA; Ruyle Memoir, 19; Warren Diary.

5. Horn, *The Army of Tennessee*, 174-175; Castel, *General Sterling Price and the Civil War in the West*, 108-109; Johnson and Buel, eds., *Battles and Leaders*, 2: 743-746; *The Mobile Register and Advertiser*, 26 Oct. 1862; Tyler to Yancy, 15 Oct. 1862, WHMC-SHSM; *The Richmond Enquirer*, 10 and 18 Oct. 1862.

6. Tyler to Yancy, 15 Oct. 1862, WHMC-SHSM; Johnson and Buel, eds., *Battles and Leaders*, 2: 760; Castel, *General Sterling Price and the Civil War in the West*, 110-111; *The Richmond Enquirer*, 18 Oct. 1862; Robbins to Family, 16 Oct. 1862, ML; Bannon Diary.

7. Compiled Missouri Confederate Service Records, RG 109, NA; Bannon Diary, SCL; Camp Jackson Papers, MHS; Robbins to Family, 16 Oct. 1862, ML: *The Richmond Enquirer*, 10 Oct. 1862; Mesker Scrapbook, MHS.

8. Calkins, ed., "From Elk Horn to Vicksburg," *CWH*, 34; Ruyle Memoir, 19-20; Tyler to Yancy, 15 Oct. 1862, WHMC-SHSM.

9. *O.R.*, 17: ser. 1, pt. 1, 390; Robbins to Family, 16 Oct. 1862, ML; Castel, *General Sterling Price and the Civil War in the West*, 111-113; Tyler to Yancy, 15 Oct. 1862, WHMC-SHSM; Ruyle Memoir, 19-20; Johnson and Buel, eds., *Battles and Leaders*, 2: 743-748; Calkins, ed., "From Elk Horn to Vicksburg," *CWH*, 34-35; Robbins to Family, 16 Oct. 1862, ML; Sam Dunlap Diary; Bevier, *History of the First and Second Missouri Confederate Brigades*, 149-150.

10. Tyler to Yancy, 15 Oct. 1862; WHMC-SHSM; Anderson, *Memoirs*, 233-236; Kavanaugh Memoir, 25, WHMC-SHSM; Ruyle Memoir, 20; *The Richmond Enquirer*, 7 Oct. 1862; Compiled Missouri Confederate Service Records, RG 109, NA; Thomas Hogan to Father, 12 Oct. 1862, Box 3, Civil War Collection, Missouri Historical Society; *The Mobile Register and Advertiser*, 23 Oct. 1862; *The Intelligencer*, 8 Oct. 1862.

11. Bannon Diary, SCL; Hogan to Father, 12 Oct. 1862, MHS; Dyson to Wife, 14 Oct. 1862, WHMC-SHSM; Anderson, *Memoirs*, 235-236; Kavanaugh Memoir, 26, WHMC-SHSM; Compiled Missouri Confederate Service Records, RG 109, NA; Calkins, ed., "From Elk Horn to Vicksburg," *CWH*, 35; Ruyle Memoir, 20; Bevier, *History of the First and Second Missouri Confederate Brigades*, 340; *History of Clay and Platte Counties*, Missouri, 674-675; *The Memphis Daily Appeal*, 18 Oct. 1862; *The Richmond Enquirer*, 10 Oct. 1862; John H. Burgin to W. Skaggs, 25 May 1925, Skaggs Collection, AHC; Boyce, "Military Organizations of St. Louis," Manuscript, 72-73, MHS; *O.R.*, 17: pt. 1, 262; Robbins to Family, 16 Oct. 1862, ML; Bannon, "Experiences of a Confederate Army Chaplain," 201-222.

12. Kavanaugh Memoir, 27, WHMC-SHSM; *The Richmond Enquirer*, 17 Oct. 1862; Hogan to Father, 12 Oct. 1862, MHS; Anderson, *Memoirs*, 236; *The Mississippian*, 26 Nov. 1862; Calkins, ed., "From Elk Horn to Vicksburg," *CWH*, 35; A. M. Bedford to Mrs. Mary Bedford, Bedford Family Papers, Western Historical Manuscript Collection-State Historical Society of Missouri.

13. *The Memphis Daily Appeal*, 18 Oct. 1862; Anderson, *Memoirs*, 237; Johnson and Buel, eds., *Battles and Leaders*, 2: 744; "Diary of Lieut. Col. Hubbell of 3d Regiment Missouri Infantry, C.S.A.," *The Land We Love*, (1868-1869), 6: 101; United Daughters of the Confederacy, Missouri Chapter, *Reminiscences of the Women of Missouri During the Sixties*, (Jefferson City, 1901), 60.

14. Castel, *General Sterling Price and the Civil War in the West*, 114-116: *The Mississippian*, 22 Oct. 1862; Greene, *The Mississippi*, 45-47; Johnson and Buel, eds., *Battles and Leaders*, 2: 759-760; John B. Bannon, "Experiences of a Confederate Army Chaplain," *Letters and Notices of the English Jesuit Province*, 34: 1866-1868, 202.

15. Castel, *General Sterling Price and the Civil War in the West*, 115-116; Bradley, *The Confederate Mail Carrier*, 73; Ruyle Memoir, 20; Bannon, "Experiences of a Confederate Army Chaplain," 202.

16. Anderson, *Memoirs*, 237; Ruyle Memoir, 20-21; Cockrell Scrapbook, 4: WHMC-SHSM; Hogan to Father, 12 Oct. 1862, MHS; Kavanaugh Memoir, 27, WHMC-SHSM.

17. Anderson, *Memoirs*, 237: Cockrell Scrapbook, 4: WHMC-SHSM; Kavanaugh Memoir, 27, WHMC-SHSM; Hogan to Father, 12 Oct. 1862, MHS; *O.R.*, 17: ser. 1, pt. 1, 259.

18. Bradley, *The Confederate Mail Carrier*, 73; Bevier, *History of the First and Second Missouri Confederate Brigades*, 341; Hogan to Father, Oct. 12, 1862, MHS; *The Richmond Enquirer*, Oc. 17, 1862; Johnson and Buel, eds., *Battles and Leaders*, 2: 238, 240, 258-260, 391, 741, 759; Claude Gentry, *The Battle of Corinth*, (Baldwyn, 1976), 30; *O.R.*, 17: ser. 1, pt. 1, 215, 238, 240-241; Evert Augustus Duychinck, *National History of the War for the Union*, (3 vols.; New York, 1861-1865), 2: 623-624; Cockrell Scrapbook, 4: WHMC-SHSM; *The Memphis Daily Appeal*, 18 Oct. 1862; Charles F. Hubert, *History of the Fiftieth Illinois Infantry*, (Kansas City, 1894), 142; Compiled Missouri Service Records, RG 109, NA; "An Infantryman at Corinth: The Diary of Charles Cowell," *Civil War Times Illustrated*, XIII, (Nov. 1974), 12.

19. Bevier, History of the First and Second Missouri Confederate Brigades, 153; *O.R.*, 17: ser. 1, pt. 1, 260, 273-274, 391; Hogan to Father, Oct. 12, 1862, MHS; Johnson and Buel, eds., *Battles and Leaders*, 2: 749; Tyler to Yancy, 15 Oct. 1862, WHMC-SHSM; "Diary of Lieut. Col. Hubbell of 3d Regiment Missouri Infantry, C.S.A.," *The Land We Love*, 101.

20. *The Memphis Daily Appeal*, 18 Oct. 1862; Hubert, *History of the Fiftieth Illinois Infantry*, 142; Ruyle Memoir, 21; Anderson, *Memoirs*, 237; Johnson and Buel, eds., *Battles and Leaders*, 2: 759; *O.R.*, 17: ser. 1, pt. 1, 238, 240, 258-260; *The Richmond Enquirer*, 18 Oct. 1862.

21. Bevier, *History of the First and Second Missouri Confederate Brigades*, 341; *O.R.*, 17: ser. 1, pt. 1, 215, 231, 238, 240; *The Richmond Enquirer*, 17 and 18 Oct. 1862; Compiled Missouri Confederate Service Records, RG 109, NA; Anderson, *Memoirs*, 240; *The Memphis Daily Appeal*, 18 Oct. 1862.

22. Adjutant General of Missouri Service Records; "Diary of Lieut. Col. Hubbell of 3d Regiment Missouri Infantry, C.S.A.," *The Land We Love*, 101; Hubbell Family Papers in private collection of Mrs. Leon Rice Taylor, Richmond, Missouri; Bevier, *History of the First and Second Missouri Confederate Brigades*, 155; *History of Ray County, Missouri*, 776; Compiled Missouri Confederate Service Records, RG 109, NA.

23. Bevier, *History of the First and Second Missouri Confederate Brigades*, 156; "Diary of Lieut. Col. Hubbell of 3d Regiment Missouri Infantry, C.S.A.," *The Land We Love*, 101; *History of Carroll County, Missouri*, 504-505; Williamson, *South of the Middle Border*, 101-102; Joe Lee Bomar, "The Audrain County Flag," *Confederate Veteran*, 36: (1928), 98.

24. Hubert, *History of the Fiftieth Illinois Infantry*, 142; Greene, *The Mississippi*, 49-50; Robbins to Family, 16 Oct. 1862, ML; Tyler to Yancy, 15 Oct. 1862, WHMC-SHSM; *The Mobile Register and Advertiser*, 15 Oct. 1862; Johnson and Buel, eds., *Battles and Leaders*, 2: 759; Calkins, ed., "From Elk Horn to Vicksburg," *CWH*, 35; Compiled Missouri Confederate Service Records, RG 109, NA; *O.R.*, 17: ser. 1, pt. 1, 209, 238, 241; Joe Lee Bomar, "The Audrain County Flag," *C.V.*, 98-99; Henry M. Alden and Alfred H. Guernsey, eds., *Harper's Pictorial History of the Civil War*, (New York, 1977), 317; Comte de Paris, *The Civil War in America*, (Philadelphia, 1876), 2: 411-412; *The Memphis Daily Appeal*, 18 Oct. 1862; *The Richmond Enquirer*, 18 Oct. 1862.

25. Johnson and Buel, eds., *Battles and Leaders*, 2: 749, 759; Ruyle Memoir, 21-22; Robbins to Family, 16 Oct. 1862, ML; Tyler to Yancy, 15 Oct. 1862, WHMC-SHSM; Anderson, *Memoirs*, 237; *O.R.*, 17: ser. 1, pt. 1, 206, 237-238, 241, 271, 391; Bevier, *History of the First and Second Missouri Confederate Brigades*, 152-153, 341; *The Mobile Register and Advertiser*, 4 Nov. 1862; "Diary of Lieut. Col. Hubbell of 3d Regiment Missouri Infantry, C.S.A.," *The Land We Love*, 101; *The Richmond Enquirer*, 10 and 18, 1862; Calkins, ed., "From Elk Horn to Vicksburg," *CWH*, 35; *The Memphis Daily Appeal*, 18 Oct. 1862.

26. Calkins, ed., "From Elk Horn to Vicksburg," *CWH*, 35; *The Mobile Register and Advertiser*, 15 Oct. 1862; Anderson, *Memoirs*, 237; Bevier, *History of the First and Second Missouri Confederate Brigades*, 341-342; Ruyle Memoir, 21; Duychinck, *National History of the War for the Union*, 2: 625; *O.R.*, 17: 206, 238, 241, 259-260; Tyler to Yancy, 15 Oct. 1862, WHMC-SHSM; Robbins to Family, 16 Oct. 1862, ML; Oscar Lawrence Jackson, *The Colonel's Diary*, (Sharon, 1922), 83-84; *The Intelligencer*, 10 Oct. 1862.

27. William M. Lamers, *The Edge of Glory: A Biography of General William S. Rosecrans*, (New York, 1961), 149, 155; *O.R.*, 17: ser. 1, pt. 1, 215, 231, 238, 241, 274-275; *The Richmond Enquirer*, 17 and 18 Oct. 1862; Alden and Guernsey, eds., *Harper's Pictorial History of the Civil War*, 317; Robbins to Family, 16 Oct. 1862, ML; Tyler to Yancy, 15 Oct. 1862, WHMC-SHSM; Castel, *General Sterling Price and the Civil War in the West*, 115-116; Ruyle Memoir, 21; *The Mobile Register and Advertiser*, 15 Oct. 1862 and 20 Nov. 1862; Johnson and Buel, eds., *Battles and Leaders*, 2: 749; Bevier, *History of the First and Second Missouri Confederate Brigades*, 341-342; Duychinck, *National History of the War for the Union*, 2: 625; *The Intelligencer*, 10 Oct. 1862.

28. *The Memphis Daily Appeal*, 18 Oct. 1862; Tyler to Yancy, 15 Oct. 1862, WHMC-SHSM; *O.R.*, 17: ser. 1, pt. 1, 206; Ruyle Memoir, 21; Hogan to Father, 12 Oct. 1862, MHS; Bevier, *History of the First and Second Missouri Confederate Brigades*, 154, 215, 341-342; Johnson and Buel, eds., *Battles and Leaders*, 2: 750; *The Richmond Enquirer*, 18 Oct. 1862, 29. *The Memphis Daily Appeal*, 18 Oct. 1862.

29. Bevier, *History of the First and Second Missouri Confederate Brigades*, 154, 341-342; *O.R.*, 17: ser. 1, pt. 1, 391; Ruyle Memoir, 21; *The Richmond Enquirer*, 18 Oct. 1862.

30. *O.R.*, 17: ser. 1, pt. 1, 391; Ruyle Memoir, 21; Tyler to Yancy, 15 Oct. 1862, WHMC-SHSM; *The Memphis Daily Appeal*, 18 Oct. 1862; "Diary of Lieut. Col. Hubbell of 3d Regiment Missouri Infantry, C.S.A.," *The Land We Love*, 101; Compiled Missouri Confederate Service Records, RG 109, NA; Calkins, ed., "From Elk Horn to Vicksburg," *CWH*, 35; M. O. Frost, *Regimental History of the Tenth Missouri Volunteer Infantry*, (Topeka, 1892), 36-37.

31. Frost, *Regimental History of the Tenth Missouri Volunteer Infantry*, 42; Tyler to Yancy, 15 Oct. 1862, WHMC-SHSM; *The Chattanooga Daily Rebel*, 2 June 1863; Anderson, *Memoirs*, 237-238; *The Mississippian*, 14 Nov. 1862; Maury, "Campaign Against Grant in North Mississippi," *SHSP*, 299; *The Memphis Daily Appeal*, 18 Oct. 1862; *The Richmond Enquirer*, 18 Oct. 1862; Hubbell, "Diary of Lieut. Col. Hubbell of 3d Regiment Missouri Infantry, C.S.A.," 104; Bevier, *History of the First and Second Missouri Confederate Brigades*, 341-342, 443; Compiled Missouri Confederate Service Records, RG 109, NA; Warren Diary; Ruyle Memoir, 21; Robbins to Family, 16 Oct. 1862, ML; *Richmond Whig*, 9 Apr. 1862; James E. Payne, *History of the Fifth Missouri Volunteer Infantry*, (Press of James E. Payne, 1899), 36.

Chapter Seven: Withdrawal and Reorganization

1. Bannon Diary, SCL; Bevier, *History of the First and Second Missouri Confederate Brigades*, 148; *The Mobile Daily Appeal*, 15 Oct. 1862; Yancy to Tyler, 15 Oct. 1862, WHMC-SHSM; George Elliott Journal, 21-22, Tennessee State Library and Archives, Nashville, Tennessee; Castel, *General Sterling Price and the Civil War in the West*, 119-120; *The Richmond Enquirer*, 17 and 18 Oct. 1862; Maury, "Campaign Against Grant in North Mississippi," *SHSP*, 302, 305.

2. Castel, *General Sterling Price and the Civil War in the West*, 120-121; Bevier, *History of the First and Second Missouri Confederate Brigades*, 160, 343-345; Pat Henry, "Major General John S. Bowen," *Confederate Veteran*, 22: (1914), 171; Bowen Papers, MHS; *The Mobile Register and Advertiser*, 23 Oct. 1862; Maury, "Campaign Against Grant in North Mississippi," *SHSP*, 302-303; *The Richmond Enquirer*, 17 and 18 Oct. 1862.

3. Anderson, *Memoirs*, 240-242; Cockrell Scrapbook, 4: WHMC-SHSM; *The Mobile Register and Advertiser*, 23 Oct. 1862 and 5 Nov. 1862; Bevier, *History of the First and Second Missouri Confederate Brigades*, 343-345; Cockrell Scrapbook, 4, WHMC-SHSM; Cockrell Scrapbook, MHS; John L. Wakelyn, *Biographical Dictionary of the Confederacy*, (Westport, 1977), 143; Compiled Missouri Confederate Service Records, RG 109, NA.

4. Bannon Diary, SCL; Bevier, *History of the First and Second Missouri Confederate Brigades*, 345-346; Compiled Missouri Confederate Service Records, RG 109, NA; Calkins, ed., "From Elk Horn to Vicksburg," *CWH*, 35; Anderson, *Memoirs*, 242; Castel, *General Sterling Price and the Civil War in the West*, 304; James Gordon, "The Battle and Retreat from Corinth," *Mississippi Historical Society Publications*, 4: (1901), 71.

5. Bevier, *History of the First and Second Missouri Confederate Brigades*, 156-157; "Diary of Lieut. Col. Hubbell of 3d Regiment Missouri Infantry, C.S.A.," *The Land We Love*, 102-103; Calkins, ed., "From Elk Horn to Vicksburg," *CWH*, 36; Ruyle Memoir, 23; Maury, "Campaign Against Grant in North Mississippi," *SHSP*, 304-305; Elliott Journal, 20-21, TSLA; Compiled Missouri Confederate Service Records, RG 109, NA; Williamson, *South of the Middle Border*, 102-103; *History of Carroll County, Missouri*, 504-505; Anderson, *Memoirs*, 247.

6. Compiled Missouri Confederate Service Records, RG 109, NA; "Diary of Lieut. Col. Hubbell of 3d Regiment Missouri Infantry, C.S.A.," *The Land We Love*, 97-105; Hubbell, "Personal Reminiscences," 1-2, 4, 9-10, 13, MHS; Mary Sue Graham, Hot Springs, Arkansas, to author, 23 June 1989; T. M. Anderson to W. A. Everman, 14 Oct. 1914, Civil War Papers, Box 9, Missouri Historical Society; *Portrait and Biographical Record and History of Clay, Ray, Carroll, Chariton, and Linn Counties, Missouri*, 279-280; Mrs. Leon Rice Taylor, Richmond, Missouri, to author, 15 Jan. 1989 and Hubbell Family Papers; *Memphis Appeal*, 18 Oct. 1862; Compiled Missouri Confederate Service Records, RG 109, NA.

7. Compiled Missouri Confederate Service Records, RG 109, NA.

8. Connelly, *Civil War Tennessee*, 54-57; *The Memphis Daily Appeal*, 30 Oct. 1862; Horn, *The Army of Tennessee*, 185-189; Maury, "Campaign Against Grant in North Mississippi," *SHSP*, 305; Rawley, *Turning Points of the Civil War*, 100-101.

9. Anderson, *Memoirs*, 245-246; *The Mobile Register and Appeal*, 2 Nov. 1862 and 16 Jan. 1863; Robbins to Sister, 19 Oct. 1862, ML; Compiled Missouri Confederate Service Records, RG 109, NA; *O.R.*, 17: ser. 1, pt. 2, 733, 736; *The Memphis Daily Appeal*, 25 Oct. 1862; Joseph Boyce Scrapbook, Missouri Historical Society.

10. Anderson, *Memoirs*, 388; Compiled Missouri Confederate Service Records, RG 109, NA; Moore, *Confederate Military History, Missouri*, 12: 86; Boyce Scrapbook, MHS; Civil War Papers, private collection of H. Riley Bock, New Madrid, Missouri; H. Riley Bock, "Confederate Col. A. C. Riley, His Report and Letters, Part I," *Missouri Historical Review*, 85: (Jan. 1991), 158-161, 178-179; H. Riley Bock, "Confederate Col. A. C. Riley, His Report and Letters, Part II," *Missouri Historical Review*, 85: (Apr. 1992), 264-265, 268.

11. Compiled Missouri Confederate Service Records, RG 109, NA; "Roster of Field and Line Officers, First Missouri Confederate Infantry," Box No. 2, Civil War Papers, Missouri Historical Society; Bock, "Confederate Col. A. C. Riley, His Reports and Letters, Part II," *MHR*, 268.

12. Riley Family Papers of H. Riley Bock; *History of Southeast Missouri*, 908-909; Boyce Scrapbook, MHS; Isabel McMeekin, *Louisville: The Gateway City*, (New York, 1946), 208; Compiled Missouri Confederate Service Records, RG 109, NA; Walter B. Stevens, *St. Louis: The Fourth City 1764-1909*, (St. Louis, 1909), 834-835.

13. Compiled Missouri Confederate Service Records, RG 109, NA; "Roster of Field and Line Officers, First Missouri Confederate Infantry," MHS; Eliot, *West Point in the Confederacy*, 418-419; *The St. Louis Missouri Republican*, 5 Dec. 1884 and 2 and 24 Nov. 1877; Babcock Scrapbook, MHS; Boyce, "Military Organizations of St. Louis," 11-13, MHS; Bannon Diary, SCL; *The Memphis Daily Appeal*, 23 Apr. 1862; W. J. MacDonald, "The Missouri River and Its Victims: Vessels Wrecked from the Beginning," *Missouri Historical Review*, 21: (1927), 597; List of Exchanged Camp Jackson Prisoners, 1861, p. 1, Camp Jackson Papers, MHS; Hopewell, *The History of Camp Jackson*, 26; Boyce Scrapbook, MHS.

14. Kennerly, *Persimmon Hill*, 33, 91, 178-179, 239-243; Compiled Missouri Confederate Service Records, RG 109, NA; Kearny-Kennerly Scrapbook, 1 and 2: Missouri Historical Society; Frederic L. Billion, *Annals of St. Louis in its Territorial Days from 1804 to 1821*, (St. Louis, 1888), 82, 266-269; Kennerly Papers, Missouri Historical Society; St. Peters, *Memorial Volume of the Diamond Jubilee of St. Louis University*, 274; *The St. Louis Missouri Republican*, 14 Dec. 1860 and 10 Nov. 1883 and 28 Dec. 1886; List of Exchanged Camp Jackson Prisoners, 1861, 2, MHS; Camp Jackson Papers, MHS; Miscellaneous papers in the Camp Jackson Papers, MHS; *The Mobile Register and Advertiser*, 16 Jan. 1863; Robbins to Sister, 21 Nov. 1862, ML; W. J. Smith to Mrs. Bowen 23 Mar. 1893, Bowen Papers, MHS; Boyce, "The Flags of the First Missouri Confederate Infantry," MHS; Deborah Isaac, "Confederate Days in St. Louis," newspaper clippings, Missouri Historical Society; Meyer, *The Heritage of Missouri*, 343; J. G. Randall, *The Civil War And Reconstruction*, (New York, 1937), 326; Bevier, *History of the First and Second Missouri Confederate Brigades*, 84.

15. Compiled Missouri Confederate Service Records, RG 109, NA; Moore, *Confederate Military History, Missouri*, 12: 287-288; Anderson, *Memoirs*, 345; Elliott Journal, 13, TSLA; Bevier, *History of the First and Second Missouri Confederate Brigades*, 212; *O.R.*, 8: ser. 1, pt. 1, 260, 308; "Col. Eugene Erwin," *Confederate Veteran*, 4: (1896), 264; Bearss, "The Battle of Pea Ridge," *AI*, 36, (1963), 28; "Recreation in Army Life," *Confederate Veteran*, 38: (1930), 388; Payne, *History of the Fifth Missouri Volunteer Infantry*, 24; Richard M. McMurry, *John Bell Hood and the War For Southern Independence*, (Lexington, 1982), 3, 6.

16. *The Memphis Daily Appeal*, 19 July 1862 and 8 and 22 Oct. 1862; Bannon Diary, SCL; *O.R.*, 17: ser. 1, pt. 1, 382-383; Cook, *The Border and the Buffalo*, 9; Adjutant General of Missouri Service Records; James E. Payne, "The Sixth Missouri at Corinth," *Confederate Veteran*, 36: (1928), 462-465; Elliott Journal, 13, 21-22, TSLA; Compiled Missouri Confederate Service Records, RG 109, NA; "Skylarking along the Line," *Confederate Veteran*, 38: (1930), 96; *The Mobile Register and Advertiser*, 8 Oct. 1862; Jerry Ponder, *The History of Ripley County, Missouri*, (1987), 44, 50, 56.

17. *O.R.*, 17: ser. 1, pt. 1, 382; Compiled Missouri Confederate Service Records, RG 109, NA; Johnson and Buel, eds., *Battles and Leaders*, 1: 270-271; *The St. Louis Missouri Republican*, 14. Dec. 1860; W. O. Coleman to William Skaggs, 27 Oct. 1909, Skaggs Collection, AHC; F. R. Noe, "Scattered Remnant of a Company," *Confederate Veteran*, 11: (1903), 16; J. J. Sitton to William Skaggs, 19 Jan. 1914, Skaggs Collection, AHC; *The Mobile Register and Advertiser*, 8 Oct. 1862; Meyer, *The Heritage of Missouri*, 343.

18. Compiled Missouri Confederate Service Records, RG 109, NA; *O.R.*, 8: ser. 1, 328-329; *Portrait and Biographical Record of Buchanan and Clinton Counties, Missouri*, 135-136; John S. Kelly to William Skaggs, Skaggs Collection, AHC; Alexander H. Waller, *History of Randolph County, Missouri*, (Topeka, 1920), 510.

19. Compiled Missouri Confederate Service Records, RG 109, NA; Warren Diary; Anderson, *Memoirs*, 245-246; William Snyder to Parents, 4 Jan. 1863, Bock Collection; Joseph Boyce to Hawes Smith, 18 Jan. 1864, Boyce Papers, MHS.

20. Compiled Missouri Confederate Service Records, RG 109, NA; Brauckman Scrapbook, MHS; *The St. Louis Daily Globe*, 19 Oct. 1899; Williams, ed., *History of Northeast Missouri*, 2: 1018; *History of Cole, Moniteau, Morgan, Benton, Miller, Maries, and Osage Counties, Missouri*, 254; Warren Family Papers in private collection of Warren Guibor, Manchester, Missouri; *The Mobile Register and Advertiser*, 2 Nov. 1862; St. Peters, *Memorial Volume of the Diamond Jubilee of St. Louis University*, 262; Moore, *Confederate Military History, Missouri*, 12: 307-308, *The St. Louis Missouri Republican*, 14 Dec. 1860 and 4 July 1885; *State of Missouri House of Representatives Journal, 21st Assembly, 1st Session*, 762; "The Storey (sic) of 'Guibor's Battery, C.S.A.'," Box 1, Civil War Papers, Missouri Historical Society; *O.R.*, 1: ser. 2, 556; *O.R.*, 24: ser. 1, pt. 1, 705; Alden McLellan to Joseph Boyce, 20 Mar. 1919, Civil War Papers, MHS.

21. Compiled Missouri Confederate Service Records, RG 109, NA; Landis information, private collection of Wilbur P. McDonald, St. Joseph, Missouri; "Landis' Battery," 183, Bowen Papers, MHS; *The Memphis Daily Appeal*, 30 June 1861 and 22 Oct. 1862; John B. Sampson, DeKalb, Missouri, interview with author, September 1, 1989 and Robert C. Dunlap Diary; Edward C. Robbins, "Landis Battery," Civil War Papers, Box NO. 1, MHS; Williams, ed., *History of Northwest Missouri*, 1: 364; Chris L. Rutt, compiler, *History of Buchanan County and the City of St. Joseph and Representative Citizens*, (Chicago, 1904) 160; Buchanan County Census, 1860, Eighth United States Census; *The Mobile Register and Advertiser*, 8 Oct. 1862; Logan, *Old Saint Jo: Gateway to the West*, 292-294; Ruyle Memoir, 25; Landis Family Papers in private collection of Walter Austill Landis, Jr., Faucett, Missouri; Henry Hance to Eve, 15 June 1864, Robbins Collection, ML.

Chapter Eight: Winter Quarters

1. *The Daily Whig*, 13 and 24 Feb. 1863; Connelly, *Civil War Tennessee*, 54-57; Johnson and Buel, eds., *Battles and Leaders*, 3: 493; Thomas Lawrence Connelly, *Autumn of Glory: The Army of Tennessee, 1862-1865*, (Baton Rouge, 1967), 4; Grant, *Personal Memoirs of U. S. Grant*, (New York, 1885), 220; *The Memphis Daily Appeal*, 14 Nov. 1862; Bruce Catton, *Grant Moves South*, (Boston, 1960), 327-329; *The Mobile Register and Advertiser*, 14 Nov. 1862; *The Chattanooga Daily Rebel*, 12 and 14 Dec. 1862; Jones, *Civil War Command And Strategy*, 104-109.

2. Maury, "Recollections of Campaign Against Grant in North Mississippi," *SHSP*, 305; Bevier, *History of the First and Second Missouri Confederate Brigades*, 182-183; Compiled Missouri Confederate Service Records, RG 109, NA; Ruyle Memoir, 23-24; Simpson Diary, WHMC-SHSM; *The Memphis Daily Appeal*, 25 Nov. 1862 and 4 and 7 Mar. 1863; *The Chattanooga Daily Rebel*, 16 and 17 Oct. 1862; *The Mobile Register and Advertiser*, 14, 15, 19, and 26 Oct. 1862; 14, 21 and 27, 1862 and 19 Dec. 1862; *The Mississippian*, 12 and 19 Nov. 1862; Jones, *Civil War Command And Strategy*, 104-109; Michael B. Ballard, *Pemberton: A Biography*, (Jackson, 1991), 27-35, 114-118, 120.

3. Compiled Missouri Confederate Service Records, RG 109, NA; Maury, "Recollections of Campaign Against Grant in North Mississippi," *SHSP*, 305; Simpson Diary, WHMC-SHSM; Ruyle Memoir, 25; Elliott Journal, 33, TSLA; Catton, *Grant Moves South*, 340-341; Ballard, *Pemberton*, 125.

4. Eaton, *Jefferson Davis*, 174-183; *The Daily Whig*, 30 Jan. 1863; *The Mobile Register and Advertiser*, 18 Dec. 1862; Jones, *Civil War Command And Strategy*, 21-22.

5. Compiled Missouri Confederate Service Records, RG 109, NA; Simpson Diary, WHMC-SHSM; William Snyder to Parents, 4 Jan. 1863, Bock Collection; Bevier, *History of the First and Second Missouri Confederate Brigades*, 166; Ruyle Memoir, 25; Warren Diary; Ballard, *Pemberton*, 121; Warren to Father, 10 Jan. 1863; Anders, *Confederate Roll of Honor: Missouri*, vii.

6. Compiled Missouri Confederate Service Records, RG 109, NA; William E. Nichols to Sister, 10 Dec. 1862, private collection of Lily Hazel Bates, Palmyra, Missouri.

7. Robbins, 30 Dec. 1862 and 4 Jan. 1863 to Family, ML; John T. Appler Diary, 1, Missouri Historical Society; William Snyder to Parents, 4 Jan. 1863, Bock Collection; Reynolds, "Gen. Sterling Price and the Confederacy," 46-50, MHS; *The Mississippian*, 20 Nov. 1862 and 4 and 9 Jan. 1863; Ruyle Memoir, 25; Simpson Diary, WHMC-SHSM; Elliott Journal, 35, TSLA; Warren to Father, 10 Jan. 1863, MHS; Castel, *General Sterling Price and the Civil War in the West*, 138.

8. Ruyle Memoir, 25; Appler Diary, 1, MHS; Francis Marion Cockrell to Gen. Samuel Cooper, 12 Sept. 1863, John Bowen Letter Book, Virginia Historical Society, Richmond, Virginia; Simpson Diary, WHMC-SHSM. *The Mobile Register and Advertiser*, 30 Jan. 1862.

9. Appler Diary, 2-3, 5, MHS; Warren Diary; *The Mississippian*, 26 Nov. 1862; Adjutant General of Missouri Service Records; *The Mobile Register and Advertiser*, 8 and 20 Nov. 1862 and 13 Dec. 1862.

10. Compiled Missouri Confederate Service Records, RG 109, NA; Anderson, *Memoirs*, 246; "Diary of Lieut. Col. Hubbell of 3d Regiment Missouri Infantry, C.S.A.," *The Land We Love*, 101; *The Memphis Daily Appeal*, 18 Oct. 1862.

11. Compiled Missouri Confederate Service Records, RG 109, NA; *The Mobile Register and Advertiser*, 2 Nov. 1862.

12. Compiled Missouri Confederate Service Records, RG 109, NA; Calkins, ed., "From Elk Horn to Vicksburg," *CWH*, 42; Miller Scrapbook, WHMC-SHSM.

13. Compiled Missouri Confederate Service Records, RG 109, NA; Bowen Papers, MHS; *The Courier*, 12 Jan. 1861; *The Mississippian*, 17 Nov. 1862; *History of Vernon County, Missouri*, 1: 264, 272; "Sketch-General Bowen's Life," Bowen Papers, MHS; Babcock Scrapbook, MHS; Brauckman Scrapbook, MHS; De Witt Hunter to John F. Snyder, 21 Jan. 1861, John F. Snyder Collection, Missouri Historical Society; "Missouri" Song, Bowen Papers, MHS; Chatham County, Georgia, 1850 and 1860 Census Records; *The Memphis Daily Appeal*, 8 Apr. 1862; Simpson Diary, WHMC-SHSM; Appler Diary, 8, MHS. Much like General Little, General Bowen was an enigma, a product of the tidewater merchant class of Georgia's Atlantic coast, who was now leading yeomen farmers of the western frontier in the middle of Mississippi. But the mix could not have produced higher-yielding results. Born just southeast of Savannah, Georgia, amid the lowlands of the salt marshes along the Atlantic, Bowen hailed from upper middle-class roots, but his ancestors had been among the planter aristocracy. What would most separate the Bowen from the largely mediocre Confederate officer corps in the West was his strategic insight, tactical brilliance, and competence.

14. Appler Diary, 5-9, MHS; Warren Diary; Kavanaugh Memoir, 34, WHMC-SHSM; Ruyle Memoir, 26-27.

15. Compiled Missouri Confederate Service Records, RG 109, NA; Elliott Journal, 44, TSLA; Ruyle Memoir, 27-28; Appler Diary, 10, MHS; Loughborough, *My Cave Life at Vicksburg*, 185-186; Dyson to Wife, n.d., WHMC-SHSM; Robbins to Father, 30 Dec. 1862, ML.

16. Bevier, *History of the First and Second Missouri Confederate Brigades*, 168-169; "Diary of Lieut. Col. Hubbell of 3d Missouri Regiment, C.S.A.," *The Land We Love*, 105; *The St. Louis Missouri Republican*, 17 Sept. 1886; Edwin C. Bearss, "Grand Gulf's Role in the Civil War," *Civil War History*, 5: (1959), 14-15; *The Memphis Daily Appeal*, 3 July 1862; Dyson to Wife, 8 June 1863, WHMC-SHSM.

17. Appler Diary, 10-11, MHS; John S. Bowen to Colonel Humphries, 14 Mar. 1863, Bowen Letter Book, VHS; Elliott Journal, 44-45, 49, TSLA; *The Memphis Daily Appeal*, 21 Mar. 1863; *The St. Louis Missouri Republican*, 6 Sept. 1884 and 17 Sept. 1886; Ruyle Memoir, 28; David D. Porter, *The Naval History of the Civil War*, (New York, 1886), 313; *The Daily Whig*, 18 and 30 Apr. 1863.

18. Bannon Diary, SCL; Elliott Diary, 49, TSLA; Compiled Missouri Confederate Service Records, RG 109, NA; Warren Guibor Papers, *The St. Louis Missouri Republican*, 17 Sept. 1886; Mike Casey to Family, 6 Apr. 1863, Robbins Collection, ML; Appler Diary, 12, MHS; *The Memphis Daily Appeal*, 6 and 11 Apr. 1863.

19. Ruyle Memoir, 27; Reynolds, "Gen. Sterling Price and the Confederacy," 48, 66-68, MHS.

Chapter Nine: Louisiana Expedition

1. Johnson and Buel, eds., *Battles and Leaders*, 3: 493-494; Jones, *Civil War Command And Strategy*, 159.

2. Catton, *Grant Moves South*, 406-410; Jones, *Civil War Command And Strategy*, 159-160; Bearss, *Grant Strikes A Fatal Blow*, 21-25.

3. Boatner, *The Civil War Dictionary*, 525; *O.R.*, 24: ser. 1, pt. 1, 139.

4. *O.R.*, 24: ser. 1, pt. 1, 139.

5. Ibid., 571; Mike Casey to Family, 6 Apr. 1863, Robbins Collection, MJ; Anderson, *Memoirs*, 282; Bearss, *The Campaign For Vicksburg: Grant Strikes A Fatal Blow*, 2: (Dayton, 1986), 26; *The Daily Whig*, 16, 22 and 29 Apr. 1863.

6. *O.R.*, 24: ser. 1, pt. 1, 139; *The Daily Whig*, 22 and 29 Apr. 1863; John D. Winters, *The Civil War in Louisiana*, (Baton Rouge, 1991), 189.

7. *O.R.*, 24: ser. 1, pt. 1, 139; *The Daily Whig*, 25 July 1863; Winters, *The Civil War in Louisiana*, 189.

8. Casey to Family, 6 Apr. 1863, Robbins Collection, ML; *The Daily Whig*, 25 April 1863.

9. Compiled Missouri Confederate Service Records, RG 109, NA; War Department Collection of Confederate Records, Chapter 2, 274: Military Departments, Letter Book, Brigadier General John S. Bowen's Command, August 1862-November 1863, National Archives, Washington, D.C., Reports No. 26-28.

10. Bowen Letter Book, Reports No. 26-28, NA.

11. Ibid., Report No. 31; Casey to Family, 6 Apr. 1863, Robbins Collection, ML; Anderson, *Memoirs*, 280; "Personal Memoir of I. V. Smith," p. 26, WHMC-SHSM; Bradley, *The Confederate Mail Carrier*, 93; Bowen to Francis M. Cockrell, 11 Apr. 1863, Bowen Letter Book, VHS.

12. Casey to Family, 6 Apr. 1863, Robbins Collection, ML. Bowen Letter Book, Report No. 30, NA; Appler Diary, 12, MHS.

13. Appler Diary, 12, MHS; Casey to Family, 6 Apr. 1863, Robbins Collection, ML; Anderson, *Memoirs*, 281.

14. Boatner, *Civil War Dictionary*, 613; Bearss, *Grant Strikes A Fatal Blow*, 25; Bowen Letter Book, Reports No. 33, 34, NA.

15. Appler Diary, 12-13, MHS; Anderson, *Memoirs*, 282; *O.R.*, 24: ser. 1, pt. 1, 188.

16. *O.R.*, 24: ser. 1, pt. 1, 139, 188, 492; Bradley, *The Confederate Mail Carrier*, 93; "Personal Memoir of I. V. Smith," 26, WHMC-SHSM; Anderson, *Memoirs*, 282; Appler Diary, 13, MHS; John N. Edwards, *Shelby and His Men: or, The War in the West*, (Cincinnati, 1867), 381.

17. Anderson, *Memoirs*, 282; "Personal Memoir of I. V. Smith," 26, WHMC-SHSM.

18. Bowen Letter Book, Report No. 36, NA; *The Daily Whig*, 16 Apr. 1863; Winters, *The Civil War in Louisiana*, 189.

19. *O.R.*, 24: ser. 1, pt. 3, 714, 720; "Personal Memoir of I. V. Smith," 26, WHMC-SHSM; Bevier, *History of the First and Second Missouri Confederate Brigades*, 408-409.

20. Bevier, *History of the First and Second Missouri Confederate Brigades*, 408; Mary Ann Anderson, ed., *The Civil War Diary of Allen Greer*, (New York, 1977), 94; Winters, *The Civil War in Louisiana*, 192.

21. Appler Diary, 13, MHS.

22. *O.R.*, 24: ser. 1, pt. 1, 139-140; Bearss, *Grant Strikes A Fatal Blow*, 31; *The Daily Whig*, 16 Apr. 1863.

23. Appler Diary, 13, MHS; Bearss, *Grant Strikes A Fatal Blow*, 36; *O.R.*, 24: ser. 1, pt. 1, 140; *The Daily Whig*, 16 Apr. 1863.

24. *O.R.*, 24: ser. 1, pt. 1, 490-492; Bearss, *Grant Strikes A Fatal Blow*, 36; *The Daily Whig*, 16 and 25 Apr. 1863; Winters, *The Civil War in Louisiana*, 189.

25. Appler Diary, 13, MHS; *O.R.*, 24: ser. 1, pt. 1, 188, 492-493; *The Memphis Daily Appeal*, 11 and 25 Apr. 1863; *The Daily Whig*, 16 Apr. 1863.

26. *O.R.*, 24: ser. 1, pt. 1, 140, 490, 493; Compiled Missouri Service Records, RG 109, NA; Appler Diary, 13, MHS; Bearss, *Grant Strikes a Fatal Blow*, 37-38; *The Memphis Daily Appeal*, 10, 11 and 17 Apr. 1863; *The Daily Whig*, 16 Apr. 1863.

27. Appler Diary, 13, MHS; *O.R.*, 24: ser. 1, pt. 3, 731; *The Memphis Daily Appeal*, 10 and 11 Apr. 1863.

28. Bearss, *Grant Strikes A Fatal Blow*, 89; *O.R.*, 24: ser. 1, pt. 3, 731; *The Memphis Daily Appeal*, 10, 11 and 16 Apr. 1863; *The Daily Whig*, 16 Apr. 1863.

29. Appler Diary, 13, MHS.

30. *O.R.*, 24: ser. 1, pt. 1, 140.

31. Ibid., 492; Appler Diary, 13, MHS; Bevier, *History of the First and Second Missouri Confederate Brigades*, 171; Anderson, *Memoirs*, 283.

32. Appler Diary, 13, MHS; *The Daily Whig*, 25 Apr. 1863.

33. *O.R.*, 24: ser. 1, pt. 1, 140.

34. Ibid., 493; Appler Diary, 13, MHS.

35. Bearss, *Grant Strikes A Fatal Blow*, 36, 38, 40; *O.R.*, 24: ser. 1, pt. 1, 139-140, 188, 493; Anderson, *Memoirs*, 284-285.

36. *O.R.*, 24: ser. 1, pt. 1, 140, 494, 497; Paul H. Hass, ed., "The Vicksburg Diary of Henry Clab Warmouth," *Journal of Mississippi History*, 31: (1969), 341; Winters, *The Civil War in Louisiana*, 189, 192; *O.R.*, 24: ser. 1, pt. 3, 736-737, 743-745; Bowen to Memminger, 11 Apr. 1863, Bowen Letter Book, VHS; Bowen to Cockrell, 11 Apr. 1863, Bowen Letter Book, VHS.

37. Appler Diary, 13, MHS.

38. Ibid., 13-14, *O.R.*, 24: ser. 1, pt. 1, 188, 496-497; Hass, ed., "The Vicksburg Diary of Henry Clab Warmouth," *JMH*, 341; Anderson, *Memoirs*, 284; Bradley, *The Confederate Mail Carrier*, 94; Winters, *The Civil War in Louisiana*, 192.

39. Appler Diary, 13-14, MHS; Anderson, *Memoirs*, 284.

40. Bevier, *History of the First and Second Missouri Confederate Brigades*, 409; Appler Diary, 13-14, MHS; *O.R.*, 24: ser. 1, pt. 1, 140; Elliott Journal, 54, TSLA.

41. Anderson, *Memoirs*, 284; Appler Diary, 13-14, MHS; Bevier, *History of the First and Second Missouri Confederate Brigades*, 171; Bradley, *The Confederate Mail Carrier*, 93-94; *O.R.*, 24: ser. 1, pt. 1, 188, 496.

42. *O.R.*, 24: ser. 1, pt. 1, 140, 494, 497; Winters, *The Civil War in Louisiana*, 192.

43. Ibid., 140, 494; Appler Diary, 14, MHS; Anderson, *Memoirs*, 284.

44. Appler Diary, 13-14, MHS; *O.R.*, 24: ser. 1, pt. 1, 140; Elliott Journal, 54, TSLA.

45. Appler Diary, 13-14, MHS; Anderson, *Memoirs*, 284-285; Bearss, *Grant Strikes A Fatal Blow*, 40; Bevier, *History of the First and Second Missouri Confederate Brigades*, 409; *O.R.*, 24: ser. 1, pt. 1, 140, 494; Elliott Journal, 54, TSLA.

46. Appler Diary, 14, MHS.

47. Anderson, *Memoirs*, 285.

48. Ibid; Bevier, *History of the First and Second Missouri Confederate Brigades*, 409.

49. Anderson, *Memoirs*, 285; Appler Diary, 14, MHS; Bearss, *Grant Strikes A Fatal Blow*, 40; *O.R.*, 24: ser. 1, pt. 1, 140, 494.

50. Appler Diary, 14, MHS.

51. Ibid., Bevier, *History of the First and Second Missouri Confederate Brigades*, 172, 409; Anderson, *Memoirs*, 285; Bearss, *Grant Strikes A Fatal Blow*, 40; Bowen Letter Book, Report No. 42, NA; Elliott Journal, 54, TSLA.

52. Appler Diary, 14, MHS.

53. *O.R.*, 24: ser. 1, pt. 1, 497.

54. Adjutant General of Missouri Service Records.

55. Catton, *Grant Moves South*, 414-415; Bowen Letter Book, Report No. 41, NA.

56. Bradley, *The Confederate Mail Carrier*, 94; *The Daily Whig*, 16. Apr. 1863; Winters, *The Civil War in Louisiana*, 192.

57. "Personal Memoir of I. V. Smith," 26, WHMC-SHSM.

58. Bradley, *The Confederate Mail Carrier*, 94; Anderson, Memoirs, 287.

59. Anderson, *Memoirs*, 287-288; Bradley, *The Confederate Mail Carrier*, 94; Winters, *The Civil War in Louisiana*, 192; *O.R.*, 24: ser. 1, pt. 3, 111, 755; Compiled Missouri Confederate Service Records, RG 109, NA.

60. Anderson, *Memoirs*, 287.

61. Ibid., 288; Bevier, *History of the First and Second Missouri Confederate Brigades*, 409; Albert O. Allen to Pinnell, 3 Dec. 1863, private collection of H. Riley Bock; Winters, *The Civil War in Louisiana*, 193-194.

62. Bradley, *The Confederate Mail Carrier*, 94.

63. Bevier, *History of the First and Second Missouri Confederate Brigades*, 410.

64. "Personal Memoir of I. V. Smith," 26, WHMC-SHSM.

65. Ibid.; Bevier, *History of the First and Second Missouri Confederate Brigades*, 410; Bradley, *The Confederate Mail Carrier*, 94; Appler Diary, 14, MHS; *The Memphis Daily Appeal*, 19 and 25 Apr. 1863; Compiled Missouri Confederate Service Records, RG 109, NA.

66. *O.R.*, 24: ser. 1, pt. 3, 792-793; Larry J. Daniel, "Bruinsburg: Missed Opportunity or Postwar Rhetoric?" *Civil War History*, 32: (1986), 257, 261; Bowen to Memminger, 11 Apr. 1863, Bowen Letter Book, VHS; Bowen to Cockrell, 11 Apr. 1863, Bowen Letter Book, VHS.

67. *The Daily Whig*, 16 Apr. 1863.

Chapter Ten: Fatal Spring in Claiborne County

1. Bannon Diary, SCL; Compiled Missouri Confederate Service Records, RG 109, NA; *The Savannah, Georgia, Republican*, 6 May 1863; John S. Bowen to John C. Pemberton, 20 Apr. 1863, Bowen Letter Book, VHS; Miller Scrapbook, WHMC-SHSM.

2. *The Daily Whig*, 30 Apr. 1863; Ballard, *Pemberton*, 132, 134-140.

3. *The St. Louis Missouri Republican*, 5 Dec. 1885 and 17 Sept. 1886; Elliott Journal, 50, TSLA; *The Daily Whig*, 30 Apr. 1863; *O.R.*, 24: ser. 1, pt. 1, 30-33; *O.R.*, 24: ser. 1, pt. 3, 231; Hogan to Father, 22 July 1863, MHS; Howard Michael Madaus and Robert D. Needham, *The Battle Flags of the Confederate Army of Tennessee*, (Milwaukee, 1976), 17, 44; William

M. Fowler, Jr., *Under Two Flags: The American Navy in the Civil War*, (New York, 1990), 214, 216; Drew Gilpin Faust, *The Creation of Confederate Nationalism: Ideology and Identity in the Civil War South*, (Baton Rouge, 1988), 22-31.

4. Bearss, *Grant Strikes A Fatal Blow*, 2: 258-259; Boyce Scrapbook, MHS; Elliott Journal, 57, TSLA; *O.R.*, 24: ser. 1, pt. 1, 257-258, 328.

5. James E. Payne Memoir of Grand Gulf and Port Gibson, Vicksburg National Military Park Archives; "Personal Memoir of I. V. Smith," WHMC-SHSM; *The St. Louis Missouri Republican*, 17 Sept. 1886; Anderson, *Memoirs*, 293-294; Elliott Journal, 57, TSLA; Bearss, *Grant Strikes A Fatal Blow*, 307-308; Compiled Missouri Confederate Service Records, RG 109, NA; Kavanaugh Memoir, 36-37, WHMC-SHSM; Hogan to Father, 22 July 1863, MHS; *O.R.*, 24: ser. 1, pt. 1, 82, 668; Fowler, *Under Two Flags*, 216; Greene, *The Mississippi*, 124.

6. Elliott Journal, 57, TSLA; *The St. Louis Missouri Republican*, 17 Sept. 1886; *O.R.*, 24: ser. 1, pt. 1, 82; Hogan to Father, 22 July 1862, MHS; "Personal Memoir of I. V. Smith," 26, TSLA; Bearss, *Grant Strikes A Fatal Blow*, 311-312; Greene, *The Mississippi*, 124; Compiled Missouri Confederate Service Records, RG 109, NA.

7. *O.R.*, 24: ser. 1, pt. 1, 33, 83; Porter, *The Naval History of the Civil War*, 317; Hogan to Father, 22 July 1863, MHS; Bearss, *Grant Strikes A Fatal Blow*, 310-315; Anderson, *Memoirs*, 294; Compiled Missouri Confederate Service Records, RG 109, NA; Elliott Journal, 57, TSLA; *The St. Louis Missouri Republican*, 17 Sept. 1886.

8. Hogan to Father, 22 July 1863, MHS; Anderson, *Memoirs*, 294; Bannon Diary, SCL; "Personal Memoir of I. V. Smith," 26, TSLA; *The Memphis Daily Appeal*, 30 Apr. 1863; Elliott Journal, 57, TSLA; *The Daily Whig*, 30 Apr. 1863; *The Savannah Republican*, 6 May 1863; *The St. Louis Missouri Republican*, 17 Sept. 1886; Compiled Missouri Confederate Service Records, RG 109, NA.

9. John S. Bowen to R. W. Memminger, 2 May 1863 and 4 June 1863, Bowen Letter Book, VHS; *The Daily Whig*, 18 Apr. 1863; Hogan to Father, 22 July 1863, MHS; Elliott Journal, 57, TSLA; *The St. Louis Missouri Republican*, 17 Sept. 1886; Bannon Diary, SCL; Ulysses S. Grant to William T. Sherman, 27 Apr. 1863, William K. Bixby Collection, Missouri Historical Society; *O.R.*, 24: ser. 1, pt. 1, 257, 328; Johnson and Buel, eds., *Battles and Leaders*, 3: 477-478, 496, 549-550; Samuel Carter, III, *The Final Fortress: The Campaign For Vicksburg 1862-1863*, (New York, 1980), 182; John C. Pemberton, III, *Pemberton: Defender of Vicksburg*, (Chapel Hill, 1976), 11; *The Memphis Daily Appeal*, 30 Apr. 1863 and 4 May 1863.

10. Elliott Journal, 57, TSLA; Bannon Diary, SCL; *The Memphis Daily Appeal*, 1, 5 and 9 May 1863; *O.R.*, 24: ser. 1, pt. 1, 663, 672; Elliott Journal, 57, TSLA; *The St. Louis Missouri Republican*, 17 Sept. 1886; Bowen to Memminger, 2 May and 4 June 1863; Bowen Letter Book, VHS.

11. *O.R.*, 24: ser. 1, pt. 1, 663, 670, 672, 673-676; Bowen to Memminger, 2 May and 4 June 1863, Bowen Letter Book, VHS; *The Memphis Daily Appeal*, 9 May 1863; Bearss, *Grant Strikes A Fatal Blow*, 346, 348, 353, 405; Bowen Report No. 52, Bowen Letter Book, NA.

12. *O.R.*, 24: ser. 1, pt. 1, 657, 668-669; Bowen to Memminger, 2 May and 4 June 1863, Bowen Letter Book, VHS; Elliott Journal, 57, TSLA; Compiled Missouri Confederate Service Records, RG 109, NA; *The St. Louis Missouri Republican*, 4 July 1885 and 17 Sept. 1886; Payne Memoir, VNMPA; Bearss, *Grant Strikes A Fatal Blow*, 349-350, 384, 405-407; "Personal Memoir of I. V. Smith," 27, TSLA.

13. *O.R.*, 24: ser. 1, pt. 1, 668, 670; Payne Memoir, VNMPA; *The Memphis Daily Appeal*, 9 May 1863; "Personal Memoir of I. V. Smith," 27, TSLA; Bowen to Memminger, 2 May and 4 June 1863, Bowen Letter Book, VHS; Bearss, *Grant Strikes A Fatal Blow*, 382-384, 367.

14. *O.R.*, 24: ser. 1, pt. 1, 670-673, 679-681; *The Intelligencer*, 10 May 1863; Bowen to Memminger, 2 May and 4 June 1863, Bowen Letter Book, VHS; Payne Memoir, VNMPA; Bearss, *Grant Strikes A Fatal Blow*, 368-369; *The Memphis Daily Appeal*, 26 Mar. 1863, 6 and 9 May 1863.

15. *The Memphis Daily Appeal*, 26 Mar. 1863 and 9 May 1863; *O.R.*, 24: ser. 1, pt. 1, 586-587, 670-674; *The Savannah Republican*, 6 and 22 May 1863; Payne Memoir, VNMPA; Elliott Journal, 58, TSLA; Earl S. Miers, *The Web of Victory: Grant at Vicksburg*, (Baton Rouge, 1955), 156-157; Compiled Missouri Confederate Service Records, RG 109, NA; Edwin C. Bearss, Arlington, Virginia, to author, 15 Jan. 1985; Hass, ed., "The Vicksburg Diary of Henry Clab Warmouth," *Journal of Mississippi History*, 65; Edgar L. Erickson, ed., "With Grant at Vicksburg: From the Civil War Diary of Captain Charles E. Wilcox," *Journal of the Illinois State Historical Society*, 30: (1938), 474; *The St. Louis Missouri Republican*, 17 Sept. 1886.

16. *O.R.*, 24: ser. 1, pt. 1, 668, 673-675; Bowen to Memminger, 2 May and 4 June 1863, Bowen Letter Book, VHS; "Personal Memoir of I. V. Smith," 27, WHMC-SHSM; Bevier, *History of the First and Second Missouri Confederate Brigades*, 145; Bearss, *Grant Strikes A Fatal Blow*, 384-385.

17. Bearss, *Grant Strikes A Fatal Blow*, 388-391; *O.R.*, 24: ser. 1, pt. 1, 659; Bowen to Memminger, 2 May and 4 June 1863, Bowen Letter Book, VHS.

18. Bearss, *Grant Strikes A Fatal Blow*, 389-391; Bowen to Memminger, 2 May and 4 June 1863, Bowen Letter Book, VHS; Bevier, *History of the First and Second Missouri Confederate Brigades*, 414-416; *O.R.*, 24: ser. 1, pt. 1, 664; "Personal Memoir of I. V. Smith," 27, WHMC-SHSM; "Consolidated Provision Return For First Brigade, May 1-May 10, 1863," Roster Sheet, National Archives; Ballard, *Pemberton*, 160-161.

Chapter Eleven: A Desperate Gamble

1. Anderson, *Memoirs*, 297-298; *O.R.*, 24: ser. 1, pt. 1, 603-604, 668-669; Bearss, *Grant Strikes A Fatal Blow*, 389-391; Jefferson Davis, *The Rise and Fall of the Confederate Government*, (New York, 1881), 398; Bevier, *The History of the First and Second Missouri Confederate Brigades*, 180, 416; "Personal Memoir of I. V. Smith," 27, WHMC-SHSM; Bowen to Memminger, 2 May and 4 June 1863, Bowen Letter Book, VHS.

2. Bearss, *Grant Strikes A Fatal Blow*, 389-391; Anderson, *Memoirs*, 298; "Personal Memoir of I. V. Smith," 27, WHMC-SHSM; *O.R.*, 24: ser. 1, pt. 1, 603-605, 668; Edwin C. Bearss 1958, "Battle of Port Gibson," Map, Bearss Collection, Arlington, Virginia; Frances H. Kennedy, ed., *The Civil War Battlefield Guide*, (Boston, 1990), 138.

3. Bearss 1958 "Battle of Port Gibson," Map; *O.R.*, 24: ser. 1, pt. 1, 668-669; Anderson, *Memoirs*, 298; "Personal Memoir of I. V. Smith," 27, WHMC-SHSM; Bevier, *History of the First and Second Missouri Confederate Brigades*, 178-179, 416-417; *The Memphis Daily Appeal*, 9 May 1863; Bearss, *Grant Strikes A Fatal Blow*, 391-392.

4. Bearss 1958 "Battle of Port Gibson," Map; Anderson, *Memoirs*, 298; "Personal Memoir of I. V. Smith," 27, WHMC-SHSM; Bowen to Memminger, 2 May and 4 June 1863, Bowen Letter Book, VHS; Bevier, *History of the First and Second Missouri Confederate Brigades*, 178-179, 416-417.

5. *O.R.*, 24: ser. 1, pt. 1, 605, 610-611, 668-669; Bevier, *History of the First and Second Missouri Confederate Brigades*, 178-179, 416-417; Bearss 1958 "Battle of Port Gibson," Map; Bearss, *Grant Strikes A Fatal Blow*, 391-392, 406-407, 642-645; Bowen to Memminger, 2 May and 4 June 1863, Bowen Letter Book, VHS.

6. Bearss, *Grant Strikes A Fatal Blow*, 391-392; *O.R.*, 24: ser. 1, pt. 1, 603-607, 668-669; Anderson, *Memoirs*, 298; Bevier, *History of the First and Second Missouri Confederate Brigades*, 416; Bearss 1958 "Battle of Port Gibson," Map; "Personal Memoir of I. V. Smith," 27, WHMC-SHSM; Kennedy, ed., *The Civil War Battlefield Guide*, 138.

7. *The Memphis Daily Appeal*, 9 May 1863; Bevier, *History of the First and Second Missouri Confederate Brigades*, 178-179, 353; Bearss, *Grant Strikes A Fatal Blow*, 391-392; *O.R.*, 24: ser. 1, pt. 1, 583, 605, 611; Hogan to Father, 22 July 1863, MHS; "Personal Memoir of I. V. Smith," 27, WHMC-SHSM.

8. *O.R.*, 24: ser. 1, pt. 1, 606-607, 611, 669; Bearss, *Grant Strikes A Fatal Blow*, 391-392; Bevier, *History of the First and Second Missouri Confederate Brigades*, 178-179, 416-417; "Personal Memoir of I. V. Smith," 27, WHMC-SHSM; Anderson, *Memoirs*, 298.

9. *The Daily Whig*, 2 May 1863; *O.R.*, 24: ser. 1, pt. 1, 611, 668-669; "Personal Memoir of I. V. Smith," 27, WHMC-SHSM; Anderson, *Memoir*, 298; Bevier, *History of the First and Second Missouri Confederate Brigades*, 178-179, 416-417; *The Memphis Daily Appeal*, 4 and 9 May 1863; Hogan to Father, 22 July 1863, MHS; Cockrell Scrapbook, 4: WHMC-SHSM; Kennedy, *The Civil War Battlefield Guide*, 138.

10. Bearss 1958 "Battle of Port Gibson," Map; *O.R.*, 24: ser. 1, pt. 1, 603, 606-608; Bearss, *Grant Strikes A Fatal Blow*, 391-392, 403.

11. "Personal Memoirs of I. V. Smith," 27, WHMC-SHSM, *O.R.*, 24: ser. 1, pt. 1, 607-613, 626-627; Bevier, *History of the First and Second Missouri Confederate Brigades*, 179, 416-417; "Personal Memoir of I. V. Smith," 27, WHMC-SHSM.

12. Bearss, *Grant Strikes A Fatal Blow*, 391-392; *O.R.*, 24: ser. 1, pt. 1, 607, 612, 668-669; "Personal Memoir of I. V. Smith," 27, WHMC-SHSM; Bevier, *History of the First and Second Missouri Confederate Brigades*, 178-179, 416-417; Bearss 1958 "Battle of Port Gibson," Map.

13. Bearss, *Grant Strikes A Fatal Blow*, 393; *The Savannah Republican*, 13 May 1863; Bevier, *History of the First and Second Missouri Confederate Brigades*, 178, 416; "Personal Memoir of I. V. Smith," 27, WHMC-SHSM; Bowen to Memminger, 2 May and 4 June 1863, Bowen Letter Book, VHS; *O.R.*, 24: ser. 1, pt. 1, 668.

14. Erickson, "With Grant at Vicksburg," *Journal of the Illinois State Historical Society*," 474; Johnson and Buel, eds., *Battles and Leaders*, 1: 337; "Personal Memoirs of I. V. Smith," 27, WHMC-SHSM; *O.R.*, 24: ser. 1, pt. 1, 607, 627; Bearss, *Grant Strikes A Fatal Blow*, 39.

15. *O.R.*, 24: ser. 1, pt. 1, 604-605, 607-608; "Personal Memoir of I. V. Smith," 27, WHMC-SHSM; Bowen to Memminger, 2 May and 4 June 1863, Bowen Letter Book, VHS.

16. Bearss, *Grant Strikes A Fatal Blow*, 392-393; *The Savannah Republican*, 13 May 1863; Bevier, *History of the First and Second Missouri Confederate Brigades*, 178-179, 417-418; *O.R.*, 24: ser. 1, pt. 1, 668-669; Bowen to Memminger, 2 May and 4 June 1863, Bowen Letter Book, VHS.

17. Compiled Missouri Confederate Service Records, RG 109, NA; "Personal Memoir of I. V. Smith," 27, WHMC-SHSM; Bearss, *Grant Strikes A Fatal Blow*, 392-393; *O.R.*, 24: ser. 1, pt. 1, 612.

18. Bevier, *History of the First and Second Missouri Confederate Brigades*, 417; "Personal Memoir of I. V. Smith," 27, WHMC-SHSM; *O.R.*, 24: ser. 1, pt. 1, 612, 669; Bowen to Memminger, 2 May and 4 June 1863, Bowen Letter Book, VHS.

19. "Personal Memoir of I. V. Smith," 27, WHMC-SHSM; *O.R.*, 24: ser. 1, pt. 1, 669; Bevier, *History of the First and Second Missouri Confederate Brigades*, 417; Compiled Missouri Confederate Service Records, RG 109, NA; Leathers Family Papers, private collection of Dorothy Voncille Liedorff Schmedake, Callao, Missouri; *History of Monroe and Shelby Counties, Missouri*, 1150-1151; *General History of Macon County, Missouri*, 145, 178; Doris Gatterman, Callao, Missouri, to author, 10 Feb. 1989; Dorothy Schmedake to author, 9 Jan. 1989.

20. Compiled Missouri Confederate Service Records, RG 109, NA; *O.R.*, 24: ser. 1, pt. 1, 604, 612; "Personal Memoir of I. V. Smith," 27, WHMC-SHSM; Bowen to Memminger, 2 May and 4 June 1863, Bowen Letter Book, VHS.

21. Compiled Missouri Confederate Service Records, RG 109, NA; Bevier, *History of the Missouri Confederate Brigades*, 180, 417; *The Memphis Daily Appeal*, 6 and 9 May 1863; Hogan to Father, 22 July 1863, MHS; "Personal Memoir of I. V. Smith," 28, WHMC-SHSM; *The Savannah Republican*, 13 May 1863; Bowen to Memminger, 2 May and 4 June 1863, Bowen Letter Book, VHS.

22. *O.R.*, 24: ser. 1, pt. 1, 666, 670-675; Payne Memoir, VNMPA; Elliott Journal, 58, TSLA; *The Memphis Daily Appeal*, 9 May 1863; Bowen to Memminger, 2 May 1863, Bowen Letter Book, VHS; Compiled Missouri Confederate Service Records, RG 109, NA.

23. *The Memphis Daily Appeal*, 9 May 1863; *O.R.*, 24: ser. 1, pt. 1, 670-671, 673-674; Elliott Journal, 58, TSLA; Payne Memoir, VNMPA; Bevier, *History of the First and Second Missouri Brigades*, 180; Bearss, *Grant Strikes A Fatal Blow*, 371-372; Bowen to Memminger, 2 May 1863, Bowen Letter Book, VHS.

24. Compiled Missouri Confederate Service Records, RG 109, NA; Elliott Journal, 58, TSLA; Payne Memoir, VNMPA; *O.R.*, 24; ser. 1, pt. 1, 670-671; *The Savannah Republican*, 13 May 1863; *The Memphis Daily Appeal*, 9 May 1863; Donald Lewis Osborn, *Tales of the Amarugia Highlands of Cass County, Missouri*, (Lee's Summitt, 1972), 1-5; *O.R.*, 24: ser. 1, pt. 1, 587.

25. Compiled Missouri Confederate Service Records, RG 109, NA; *O.R.*, 24: ser. 1, pt. 1, 587; Elliott Journal, 58, TSLA; James A. Payne, "From Missouri," *Confederate Veteran*, 38: (1930), 366; Emily Crawford to Elizabeth Lewis, 11 June 1863, private collection of Charles Sullivan, Pascagoula, Mississippi; Bearss, *Grant Strikes A Fatal Blow*, 397.

26. *The Savannah Republican*, 13 May 1863; *O.R.*, 24: ser. 1, pt. 1, 670-671, 674-675; Elliott Journal, 58, TSLA; Payne Memoir, VNMPA; *The Memphis Daily Appeal*, 9 May 1863.

27. "Personal Memoir of I. V. Smith," 28, WHMC-SHSM; Bowen to Memminger, 4 and 6 June 1863, Bowen Letter Book, VHS; Payne Memoir, VNMPA; *O.R.*, 24: ser. 1, pt. 1, 669, 670-671; Elliott Journal, 58, TSLA; *The Memphis Daily Appeal*, 6 and 9 May 1863; Bannon Diary, SCL; Bevier, *History of the First and Second Missouri Confederate Brigades*, 181, 419; Hogan to Father, 22 July 1863, MHS.

28. Hogan to Father, 22 July 1863, MHS; Elliott Journal, 58, TSLA; *O.R.*, 24: ser. 1, pt. 1, 670-671, 675; "Personal Memoir of I. V. Smith," 28, WHMC-SHSM; Payne Memoir, VNMPA; *The Savannah Republican*, 13 May 1863; Bowen to Memminger, 2 May and 4 and 6 June 1863, Bowen Letter Book, VHS; *The Memphis Daily Appeal*, 4, 5 and 6 May 1863; *The Mobile Register and Advertiser*, 4 May 1863; Compiled Missouri Confederate Service Records, RG 109, NA; Paxton, *Annals of Platte County, Missouri*, 316-317; *Platte County Argus*, 17 Aug. 1916; *History of Clay and Platte Counties, Missouri*, 676-677; James Synnamon, "A Veteran With Many Wounds," *Confederate Veteran*, 21: (1913), 582.

Chapter Twelve: To the Hill of No Return

1. Bannon Diary, SCL; Elliott Journal, 58, TSLA; Compiled Missouri Confederate Service Records, RG 109, NA; Bevier, *History of the First and Second Missouri Confederate Brigades*, 419; Bowen to Memminger, Bowen Letter Book, VHS; *O.R.*, 24: ser. 1, pt. 1, 669, 683; Ballard, *Pemberton*, 146-147; Bearss, *Grant Strikes A Fatal Blow*, 412-413.

2. *The St. Louis Missouri Republican*, 17 Sept., 1886; Anderson, *Memoirs*, 299; Elliott Journal, 58; Fowler, *Under Two Flags*, 216-217; *O.R.*, 24: ser. 1, pt. 1, 666; Bannon Diary, SCL; Bowen to Memminger, 2 May and 4 June 1863, Bowen Letter Book, VHS; Bevier, *History of the First and Second Missouri Confederate Brigades*, 181-182; *The Memphis Daily Appeal*, 6 and 19 May 1863.

3. Compiled Missouri Confederate Service Records, RG 109, NA; *The Mobile Register and Advertiser*, 19 Nov. 1863; Crawford to Lewis, 11 June 1863; James W. Thompson, Jackson, Mississippi, to author, 27 Jan. 1989; *The St. Louis Missouri Republican*, 17 Sept. 1886; Bowen to Memminger, 4 June 1863, Bowen Letter Book, VHS; *The Memphis Daily Appeal*, 6 and 28 Apr. 1863 and 6 and 9 May 1863; Lewis Family Papers, private collection of Leroy R. Lewis, Chatham, New Jersey.

4. Crawford to Lewis, 11 June 1863; Robbins to Family, 30 Dec. 1862, Robbins Collection, ML; *The Weekly Mississippian*, 25 Nov. 1862; "Diary of Lieut. Col. Hubbell of 3d Regiment Missouri Infantry, C.S.A.," *The Land We Love*, 105.

5. Elliott Journal, 58, TSLA; Compiled Missouri Confederate Service Records, RG 109, NA; Anderson, *Memoirs*, 299-301; Ruyle Memoir, 29; *The St. Louis Missouri Republican*, 17 Sept. 1886; Bearss, *Grant Strikes A Fatal Blow*, 422; Bowen to Memminger, 2 May and 4 June 1863, Bowen Letter Book, VHS; Bevier, *History of the First and Second Missouri Confederate Brigades*, 181-182; *The Memphis Daily Appeal*, 6 and 9 May 1863.

6. Anderson, *Memoirs*, 301-302; Bevier, *History of the First and Second Missouri Confederate Brigades*, 181-182; "Personal Memoir of I. V. Smith," 28, WHMC-SHSM; Appler Diary, 16, MHS; Bearss, *Grant Strikes A Fatal Blow*, 423.

7. Bearss, *Grant Strikes A Fatal Blow*, 423, 425, 427; Anderson, *Memoirs*, 302-303; Leavy Journal, 13, VNMPA; Compiled Missouri Confederate Service Records, RG 109, NA; Riley to Cockrell, 1 July 1863; *O.R.*, 24: ser. 1, pt. 1, 669.

8. Anderson, *Memoirs*, 303-305; Elliott Journal, 59, TSLA; Appler, 16, MHS; "Personal Memoir of I. V. Smith," 28, WHMC-SHSM; *The Memphis Register and Advertiser*, 6 May 1863.

9. Elliott Journal, 59, TSLA; *The St. Louis Missouri Republican*, 17 Sept. 1886; Appler Diary, 16, MHS; *The Memphis Daily Appeal*, 9 May 1863; Catton, *Grant Moves South*, 428-430; Grant, *Personal Memoirs of U. S. Grant*, 258-260; Ballard, *Pemberton*, 147; Bearss, *Grant Strikes A Fatal Blow*, 480-481.

10. Bannon Diary, SCL; Anderson, *Memoirs*, 306; Hogan to Father, 22 July 1863, MHS; "Personal Memoir of I. V. Smith," 28, WHMC-SHSM; Appler Diary, 16, MHS; *The Savannah Republican*, 22 May 1863; *O.R.*, 24: ser. 1, pt. 3, 428-430; Bowen to Memminger, 6 June 1863, Bowen Letter Book, VHS.

11. Elliott, 59, TSLA; Anderson, *Memoirs*, 306-307; *O.R.*, 24: ser. 1, pt. 3, 834; *The Richmond Enquirer*, 13 Aug. 1863; Compiled Missouri Confederate Service Records, RG 109, NA; Bevier, *History of the First and Second Missouri Confederate Brigades*, 13-14, 18-21; Bowen to Memminger, 11 May 1863, Bowen Letter Book, VHS; *The Intelligencer*, 12 June 1863; *The Daily Whig*, 11 Feb. 1863; Bearss, *Grant Strikes A Fatal Blow*, 454; Appler Diary, 16-17, MHS; Robbins to Family, 4 Jan. 1863, Robbins Collection, ML; *The Chattanooga Daily Rebel*, 18 Oct. 1862; Fellman, *Inside War*, v, vi, xv-xviii; *The Memphis Daily Appeal*, 24 Feb. 1863 and June 6 1863; S.H.M. Byers, *With Fire and Sword*, (New York, 1911), 14; Mesker Scrapbook, 1: MHS; "Report of the Proceeding of the Ex-Confederate Association of Missouri in its Second Annual Meeting at Sedalia, Pettis County, Missouri, Aug. 15, 16, 1882," Missouri Historical Society.

12. St. Peters, *Memorial Volume of the Diamond Jubilee of St. Louis University*, 213; *History of Clay and Platte Counties*, Missouri, 295-296; Compiled Missouri Confederate Service Records, RG 109, NA; *Portrait and Biographical Record of Clay, Ray, Carroll, Chariton, and Linn Counties, Missouri*, 151-152; *The Memphis Daily Appeal*, 28 Apr. 1863; *History of Henry and St. Clair Counties, Missouri*, (St. Joseph, 1883), 502-505; "Maj. John H. Britts," *Confederate Veteran*, 18: (1910), 36; William Barnaby Faherty, *Better the Dream, Saint Louis: University and Community, 1818-1968*, (St. Louis, 1968), xiii, 28, 39, 52, 54-55, 59-62, 72, 85, 88-89, 108-109, 126, 135, 139-140.

13. *The St. Louis Missouri Republican*, 17 Sept. 1886 and 5 Dec. 1884; Catton, *Grant Moves South*, 438-443; Richard E. Beringer, Herman Hattaway, Archer Jones, and William N. Still, Jr., *The Elements of Confederate Defeat: Nationalism, War Aims and Religion*, (Athens, 1988), 111-113; *The Memphis Daily Appeal*, 11 June 1863; Ruyle Memoir, 30; Fisher Diary, 1, MHS; Johnson and Buel, eds., *Battles and Leaders*, 3: 502-507; *The Mobile Register and Advertiser*, 17, 19 and 22 May 1863; Appler Diary, 17, MHS; *The Intelligencer*, 21 July 1863; Rawley, *Turning Points of the Civil War*, 153, 160; Ballard, *Pemberton*, 152; Jones, *Civil War Command And Strategy*, 112, 160-161.

14. Appler Diary, 17, MHS; *O.R.*, 24: ser. 1, pt. 1, 261 and *O.R.*, 24: ser. 1, pt. 2, 110, 114; Leavy Journal, 12, VNMPA; *The Richmond Enquirer*, 12 June 1863; "Personal Memoir of I. V. Smith," 28, WHMC-SHSM; Ballard, *Pemberton*, 151, 154-155; Fisher Diary, 1, MHS; Beringer, Hattaway, Jones and Still, *The Elements of Confederate Defeat*, 112-113.

15. Hogan to Father, 22 July 1863, MHS; Appler Diary, 17, MHS; "Personal Memoir of I. V. Smith," 28, WHMC-SHSM; *The Richmond Enquirer*, 12 June 1863; Pemberton, *Pemberton, Defender of Vicksburg*, 150; *The Mobile Advertiser and Register*, 11 June 1863; Johnson and Buel, eds., *Battles and Leaders*, 3: 508; *The St. Louis Missouri Republican*, 5 Dec. 1884; Bearss, *Grant Strikes A Fatal Blow*, 561-567, 573, 576-577; Ballard, *Pemberton*, 154-157; Fisher Diary 1, MHS; *O.R.*, 24: ser. 1, pt. 1, 125, 261-262; Ruyle Memoir, 30.

16. Appler Diary, 17, MHS; Ruyle Memoir, 30; Bannon, "Experiences of a Confederate Army Chaplain," 203-210; Fisher Diary, 1, MHS; "Personal Memoir of I. V. Smith," 28, WHMC-SHSM.

17. Johnson and Buel, eds., *Battles and Leaders*, 3: 508-509; Hogan to Father, 22 July 1863, MHS; Bearss, *Grant Strikes A Fatal Blow*, 576-577; Ruyle Memoir, 30; *The Mobile Register and Advertiser*, 11 June 1863; "Personal Memoir of I. V. Smith," 28, WHMC-SHSM; Ballard, *Pemberton*, 158-159; "Original Letters and Reports Regarding the Siege of Vicksburg," Bixby Collection, Missouri Historical Society; *The Richmond Enquirer*, 12 June 1863; Pemberton, *Pemberton, Defender of Vicksburg*, 154-155.

Chapter Thirteen: Champion Hill

1. *O.R.*, 24: ser. 1, pt. 1, 263; *O.R.*, 24: ser. 1, pt. 2, 93-94, 125-127.

2. Johnson and Buel, eds., *Battles and Leaders*, 3: 509; Bowen Letter Book, Report No. 84, NA; *The Mobile Register and Advertiser*, 11 June 1863; Ballard, *Pemberton*, 160-162; Bearss, *Grant Strikes A Fatal Blow*, 586-587; *The Richmond Enquirer*, 12 June 1863; Ruyle Memoir, 30; *The St. Louis Missouri Republican*, 5 Dec. 1884; *O.R.*, 24: ser. 1, pt. 1, 87, 263.

3. Anderson, *Memoirs*, 310-311; Bearss, *Grant Strikes A Fatal Blow*, 583-584; Riley to Cockrell, 1 July 1863; Kavanaugh Memoir, 29, WHMC-SHSM; Ruyle Memoir, 30; Samuel Dunlap Diary, 211-212, WHMC-SHSM; *The St. Louis Missouri Republican*, 5 Dec. 1884; "Personal Memoir of I. V. Smith," 28, WHMC-SHSM; *O.R.*, 24: ser. 1, pt. 2, 110.

4. Compiled Missouri Confederate Service Records, RG 109, NA; Anderson, *Memoirs*, 310-311; *O.R.*, 24: ser. 1, pt. 2, 110; Riley to Cockrell, 1 July 1863; *The St. Louis Missouri Republican*, 4 Dec. 1884.

5. Compiled Missouri Confederate Service Records, RG 109, NA; Anderson, *Memoirs*, 310-311; Ruyle Memoir, 30; Riley to Cockrell, 1 July 1863; Hubbell Family Papers in the private collection of Mrs. Leon Rice Taylor; "Personal Memoir of I. V. Smith," 28, WHMC-SHSM; *The St. Louis Missouri Republican*, 5 Dec. 1884; Bearss, *Grant Strikes A Fatal Blow*, 584.

6. Samuel Dunlap Diary, 211-212, WHMC-SHSM; Riley to Cockrell, 1 July 1863; Ruyle Memoir, 30; Anderson, *Memoirs*, 310-311; *The St. Louis Missouri Republican*, 5 Dec. 1884 and 1 Jan. 1887; "Personal Memoir of I. V. Smith," 28, WHMC-SHSM; *O.R.*, 24: ser. 1, pt. 2, 110.

7. *The Richmond Enquirer*, 11 June 1863; Bearss, *Grant Strikes A Fatal Blow*, 586-587, 591-592, 641; *O.R.*, 24: ser. 1, pt. 2, 93-94; *The St. Louis Missouri Republican*, 5 Dec. 1884; *The Mobile Register and Advertiser*, 11 June 1863; *The Intelligencer*, 9 June 1863; Herman Hattaway, *General Stephen D. Lee*, (Jackson, 1976), 86-87.

8. Ruyle Memoir, 30; *The Mobile Register and Advertiser*, 11 June 1863; Fisher Diary, 1, MHS; *The St. Louis Missouri Republican*, 5 Dec. 1884; Bearss, *Grant Strikes A Fatal Blow*, 596-600, 605-607; Edwin C. Bearss, *Decision in Mississippi*, (Little Rock, 1962), 246-250, 260-263; Elliott Journal, 60, TSLA; *The Richmond Enquirer*, 12 June 1863; "Personal Memoir of I. V. Smith," 28, WHMC-SHSM; *O.R.*, 24: ser. 1, pt. 2, 94-95 and *O.R.*, 24: ser. 1, pt. 1, 640; *The Memphis Daily Appeal*, 11 June 1863.

9. Elliott Journal, 60, TSLA; *The Richmond Enquirer*, 12 June 1863; Bearss, *Decision in Mississippi*, 246-250, 260-263; *The Vicksburg, Daily Herald*, 5 Oct. 1902; Ruyle 30; Fisher Diary, 1, MHS; *The St. Louis Missouri Republican*, 5 Dec. 1884; "Personal Memoir of I. V. Smith," 28, WHMC-SHSM; Bearss, *Grant Strikes A Fatal Blow*, 596-600, 605-607; *The Mobile Register and Advertiser*, 11 June 1863; *The Memphis Daily Appeal*, 11 June 1863.

10. Samuel Dunlap Diary, 211-212, WHMC-SHSM; Bearss, *Grant Strikes A Fatal Blow*, 607-608, 641; Leavy Journal, 13, VNMPA; *The Daily Herald*, 5 Oct. 1902; "Personal Memoir of I. V. Smith," 28, WHMC-SHSM; Elliott Journal, 60, TSLA; Riley to Cockrell, 1 July 1863; *The Mobile Register and Advertiser*, 11 June 1863; Fisher Diary, 1, MHS; Ruyle Memoir, 30; *The St. Louis Missouri Republican*, 5 Dec. 1884; *O.R.*, 24: ser. 1, pt. 2, 110-111; *The Richmond Enquirer*, 12 June 1863.

11. Fisher Diary, 1, MHS; Ruyle Memoir, 30; Bearss, *Grant Strikes A Fatal Blow*, 608; *The Mobile Register and Advertiser*, 7 June 1863; "Personal Memoir of I. V. Smith," 28, WHMC-SHSM; *O.R.*, 24: ser. 1, pt. 2, 110; Hogan to Father, 22 July 1863, MHS; Leavy Journal, 13, 15, VNMPA; *The Intelligencer*, 9 June 1863 and 6 Aug. 1863; Elliott Journal, 60, TSLA; *The St. Louis Missouri Republican*, 5 Dec. 1884.

12. Compiled Missouri Confederate Service Records, RG 109, NA; *The Mobile Register and Advertiser*, 11 June 1863; Fisher Diary, 1, MHS; Ruyle Memoir, 30; *The Intelligencer*, 9 June 1863; *The Memphis Daily Appeal*, 11 June 1863; *The St. Louis Missouri Republican*, 5 Dec. 1884.

13. Ruyle Memoir, 30-31; *O.R.*, 24: ser. 1, pt. 2, 106, 110-111; *The Memphis Daily Appeal*, 11 June 1863; Compiled Missouri Confederate Service Records, RG 109, NA; *History of Randolph and Macon Counties, Missouri*, 863-864.

14. *History of Randolph and Macon Counties, Missouri*, 863-864; *O.R.*, 24: ser. 1, pt. 2, 110-111; Ruyle Memoir, 30-31; "Personal Memoir of I. V. Smith," 28, WHMC-SHSM; Compiled Missouri Confederate Service Records, RG 109, NA.

15. "Personal Memoir of I. V. Smith," 28, WHMC-SHSM; Bevier, *History of the First and Second Missouri Confederate Brigades*, 14; *O.R.*, 24: ser. 1, pt. 2, 110-111; *History of Randolph and Macon Counties, Missouri*, 863-864; Compiled Missouri Confederate Service Records, RG 109, NA; Riley to Cockrell, 1 July 1863.

16. "Personal Memoir of I. V. Smith," 28, WHMC-SHSM; *O.R.*, 24: ser. 1, pt. 2, 110-111; Compiled Missouri Confederate Service Records, RG 109, NA; *History of Randolph and Macon Counties, Missouri*, 863-864.

17. *O.R.*, 24: ser. 1, pt. 2, 110-111; Riley to Cockrell, 1 July 1863; Anderson, *Memoirs*, 311; Ruyle Memoir, 30-31; Fisher, 1, MHS; *History of Boone County, Missouri*, (St. Louis, 1882), 905-906.

18. *O.R.*, 24: ser. 1, pt. 2, 110-111, 118-119; Anderson, *Memoirs*, 311-312; Riley to Cockrell, 1 July 1863; Ruyle Memoir, 30-31; Stephen D. Lee, "The Campaign of Vicksburg, Mississippi in 1863-from April 15th to and Including the Battle of Champion Hills, or Baker's Creek, May 16th, 1863," *Publications of the Mississippi Historical Society*, 3: (1900), 47.

19. *O.R.*, 24: ser. 1, pt. 2, 118-119; Samuel Dunlap Diary, 211-212, WHMC-SHSM; Anderson, *Memoirs*, 312; Isaac, "Confederate Days in St. Louis," MHS.

20. Simpson Diary, WHMC-SHSM; *The St. Louis Missouri Republican*, 5 Dec. 1884; Warren Diary; *O.R.*, 24: ser. 1, pt. 1, 669; Kavanaugh Memoir, 39, WHMC-SHSM; Compiled Missouri Confederate Service Records, RG 109, NA; Bevier, *History of the First and Second Missouri Confederate Brigades*, 13-14, 19-21, 276; Lee, "The Campaign of Vicksburg, Mississippi," *PMHS*, 47; Anderson, *Memoirs*, 306-307; Lemmon Family Papers.

21. Compiled Missouri Confederate Service Records, RG 109, NA.

22. "Ex-Confederate Association of Missouri Reunion, Ninth Annual Meeting, Kansas City, Aug. 19-20, 1891," 21.

23. *O.R.*, 24: ser. 1, pt. 2, 110-111.

24. Ibid., 95-96, 110-111; "Personal Memoir of I. V. Smith," 28, WHMC-SHSM; Bearss, *Grant Strikes A Fatal Blow*, 607-609; Compiled Missouri Confederate Service Records, RG 109, NA; Payne, "Missouri Troops in the Vicksburg Campaign," *Confederate Veteran*, 340-341.

25. Anderson, *Memoirs*, 311-312; *O.R.*, 24: ser. 1, pt. 2, 110-111.

26. Bevier, *History of the First and Second Missouri Confederate Brigades*, 167; Ruyle Memoir, 31; *O.R.*, 24: ser. 1, pt. 2, 110-111; "Personal Memoir of I. V. Smith," 29, WHMC-SHSM.

27. Edwin C. Bearss to author, 15 Jan. 1985; "Personal Memoir of I. V. Smith," 29, WHMC-SHSM; *O.R.*, 24: ser. 1, pt. 2, 110-111; Bevier, *History of the First and Second Missouri Confederate Brigades*, 424; S. Wentworth Stevenson, "A Southern Campaign," The Ladies Benevolent and Industrial Sallymag Society, (Charlottetown, 1868), 112.

28. Bearss, *Grant Strikes A Fatal Blow*, 606, 609-610; "Personal Memoir of I. V. Smith," 29, WHMC-SHSM; *O.R.*, 24: ser. 1, pt. 2, 42, 55.

29. Ruyle Memoir, 31; *The Memphis Daily Appeal*, 11 June 1863; Hogan to Father, 22 July 1863, MHS; *The Richmond Enquirer*, 12 June 1863; United States Department of the Interior Geological Survey of Hinds County, Mississippi, Topographical Sheet.

30. Ruyle Memoir, 31; Compiled Missouri Confederate Service Records, RG 109; NA; Phillip Thomas Tucker, "The History of the First Missouri Confederate Brigade, 1862-1865," Central Missouri State University, Warrensburg, Missouri, M.A. Thesis, 1983, 124; Lily Hazel Bates Papers; Kathleen White Miles, *Bitter Ground: The Civil War in Missouri's Golden Valley, Benton, Henry and St. Clair Counties*, (Warsaw, 1971), 317-319.

31. *O.R.*, 24: ser. 1, pt. 2, 49-51; Ruyle Memoir, 31; *The Memphis Daily Appeal*, 11 June 1863; *History of the Sixteenth Battery of Ohio Volunteer Light Artillery, U.S.A.*, (n.p., 1906), 58.

32. Compiled Missouri Confederate Service Records, RG 109, NA; Anderson, *Memoirs*, 310; "Diary of Lt. Col. Hubbell of 3d Regiment Missouri Infantry, C.S.A.," *The Land We Love*, 105; *O.R.*, 24: ser. 1, pt. 2, 110; Hubbell, "Personal Reminiscences," 13-14, 16; T. M. Anderson to W. A. Everman, 29 Sept. 1914 and 14 Oct. 1914, Box 9, Civil War Papers, Missouri Historical Society; Mrs. Leon Rice Taylor Papers.

33. *History of Ray County, Missouri*, 776; Compiled Missouri Confederate Service Records, RG 109, NA; "Diary of Lieut. Col. Hubbell of 3d Regiment Missouri Infantry, C.S.A." *The Land We Love*, 105; Mrs. Leon Rice Taylor interview with author, 16 June 1989.

34. Compiled Missouri Confederate Service Records, RG 109, NA; Anderson, *Memoirs*, 313; Riley to Cockrell, 1 July 1863; Bevier, *History of the First and Second Missouri Confederate Brigade*, 425-426.

35. Hogan to Father, 22 July 1863, MHS; *O.R.*, 24: ser. 1, pt. 2, 110-111; Riley to Cockrell, 1 July 1863; Ruyle Memoir, 31; "Personal Memoir of I. V. Smith," 29, WHMC-SHSM.

36. Ruyle Memoir, 31; *O.R.*, 24: ser. 1, pt. 2, 44, 56; Hogan to Father 22 July 1863, MHS; *The Memphis Daily Appeal*, 11 June 1863; David F. Lenox, "Memoirs of a Missouri Confederate Soldier," Missouri Historical Society.

37. *O.R.*, 24: ser. 1, pt. 2, 49-50, 88, 110-111; *History of the Sixteenth Battery of Ohio Volunteer Light Artillery*, 50-52; Anderson, *Memoirs*, 313; T. M. Eddy, *Patriotism of Illinois*, (Chicago, 1865), 2: 463; *The St. Louis Missouri Republican*, 5 Dec. 1884; Bearss, *Grant Strikes A Fatal Blow*, 611; *The Memphis Daily Appeal*, 11 June 1863; Bevier, *History of the First and Second Missouri Confederate Brigades*, 425-426; Hogan to Father, 22 July 1863, MHS.

38. *O.R.*, 24: ser. 1, pt. 2, 110-111, 115-120; Bearss, *Grant Strikes A Fatal Blow*, 611-612; Riley to Cockrell, 1 July 1863; Fisher Diary, 1, MHS; *The St. Louis Missouri Republican*, 5 Dec. 1884; Elliott Journal, 60, TSLA.

39. Elliott Journal, 60, TSLA; Hogan to Father, 1 July 1863, MHS; Bearss, *Grant Strikes A Fatal Blow*, 611-615; Herb Phillips, *Champion Hill*, (Champion Hill Battlefield Foundation, n.d.), 11; Kavanaugh Memoir, 38, WHMC-SHSM; Leavy Journal, 12-13, VNMPA; *The St. Louis Missouri Republican*, 5 Dec. 1884.

40. *O.R.*, 24: ser. 1, pt. 2, 115-120; *The Daily Herald*, 5 Oct. 1902; Bearss, *Grant Strikes A Fatal Blow*, 613; Leavy Journal, 12-13, VNMPA.

41. Anderson, *Memoirs*, 313; Bevier, *History of the First and Second Missouri Confederate Brigades*, 14; Bob Priddy, *Across the Wide Missouri*, (2 vols., Independence, 1982-1984), 1: 292; *The St. Louis Missouri Republican*, 5 Dec. 1884.

42. Bevier, *History of the First and Second Missouri Confederate Brigades*, 426; Anderson, *Memoirs*, 313; Kavanaugh Memoir, 38, WHMC-SHSM; *O.R.*, 24: ser. 1, pt. 1, 724, 730-731; *The Memphis Daily Appeal*, 11 June 1863; T. B. Sproul, *Confederate Veteran*, 7: (1894), 199; *The St. Louis Missouri Republican*, 5 Dec. 1884; Ruyle Memoir, 31.

43. Kavanaugh Memoir, 38, WHMC-SHSM; Byers, *With Fire and Sword*, 76-77; *O.R.*, 24: ser. 1, pt. 1, 724; *The Memphis Appeal*, 11 June 1863; Ruyle Memoir, 31; *The St. Louis Missouri Republican*, 5 Dec. 1884; Hogan to Father, 22 July 1863, MHS.

44. Hogan to Father, 22 July 1863, MHS; *O.R.*, 24: ser. 1, pt. 2, 110-111; *The St. Louis Missouri Republican*, 5 Dec. 1863; Kavanaugh Memoir, 38, WHMC-SHSM; Bearss, *Grant Strikes A Fatal Blow*, 614; Riley to Cockrell, 1 July 1863; *O.R.*, 24: ser. 1, pt. 2, 110-111.

45. Riley to Cockrell, 1 July 1863; *O.R.*, 24: ser. 1, pt. 2, 119.

46. Riley to Cockrell, 1 July 1863; *O.R.*, 24: ser. 1, pt. 2, 112; S.C. Trigg, "Fighting Around Vicksburg," *Confederate Veteran*, 12: (1904), 120; Bearss, *Grant Strikes A Fatal Blow*, 614-615; Payne, "Missouri Troops in the Vicksburg Campaign," *C.V.*, 341; *The St. Louis Missouri Republican*, 5 Dec. 1884; H. Riley Bock Papers; Boyce, "The Flags of the First Missouri Confederate Infantry," MHS; Byers, *With Fire and Sword*, 79.

47. Riley to Cockrell, 1 July 1863; *O.R.*, 24: ser. 1, pt. 2, 112; Compiled Missouri Confederate Service Records, RG 109, NA; *The St. Louis Missouri Republican*, 5 Dec. 1884; *O.R.*, 24: pt. 2, 112; *O.R.*, 38: ser. 1, pt. 3, 919; Lewis Kennerly to Sister, 3 Oct. 1863, Bowen Papers, MHS; Joseph Boyce to Hawes Smith, 18 Jan. 1864, Boyce Papers, MHS; Joseph Boyce to Isaac J. Fowler, 10 May 1913, Boyce Papers, MHS.

48. Bearss, *Grant Strikes A Fatal Blow*, 614-616; J. B. Sanborn, *Memoirs of George B. Boomer*, (Boston, 1864), 281; *History of the Sixteenth Battery of Ohio Volunteer Light Artillery*, 56; *O.R.*, 24: pt. 2, 44; Riley to Cockrell, 1 July 1863; *The Memphis Daily Appeal*, 11 June 1863.

49. Bearss, *Grant Strikes A Fatal Blow*, 616; *O.R.*, 24: pt. 2, 44, 111, 119; *The St. Louis Missouri Republican*, 5 Dec. 1884; Elliott Journal, 60, TSLA; Hogan to Father, 22 July 1863, MHS; Bevier, *History of the First and Second Missouri Confederate Brigades*, 426; Riley to Cockrell, 1 July 1863; Anderson, *Memoirs*, 313-314; *O.R.*, 24: ser. 1, pt. 1, 718; Champ Clark Scrapbook, 15: Champ Clark Papers, WHMC-SHSM; Ruyle Memoir, 31; Boyce 8 Mar. 1914 Paper on Bannon, MHS.

50. *The St. Louis Missouri Republican*, 5 Dec. 1884; Leavy Journal, 13, VNMPA; Ballard, *Pemberton*, 163-164; Hogan to Father, 22 July 1863, MHS; Bevier, *History of the First and Second Missouri Confederate Brigades*, 189; Bearss, *Grant Strikes A Fatal Blow*, 609-617; Anderson, *Memoirs*, 313; "Personal Memoir of I. V. Smith," 29, WHMC-SHSM; *The Daily Herald*, 5 Oct. 1902; *O.R.*, 24: ser. 1, pt. 2, 111; Riley to Cockrell, 1 July 1863.

51. Compiled Missouri Confederate Service Records, RG 109, NA; Bevier, *History of the First and Second Missouri Confederate Brigades*, 225-226; "Captain C.M.B. Thurmond's War Record," Civil War Papers, 1900-1962, Missouri Historical Society; Riley to Cockrell, 1 July 1863.

52. *O.R.*, 24: ser. 1, pt. 2, 111-112, 116-117; Bevier, *History of the First and Second Missouri Confederate Brigades*, 192, 426; Anderson, *Memoirs*, 315; Hogan to Father, 22 July 1863, MHS.

53. Robert C. Dunlap Diary; Bearss, *Grant Strikes A Fatal Blow*, 621, 623; *The St. Louis Missouri Republican*, 5 Dec. 1884; "Personal Memoir of I. V. Smith," 29, WHMC-SHSM; Anderson, *Memoirs*, 314; Walter A. Landis to author, 4 Nov. 1988; *The Memphis Daily Appeal*, 11 June 1863; Robbins, "Landis Battery," MHS.

54. *O.R.*, 24: ser. 1, pt. 2, 111-112, 117, 119; *The Richmond Enquirer*, 12 June 1863; Bearss, *Grant Strikes A Fatal Blow*, 623-628.

55. Leavy Journal, 13, VNMPA; Anderson, *Memoirs*, 314-315; *O.R.*, 24: ser. 1, pt. 2, 111-112; *The Richmond Enquirer*, 12 June 1863.

56. *O.R.*, 24: ser. 1, pt. 2, 112; Hogan to Father, 22 July 1863, MHS; Anderson, *Memoirs*, 315; *The Memphis Daily Appeal*, 11 June 1863; Johnson and Buel, eds., *Battles and Leaders*, 3: 487.

57. Leavy Journal, 13, VNMPA; Bearss, *Grant Strikes A Fatal Blow*, 641; Anderson, *Memoirs*, 314; *O.R.*, 24: ser. 1, pt. 2, 111-112.

58. Bearss, *Grant Strikes A Fatal Blow*, 642, 645; Johnson and Buel, eds., *Battles and Leaders of the Civil War*, 3: 512.

59. Byers, *With Fire and Sword*, 84.

Chapter Fourteen: Last Stand on the Mississippi

1. Henry Cheavens Journal, Western Historical Manuscript Collection-State Historical Society of Missouri: Leavy Journal, 14-15, VNMPA; Fisher Diary, 1, MHS; Hogan to Father, 22 July 1863, MHS; *O.R.*, 24: ser. 1, pt. 2, 72, 113; *O.R.*, 24: ser. 1, pt. 1, 267; Bevier, *History of the First and Second Missouri Confederate Brigades*, 426; Bearss, *Grant Strikes A Fatal Blow*, 664; "Personal Memoir of I. V. Smith," 29, WHMC-SHSM; *The St. Louis Missouri Republican*, 5 Dec. 1884; Anderson, *Memoirs*, 315; Compiled Missouri Confederate Service Records, RG 109, NA.

2. *The Memphis Daily Appeal*, 11 June 1861, 15 Dec. 1862 and 29 July 1863; "Personal Memoir of I. V. Smith," 29, WHMC-SHSM; Leavy Journal, 14-15, VNMPA; Bearss, *Grant Strikes A Fatal Blow*, 654, 664; *The St. Louis Missouri Republican*, 5 Dec. 1884; *The Chattanooga Daily Rebel*, 29 July 1863; *O.R.*, 24: ser. 1, pt. 2, 113-119, 266-267; *The Daily Whig*, 8 Jan. 1863; Carl N. Degler, *The Other South: Southern Dissenters in the Nineteenth Century*, (New York, 1974), 173-174.

3. Robert C. Dunlap Diary; Bevier, *History of the First and Second Missouri Confederate Brigades*, 426-427; *O.R.*, 24: ser. 1, pt. 2, 72; Johnson and Buel, eds., *Battles and Leaders*, 3: 487: "Personal Memoir of I. V. Smith," 29, WHMC-SHSM; *The St. Louis Missouri Republican*, 5 Dec. 1884; Kavanaugh Memoir, 39, WHMC-SHSM.

4. Hogan to Father, 22 July 1863, MHS; Bearss, *Grant Strikes A Fatal Blow*, 655, 670; *O.R.*, 24: ser. 1, pt. 2, 113; *The Memphis Daily Appeal*, 11 June 1863; Bannon Diary, SCL; *The St. Louis Missouri Republican*, 5 Dec. 1884.

5. Hogan to Father, 22 July 1863, MHS; Bearss, *Grant Strikes A Fatal Blow*, 670-675; "Personal Memoir of I. V. Smith," 29, WHMC-SHSM; Fisher Diary, 1, MHS; *The Memphis Daily Appeal*, 11 June 1863; *O.R.*, ser. 1, pt. 2, 113, 136-138; *The St. Louis Missouri Republican*, 5 Dec. 1884.

6. Bevier, *History of the First and Second Missouri Confederate Brigades*, 426-427; Cheavens Journal, WHMC-SHSM; "Personal Memoir of I. V. Smith," 29, WHMC-SHSM; *The Memphis Daily Appeal*, 11 June 1863; "James Synnamon," *Confederate Veteran* 21 (1913), 582; Hogan to Father, 22 July 1863, MHS; *The St. Louis Missouri Republican*, 5 Dec. 1884; *O.R.*, 24: ser. 1, pt. 2, 113; Compiled Missouri Confederate Records, RG 109, NA.

7. "Personal Memoir of I. V. Smith," 29-30, WHMC-SHSM; "From Elkhorn to Vicksburg," *CWH*, 43; Leavy Journal, 12, VNMPA; Compiled Missouri Confederate Service Records, RG 109, NA; Madaus and Needham, *The Battle Flags of the Confederate Army of Tennessee*, 44; Anderson, *Memoirs*, 318; *The Memphis Daily Appeal*, 11 June 1863; *O.R.*, 24: ser. 1, pt. 2, 113, 119-120; "Confederate Battle Flags of the Wisconsin Historical Society" Report, (Madison, 1906), n.p.

8. Hogan to Father, 22 July 1863, MHS; "Personal Memoir of I. V. Smith," 29-30, WHMC-SHSM; Compiled Missouri Confederate Service Records, RG 109, NA; Kavanaugh Memoir, 29, WHMC-SHSM; Samuel Dunlap Diary, 215, WHMC-SHSM; *The St. Louis Missouri Republican*, 5 Dec. 1884; *O.R.*, 24, ser. 1, pt. 2, 113-114.

9. Anderson, *Memoirs*, 318-320; *The Vandalia, Missouri, Leader*, 5 July 1918; Compiled Missouri Confederate Service Records, RG 109, NA; Williams, ed., *History of Northeast Missouri*, 2: 894-895; "Personal Memoir of I. V. Smith," 29, WHMC-SHSM; *O.R.*, 24: ser. 1, pt. 2, 113-114; *The St. Louis Missouri Republican*, 5 Dec. 1884; *O.R.*, 24: ser. 1, pt. 2, 113-114.

10. Bearss, *Grant Strikes A Fatal Blow*, 677; Compiled Missouri Confederate Service Records, RG 109, NA; Samuel Dunlap Diary, 216, WHMC-SHSM; Leavy Journal, 15, VNMPA: *O.R.*, 24: ser. 1, pt. 2, 113-114, 400-401, 418; *The Memphis Daily Appeal*, 11 June 1863; "James Synnamon," *C.V.*, 582.

11. Fisher, 1, MHS; *The Memphis Daily Appeal*, 11 June 1863; Bearss, *Grant Strikes A Fatal Blow*, 675; Anderson, *Memoirs*, 319; "Personal Memoir of I. V. Smith," 30, WHMC-SHSM; Johnson and Buel, eds., *Battles and Leaders*, 3: 515; Hogan to Father, 22 July 1863, MHS; *O.R.*, 24: ser. 1, pt. 1, 617; *O.R.*, 24: ser. 1, pt. 2, 113-114, 120; *The St. Louis Missouri Republican*, 5 Dec. 1884.

12. *The Mobile Register and Advertiser*, 30 May 1863; Loughborough, *My Cave Life In Vicksburg*, 44; *The St. Louis Missouri Republican*, 5 Dec. 1884.

13. *The Memphis Daily Appeal*, 11 June 1863; Hogan to Father, 22 July 1863, MHS; Robert C. Dunlap Diary; Robert W. Noble, *Battle of Pea Ridge, or Elk Horn Tavern: War Papers and Personal Reminiscences*, (St. Louis, 1892) 1: 240; *The St. Louis Missouri Republican*, 5 Dec. 1884.

14. Compiled Missouri Confederate Service Records, RG 109, NA; *The St. Louis Missouri Republican*, 5 Dec. 1884; Francis Christian Clewell to Mother, 15 Feb. 1863, "Letters From A Southern Soldier," Gertrude Jenkins Papers, 1859-1908, William R. Perkins Library, Duke University, Durham, North Carolina.

15. *The Atlanta Intelligencer*, 4 and 25 June 1863; *The Richmond Enquirer*, 30 May 1863; *The Memphis Daily Appeal*, 17 Nov. 1862; *The Mobile Register and Advertiser*, 25 Feb. 1863; *The Daily Whig*, 7 and 30 Jan. 1863, 13, 24 and 26 Feb. 1863, 6, 11, and 28 Mar. 1863 and 18 Apr. 1863; Jones, *Civil War Command And Strategy*, 21-22.

16. *The Memphis Daily Appeal*, 25 Feb. 1863.

17. Kavanaugh Memoir, 39, WHMC-SHSM; Hogan to Father, 22 July 1863, MHS; *The Mobile Register and Advertiser*, 19 July 1863; Cockrell Scrapbook, 4: WHMC-SHSM; *O.R.*, 24: ser. 1, pt. 2, 414; Anderson, *Memoirs*, 327; Fisher Diary, 2, MHS; Elliott Journal, 61, TSLA; *The St. Louis Missouri Republican*, 5 Dec. 1884; *The Chattanooga Daily Rebel*, 29 July 1863.

18. *The Savannah Republican*, 18 Aug. 1863; Amos C. Riley to Francis M. Cockrell, 26 July 1863, private collection of H. Riley Bock collection, New Madrid, Missouri; Ruyle Memoir, 33; Leavy Journal, 21, 34, VNMPA; Compiled Missouri Confederate Service Records, RG 109, NA; *The Mobile Register and Advertiser*, 19 July 1863; Anderson, *Memoirs*, 342; Edwin C. Bearss, *The Campaign For Vicksburg: Unvexed to the Sea*, (Dayton, 1986), 3:1079.

19. *O.R.*, 24: ser. 1, pt. 2, 414-415; *The St. Louis Missouri Republican*, 5 Dec. 1884; Fisher Diary, 2, MHS; *The Savannah Republican*, 18 Aug. 1863; Riley to Cockrell, 26 July 1863; Bearss, *Unvexed to the Sea*, 761; Elliott Journal, 61, TSLA; "Personal Memoir of I. V. Smith," 20, WHMC-SHSM; Johnson and Buel, eds., *Battles and Leaders*, 3: 517; *The Memphis Daily Appeal*, 10 June 1863; *The Mobile Register and Advertiser*, 19 July 1863; *The Chattanooga Daily Rebel*, 29 July 1863.

20. *O.R.*, 24: ser. 1, pt. 2, 414-415; *The Mobile Register and Advertiser*, 19 July 1863; Riley to Cockrell, 26 July 1863; Fisher Diary, 2, MHS; Ruyle Memoir, 32; *The St. Louis Missouri Republican*, 5 Dec. 1884; Bevier, *History of the First and Second Missouri Confederate Brigades*, 202; Boyce, "The Flags of the First Missouri Confederate Infantry," MHS; *The Savannah Republican*, 18 Aug. 1863.

21. Kavanaugh Memoir, 40, WHMC-SHSM; *O.R.*, 24: ser. 1, pt. 2, 414-415.

22. *O.R.*, 24: ser. 1, pt. 2, 414-415, 257-258, 262-264; *The Memphis Daily Appeal*, 10 June 1863; Kavanaugh Memoir, 40, WHMC-SHSM; *The St. Louis Missouri Republican*, 5 Dec. 1884; "Personal Memoir of I. V. Smith," 20, WHMC-SHSM; Robbins to Family, 24 Jan. 1863, ML; Fisher Diary, 2, MHS; Hogan to Father, 22 July 1863, MHS; Bearss, *Unvexed to the Sea*, 761-764.

23. Miers, *The Web of Victory*, 204-205; *O.R.*, 24: ser. 1, pt. 2, 414-415; Hogan to Father, 22 July 1863, MHS; Kavanaugh Memoir, 41, WHMC-SHSM; *The Memphis Daily Appeal*, 10 June 1863; *The St. Louis Missouri Republican*, 5 Dec. 1884; Bearss, *Unvexed to the Sea*, 773; *The Mobile Register and Advertiser*, 19 July 1863.

24. Compiled Missouri Confederate Service Records, RG 109, NA; *O.R.*, 24: ser. 1, pt. 2, 415; *History of St. Charles, Montgomery and Warren Counties, Missouri*, (St. Louis, 1885), 179-180, 294.

25. Bearss, *Unvexed to the Sea*, 767; Anderson, *Memoirs*, 329; *The St. Louis Missouri Republican*, 5 Dec. 1884.

26. *O.R.*, 24: ser. 1, pt. 2, 415, 417; *The Memphis Daily Appeal*, 27 July 1863; Fisher Diary, 2, MHS; Bearss, *Unvexed to the Sea*, 780-785; Robert Dunlap Diary; *The St. Louis Missouri Republican*, 5 Dec. 1884; Riley to Cockrell, 26 July 1863; *The Savannah Republican*, 18 Aug. 1863; Compiled Missouri Confederate Service Records, RG 109, NA.

Chapter Fifteen: The Siege of Vicksburg

1. *O.R.*, 24: ser. 1, pt. 2, 414-415; "Personal Memoir of I. V. Smith," 30, WHMC-SHSM; Fisher Diary, 2, MHS; Elliott Journal, 61, TSLA; Miers, *The Web of Victory*, 206; Johnson and Buel, eds., *Battles and Leaders*, 3: 518; *The Savannah Republican*, 18 Aug. 1863; *The Memphis Daily Appeal*, 10 June 1863 and 14 July 1863; *The St. Louis Missouri Republican*, 5 Dec. 1884; *The Mobile Register and Advertiser*, 19 July 1863.

2. Bearss, *Unvexed to the Sea*, 787-788, 813-814, 816: footnote no. 8; *O.R.*, 24: ser. 1, pt. 2, 415; Riley to Cockrell, 26 July 1863; Fisher Diary, 2, MHS; "Personal Memoir of I. V. Smith," 30, WHMC-SHSM; *The St. Louis Missouri Republican*, 5 Dec. 1884; *The Savannah Republican*, 18 Aug. 1863; *The Mobile Register and Advertiser*, 19 July 1863; *The Memphis Daily Appeal*, 14 July 1863.

3. Bearss, *Unvexed to the Sea*, 844; Elliott Journal, 61, TSLA; *The Savannah Republican*, 18 Aug. 1863; "Personal Memoir of I. V. Smith," 30, WHMC-SHSM; Fisher Diary, 2, MHS; *The St. Louis Missouri Republican*, 5 Dec. 1884; *O.R.*, 24: ser. 1, pt. 2, 257-258, 273, 415; *The Memphis Daily Appeal*, 10 June 1863; Hogan to Father, 22 July 1863, MHS; *The Mobile Register and Advertiser*, 30 May 1863.

4. *O.R.*, 24: ser. 1, pt. 2, 415; *The Savannah Republican*, 18 Aug. 1863; Hogan to Father, 22 July 1863, MHS; Fisher Diary, 2, MHS; "Personal Memoir of I. V. Smith," 30, WHMC-SHSM; Compiled Missouri Confederate Service Records, RG 109, NA; Pauline E. Brown, Richmond, Missouri, to author, 23 June 1986; *The St. Louis Missouri Republican*, 5 Dec. 1884; Elliott Journal, 62, TSLA.

5. Riley to Cockrell, 26 July 1863; *The St. Louis Missouri Republican*, 5 Dec. 1884; Fisher, 2, MHS; Compiled Missouri Confederate Service Records, RG 109, NA; *O.R.*, 24: ser. 1, pt. 2, 257; Joseph Boyce, "What Flag was This?," *Confederate Veteran*, 27: (1919), 235; Anderson, *Memoirs*, 331-332; Moore, *Confederate Military History, Missouri*, 12: 123.

6. *O.R.*, 24: ser. 1, pt. 2, 415; Compiled Missouri Confederate Service Records, RG 109, NA; *The Savannah Republican*, 17 Aug. 1863; Joseph B. Mitchell, *The Badge of Gallantry*, (New York, 1968), 113, 119-120; *The St. Louis Missouri Republican*, 5 Dec. 1884; Webb, *Battles and Biographies of Missourians*, 359-360; Bevier, *History of the First and Second Missouri Confederate Brigades*, 84: "Personal Memoir of I. V. Smith," 30, WHMC-SHSM; Anderson, *Memoirs*, 331-332; W. J. Ervin, "Genius and Heroism of Lieut. K. H. Faulkner," *Confederate Veteran* 14: (1906), 497; Miers, *The Web of Victory*, 214; Bearss, *Unvexed to the Sea*, 858.

7. "Personal Memoir of I. V. Smith," 30, WHMC-SHSM; *The Savannah Republican*, 17 Aug. 1863; *O.R.*, 24: ser. 1, pt. 2, 415; Compiled Missouri Confederate Service Records, RG 109, NA; Leita Barkley to Mrs. Watkins, 3 Feb. 1955, Marie Oliver Watkins Papers, WHMC-SHSM; Watkins and Watkins, *Tearin' Through the Wilderness, Missouri Pioneer Episodes and Genealogy of the Watkins Family of Virginia and Missouri, 1822-1885*, 83, 87.

8. Fisher Diary, 2, MHS; *The Savannah Republican*, 18 Aug. 1863; Anderson, *Memoirs*, 333-334; C. A. Powell, "Brother Fought Against Brother," *Confederate Veteran* 10: (1902), 463; Emma Balfour, *Vicksburg, A City Under Siege: Diary of Emma Balfour, May 16, 1863-June 2, 1863*, (private printer, 1983), n.p.; *The St. Louis Missouri Republican*, 5 Dec. 1884; Kenneth Trist Urquhart, ed., *Vicksburg: Southern City Under Siege, William Lovelace Foster's Letter Describing the Defense and Surrender of the Confederate Fortress on the Mississippi*, (New Orleans, 1980), 21; S. C. Trigg, "Fighting Around Vicksburg," *Confederate Veteran*, 12: (1904), 120; "Genius and Heroism of Lieut. K. H. Faulkner," *C.V.*, 497.

9. *O.R.*, 24: ser. 1, pt. 2, 415; Elliott Journal, 61-65, TSLA; Fisher Diary, 2-6, MHS; *The St. Louis Missouri Republican*, 5 Dec. 1884; Compiled Missouri Confederate Service Records, RG 109, NA.

10. Fisher Diary, 3-4, MHS; Ruyle Memoir, 33; Leavy Journal, 23-24, VNMPA; Moore, ed., *The Rebellion Record*, 7: 172; *The Mobile Register and Advertiser*, 19 July 1863; *The St. Louis Missouri Republican*, 5 Dec. 1884; *The Intelligencer*, 11 June 1863 and 21 July 1863.

11. James E. Payne, "Recreation in Army Life," *Confederate Veteran*, 38: (1930), 388.

12. Compiled Missouri Confederate Service Records, RG 109, NA; Fisher Diary, 3-5, 7, MHS; *The Memphis Daily Appeal*, 27 July 1863; Hogan to Father, 22 July 1863, MHS; *The Richmond Enquirer*, 5 June and 1 July 1863; Elliott Journal, 63-64, TSLA; Moore, ed., *The Rebellion Record*, 7: 171-172; Edwin B. Coddington, *The Gettysburg Campaign: A Study in Command*, (New York, 1984), 4-11.

13. Quaife, ed., *Absalom Grimes*, 124-126; "Facts Concerning Albert Carlisle Mitchell," including Absalom Grimes Sketch, Absalom Grimes Papers, MHS; Compiled Missouri Confederate Service Records, RG 109, NA.

14. Elliott Journal, 61-62, TSLA; *History of Clay and Platte Counties*, Missouri, 678-679; Compiled Missouri Confederate Service Records, RG 109, NA.

15. Moore, ed., *The Rebellion Record*, 7: 172; Elliott Journal, 65, TSLA; *The St. Louis Missouri Republican*, 5 Dec. 1884.

16. Compiled Missouri Confederate Service Records, RG 109, NA; Leavy Journal, 23-24, VNMPA; *History of Henry and St. Clair Counties, Missouri*, 503-504; Fisher Diary, 4-5, MHS; Bearss, *Unvexed to the Sea*, 1261; *The St. Louis Missouri Republican*, 5 Dec. 1884; "Maj. John H. Britts," *Confederate Veteran*, 18, (1910), 36: Boyce 8 Mar. 1914 Bannon Paper, MHS.

17. Leavy, 21-22, VNMPA; Compiled Missouri Confederate Service Records, RG 109, NA; Fisher Diary, 3, MHS.

18. *The Mobile Advertiser and Register*, 19 July 1863; Miers, *The Web of Victory*, 280-281; Fisher Diary, 6, MHS; Moore, ed., *The Rebellion Record*, 7: Fisher Diary, 6, MHS; *O.R.*, 24: ser. 1, pt. 2, 376; Richard Wheeler, *The Siege of Vicksburg*, (New York, 1978), 221; Joseph O. Jackson, ed., *Some of the Boys...": The Civil War Letters of Isaac Jackson, 1862-1865*, (Carbondale, 1960), 107.

19. Eddy, *Patriotism of Illinois*, 471; *The Mobile Register and Advertiser*, 19 July 1863; Elliott Journal, 65, TSLA; Johnson and Buel, eds., *Battles and Leaders*, 3: 491; *O.R.*, 24: ser. 1, pt. 2, 293-294, 333, 415-416; Fisher Diary, 6, MHS; *The Richmond Enquirer*, 14 Aug. 1863.

20. *O.R.*, 24: ser. 1, pt. 2, 415-416; Tunnard, *A Southern Record*, 258-260; *The Richmond Enquirer*, 14 Aug. 1863; Fisher 7, MHS; Elliott Journal, 65, TSLA; *The Mobile Register and Advertiser*, 19 July 1863; Moore, ed., *The Rebellion Record*, 7: 173; Payne, "Missouri Troops in the Vicksburg Campaign," *C.V.*, 378-379; Kavanaugh Memoir, 43, WHMC-SHSM; Compiled Missouri Confederate Service Records, RG 109, NA.

21. Tunnard, *A Southern Record*, 258-260; Moore, ed., *The Rebellion Record*, 7: 173, 203; *O.R.*, 24: ser. 1, pt. 2, 415; Bearss, *Unvexed to the Sea*, 821; Compiled Missouri Confederate Service Records, RG 109, NA; Necrology Scrapbook, No. 11c, 106, Missouri Historical Society.

22. Ruyle Memoir, 32-33; Hogan to Father, 22 July 1863, MHS; Elliott Journal, 65, TSLA; Moore, ed., *The Rebellion Record*, 7: 173; *O.R.*, 24: ser. 1, pt. 2, 415.

23. Fisher, 6, MHS; Hogan to Father, 22 July 1863, MHS; *O.R.*, 24: ser. 1, pt. 2, 372, 416; Elliott Journal, 65, TSLA; Moore, ed., *The Rebellion Record*, 7: 173; Bevier, *History of the First and Second Missouri Confederate Brigades*, 84.

24. Kenny, "Father John Bannon, S.J.," 94.

25. Elliott Journal, 65, TSLA; Moore, ed., *The Rebellion Record*, 7: 173; Anderson, *Memoirs*, 355; Compiled Missouri Confederate Service Records, RG 109, NA; *The St. Louis Missouri Republican*, 5 Dec. 1884; *O.R.*, 24: ser. 1, pt. 2, 416; Hogan to Father, 22 July 1863, MHS; Fisher 7, MHS; Leavy, 38, VNMPA; Lida Lord Reed, "A Woman's Experiences During the Siege of Vicksburg," *The Century Magazine*, 61: (1901), 926; Johnson and Buel, eds., *Battles and Leaders*, 3: 491; *O.R.*, 24: ser. 1, pt. 2, 202-203; Kavanaugh *Memoir*, 44, WHMC-SHSM; *The Richmond Enquirer*, 14 Aug. 1863; "Personal Memoir of I. V. Smith," 31, WHMC-SHSM; Robert Dunlap Diary.

26. Elliott Journal, 66, TSLA; Anderson, *Memoirs*, 346; *The Mobile Advertiser and Register*, 19 July 1863; Compiled Missouri Confederate Service Records, RG 109, NA; *The Richmond Enquirer*, 14 Aug. 1863; Leavy Journal, 37, VNMPA; Fisher Diary, 3, 6-7, MHS; James J. Pillar, *The Catholic Church in Mississippi, 1837-1865*, (New Orleans, 1964), 258.

27. Hogan to Father, 22 July 1863, MHS; Bannon Diary, SCL; Boyce 8 Mar. 1914 Bannon Paper, MHS; Pillar, *The Catholic Church in Mississippi*, 258; M. J. Mulvihill, *Vicksburg and Warren County, Mississippi, Tunica Indians, Quebec Missionaries, Civil War Veterans*, (Vicksburg, 1931), 75; *The Richmond Enquirer*, 14 Aug. 1863.

28. Compiled Missouri Confederate Service Records, RG 109, NA; Webb, *Battles and Biographies of Missourians*, 359; Payne, "Missouri Troops in the Vicksburg Campaign," *CV*, 378; Moore, ed., *The Rebellion Record*, 7: 173; Elliott Journal, 66, TSLA; Fisher, 7, MHS; Kavanaugh Memoir, 42, WHMC-SHSM; *O.R.*, 24: ser. 1, pt. 2, 173, 416; *The St. Louis Missouri Republican*, 5 Dec. 1884; *The Richmond Enquirer*, 14 Aug. 1863.

29. *O.R.*, 24: ser. 1, pt. 2, 173, 416; *The St. Louis Missouri Republican*, 5 Dec. 1884; Compiled Missouri Confederate Service Records, RG 109, NA; W. N. Crenshaw to Maj. Thomas Rigby, 8 July 1901, Vicksburg National Military Park Archives; Elliott Journal, 66, TSLA; Moore, ed., *The Rebellion Record*, 7: 173; Kavanaugh Memoir, 42, WHMC-SHSM; "The Bravest Soldier," newspaper clipping, 2: Kearny-Kennerly Scrapbook, Missouri Historical Society; Compiled Missouri Confederate Service Records, RG 109, MHS; Fisher, 7, MHS; *The Centralia, Missouri, Fireside Guard*, 16 Mar. 1917; Webb, *Battles and Biographies of Missourians*, 359; "Personal Memoir of I. V. Smith," 32, WHMC-SHSM; Elliott Journal, 66, TSLA; *The Richmond Enquirer*, 14 Aug. 1863.

30. *The Centralia Fireside Guard*, 16 Mar. 1917; Cockrell Scrapbook, 4: WHMC-SHSM; Anderson, *Memoirs*, 352; Leavy Journal, 40, VNMPA; Kavanaugh Memoir, 42, WHMC-SHSM; *The St. Louis Missouri Republican*, 5 Dec. 1884.

31. Leavy Journal, 40, VNMPA; Kavanaugh Memoir, 42, WHMC-SHSM; *The Centralia Fireside Guard*, 16 Mar. 1917; Cockrell Scrapbook, 5: WHMC-SHSM; Anderson, *Memoirs*, 352; *The St. Louis Missouri Republican*, 5 Dec. 1884.

32. Cockrell to Riley, 26 July 1863; Elliott Journal, 66, TSLA; Fisher Diary, 7, MHS; *O.R.*, 24: ser. 1, pt. 2, 416; Hogan to Father, 22 July 1863, MHS; Tunnard, *A Southern Record*, 266; Kavanaugh Memoir, 42, WHMC-SHSM; *The St. Louis Missouri Republican*, 5 Dec. 1884.

33. Fisher Diary, 7-8, MHS; *The Centralia Fireside Guard*, 16 Mar. 1917; Anderson, *Memoirs*, 352; Kavanaugh Memoir, 42-43, WHMC-SHSM; Cockrell Scrapbook, 4: WHMC-SHSM; *The Richmond Enquirer*, 14 Aug. 1863; Johnson and Buel, eds., *Battles and Leaders*, 528; *The St. Louis Missouri Republican*, 5 Dec. 1884.

34. Moore, ed., *The Rebellion Record*, 7: 173; Elliott Journal, 66, TSLA; *The St. Louis Missouri Republican*, 5 Dec. 1884; Fisher Diary, 7, MHS; Compiled Missouri Confederate Service Records, RG 109, NA; Adjutant of Missouri Service Records; "J. J. Moore," *Confederate Veteran*, 34, (1926), 265; Anderson, *Memoirs*, 352-353; *The Centralia Fireside Guard*, 16 Mar. 1917; Cockrell Scrapbook, 4: WHMC-SHSM; "A Hero in the Strife," *Confederate Veteran*, (1894), 282.

35. *The Centralia Fireside Guard*, 16 Mar. 1917; Fisher Diary, 7, MHS; Anderson, *Memoirs*, 353-354; *The St. Louis Missouri Republican*, 5 Dec. 1884; Cockrell Scrapbook, 4: WHMC-SHSM; *The Richmond Enquirer*, 14 Aug. 1863; *O.R.*, 24: ser. 1, pt. 2, 294, 377; Kavanaugh Memoir, 41-42, WHMC-SHSM; *The Memphis Daily Appeal*, 17 Nov. 1862; Bearss, *Unvexed to the Sea*, 928-929; Tunnard, *A Southern Record*, 266; Johnson and Buel, eds., *Battles and Leaders of the Civil War*, 3: 491.

36. Compiled Missouri Confederate Service Records, RG 109, NA; Bannon Diary, SCL; *The Richmond Enquirer*, 14 Aug. 1863; Johnson and Buel, eds., *Battles and Leaders*, 3: 491; Kavanaugh Memoir, 41-43, WHMC-SHSM; *O.R.*, 24: ser. 1, pt. 2, 416; Fisher Diary, 8, MHS; *The St. Louis Missouri Republican*, 5 Dec. 1884; Anderson, *Memoirs*, 355; *The Centralia Fireside Guard*, 16 Mar. 1917.

37. *O.R.*, 24: ser. 1. pt. 2, 416; Kavanaugh Memoir, 43, WHMC-SHSM.

38. Cockrell Scrapbook, 4: WHMC-SHSM; Anderson, *Memoirs*, 356; *O.R.*, 24: pt. 2, 416-417; Bevier, *History of the First and Second Missouri Confederate Brigades*, 217, 433-434; Fisher, 8, MHS; Elliott Journal, 66, TSLA; Johnson and Buel, eds., *Battles and Leaders*, 3, 550; *The Richmond Enquirer*, 14 Aug. 1863; Moore, ed., *The Rebellion Record*, 7: 173; *The St. Louis Missouri Republican*, 5 Dec. 1884; Kavanaugh Memoir, 43-44, WHMC-SHSM; Adjutant General of Missouri Service Records.

39. Compiled Missouri Confederate Service Records, RG 109, NA; Foster, *Vicksburg: Southern City Under Siege*, 59; Hogan to Father, 22 July 1863, MHS; Bevier, *History of the First and Second Missouri Confederate Brigades*, 434; *The St. Louis Missouri Republican*, 5 Dec. 1884; Adjutant of Missouri Service Records; Necrology Scrapbook, No. 1k, 214.

40. Adjutant of Missouri Service Records; *The St. Louis Missouri Republican*, 5 Dec. 1884; "The Audrain County Flag," *C.V.*, 99; Boyce, "The Flags of the First Missouri Confederate Infantry," MHS; Anderson, *Memoirs*, 357.

41. Fisher Diary, 8, MHS; Bannon Diary, SCL; Anderson, *Memoirs*, 357; *The St. Louis Missouri Republican*, 5 Dec. 1884; Elliott Journal, 66, TSLA; Beringer, Hattaway, Jones and Still, *The Elements of Confederate Defeat*, 116.

42. *The Savannah Republican*, 17 Aug. 1863.

43. Elliott Journal, 55, 68, TSLA; *The Mobile Register and Advertiser*, 27 Oct. 1863; *O.R.*, 24: ser. 1, pt. 2, 417; Staff Sergeant Henry Eugene Erwin biographical sketch, Archives of The Airmen Memorial Museum, Suitland, Maryland; *The St. Louis Missouri Republican*, 19 Sept. 1863; Warren Diary; Frank Von Phul to Joseph Boyce, 5 Dec. 1914, Boyce Collection, MHS.

44. *O.R.*, 24: ser. 1, pt. 2, 417; Compiled Missouri Confederate Service Records, RG 109, NA; Cockrell to Cooper, 12 Sept. 1863, Bowen Letter Book, VHS; Dyson to Wife, 20 July 1863 and 8 June 1863, Dyson Collection, WHMC-SHSM.

45. Crenshaw to Rigby, 8 July 1901, VNMPA.

46. Fisher Diary, 9, MHS; Kavanaugh Memoir, 44-45, WHMC-SHSM; Elliott Journal, 67, TSLA; Hogan to Father, 22 July 1863, MHS; Anderson, *Memoirs*, 22 July 1863, MHS; *The St. Louis Missouri Republican*, 5 Dec. 1884; *The Mobile Register and Advertiser*, 19 July 1863.

47. Bevier, *History of the First and Second Missouri Confederate Brigades*, 353-354; Compiled Missouri Confederate Service Records, RG 109, NA; *Writer's Program of the Works Projects Administration in the State, A Guide to the "Show Me" State of Missouri*, (New York, 1941), 376; Lemmon Papers, Elliott Journal, 67, TSLA; *O.R.*, 24: ser. 1, pt. 3, 907; Quaife, ed., *Absalom Grimes*, 272; H. Riley Bock, "Jefferson Patterson, A New Madrid Black in the Civil War," *Missouri Partisan*, 5: (1989), n.p.; *The Richmond Enquirer*, 9 Apr. 1862; *University Missourian*, 14 Dec. 1915.

48. *The St. Louis Missouri Republican*, 5 Dec. 1884; Bannon Diary, SCL; Fisher Diary, 8, MHS; Compiled Missouri Confederate Service Records, RG 109, NA; *The Savannah Republican*, 9 and 20 July 1863; Bearss, *Unvexed to the Sea*, 1284-1289; Kearny-Kennerly Scrapbook, 2: MHS; *The Memphis Daily Appeal*, 17 and 18 July 1863; *The Richmond Enquirer*, 2 July 1863; Boyce, "The Flags of the First Missouri Confederate Infantry," MHS.

49. Elliott Journal, 67, TSLA; Fisher Diary, 9, MHS; *The Savannah Republican*, 9 July 1863; *The Richmond Enquirer*, 9 Apr. 1862; Jones, *Civil War Command And Strategy*, 162-163, 170-171, 236-239.

BIBLIOGRAPHY

MANUSCRIPT MATERIAL

Adjutant General of Missouri Records of Confederate Soldiers, Adjutant General's Office, Jefferson City, Missouri.

Appler, John T., Diary, Missouri Historical Society, St. Louis, Missouri.

Babcock Scrapbook, Missouri Historical Society.

Bankhead Family Papers, L. Carey Bankhead, Moberly, Missouri.

Barns, Cora N., Scrapbooks, Western Historical Manuscript Collection-State Historical Society of Missouri, Columbia, Missouri.

Bannon, John B., Diary, Yates Snowden Collection, South Caroliniana Library, University of South Carolina, Columbia, South Carolina.

Bannon, John B., Sketch, The Confederate Museum, Richmond, Virginia.

Bates, Lily Hazel, Family Papers, Palmyra, Missouri.

Bedford Family Papers, Western Historical Manuscript Collection-State Historical Society of Missouri.

Bixby, William K., Missouri Historical Society.

Blow Family Papers, Missouri Historical Society.

Riley Family Papers, H. Riley Bock, New Madrid, Missouri.

Boyce, Joseph, Scrapbook, Missouri Historical Society.

Boyce Family Collection, Edmund J. Boyce, St. Louis, Missouri.

Boyce, Joseph, Papers, Missouri Historical Society.

Boyce, Joseph, "Military Organizations of St. Louis," Missouri Historical Society.

Boyce, Joseph, "Rev. John Bannon-Chaplain Price's Missouri Confederate Division," 8 Mar. 1914, Missouri Historical Society.

Boyce, Joseph, "The Flags of the First Missouri Confederate Infantry," Missouri Historical Society.

Bowen, John Stevens, Papers, Missouri Historical Society.

Bowen, John Stevens, Letter Book, Virginia Historical Society, Richmond, Virginia.

Brauckman Scrapbook, Missouri Historical Society.

Breckenridge Scrapbooks, Missouri Historical Society.

Burbridge Family Papers, H. C. Burbridge, Jr., Jacksonville, Florida.

Camp Jackson Papers, Missouri Historical Society.

Champ Clark Papers, Western Historical Manuscript Collection-State Historical Society of Missouri.

Cheavens, Henry, Journal, Western Historical Manuscript Collection-State Historical Society of Missouri.

Compiled Service Records of Confederate Soldiers Who Served In Organizations From the State of Missouri, Record Group 109, National Archives, Washington, D.C.

Census Records of 1860 for Buchanan and Linn Counties, Missouri.

Census Records of 1850 and 1860 for Chatham County, Georgia.

Civil War Papers, Missouri Historical Society.

Clark Family Papers, Missouri Historical Society.

Cockrell, Francis Marion, Scrapbook, Missouri Historical Society.

Cockrell, Francis Marion, Scrapbooks, Western Historical Manuscript Collection-State Historical Society of Missouri.

"Consolidated Provision Return For First Brigade, May 1-May 10, 1863," Roster Sheet, National Archives, Washington, D.C.

Crawford, Emily to Elizabeth Lewis, 11 June 1863, Charles Sullivan Collection, Pascagoula, Mississippi.

Crenshaw, W. N. to Major Thomas Rigby, 8 July 1901, Vicksburg National Military Park Archives, Vicksburg, Mississippi.

Danner, Albert Carey, Family Papers, Dorothy Danner Dapointe Trabits, Mobile, Alabama.

Dunlap, Robert C., Diary and Family Papers, John B. Sampson, DeKalb, Missouri.

Dunlap, Samuel B., Diary, Western Historical Manuscript Collection-State Historical Society of Missouri.

Dyson, Absalom Roby, Collection, Western Historical Manuscript Collection-State Historical Society of Missouri-University of Missouri-St. Louis.

Elliott, George, Journal, Tennessee State Library and Archives, Nashville, Tennessee.

Engelman, George, Diary, Missouri Historical Society.

Ex-Confederate Associations of Missouri Reunion Reports, Missouri Historical Society.

Fisher, Theodore T., Diary of Siege of Vicksburg, Missouri Historical Society.

Flag Envelope, Missouri Historical Society.

Gates, Elijah, to Sterling Price, 12 July, 1862, Henry E. Huntington Library and Art Gallery, Los Angeles, California.

Grimes, Absalom, Papers, Missouri Historical Society.

Guibor Family Papers, Warren Guibor, Manchester, Missouri.

Haydon Family Collection, Dorothy Haydon-Kerr, Springfield, Missouri.

Holman, Vinson, Diary typescript, Pea Ridge National Military Park Archives, Pea Ridge, Arkansas.

Hogan, Thomas, Letters, Missouri Historical Society.

Hubbell, Richard M., "Personal Reminiscences," Missouri Historical Society.

Hubbell Family Papers, Mrs. Leon Rice Taylor, Richmond, Missouri.

Isaac, Deborah, "Confederate Days in St. Louis," Missouri Historical Society.

Jenkins, Gertrude, Papers, 1859-1908, William R. Perkins Library, Duke University, Durham, North Carolina.

Kavanaugh, William H., Papers, Western Historical Manuscript Collection-State Historical Society of Missouri.

Kearney-Kennerly Scrapbook, Missouri Historical Society.

Kennerly Family Papers, Missouri Historical Society.

Landis Family Papers, Walter Austill Landis, Jr., Faucett, Missouri.

Landis Family Papers, Wilbur P. McDonald, St. Joseph, Missouri.

Lane, Anne, to Sarah Glasgow, 20 Feb. 1864, Missouri Historical Society.

Leathers Family Papers, Dorothy Voncille Liedorff Schmedake, Callao, Missouri.

Leavy, John A., Journal, Vicksburg National Military Park Archives.

Lemmon Family Papers, Joe Lemmon, Bolivar, Missouri.

Lenox, David, F., "Memoirs of a Missouri Confederate Soldier," Missouri Historical Society.

Lewis Family Papers, Leroy R. Lewis, Chatham, New Jersey.

Little, Henry, Diary, The United States Army Military Institute, Carlisle Barracks, Pennsylvania.

Little, Henry, biographical sketch, Maryland Historical Society, Baltimore, Maryland.

Little Family Papers, Fielding L. Taylor, Virginia Beach, Virginia.

Mesker Scrapbook, Missouri Historical Society.

Miller, Edwin L., Scrapbook, 1888-1897, Western Historical Manuscript Collection-State Historical Society of Missouri.

Miscellaneous Civil War Manuscripts File, Western Historical Manuscript Collection-State Historical Society of Missouri.

Mitchell Family Papers, William F. Moore, Redstone, Alabama.

Mothershead, Joseph, Journal, Tennessee State Library and Archives.

McNamara, J. C., "An Historical Sketch of the Sixth Division-Missouri State Guard, from its Organization in 1861 to its Surrender to Shreveport, La., in 1865," Missouri Historical Society.

Necrology Scrapbooks, Missouri Historical Society.

Payne, Asa, "Story of the Battle of Pea Ridge," Pea Ridge National Military Park Archives.

Payne, James E., Memoir of Grand Gulf and Port Gibson, Vicksburg National Military Park Archives.

Reynolds, Thomas C., "Gen. Sterling Price and the Confederacy," Missouri Historical Society.

Robbins, Edward C., "Landis Battery," Missouri Historical Society.

Robbins, Edward C., Letters, Mercantile Library, St. Louis, Missouri.

Ruyle, William A., Memoir, Dee Ruyle, Bolivar, Missouri.

Samuel, David Todd to Dr. W. W. Todd, 24 Apr. 1861, Missouri Historical Society.

Shelton, Alonzo H., "Memoir of a Confederate Veteran," Archives of William Jewell College, Liberty, Missouri.

Simpson, Avington Wayne, Diary, Western Historical Manuscript Collection-State Historical Society of Missouri.

Skaggs, William, Collection of Confederate Veteran Letters, Arkansas History Commission, Little Rock, Arkansas.

"Sketch of Colonel B. A. Rives of Ray County, Missouri," Missouri Historical Society.

Smith, Isaac V., "Personal Memoir of I. V. Smith," Western Historical Manuscript Collection-State Historical Society of Missouri.

Snyder, William T., Letters, H. Riley Bock Collection, New Madrid, Missouri.

Sweeny, Dr. Thomas, Springfield, Missouri, photographic collection.

Tyler, John, Jr., to Hon. William L. Yancy, 15 Oct. 1862, Western Historical Manuscript Collection-State Historical Society of Missouri.

Voelkner, Henry, to Family, 18 Mar. 1862, Missouri Historical Society.

Walter, John F., Capsule Histories of Arkansas Military Units, Arkansas History Commission.

War Department Collection of Confederate Records, Chapter 2, vol. 274, Military Departments, Letter Book, Brigadier General John S. Bowen's Command, Aug. 1862-Nov. 1863, National Archives.

Warren, George William, Diaries and Family Papers, George William Warren, IV, Montpelier, Virginia.

Warren, George William, Letters, Diary, and Family Papers, Ellen R. Warren, Alexandria, Virginia.

Watkins, Marie Oliver Papers, 1702-1962, Western Historical Manuscript Collection-State Historical Society of Missouri.

BOOKS

Alden, Henry M., and Guernsey, eds., *Harper's Pictorial History of the Civil War*, (New York, 1977).

Anders, Leslie, *The Eighteenth Missouri*, (New York, 1968).

Anders, Leslie, ed. and compiler, *Confederate Roll of Honor: Missouri*, (Warrensburg, 1989).

Anderson, Ephraim McDowell, *Memoirs: Historical and Personal; Including the Campaigns of the First Missouri Confederate Brigade*, (St. Louis, 1868).

Anderson, Mary Ann, ed., *The Civil War Diary of Allen Greer*, (New York, 1977).

Balfour, Emma, *Vicksburg, A City Under Siege: Diary of Emma Balfour, May 16, 1863-June 2, 1863*, (private printing, 1983).

Ballard, Michael B., *Pemberton: A Biography*, (Jackson, 1991).

Balthis, Laura V., ed., *Early Recollections of George W. Dameron: Biographical Sketches of Log Cabin Pioneers*, (Huntsville, 1898).

Bearss, Edwin C., *The Campaign For Vicksburg: Grant Strikes A Fatal Blow*, (3 vols: Dayton, 1980).

Bearss, Edwin C., *The Campaign For Vicksburg: Unvexed to the Sea*, (Dayton, 1988).

Bearss, Edwin C., *Decision in Mississippi*, (Little Rock, 1962).

Beringer, Richard E., Hattaway, Herman, Jones, Archer; Still, Jr., William N., *The Elements of Confederate Defeat: Nationalism, War Aims and Religion*, (Athens, 1988).

Bevier, Robert, *History of the First and Second Missouri Confederate Brigades, 1861-1865 and from Wakarusa to Appomattox, A Military Anagraph*, (St. Louis, 1879).

Billion, Frederic L., *Annals of St. Louis in the Territorial Days from 1804 to 1821*, (St. Louis, 1888).

Boatner, Mark M., III, *The Civil War Dictionary*, (New York, 1967).

Bradley, James, *The Confederate Mail Carrier*, (Mexico, 1894).

Brownlee, Richard S., *Gray Ghosts of the Confederacy: Guerrilla Warfare in the West, 1861-1865*, (Baton Rouge, 1958).

Bryan, William S., and Rose, Robert, *A History of the Pioneer Families of Missouri*, (St. Louis, 1876).

Britton, Wiley, *The Civil War on the Border*, (New York, 1890).

Byers, S. H. M., *With Fire and Sword*, (New York, 1911).

Carter, III, Samuel, *The Final Fortress: The Campaign For Vicksburg, 1862-1863*, (New York, 1980).

Castel, Albert, *General Sterling Price and the Civil War in the West*, (Baton Rouge, 1968).

Castel, Albert, *William Clarke Quantrill: His Life and Times*, (Marietta, 1992).

Catton, Bruce, *Grant Moves South*, (Boston, 1960).

Coddington, Edwin B., *The Gettysburg Campaign: A Study in Command*, (New York, 1968).

Connelly, Thomas Lawrence, *Civil War Tennessee: Battles and Leaders*, (Knoxville, 1979).

Connelly, Thomas Lawrence, *Army of the Heartland: The Army of Tennessee, 1861-1862*, (Baton Rouge, 1971).

Connelly, Thomas Lawrence, *Autumn of Glory: The Army of Tennessee, 1862-1865*, (Baton Rouge, 1967).

Connelly, William E., *Doniphan's Expedition*, (Topeka, 1907).

Cook, John R., *The Border and the Buffalo: An Untold Story of the Southwest Plains*, (New York, 1967).

Daniel, Larry J., *Soldiering in the Army of Tennessee: A Portrait of Life in a Confederate Army*, (Chapel Hill, 1991).

Davis, Jefferson, *The Rise and Fall of the Confederate Government*, (New York, 1881).

Degler, Carl N., *The Other South: Southern Dissenters in the Nineteenth Century*, (New York, 1974).

Duychinck, Evert Augustus, *National History of the War For the Union*, (3 vols: New York, 1861-1865).

Dyer, David P., *Autobiography and Reminiscences*, (St. Louis, 1922).

Eaton, Clement, *Jefferson Davis*, (New York, 1977).

Eddy, T. M., *Patriotism of Illinois*, (Chicago, 1865).

Edwards, John N., *Shelby and His Men: or, The War in the West*, (Cincinnati, 1867).

Ehrlich, Walter, *They Have No Rights: Dred Scott's Struggle For Freedom*, (Westport, 1979).

Ellsworth, Eliot, Jr., *West Point in the Confederacy*, (New York, 1941).

Faherty, William Baraby, *Better the Dream, Saint Louis: University and Community, 1818-1968*, (St. Louis, 1968).

Faust, Drew Gilpin, *The Creation of Confederate Nationalism: Ideology and Identity in the Civil War South*, (Baton Rouge, 1988).

Fellman, Michael, *Inside War: The Guerilla Conflict in Missouri During the American Civil War*, (New York, 1989).

Fowler, William M., Jr., *Under Two Flags: The American Navy in the Civil War*, (New York, 1990).

Freeman, Douglas S., *Lee's Lieutenants: Cedar Mountain to Chancellorsville*, (New York, 1943).

Frost, M. O., *Regimental History of the Tenth Missouri Volunteer Infantry*, (Topeka, 1892).

Gentry, Claude, *The Battle of Corinth*, (Baldwyn, 1976).

Gibson, J. W., *Recollections of a Pioneer*, (St. Joseph, 1912).

Grant, Ulysses S., *Personal Memoirs of U. S. Grant*, (New York, 1885).

Gray, J. Glenn, *The Warriors: Reflection on Men in Battle*, (New York, 1967).

Greene, Francis V., *The Mississippi*, (New York, 1883).

Grenville, M. Dodge, *The Battle of Atlanta and other Campaigns, Addresses, etc.*, (Council Bluffs, 1911).

Hale, Donald R., *We Rode With Quantrill: Quantrill and the Guerrilla War*, (Clinton, 1975).

Harrell, John, *Confederate Military History, 8: Arkansas*, (Atlanta, 1899).

Hartje, Robert G., *Van Dorn: The Life and Times of a Confederate General*, (Nashville, 1967).

Harwell, Richard Barksdale, ed., *Kate: The Journal of a Confederate Nurse*, (Baton Rouge, 1959).

Hattaway, Herman, *General Stephen D. Lee*, (Jackson, 1976).

Hayes, Steven R., *A Headwaters Creek Trail*, (Pea Ridge).

Hopewell, John M., *The History of Camp Jackson*, (St. Louis, 1861).

Horn, Stanley F., *The Army of Tennessee*, (Wilmington, 1987).

Howe, Henry, *The Times of the Rebellion in the West*, (Cincinnati, 1867).

Hubert, Charles F., *History of the Fiftieth Illinois Infantry*, Kansas City, 1894).

Hunt, Alfred N., *Haiti's Influence on Antebellum America: Slumbering Volcano in the Caribbean*, (Baton Rouge, 1988).

Jackson, Oscar Lawrence, *The Colonel's Diary*, (Sharon, 1922).

Johnson, Robert Underwood and Buel, Clarence Clough, eds., *Battles and Leaders of the Civil War*, (New York, 1884-1888).

Jones, Archer, *Civil War Command And Strategy: A Process of Victory And Defeat*, (New York, 1992).

Josephy, Alvin M., Jr., *The Civil War in the American West*, (New York, 1991).

Kennedy, Francis H., ed., *The Civil War Battlefield Guide*, (Boston, 1990).

Kennerly, William C., *Persimmon Hill: A Narrative of Old St. Louis and the Far West*, (Norman, 1948).

King, James T., *A Life of General Eugene A. Carr*, (Lincoln, 1963).

Kitchens, Ben Earl, *Rosecrans Meets Price: The Battle of Iuka, Mississippi*, (Florence, 1985).

Knox, Thomas W., *The Lost Army*, (New York, 1894).

Lamers, William M., *The Edge of Glory: A Biography of General William S. Rosecrans*, (New York, 1961).

Logan, Sheridan A., *Old Saint Jo: Gateway to the West*, (St. Joseph, 1979).

Loughborough, Mary, *My Cave Life at Vicksburg*, (New York, 1864).

McElroy, John, *The Struggle For Missouri*, (Washington, 1909).

McMeekin, Isabel, *Louisville: The Gateway City*, (New York, 1946).

McMurry, Richard M., *Two Great Rebel Armies: An Essay in Confederate Military History*, (Chapel Hill, 1989).

McMurry, Richard M., *John Bell Hood and the War for Southern Independence*, (Lexington, 1982).

McPherson, James M., *Battle Cry of Freedom: The Civil War Era*, (Oxford, 1988).

McWhiney, Grady, and Jamieson, Perry D., *Attack and Die: Civil War Military Tactics and the Southern Heritage*, (University, 1982).

Madaus, Howard Michael and Needham, Robert D., *The Battle Flags of the Confederate Army of Tennessee*, (Milwaukee, 1976).

March, David D., *The History of Missouri*, (New York, 1967).

Marshall, Howard Wight, *Folk Architecture in Little Dixie: A Regional Culture in Missouri*, (Columbia, 1981).

Meyer, Duane G., *The Heritage of Missouri*, (St. Louis, 1970).

Miers, Earl S., *The Web of Victory: Grant at Vicksburg*, (Baton Rouge, 1955).

Miles, Kathleen White, *Bitter Ground: The Civil War in Missouri's Golden Valley, Benton, Henry and St. Clair Counties*, (Warsaw, 1971).

Miller, George, *Missouri's Memorable Decade 1860-1870: An Historical Sketch, Personal-Political-Religious*, (Columbia, 1898).

Millet, Allan R., Maslowski, Peter, *For the Common Defense: A Military History of the United States of America*, (New York, 1984).

Mitchell, Joseph B., *The Badge of Gallantry*, (New York, 1968).

Moore, Frank, ed., *The Rebellion Record*, (11 vols: New York, 1862-1868).

Moore, John C., *Confederate Military History, 12: Missouri*, Extended Edition, (Wilmington, 1988).

Monaghan, Jay, *Civil War on the Western Border, 1854-1865*, (New York, n.d.)

Morgan, Dale L., ed., *The Overland Diary of James A. Pritchard from Kentucky to California in 1849*, (Denver, 1959).

Mullins, Michael, *The Fremont Rifles: A History of the 37th Illinois Veteran Volunteer Infantry*, (Wilmington, 1990).

Mulvihill, M. J., Vicksburg and Warren County, Mississippi, Tunica Indians, Quebec Missionaries, Civil War Veterans, (Vicksburg, 1931).

Nevins, Allen, *Ordeal of the Union, The War For the Union: The Organized War, 1863-1864*, (8 vols: New York, 1959-1971).

Noble, Robert W., *Battle of Pea Ridge, or Elk Horn Tavern: War Papers and Personal Reminiscences*, (St. Louis, 1892).

Osborn, Donald Lewis, *Tales of the Amarugia Highlands of Cass County, Missouri*, (Lee's Summit, 1972).

Paris, Comte de, *The Civil War in America*, (Philadelphia, 1876).

Payne, James E., *History of the Fifth Missouri Volunteer Infantry*, (James E. Payne Press, 1899).

Pemberton, John C., III, *Pemberton: Defender of Vicksburg*, (Chapel Hill, 1976).

Phillips, Christopher, *Damned Yankee: The Life of General Nathaniel Lyon*, (Columbia, 1990).

Phillips, Herb, *Champion Hill*, (Champion Hill Battle Fund Foundation).

Pillar, James J., *The Catholic Church in Mississippi 1837-1865*, (New Orleans, 1964).

Pollard, Edward A., *The Lost Cause*, (New York, 1866).

Porter, David D., *The Naval History of the Civil War*, (New York, 1886).

Priddy, Bob, *Across the Wide Missouri*, (2 vols., Independence, 1982-1984).

Quaife, Milo, N., ed., *Absalom Grimes: Confederate Mail Runner*, (New Haven, 1926).

Randall, J. G., *The Civil War And Reconstruction*, (New York, 1937).

Rawley, James A., *Turning Points of the Civil War*, (Lincoln, 1989).

Reavis, L. V., *Saint Louis, the Future Great City*, (St. Louis, 1876).

Robertson, James I., Jr., *The Stonewall Brigade*, (Baton Rouge, 1963).

Rowland, Dunbar, ed., *Jefferson Davis, Constitutionalist: Letters, Papers and Speeches*, (Jackson, 1923).

Royster, Charles, *A Revolutionary People At War: The Continental Army and American Character, 1775-1783*, (New York, 1979).

Sanborn, J. B., *Memoirs of George B. Boomer*, (Boston, 1864).

Stevens, Walter B., *St. Louis: The Fourth City, 1764-1909*, (St. Louis, 1909).

St. Peters, Robert, *Memorial Volume of the Diamond Jubilee of St. Louis University*, (St. Louis, 1904).

Sunderland, Glenn W., *Five Days to Glory*, (New York, 1970).

Tunnard, William H., *A Southern Record: The History of the Third Louisiana Infantry*, (Dayton, 1970).

Urquhart, Kenneth Trist, ed., *Vicksburg: Southern City Under Siege: William Lovelace Foster's Letters Describing the Defense and Surrender of the Confederate Fortress on the Mississippi*, (New Orleans, 1980).

Wakelyn, Jon L., *Biographical Dictionary of the Confederacy*, (Westport, 1977).

Warner, Ezra, Jr., *General in Gray: Lives of the Confederate Commanders*, (Baton Rouge, 1959).

Watkins, Marie Oliver, and Watkins, Helen, *Tearin' Through the Wilderness: Missouri Pioneer Episodes and Genealogy of the Watkins Family of Virginia and Missouri*, (Charleston, 1957).

Web, William L., *Battles and Biographies of Missourians*, (Kansas City, 1900).

Wheeler, Richard, *The Siege of Vicksburg*, (New York, 1978).

Wickersham, John T., *The Gray and the Blue*, (Berkeley, 1915).

Williams, Walter, ed., *History of Northwest Missouri*, (Chicago, 1913).

Williams, Walter, ed., *History of Northeast Missouri*, (Chicago, 1913).

Williamson, Hugh P., *South of the Middle Border*, (Philadelphia, 1946).

Winters, John D., *The Civil War In Louisiana*, (Baton Rouge, 1963).

Woodworth, Steven E., *Jefferson Davis And His Generals: The Failure of Confederate Command in the West*, (Lawrence, 1990).

Wright, Robert K., *The Continental Army*, (Washington, D.C., 1983).

Yearns, W. Buck, ed., *The Confederate Governors*, (Athens, 1985).

MISSOURI COUNTY HISTORIES

Cockrell, Ewing, *History of Johnson County, Missouri*, (Topeka, 1918).

General History of Macon County, Missouri, (Chicago, 1910).

History of Andrew and DeKalb Counties, Missouri, (Chicago, 1888).

History of Carroll County, Missouri, (St. Louis, 1881).

History of Boone County, Missouri, (St. Louis, 1882).

History of Clay and Platte Counties, Missouri, (St. Louis, 1885).

History of Cole, Moniteau, Morgan, Benton, Miller, Maries and Osage Counties, Missouri, (Chicago, 1889).

History of Henry and St. Clair Counties, Missouri, (St. Joseph, 1883).

History of Laclede, Cedar, Dallas, Webster, Wright and Texas Counties, Missouri, (Chicago, 1889).

History of Lafayette County, Missouri, (St. Louis, 1881).

History of Lincoln County, Missouri, (Chicago, 1888).

History of Monroe and Shelby Counties, Missouri, (St. Louis, 1884).

History of Newton, Lawrence, Barry and McDonald Counties, Missouri, (Chicago, 1888).

History of Pike County, Missouri, (Des Moines, 1883).

History of Randolph and Macon Counties, Missouri, (St. Louis, 1884).

History of Ray County, Missouri, (St. Louis, 1881).

History of Southeast Missouri, (Chicago, 1888).

History of St. Charles, Montgomery and Warren Counties, Missouri, (St. Louis, 1885).

Johnson, J. B., *History of Vernon County, Missouri*, (2 vols: Chicago, 1911).

Keith, Clayton, *Military History of Pike County, Missouri*, (Louisiana, 1915).

Paxton, William M., *Annals of Platte County, Missouri*, (Kansas City, 1897).

Ponder, Jerry, *The History of Ripley County, Missouri*, (1987).

Portrait and Biographical Record of Clay, Ray, Carroll, Chariton, and Linn Counties, Missouri, (Chicago, 1893).

Portrait and Biographical Record of Johnson and Pettis Counties, Missouri, (Chicago, 1895).

Portrait and Biographical Record of Buchanan and Clinton Counties, Missouri, (Chicago, 1893).

Rutt, Chris L., *History of Buchanan County and the City of St. Joseph, Missouri, and Representative Citizens*, (Chicago, 1904).

Waller, Alexander H., *History of Randolph County, Missouri*, (Chicago, 1895).

ARTICLES

"An Infantryman at Corinth: The Diary of Charles Cowell," *Civil War Times Illustrated*, 13: (1974).

Bannon, John B., "Experiences of a Confederate Army Chaplain," *Letters and Notices of the English Jesuit Province*, 34: (1866-1868).

Bailey, Anne J., "The Abandoned Western Theater: Confederate National Policy Toward the Trans-Mississippi Region," *Journal of Confederate History*, 5: (1990).

Barr, Alwyn, "Confederate Artillery in Arkansas," *Arkansas Historical Quarterly*, 21: (1962).

Bearss, Edwin C., "The Battle of Pea Ridge," *Annals of Iowa*, 36: (1962).

Bearss, Edwin C., "The Battle of Pea Ridge," *Arkansas Historical Quarterly*, 37: (1963-1964).

Bearss, Edwin C., "The First Day at Pea Ridge, March 7, 1862," *Arkansas Historical Quarterly*, 17: (1958).

Bearss, Edwin C., "Grand Gulf's Role in the Civil War," *Civil War History*, 5: (1959).

Bock, H. Riley, "Jefferson Patterson, A New Madrid Black in the Civil War," *Missouri Partisan*, 5: (1989).

Bock, H. Riley, "Confederate Col. A. C. Riley, His Reports and Letters, Part I," *Missouri Historical Review*, 85: (1991).

Bock, H. Riley, "Confederate Col. A. C. Riley, His Reports and Letters, Part II," Missouri Historical Review, 85: (1992).

Bond, John W., "The History of Elkhorn Tavern" *Arkansas Historical Quarterly*, 21: (1962).

Boyce, Joseph, "What Flag was This?" *Confederate Veteran*, 27: (1919).

Bomar, Joe Lee, "The Audrain County Flag," *Confederate Veteran*, 36: (1928).

Brown, Walter, "Pea Ridge: Gettysburg of the West," *Arkansas Historical Quarterly*, 15: (1956).

Calkins, Homer L., ed., "From Elk Horn to Vicksburg: James Fauntleroy's Diary of the Year 1862," *Civil War History*, 2: (1956).

Castel, Albert, "A New View of the Battle of Pea Ridge," *Missouri Historical Review*, 62: (1968).

Carter, Harvey L., and Peterson, Norma L., "William S. Stewart Letters: January 13, 1861, to December 4, 1862," *Missouri Historical Review*, 61: (1967).

Clark, Kimball, "The Epic March of Doniphan's Missourians," *Missouri Historical Review*, 80: (1986).

Cook, George, "Neosho...Its Part in the Confederate Dream," *Gateway Magazine*, 2: (1981).

Daniel, Larry T., "Bruinsburg: Missed Opportunity or Postwar Rhetoric?" *Civil War History*, 32: (1986).

Erickson, Edgar L., "With Grant at Vicksburg: From the Civil War Diary of Captain Charles E. Wilcox," *Journal of the Illinois State Historical Society*, 30: (1938).

Ervin, W. J., "Genius and Heroism of Lieut. K. H. Faulkner," *Confederate Veteran*, 14: (1906).

Gerber, John, "Twain's 'Private Campaign'," *Civil War History*, 1: (1955).

Gordon, James, "The Battle and Retreat from Corinth," *Mississippi Historical Society Publications*, 4: (1901).

Grover, George S., "Col. Benjamin Whiteman Grover," *Missouri Historical Review*, 1: (1907).

Grover, Benjamin Whiteman, "Civil War in Missouri," *Missouri Historical Review*, 8: (1913).

Gunn, Jack W., "The Battle of Iuka," *Journal of Mississippi History*, 24: (1962).

Hallock, Judith Lee, " 'Lethal and Debilitating' ": The Southern Disease Environment as a Factor in Confederate Defeat," *Journal of Confederate History*, 7: (1991).

Hass, Paul H., ed., "The Vicksburg Diary of Henry Clab Warmouth," *Journal of Mississippi History*, 31: (1969).

Henry, Pat, "Major General John S. Bowen," *Confederate Veteran*, 22: (1914).

Irwin, Ray W., "Missouri in Crisis: The Journal of Captain Albert Tracy; 1861," *The Missouri Historical Review*, 51: (1956).

Kirkpatrick, Arthur Roy, "The Admission of Missouri to the Confederacy," *Missouri Historical Review*, 55: (1961).

Lee, Stephen D., "The Campaign of Vicksburg, Miss. in 1863-from April 15th to and Including the Battle of Champion Hills, or Baker's Creek, May 16th 1863," *Publications of the Mississippi Historical Society*, 3: (1900).

MacDonald, "The Missouri River and Its Victims: Vessels Wrecked from the Beginning," *Missouri Historical Review*, 21: (1927).

Maury, Dabney H., "Campaign Against Grant in North Mississippi," *Southern Historical Society Papers*, 13: (January-December, 1885).

Maury, Dabney H., "Recollections of the Elkhorn Campaign," *Southern Historical Society Papers*, 2: (1876).

Missouri Partisan, Journal of Missouri Division, Sons of Confederate Veterans, 7: (Summer/Fall 1991).

Mitchell, W. A., "The Confederate Mail Carrier," *Confederate Veteran*, 22: (1914).

Noe, F. R., "Scattered Remnant of a Company," *Confederate Veteran*, 11: (1903).

Payne, James E., "Recreation in Army Life," *Confederate Veteran*, 38: (1930).

Payne, James E., "The Sixth Missouri at Corinth," *Confederate Veteran*, 36: (1928).

Payne, James E., "Skylarking Along the Line," *Confederate Veteran*, 38: (1930).

Payne, James E., "From Missouri," *Confederate Veteran*, 38: (1930).

Payne, James E., "Missouri Troops in the Vicksburg Campaign," *Confederate Veteran*, 36: (1928).

Payne, James E., "Fighting John Brown at Osawatomie," *Confederate Veteran*, 28: (1920).

Payne, James E., "Early Days of War in Missouri," *Confederate Veteran*, 38: (1931).

Powell, C.A., "Brother Fought Against Brother," *Confederate Veteran*, 10: (1902).

"Vicksburg," *The Century Magazine*, 61: (1901).

Roher, Walter A., "Confederate Generals-the View from Below," *Civil War Times Illustrated*, (1979).

Shoemaker, Floyd C., "Missouri-Heir of Southern Tradition and Individuality," *Missouri Historical Review*, 36: (1942).

Sproul, T. B., *Confederate Veteran*, 7: (1894).

Stadler, Francis Hurd, "Letters From Minoma," *The Missouri Historical Society Bulletin*, 16: 1960).

Stevenson, S. Wentworth, "A Southern Campaign," *The Ladies' Benevolent and Industrial Sallymag Society*, (1868).

Stewart, Faye L., "Battle of Pea Ridge," *Missouri Historical Review*, 22: (1928).

Synnamon, James, "A Veteran with Many Wounds," *Confederate Veteran*, 21: (1913).

Trigg, S. C., "Fighting Around Vicksburg," *Confederate Veteran*, 12: (1904).

Truman, William L., "The Battle of Elk Horn, or Pea Ridge, Arkansas," *Confederate Veteran*, 36: (1928).

Weidemeyer, J. M., "Missourians East of the Mississippi," *Confederate Veteran*, 18: (1910).

ARTICLES WITHOUT AUTHORS

"A Hero in the Strife," Confederate Veteran, (1894).

"Diary of Lieut. Col. Hubbell of 3d Regiment Missouri Infantry, C.S.A.," The Land We Love, (1868-1869).

"J. J. Moore," Confederate Veteran, 34: (1926).

"James Synnamon," Confederate Veteran, 21: (1913).

"Maj. John H. Britts," Confederate Veteran, 18: (1910).

"Rev. John Bannon," Confederate Veteran, 21: (1913).

"The Tallest Confederate: Henry C. Thruston," Civil War Times.

NEWSPAPERS

Albany, Missouri, Ledger

Bolivar, Missouri, Courier

California, Missouri, Weekly Times

Centralia, Missouri, Fireside Guard

Chattanooga, Tennessee, Daily Rebel

Daily Missouri Democrat, St. Louis, Missouri

Daily New Orleans, Louisiana, Picayune

Intelligencer, Atlanta, Georgia

Kansas City, Missouri, Times

Memphis, Tennessee, Daily Appeal

Missouri Army Argus

Mobile, Alabama, Register and Advertiser

National Tribune, New York, New York

New York, New York, Herald

Platte County, Missouri, Argus

Richmond, Missouri, Missourian

Richmond, Virginia, Enquirer

Savannah, Georgia, Republican

St. Joseph, Missouri, Gazette

St. Louis, Missouri, Daily Evening News

St. Louis, Missouri, Daily Globe

St. Louis Daily Missourian

St. Louis, Missouri, Globe-Democrat

St. Louis, Missouri, Post-Dispatch

St. Louis Missouri Republican

University Missourian

Vandalia, Missouri, Leader

Vicksburg, Mississippi, Daily Herald

Vicksburg, Mississippi, Daily Whig

Weekly, Jackson, Mississippian

PERSONAL INTERVIEWS

Evans, Marjorie, Troy, Missouri, with author, 20 Nov. 1987.

PERSONAL CORRESPONDENCE

Bearss, Edwin C., Arlington, Virginia, to author, 15 Jan. 1985.

Bock, H. Riley, New Madrid, Missouri, to author, 18 Nov. 1987 and 18 Oct. 1988.

Brown, Pauline E., Richmond, Virginia, to author, 23 June 1986.

Graham, Mary Sue, Hot Springs, Arkansas, to author, 23 June 1989.

McDonald, Wilbur P., St. Joseph, Missouri, to author, 4 Nov. 1988 and 12 Dec. 1988.

O'Connor, Gaylord, Louisiana, Missouri, to author, 21 Nov. 1985 and 29 May 1989.

St. Peters, Robert, Alton, Illinois, to author, 30 June 1985.

Thompson, James W., Jackson, Mississippi, to author, 27 Jan. 1989.

UNPUBLISHED ACADEMIC WORKS

Phillip Thomas Tucker, "A Perspective of Johnson County's Confederate Dead Who Served in the First Missouri Brigade, C.S.A., 1861-1865," 1978 Central Missouri State University, Warrensburg, Missouri, 1978 Graduate School Study.

Phillip Thomas Tucker, "The History of the First Missouri Confederate Brigade, 1862-1865," M.A. Thesis, 1983, Central Missouri State University.

Phillip Thomas Tucker, "The History of the Fifth Missouri Confederate Infantry," Ph.D. Dissertation, 1990, St. Louis University, St. Louis, Missouri.

BOOKS

Alden, Henry M., and Guernsey, eds., *Harper's Pictorial History of the Civil War*, (New York, 1977).

Anders, Leslie, *The Eighteenth Missouri*, (New York, 1968).

Anders, Leslie, ed. and compiler, *Confederate Roll of Honor:* Missouri, (Warrensburg, 1989).

Anderson, Ephraim McDowell, *Memoirs: Historical and Personal; Including the Campaigns of the First Missouri Confederate Brigade*, (St. Louis, 1868.)

Anderson, Mary Ann, ed., *The Civil War Diary of Allen Greer*, (New York, 1977).

Balfour, Emma, *Vicksburg, A City Under Siege: Diary of Emma Balfour, May 16, 1863-June 2, 1863*, (private printing, 1983).

Ballard, Michael B., *Pemberton: A Biography*, (Jackson, 1991).

Balthis, Laura V., ed., *Early Recollections of George W. Dameron: Biographical Sketches of Log Cabin Pioneers*, (Huntsville, 1898).

Bearss, Edwin C., *The Campaign For Vicksburg: Grant Strikes A Fatal Blow*, (3 vols: Dayton, 1980).

Bearss, Edwin C., *The Campaign For Vicksburg: Unvexed to the Sea*, (Dayton, 1988).

Bearss, Edwin C., *Decision in Mississippi*, (Little Rock, 1962).

Beringer, Richard E., Hattaway, Herman, Jones, Archer; Still, Jr., William N., *The Elements of Confederate Defeat: Nationalism, War Aims and Religion*, (Athens, 1988).

Bevier, Robert, *History of the First and Second Missouri Confederate Brigade, 1861-1865 and from Wakarusa to Appomattox, A Military Anagraph*, (St. Louis, 1879).

Billion, Frederic L., *Annals of St. Louis in the Territorial Days from 1804 to 1821*, (St. Louis, 1888).

Boatner, Mark M., III, *The Civil War Dictionary*, (New York, 1967).

Bradley, James, *The Confederate Mail Carrier*, (Mexico, 1894).

Brownlee, Richard S., *Gray Ghosts of the Confederacy: Guerrilla Warfare in the West, 1861-1865*, (Baton Rouge, 1958).

Bryan, William S., and Rose, Robert, *A History of the Pioneer Families of Missouri*, (St. Louis, 1876).

Britton, Wiley, *The Civil War, on the Border*, (New York, 1890).

Byers, S. H. M., *With Fire and Sword*, (New York, 1911).

Carter, III, Samuel, *The Final Fortress: The Campaign For Vicksburg, 1862-1863*, (New York, 1980).

Castel, Albert, *General Sterling Price and the Civil War in the West*, (Baton Rouge, 1968).

Castel, Albert, *Wiliam Clarke Quantrill: His Life and Times*, (Marietta, 1992).

Catton, Bruce, *Grant Moves South*, (Boston, 1960).

Coddington, Edwin B., *The Gettysburg Campaign: A Study in Command*, (New York, 1968).

Connelly, Thomas Lawrence, *Civil War Tennessee: Battles and Leaders,* (Knoxville, 1979).

Connelly, Thomas Lawrence, *Army of the Heartland: The Army of Tennessee, 1861-1862*, (Baton Rouge, 1971).

Connelly, Thomas Lawrence, *Autumn of Glory: The Army of Tennessee, 1862-1865*, (Baton Rouge, 1967).

Connelly, William E., *Doniphan's Expedition*, (Topeka, 1907).

Cook, John R., *The Border and the Buffalo: An Untold Story of the Southwest Plains*, (New York, 1967).

Compiled by Committee, *History of the Sixteenth Battery of Ohio Volunteer Light Artillery, U.S.A.*, (1906).

Daniel, Larry J., *Soldiering in the Army of Tennessee: A Portrait of Life in a Confederate Army*, (Chapel Hill, 1991).

Davis, Jefferson, *The Rise and Fall of the Confederate Government*, (New York, 1881).

Degler, Carl N., *The Other South: Southern Dissenters in the Nineteenth Century*, (New York, 1974).

Duychinck, Evert Augustus, *National History of the War For the Union*, (3 vols: New York, 1861-1865).

Dyer, David P., *Autobiography and Reminiscences*, (St. Louis, 1922).

Eaton, Clement, *Jefferson Davis*, (New York, 1977).

Eddy, T. M., *Patriotism of Illinois*, (Chicago, 1865).

Edwards, John N., *Shelby and His Men: or, The War in the West*, (Cincinnati, 1867).

Ehrlich, Walter, *They Have No Rights: Dred Scott's Struggle For Freedom*, (Westport, 1979).

Ellsworth, Eliot, Jr., *West Point in the Confederacy*, (New York, 1941).

Faherty, William Baraby, *Better the Dream, Saint Louis: University and Community, 1818-1968*, (St. Louis, 1968).

Faust, Drew Gilpin, *The Creation of Confederate Nationalism: Ideology and Identity in the Civil War South*, (Baton Rouge, 1988).

Fellman, Michael, *Inside War: The Guerilla Conflict in Missouri During the American Civil War*, (New York, 1989).

Fowler, William M., Jr., *Under Two Flags: The American Navy in the Civil War*, (New York, 1990).

Freeman, Douglas S., *Lee's Lieutenants: Cedar Mountain to Chancellorsville*, (New York, 1943).

Frost, M. O., *Regimental History of the Tenth Missouri Volunteer Infantry*, (Topeka, 1892).

Gentry, Claude, *The Battle of Corinth*, (Baldwyn, 1976).

Gibson, J. W., *Recollections of a Pioneer*, (St. Joseph, 1912).

Grant, Ulysses S., *Personal Memoirs of U. S. Grant*, (New York, 1885).

Gray, J. Glenn, *The Warriors: Reflection on Men in Battle*, (New York, 1967).

Greene, Francis V., *The Mississippi*, (New York, 1883).

Grenville, M. Dodge, *The Battle of Atlanta and other Campaigns, Addresses, etc.*, (Council Bluffs, 1911).

Hale, Donald R., *We Rode With Quantrill: Quantrill And The Guerrilla War*, (Clinton, 1975).

Harrell, John, *Confederate Military History*, 8: Arkansas, (Atlanta, 1899).

Hartje, Robert G., *Van Dorn: The Life and Times of a Confederate General*, (Nashville, 1967).

Harwell, Richard Barksdale, ed., *Kate: The Journal of a Confederate Nurse*, (Baton Rouge, 1959).

Hattaway, Herman, *General Stephen D. Lee*, (Jackson, 1976).

Hayes, Steven R., *A Headwaters Creek Trail*, (Pea Ridge).

Hopewell, John M., *The History of Camp Jackson*, (St. Louis, 1861).

Horn, Stanley F., *The Army of Tennessee*, (Wilmington, 1987).

Howe, Henry, *The Times of the Rebellion in the West*, (Cincinnati, 1867).

Hubert, Charles F., *History of the Fiftieth Illinois Infantry*, (Kansas City, 1894).

Hunt, Alfred N., *Haiti's Influence on Antebellum America: Slumbering Volcano in the Caribbean*, (Baton Rouge, 1988).

Jackson, Oscar Lawrence, *The Colonel's Diary*, (Sharon, 1922).

Johnson, Robert Underwood and Buel, Clarence Clough, eds., *Battles and Leaders of the Civil War*, (New York, 1884-1888).

Jones, Archer, *Civil War Command And Strategy: A Process of Victory And Defeat*, (New York, 1992).

Josephy, Alvin M., Jr., *The Civil War in the American West*, (New York, 1991).

Kennedy, Francis H., ed., *The Civil War Battlefield Guide*, (Boston, 1990).

Kennerly, William C., *Persimmon Hill: A Narrative of Old St. Louis and the Far West*, (Norman, 1948).

King, James T., *A Life of General Eugene A. Carr*, (Lincoln, 1963).

Kitchens, Ben Earl, *Rosecrans Meets Price: The Battle of Iuka, Mississippi*, (Florence, 1985).

Knox, Thomas W., *The Lost Army*, (New York, 1894).

Lamers, William M., *The Edge of Glory: A Biography of General William S. Rosecrans*, (New York, 1961).

Logan, Sheridan A., *Old Saint Jo: Gateway to the West* (St. Joseph, 1979).

Loughborough, Mary, *My Cave Life at Vicksburg*, (New York, 1864).

McElroy, John, *The Struggle For Missouri*, (Washington, 1909).

McMeekin, Isabel, *Louisville: The Gateway City*, (New York, 1946).

McMurry, Richard M., *Two Great Rebel Armies: An Essay in Confederate Military History*, (Chapel Hill, 1989).

McMurry, Richard M., *John Bell Hood and the War For Southern Independence*, (Lexington, 1982).

McPherson, James M., *Battle Cry of Freedom: The Civil War Era*, (Oxford, 1988).

McWhiney, Grady, and Jamieson, Perry D., *Attack and Die: Civil War Military Tactics and the Southern Heritage*, (University, 1982).

Madaus, Howard Michael and Needham, Robert D., *The Battle Flags of the Confederate Army of Tennessee*, (Milwaukee, 1976).

March, David D., *The History of Missouri*, (New York, 1967).

Marshall, Howard Wight, *Folk Architecture in Little Dixie: A Regional Culture in Missouri*, (Columbia, 1981).

Meyer, Duane G., *The Heritage of Missouri*, (St. Louis, 1970).

Miers, Earl S., *The Web of Victory: Grant at Vicksburg*, (Baton Rouge, 1955).

Miles, Kathleen White, *Bitter Ground: The Civil War in Missouri's Golden Valley, Benton, Henry and St. Clair Counties*, (Warsaw, 1971).

Miller, George, *Missouri's Memorable Decade 1860-1870: An Historical Sketch, Personal-Political-Religious*, (Columbia, 1898).

Millet, Allan R., Maslowski, Peter, *For the Common Defense: A Military History of the United States of America*, (New York, 1984).

Mitchell, Joseph B., *The Badge of Gallantry*, (New York, 1968).

Moore, Frank, ed., *The Rebellion Record*, (11 vols: New York, 1862-1868).

Moore, John C., *Confederate Military History*, 12: Missouri, Extended Edition, (Wilmington, 1988).

Monaghan, Jay, *Civil War on the Western Border, 1854-1865*, (New York, n.d.)

Morgan, Dale L., ed., *The Overland Diary of James A. Pritchard from Kentucky to California in 1849*, (Denver, 1959).

Moscow Mills Memories, (1976).

Mullins, Michael, *The Fremont Rifles: A History of the 37th Illinois Veteran Volunteer Infantry*, (Wilmington, 1990).

Mulvihill, M. J., *Vicksburg and Warren County, Mississippi, Tunica Indians, Quebec Missionaries, Civil War Veterans*, (Vicksburg, 1931).

Nevins, Allen, *Ordeal of the Union, The War For the Union: The Organized War, 1863-1864*, (8 vols: New York, 1959-1971).

Noble, Robert W., *Battle of Pea Ridge, or Elk Horn Tavern: War Papers and Personal Reminiscences*, (St. Louis, 1892).

Osborn, Donald Lewis, *Tales of the Amarugia Highlands of Cass County, Missouri*, (Lee's Summit, 1972).

Paris, Comte de, *The Civil War in America*, (Philadelphia, 1876).

Payne, James E., *History of the Fifth Missouri Volunteer Infantry*, (James E. Payne Press, 1899).

Pemberton, John C., III, *Pemberton: Defender of Vicksburg*, (Chapel Hill, 1976).

Phillips, Christopher, *Damned Yankee: The Life of General Nathaniel Lyon*, (Columbia, 1990.)

Phillips, Herb, *Champion Hill*, (Champion Hill Battlefield Foundation).

Pillar, James J., *The Catholic Church in Mississippi 1837-1865*, (New Orleans, 1964).

Pollard, Edward A., *The Lost Cause*, (New York, 1866).

Porter, David D., *The Naval History of the Civil War*, (New York, 1886).

Priddy, Bob, *Across the Wide Missouri*, (2 vols., Independence, 1982-1984).

Quaife, Milo M., ed., *Absalom Grimes: Confederate Mail Runner*, (New Haven, 1926).

Randall, J. G., *The Civil War And Reconstruction*, (New York, 1937).

Rawley, James A., *Turning Points of the Civil War*, (Lincoln, 1989).

Reavis, L. V., *Saint Louis, the Future Great City*, (St. Louis, 1876).

Robertson, James I., Jr., *The Stonewall Brigade*, (Baton Rouge, 1963).

Rowland, Dunbar, ed., *Jefferson Davis, Constitutionalist: Letters, Papers and Speeches*, (Jackson, 1923).

Royster, Charles, *A Revolutionary People At War: The Continental Army and American Character, 1775-1783*, (New York, 1979).

Sanborn, J. B., *Memoirs of George B. Boomer*, (Boston, 1864).

State of Missouri House of Representatives *Journal*, 21st Assembly, 1st Session.

State of Wisconsin, *Confederate Battle Flags of the Wisconsin Historical Society Report*, (Madison, 1906).

Stevens, Walter B., *St. Louis: The Fourth City, 1764-1909*, (St. Louis, 1909).

St. Peters, Robert, *Memorial Volume of the Diamond Jubilee of St. Louis University*, (St. Louis, 1904).

Sunderland, Glenn W., *Five Days to Glory*, (New York, 1970).

The Encyclopedia of the New West, (Marshall, 1881).

The Johnson County, Missouri, Historical Society *Bulletin*, August 1959. (Warrensburg, 1959).

The United States Biographical Dictionary, Missouri Volume, (Chicago, 1878).

The War of the Rebellion: A Compilation of the Official Records of the Union and Confederate Armies, (128 vols: Washington, D.C., 1880-1901).

Tunnard, William H., *A Southern Record: The History of the Third Louisiana Infantry*, (Dayton, 1970).

Union and Confederate Annals: The Blue and Gray in Friendship Meet and Heroic Deeds Recite, 1: (St. Louis, 1884).

United Daughters of the Confederacy, Missouri Chapter, *Reminiscences of the Women of Missouri During the Sixties*, (Jefferson City, 1901).

Urquhart, Kenneth Trist, ed., *Vicksburg: Southern City Under Siege: William Lovelace Foster's Letters Describing the Defense and Surrender of the Confederate Fortress on the Mississippi*, (New Orleans, 1980).

Wakelyn, Jon L., *Biographical Dictionary of the Confederacy*, (Westport, 1977).

Warner, Ezra, Jr., *General in Gray: Lives of the Confederate Commanders*, (Baton Rouge, 1959).

Watkins, Marie Oliver, and Watkins, Helen, *Tearin' Through the Wilderness: Missouri Pioneer Episodes and Genealogy of the Watkins Family of Virginia and Missouri*, (Charleston, 1957).

Web, William L., *Battles and Biographies of Missourians*, (Kansas City, 1900).

Wheeler, Richard, *The Siege of Vicksburg*, (New York, 1978).

Wickersham, John T., *The Gray and the Blue*, (Berkeley, 1915).

Williams, Walter, ed., *History of Northwest Missouri*, (Chicago, 1913).

Williams, Walter, ed., *History of Northeast Missouri*, (Chicago, 1913).

Williamson, Hugh P., *South of the Middle Border*, (Philadelphia, 1946).

Winters, John D., *The Civil War In Louisiana*, (Baton Rouge, 1963).

Woodworth, Steven E., *Jefferson Davis And His Generals: The Failure of Confederate Command in the West*, (Lawrence, 1990).

Wright, Robert K., *The Continental Army*, (Washington, D.C., 1983).

United States Government, Writer's Program of the Works Projects Administration in the State, *A Guide to the "Show Me" State of Missouri*, (New York, 1941).

Yearns, W. Buck, ed., *The Confederate Governors*, (Athens, 1985).

INDEX